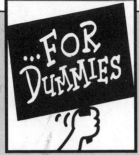
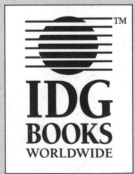

GENEALOGY ONLINE

FOR

DUMMIES®

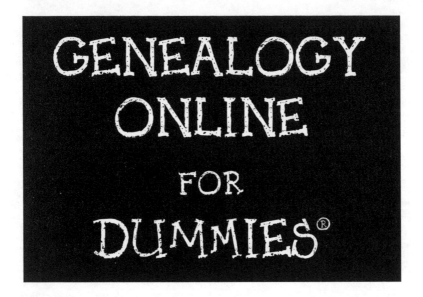

GENEALOGY ONLINE FOR DUMMIES®

by Matthew Helm and April Leigh Helm

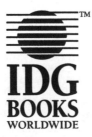

IDG Books Worldwide, Inc.
An International Data Group Company

Foster City, CA ♦ Chicago, IL ♦ Indianapolis, IN ♦ New York, NY

Genealogy Online For Dummies®

Published by
IDG Books Worldwide, Inc.
An International Data Group Company
919 E. Hillsdale Blvd.
Suite 400
Foster City, CA 94404
www.idgbooks.com (IDG Books Worldwide Web site)
www.dummies.com (Dummies Press Web site)

Library of Congress Catalog Card No.: 98-85137

ISBN: 0-7645-0377-4

Printed in the United States of America

10 9 8 7 6 5 4 3

1B/RZ/RQ/ZY/IN

Distributed in the United States by IDG Books Worldwide, Inc.

Distributed by Macmillan Canada for Canada; by Transworld Publishers Limited in the United Kingdom; by IDG Norge Books for Norway; by IDG Sweden Books for Sweden; by Woodslane Pty. Ltd. for Australia; by Woodslane Enterprises Ltd. for New Zealand; by Longman Singapore Publishers Ltd. for Singapore, Malaysia, Thailand, and Indonesia; by Simron Pty. Ltd. for South Africa; by Toppan Company Ltd. for Japan; by Distribuidora Cuspide for Argentina; by Livraria Cultura for Brazil; by Ediciencia S.A. for Ecuador; by Addison-Wesley Publishing Company for Korea; by Ediciones ZETA S.C.R. Ltda. for Peru; by WS Computer Publishing Corporation, Inc., for the Philippines; by Unalis Corporation for Taiwan; by Contemporanea de Ediciones for Venezuela; by Computer Book & Magazine Store for Puerto Rico; by Express Computer Distributors for the Caribbean and West Indies. Authorized Sales Agent: Anthony Rudkin Associates for the Middle East and North Africa.

For general information on IDG Books Worldwide's books in the U.S., please call our Consumer Customer Service department at 800-762-2974. For reseller information, including discounts and premium sales, please call our Reseller Customer Service department at 800-434-3422.

For information on where to purchase IDG Books Worldwide's books outside the U.S., please contact our International Sales department at 650-655-3200 or fax 650-655-3295.

For information on foreign language translations, please contact our Foreign & Subsidiary Rights department at 650-655-3021 or fax 650-655-3281.

For sales inquiries and special prices for bulk quantities, please contact our Sales department at 650-655-3200 or write to the address above.

For information on using IDG Books Worldwide's books in the classroom or for ordering examination copies, please contact our Educational Sales department at 800-434-2086 or fax 317-596-5499.

For press review copies, author interviews, or other publicity information, please contact our Public Relations department at 650-655-3000 or fax 650-655-3299.

For authorization to photocopy items for corporate, personal, or educational use, please contact Copyright Clearance Center, 222 Rosewood Drive, Danvers, MA 01923, or fax 978-750-4470.

About the Authors

Matthew Helm is currently the Director of Human Resource Information Systems at the University of Illinois. Also, he is the Executive Vice President and Chief Technology Officer for Toolbox Internet Marketing Services, Inc., and publisher of the Journal of Online Genealogy. He is the creator and maintainer of Helm's Genealogy Toolbox, Helm/Helms Family Research Page, and a variety of other World Wide Web sites. Matthew has spoken at the GENTECH96, GENTECH97, Illinois State Genealogical Society conferences, and has lectured on genealogy to various other groups. Matthew holds an A.B. in History and an M.S. in Library and Information Science from the University of Illinois at Urbana-Champaign.

April Leigh Helm is the President of Toolbox Internet Marketing Services, Inc. Also, she is the editor and maintainer of the Journal of Online Genealogy. April has spoken at GENTECH97 and has lectured on genealogy and other topics for various conferences and groups. She holds a B.S. in Journalism and an Ed.M. in Higher Education Administration from the University of Illinois at Urbana-Champaign.

Although collectors for many years of notes on family members and old photographs, it was not until 1990, while living and working in the Washington, D.C. area, that the Helms began seriously researching their family lines. Upon returning to central Illinois in 1994, the Helms found themselves with limited historical and genealogical resources to continue their research. It was then that they jumped into online genealogy.

Here's a little more information about the genealogical World Wide Web sites maintained by the Helms.

- ✔ Helm's Genealogy Toolbox (`genealogy.tbox.com/`) is a comprehensive listing of genealogical sites that Matthew created and introduced to the public in 1994.

- ✔ The Journal of Online Genealogy (`www.onlinegenealogy.com/`) is an electronic magazine on the World Wide Web that focuses on the use of online resources and techniques in genealogy and family history. It was introduced in July 1996.

- ✔ The Helm/Helms Family Research Page (`genealogy.tbox.com/research/helm.html`) is a surname-focused site where genealogists can share information about their ancestors with the Helm, Helms, or derivative family names.

ABOUT IDG BOOKS WORLDWIDE

Welcome to the world of IDG Books Worldwide.

IDG Books Worldwide, Inc., is a subsidiary of International Data Group, the world's largest publisher of computer-related information and the leading global provider of information services on information technology. IDG was founded more than 25 years ago and now employs more than 8,500 people worldwide. IDG publishes more than 275 computer publications in over 75 countries (see listing below). More than 90 million people read one or more IDG publications each month.

Launched in 1990, IDG Books Worldwide is today the #1 publisher of best-selling computer books in the United States. We are proud to have received eight awards from the Computer Press Association in recognition of editorial excellence and three from *Computer Currents'* First Annual Readers' Choice Awards. Our best-selling *...For Dummies*® series has more than 50 million copies in print with translations in 38 languages. IDG Books Worldwide, through a joint venture with IDG's Hi-Tech Beijing, became the first U.S. publisher to publish a computer book in the People's Republic of China. In record time, IDG Books Worldwide has become the first choice for millions of readers around the world who want to learn how to better manage their businesses.

Our mission is simple: Every one of our books is designed to bring extra value and skill-building instructions to the reader. Our books are written by experts who understand and care about our readers. The knowledge base of our editorial staff comes from years of experience in publishing, education, and journalism — experience we use to produce books for the '90s. In short, we care about books, so we attract the best people. We devote special attention to details such as audience, interior design, use of icons, and illustrations. And because we use an efficient process of authoring, editing, and desktop publishing our books electronically, we can spend more time ensuring superior content and spend less time on the technicalities of making books.

You can count on our commitment to deliver high-quality books at competitive prices on topics you want to read about. At IDG Books Worldwide, we continue in the IDG tradition of delivering quality for more than 25 years. You'll find no better book on a subject than one from IDG Books Worldwide.

John Kilcullen
CEO
IDG Books Worldwide, Inc.

Steven Berkowitz
President and Publisher
IDG Books Worldwide, Inc.

Eighth Annual Computer Press Awards ≥1992

WINNER
Ninth Annual Computer Press Awards ≥1993

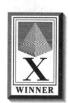

WINNER
Tenth Annual Computer Press Awards ≥1994

WINNER
Eleventh Annual Computer Press Awards ≥1995

IDG Books Worldwide, Inc., is a subsidiary of International Data Group, the world's largest publisher of computer-related information and the leading global provider of information services on information technology. International Data Group publishes over 275 computer publications in over 75 countries. More than 90 million people read one or more International Data Group publications each month. International Data Group's publications include: **ARGENTINA:** Buyer's Guide, Computerworld Argentina, PC World Argentina; **AUSTRALIA:** Australian Macworld, Australian PC World, Australian Reseller News, Computerworld, IT Casebook, Network World, Publish, Webmaster; **AUSTRIA:** Computerwelt Österreich, Networks Austria, PC Tip Austria; **BANGLADESH:** PC World Bangladesh; **BELARUS:** PC World Belarus; **BELGIUM:** Data News; **BRAZIL:** Annuário de Informática, Computerworld, Connections, Macworld, PC Player, PC World, Publish, Reseller News, Supergamepower; **BULGARIA:** Computerworld Bulgaria, Network World Bulgaria, PC & MacWorld Bulgaria; **CANADA:** CIO Canada, Client/Server World, ComputerWorld Canada, InfoWorld Canada, NetworkWorld Canada, WebWorld; **CHILE:** Computerworld Chile, PC World Chile; **COLOMBIA:** Computerworld Colombia, PC World Colombia; **COSTA RICA:** PC World Centro America; **THE CZECH AND SLOVAK REPUBLICS:** Computerworld Czechoslovakia, Macworld Czech Republic, PC World Czechoslovakia; **DENMARK:** Communications World Danmark, Computerworld Danmark, Macworld Danmark, PC World Danmark, Techworld Denmark; **DOMINICAN REPUBLIC:** PC World Republica Dominicana; **ECUADOR:** PC World Ecuador; **EGYPT:** Computerworld Middle East, PC World Middle East; **EL SALVADOR:** PC World Centro America; **FINLAND:** MikroPC, Tietoverkko, Tietoviikko; **FRANCE:** Distributique, Hebdo, Info PC, Le Monde Informatique, Macworld, Reseaux & Telecoms, WebMaster France; **GERMANY:** Computer Partner, Computerwoche, Computerwoche Extra, Computerwoche FOCUS, Global Online, Macwelt, PC Welt; **GREECE:** Amiga Computing, GamePro Greece, Multimedia World; **GUATEMALA:** PC World Centro America; **HONDURAS:** PC World Centro America; **HONG KONG:** Computerworld Hong Kong, PC World Hong Kong, Publish in Asia; **HUNGARY:** ABCD CD-ROM, Computerworld Szamitastechnika, Internetto online Magazine, PC World Hungary, PC-X Magazin Hungary; **ICELAND:** Tolvuheimur PC World Island; **INDIA:** Information Communications World, Information Systems Computerworld, PC World India, Publish in Asia; **INDONESIA:** InfoKomputer PC World, Komputek Computerworld, Publish in Asia; **IRELAND:** ComputerScope, PC Live!; **ISRAEL:** Macworld Israel, People & Computers/Computerworld; **ITALY:** Computerworld Italia, Macworld Italia, Networking Italia, PC World Italia; **JAPAN:** DTP World, Macworld Japan, Nikkei Personal Computing, OS/2 World Japan, SunWorld Japan, Windows NT World, Windows World Japan; **KENYA:** PC World East African; **KOREA:** Hi-Tech Information, Macworld Korea, PC World Korea; **MACEDONIA:** PC World Macedonia; **MALAYSIA:** Computerworld Malaysia, PC World Malaysia, Publish in Asia; **MALTA:** PC World Malta; **MEXICO:** Computerworld Mexico, PC World Mexico; **MYANMAR:** PC World Myanmar; **NETHERLANDS:** Computer! Totaal, LAN Internetworking Magazine, LAN World Buyers Guide, Macworld Netherlands, Net, WebWereld; **NEW ZEALAND:** Absolute Beginners Guide and Plain & Simple Series, Computer Buyer, Computer Industry Directory, Computerworld New Zealand, MTB, Network World, PC World New Zealand; **NICARAGUA:** PC World Centro America; **NORWAY:** Computerworld Norge, CW Rapport, Datamagasinet, Financial Rapport, Kursguide Norge, Macworld Norge, Multimediaworld Norge, PC World Ekspress Norge, PC World Nettverk, PC World Norge, PC World ProduktGuide Norge; **PAKISTAN:** Computerworld Pakistan; **PANAMA:** PC World Panama; **PEOPLE'S REPUBLIC OF CHINA:** China Computer Users, China Computerworld, China InfoWorld, China Telecom World Weekly, Computer & Communication, Electronic Design China, Electronics Today, Electronics Weekly, Game Software, PC World China, Popular Computer Week, Software Weekly, Software World, Telecom World; **PERU:** Computerworld Peru, PC World Profesional Peru, PC World SoHo Peru; **PHILIPPINES:** Click!, Computerworld Philippines, PC World Philippines, Publish in Asia; **POLAND:** Computerworld Poland, Computerworld Special Report Poland, Cyber, Macworld Poland, Networld Poland, PC World Komputer; **PORTUGAL:** Cerebro/PC World, Computerworld/Correio Informático, Dealer World Portugal, Mac*In/PC*In Portugal, Multimedia World; **PUERTO RICO:** PC World Puerto Rico; **ROMANIA:** Computerworld Romania, PC World Romania, Telecom Romania; **RUSSIA:** Computerworld Russia, Mir PK, Publish, Seti; **SINGAPORE:** Computerworld Singapore, PC World Singapore, Publish in Asia; **SLOVENIA:** Monitor; **SOUTH AFRICA:** Computing SA, Network World SA, Software World SA; **SPAIN:** Communicaciones World España, Computerworld España, Dealer World España, Macworld España, PC World España; **SRI LANKA:** Infolink PC World; **SWEDEN:** CAP&Design, Computer Sweden, Corporate Computing Sweden, Internetworld Sweden, it.branschen, Macworld Sweden, MaxiData Sweden, MikroDatorn, Nätverk & Kommunikation, PC World Sweden, PCAktiv, Windows World Sweden; **SWITZERLAND:** Computerworld Schweiz, Macworld Schweiz, PCtip; **TAIWAN:** Computerworld Taiwan, Macworld Taiwan, NEW ViSiON/Publish, PC World Taiwan, Windows World Taiwan; **THAILAND:** Publish in Asia, Thai Computerworld; **TURKEY:** Computerworld Turkiye, Macworld Turkiye, Network World Turkiye, PC World Turkiye; **UKRAINE:** Computerworld Kiev, Multimedia World Ukraine, PC World Ukraine; **UNITED KINGDOM:** Acorn User UK, Amiga Action UK, Amiga Computing UK, Apple Talk UK, Computing, Macworld, Parents and Computers UK, PC Advisor, PC Home, PSX Pro, The WEB; **UNITED STATES:** Cable in the Classroom, CIO Magazine, Computerworld, DOS World, Federal Computer Week, GamePro Magazine, InfoWorld, I-Way, Macworld, Network World, PC Games, PC World, Publish, Video Event, THE WEB Magazine, and WebMaster; online webzines: JavaWorld, NetscapeWorld, and SunWorld Online; **URUGUAY:** InfoWorld Uruguay; **VENEZUELA:** Computerworld Venezuela, PC World Venezuela; and **VIETNAM:** PC World Vietnam. 5/7/98

Dedication

For the littlest Helm, Brynn Kyleakin (who graciously held off the impending arrival until after we finished this book and who gives us even more reason to continue our own genealogical pursuits)

Authors' Acknowledgments

We wish to acknowledge the following people, without whom this book wouldn't exist.

Lisa Swayne and Jill Pisoni, who sought us out to write the book.

Alan Mann, a leader in the genealogical community whose opinion we greatly respect.

Bill, Ryan, Andrea, Heather, Carmen, Paula, Colleen, Patricia, Tammy, Linda, Stacey, and Rowena who have logged a lot of hours editing the book and putting together the CD-ROM.

Our respective parents and ancestors, without whom our own genealogies would not be possible.

Publisher's Acknowledgments

We're proud of this book; please register your comments through our IDG Books Worldwide Online Registration Form located at http://my2cents.dummies.com.

Some of the people who helped bring this book to market include the following:

Acquisitions, Development, and Editorial

Project Editors: Bill Helling, Ryan Rader

Senior Acquisitions Editor: Jill Pisoni

Permissions Editor: Heather Heath Dismore

Associate Permissions Editor:
Carmen Krikorian

Copy Editor: Andrea C. Boucher

Technical Editor: Alan Mann

Media Development Technical Editor:
Joell Smith

Editorial Manager: Elaine Brush

Media Development Manager: Joyce Pepple

Editorial Assistant: Paul E. Kuzmic

Production

Project Coordinator: Cindy L. Phipps

Layout and Graphics: Lou Boudreau, Angela F. Hunckler, Todd Klemme, Jane E. Martin, Brent Savage, Kate Snell

Proofreaders: Christine Berman, Arielle Carole Menelle, Nancy Price, Rebecca Senninger, Janet M. Withers

Indexer: Sharon Hilgenberg

Special Help
Linda S. Stark, Rowena Rappaport, Tamara Castleman, Paula Lowell, Patricia Yuu Pan, Stacey Riebsomer, Colleen Williams

Precision Graphics

General and Administrative

IDG Books Worldwide, Inc.: John Kilcullen, CEO; Steven Berkowitz, President and Publisher

IDG Books Technology Publishing: Brenda McLaughlin, Senior Vice President and Group Publisher

Dummies Technology Press and Dummies Editorial: Diane Graves Steele, Vice President and Associate Publisher; Mary Bednarek, Director of Acquisitions and Product Development; Kristin A. Cocks, Editorial Director

Dummies Trade Press: Kathleen A. Welton, Vice President and Publisher; Kevin Thornton, Acquisitions Manager

IDG Books Production for Dummies Press: Michael R. Britton, Vice President of Production and Creative Services; Cindy L. Phipps, Manager of Project Coordination, Production Proofreading, and Indexing; Kathie S. Schutte, Supervisor of Page Layout; Shelley Lea, Supervisor of Graphics and Design; Debbie J. Gates, Production Systems Specialist; Robert Springer, Supervisor of Proofreading; Debbie Stailey, Special Projects Coordinator; Tony Augsburger, Supervisor of Reprints and Bluelines

Dummies Packaging and Book Design: Robin Seaman, Creative Director; Kavish + Kavish, Cover Design

♦

The publisher would like to give special thanks to Patrick J. McGovern, without whom this book would not have been possible.

♦

Contents at a Glance

Cartoons at a Glance

By Rich Tennant

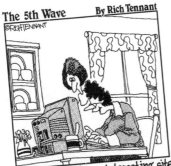

"It's really quite an interesting site. There's roller coaster action, suspense, and drama where skill and strategy are matched against winning and losing. And I thought researching genealogy online would be dull."

page 223

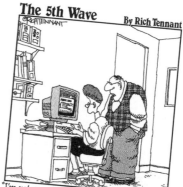

"I'm not sure I want to be claimed by a family whose home page has a link to the Zang Zone."

page 249

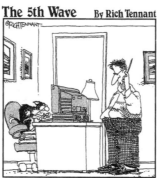

"Well, she now claims she's a descendant of the royal Egyptian line of cats, but I'm not buying that just yet."

page 7

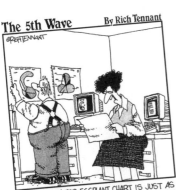

"WELL, SHOOT! THIS EGGPLANT CHART IS JUST AS CONFUSING AS THE BUTTERNUT SQUASH CHART AND THE GOURD CHART. CAN'T YOU JUST MAKE A PIE CHART LIKE EVERYONE ELSE?"

page 147

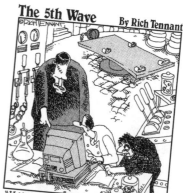

"Hold your horses. It takes time to locate the ancestors for someone of your background."

page 89

Fax: 978-546-7747 • E-mail: the5wave@tiac.net

Table of Contents

· ·

Introduction

● ●

*O*ver the past couple of years, interest in genealogical research seems to have boomed! Everywhere you turn, magazines and newspapers are running stories and columns about family history. Computer use and the rise of the Internet have helped encourage this growing interest and changed the nature of genealogy. To be a genealogist these days does not necessarily mean that you have to pack the kids in the car and travel a thousand miles to find details on that elusive ancestor. In fact, at times you don't even have to leave the comfort of your home in order to discover valuable information.

If you have an interest in genealogy, a wealth of information is at your fingertips. You can correspond with family members who live in far-off lands. You can research the history of a particular area without setting foot outside your home. You can discover resources you never suspected would help you in your pursuit of your family history. And you can do all of it using your computer and a little hook-up to the Internet.

Having so many resources available on the Internet is great, but you have to be careful not to overload yourself with information and get so frustrated that your interest in genealogy becomes a burden. The number of genealogy-related sites on the Internet is growing so rapidly that becoming over-whelmed is an easy thing to do. This is where we come in to help you.

Of course, you're probably asking yourself how this book differs from the many other genealogy books on the shelf. Some books tell you only the traditional methods of genealogical research — which have you traveling hundreds of miles to visit courthouses and using the good old typewriter to summarize your results. Unfortunately, these books miss the many opportunities that online research provides. Other books that do cover online genealogy tend to group resources by how users access them (all FTP sites are listed together, all World Wide Web sites are listed together, and so on), rather than telling you how you can integrate the many Internet resources to achieve your genealogical goal. As genealogists, we understand that re-searchers do not conduct searches by trying, for example, all the FTP sites and then all the World Wide Web sites. We search by looking for surnames or places anywhere we can find them — through FTP sites, World Wide Web sites, e-mail, newsgroups, or whatever.

Also, some books become too computer heavy — giving you lots of overkill about the ins and outs of each kind of Internet resource — and neglecting to help you with basic research techniques online and offline that you need to

successfully meet your goal. We don't want you to have a bad experience online. So rather than focus on just one thing — genealogy or online resources — we've tried to balance the act. In this book, we show you how to integrate genealogical research with the use of online resources so that you can learn to effectively and efficiently use your computer and the Internet in your family research.

Is This Book for You?

In writing this book, we made a couple of assumptions. (We know, you're never supposed to assume anything about anyone, so we broke a rule right off the bat! We apologize for being so rude.) If you fit one of these assumptions, this book is for you:

- ✔ You've done at least a little genealogy groundwork, and now you're ready to use the Internet to pursue (and better prepare yourself) for your genealogy both online and offline.

- ✔ You have at least a little computer experience, are now interested in pursuing your family tree, and want to know where and how to start.

- ✔ You have a little experience in genealogy and some experience with computers, but you want to learn how to put them together.

Of course, you can have a lot of computer experience and be a novice to genealogy or to online genealogy and still benefit from this book. In this case, you may still want to skim some of the basic sections on computers and the Internet in case you can find something else you can use.

Becoming an Official Genealogist

What are the requirements for becoming an official genealogist? Well, do you have a mirror nearby? If so, go to the mirror and look at yourself. Now say out loud, "I declare myself an official genealogist." There you go. It's official — you're a genealogist, and it's time to get started pulling together the puzzle pieces of your family history.

Seriously, being a genealogist has no formal requirements. You simply need an interest in your ancestry and a willingness to devote the rest of your life to pursuing information and documents.

How This Book Is Organized

To help you get a better picture of what this book has to offer to you, we explain a little about how it's organized and what you can expect to find in each part.

Before we get into each of the parts, we must tell you that we're aware that you may not read this book from cover to cover, in order. (No, you're not hurting our feelings by skipping through the sections looking only for information you're interested in at that particular moment!) In fact, we've tried to write this book to accommodate you. Each section within a chapter is written to stand alone so that you can pick up the book and flip directly to a section that deals with what you want to know. If we think something relevant in another section can supplement your knowledge on the particular topic, we provide a note or reference telling you the other place(s) we think you should look as well. However, we've tried very hard to do this referencing in a manner that is not obnoxious to those of you who choose to read the book through, chapter by chapter in order. We hope we've succeeded in addressing both types of readers! And now, on to the parts information.

Part I: Getting Your Act Together

You need to have a good foundation before starting your online genealogical research. This part explores the fundamental family information that you need to collect first, how to form an online research plan, and getting started on the Internet searching for information about ancestors and geographic locations.

Part II: Finding the Elusive Records

Searching online for information about members of a particular ethnic or religious group can pose a great deal of difficulty even for the most skilled genealogist. Likewise, looking for a specialized type of record can do the same. For this reason, Part II examines resources that are available online to help you find those elusive ancestors.

Part III: Maximizing Research Resources

One of the most important aspects of genealogical research is using a coordinated effort to achieve success. This part takes a look at what goes into this effort, including using all available online resources, cooperating with other researchers, coordinating with groups and societies, and sharing the fruits of your research with the online community.

Part IV: The Part of Tens

Ah, the infamous Part of Tens! (Infamous because every ...*For Dummies* book has one of these sections with profound advice or lists of things to do.) Here you find a series of quick-reference chapters that give you useful genealogical hints and reminders. We've put in a list of online publications we think you should know about, some tips for creating a genealogical Web page, hints to keep your online research sailing smoothly, and a list of sites we think every beginner to genealogy should visit.

Part V: Appendixes

As you're reading along in this book (or skipping from chapter to chapter, section to section, looking over only those parts that interest you), you may have additional questions in some areas. That's why we've included the Appendixes. One helps you get some clarification or further information about going online. Another one provides definitions of many of the terms that you are likely to encounter in your genealogical research. And the last one gives you an overview of the software that we've included on the CD-ROM that accompanies this book, as well as basic instructions for installing and using it.

The Genealogy Online For Dummies Internet Directory

This directory (on the yellow paper) contains a directory of select Internet sites that are of use and interest to genealogists. You can find sites for everything — from surnames to government to geographic-specific to comprehensive genealogical indices to big search engines to commercial endeavors. For each site we identify, we provide the name, URL (Uniform Resource Locator), and a brief overview of what the site has to offer.

We want you to be able to see immediately whether a site we've identified in the directory has a particular type of information or service of interest to you. For this reason, we've created some mini-icons — or, if you prefer, *micons* (see the *Genealogy Online Internet Directory* for details).

Icons Used throughout the Book

To help you get the most out of this book, we created some icons that tell you at a glance if a section or paragraph has important information of a particular kind.

Here we refer you to other books or materials if you would like additional information.

This icon signals a Web site that has a search engine you can use to look for content within the site.

Here you can find concepts or terms that are unique to genealogy.

When you see this icon, you know we're offering advice or shortcuts to make your researching easier.

This icon points out software that is included on the CD-ROM.

We walk readers step by step through an example of something.

Look out! This is something tricky or unusual to watch for.

Your Next Step

Depending on where you're reading this introduction, your next step is one of two possibilities:

✔ You need to go to the front of the bookstore and pay for this book so that you can take it home and use it. (A lot of bookstores are pretty understanding about your sitting and reading through parts of books — that's why they provide the comfortable chairs, right? But we're not sure they would look highly upon your whipping out your laptop computer, asking to borrow an Internet connection from them, and proceeding to go through this entire book right there in the store. Then again, we could be mistaken — so use your best judgment based on your knowledge of the bookstore in which you're standing.)

    ✔ If you've already bought the book and you're at home (or wherever), you can go ahead and start reading, following the steps for the online activities in the book as they come along.

Part I
Getting Your Act Together

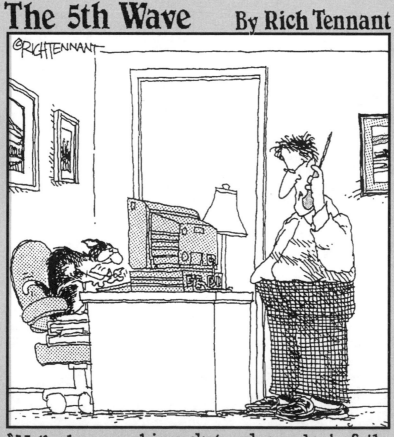

The 5th Wave By Rich Tennant

"Well, she now claims she's a descendant of the royal Egyptian line of cats, but I'm not buying that just yet."

In this part . . .

So you want to be an online genealogist? Well, you need to prepare yourself for that first research trip online by learning the basics of genealogy and how to form a research plan. When you're ready to take the online plunge, we help you find worthwhile surname and geographic-specific resources on the Internet.

Chapter 1

You Gotta Have Groundwork

In This Chapter:
▶ Interviewing your family
▶ Finding genealogical records in your home
▶ Using official records to discover your ancestors
▶ What you can find at Family History Centers

*A*lthough this is a book about researching your genealogy online, it is important to understand that several key sources of information must be found in places other than the Internet. You can use these resources to build a good foundation before you make that first trip online and to prove facts that you discover on other genealogists' Web sites. However, you can use online resources to help you find out what type of information you need to get started, and this chapter points you in the right direction.

As you venture into online genealogy, keep in mind that *you cannot complete your entire genealogy using only online resources.* (Consider this our disclaimer so that we don't get scolded by other genealogists who know what it takes to produce a solid genealogical work.) Many crucial records simply have not been transferred into an electronic format. In fact, it's best to think of online research methods as only one of many tools that you can use to gather the information for a complete picture of your ancestors.

In this chapter, we give an overview of several resources that you can rely on for information before you begin your online genealogical research and provide some links to online sites that can assist you in acquiring these resources.

Starting Your Research with What You Already Know

Sometimes, beginning genealogists start their initial search by trying to find out the identity of their great-great grandfather or their families' first immigrants. Such a strategy often becomes frustrating because they either can't find any information or they find something that they assume is true, only to find out later that the information doesn't apply to their family branch. To avoid this mess, we recommend that you conduct your genealogical research one step at a time — and that you begin your genealogical research with yourself.

Making a few notes about yourself — the biographical sketch

You already know a great deal about yourself — probably more than anyone else knows about you! (Unless you're married. Then you're sure that your spouse knows more about you, right?) You probably know your birth date, place of birth, parents' names, and where you've lived. (We recognize that not everyone knows all this information; adoptions or other extenuating circumstances may require you to do the best you can with what you know until you can discover additional information about yourself.) So, sit down at that computer, open your word processor, and begin creating an autobiographical sketch (of course, you can take out a piece of paper and start writing down all those details instead).

You can approach the sketch in several ways. Sometimes, the easiest method is to begin with current events and work back through your life. For instance, first note the basics: your current occupation, residence, and activities. Then move back to your last residence, occupation, and so on until you arrive at your birth date. Make sure that you include milestones like children's birth dates, marriage dates, military service dates, and other significant events in your life. If you prefer, you can cover your life by beginning with your birth and working forward to the present. Either way is fine, as long as all the important events are listed in the sketch.

Another method is to use 3 x 5-inch cards or a computer word processor to make notes on things that you recall over a certain period of time. Then you can arrange the cards or the paragraphs in the word-processing file to create a biographical sketch.

Finding primary sources

Although you may know a lot about yourself, someone else may have difficulty discovering these facts about you. This is where primary sources come in handy.

Primary sources are documents, oral accounts (if the account is chronologically close to the actual event), photographs, or any other items created at the time of a certain event's occurrence. For example, a primary source for your birth date would be a birth certificate. Typically, a birth certificate is prepared within a few days of the actual event, so information (like the time, date, and parents' names) is a reliable firsthand account of the event — unless, of course, someone lied about the parents' names (which occasionally occurs). For additional information on primary sources, see The Historian's Sources page at the Library of Congress site (lcweb2.loc.gov/ammem/ndlpedu/lessons/psources/pshome.html).

Some records may contain both primary and secondary sources. *Secondary sources* are those that are created a long time after the event or for which information is supplied by someone who was not an eyewitness to the event. (It is possible for a secondary source to be a person who was an eyewitness to the event but is recalling it after a significant time has passed.) For example, a death certificate contains both primary and secondary source information. The primary source information is the death date and cause of death. The facts are primary because the certificate was prepared around the time of death and the information is usually provided by a medical professional who pronounced the death. The secondary source information on the death certificate includes the birth date and place of birth of the deceased individual. These details are secondary because the certificate was issued at a time significantly later than the birth (assuming that the birth and death dates are at least a few years apart). Secondary sources do not have the degree of reliability or surety that primary sources do. Often secondary source information, such as that found on death certificates, is provided by an individual's children, descendants who may or may not know the exact date or place of birth. So, it's always a good idea to back up your secondary sources with reliable primary sources.

You can familiarize yourself with primary sources by collecting some information for your own biographical profile. Try to match up primary sources for each event in the sketch (for example, birth and marriage certificates, deeds, leases, military records, and tax records). (For more information on finding these types of documents, see the appropriate sections later in this chapter.) If you can't locate primary source documents for each event in your life, don't fret! Remember, your biographical sketch can serve as a primary source document because it is written by you and about you.

Chatting with Papa and Aunt Lola: Interviewing Your Family Members

After you complete your own biographical sketch, you will probably want to take the next step and begin interviewing your family members to collect information about them and other relatives. (You want to collect the same types of information about their lives as you provided about your own.) Your parents, brothers, sisters, grandparents, aunts, uncles, and cousins are good candidates for information about your family's most recent generations. Talking to relatives provides you with leads that you can use later to find primary sources. (For more information on primary sources, see "Finding primary sources" in the preceding section.) Family interviews can be completed in person or through a questionnaire — although we strongly recommend that they be conducted in person. (For an example of a cover letter to send your family, see www.familytreemaker.com/00000059.html.)

Here are a few tips to remember as you plan a family interview:

- ✔ Before interviewing family members, prepare a list of questions that you want to ask. Knowing what you want to achieve during the discussion can help you get started and keep your interview focused. (See the sidebar "Good interviewing questions" for some ideas).

- ✔ You may want to bring a tape recorder for the interview. However, make sure that you get the permission of each participant before you start taping.

- ✔ Use photographs and other documents to help your family member recall events.

- ✔ Try to keep your interviews to two hours or less so that you're not overwhelmed with information and the interviewee doesn't get worn out by your visit. Within two hours, you can collect a lot of information to guide you in your research. And remember, you can always do another interview if you want more information from the family member (actually, we really encourage you to do subsequent interviews — often the first interview will stimulate memories for the individual that you can then cover during another interview).

We're not sure how to politely phrase this next tip, so excuse us for being blunt. You may want to begin interviewing some of your older relatives as soon as possible, depending on their ages and health. If a family member passes on before you arrange to interview him or her, you may miss the opportunity of a lifetime to learn more about previous generations.

TIP

Good interviewing questions

Before conducting your family interview, pull together a set of questions to guide the discussion. Your planning can make the difference between an interview in which the family member stays focused or a question-and-answer session that invites bouncing from one unrelated topic to another. Here are examples of some questions that you may want to ask.

- What is your full name and do you know why you were named that?

- Where were you born and when? Do you remember any stories that your parents told you about the event?

- What do you remember about your childhood?

- Where did you go to school? Did you finish school? If not, why? (Remember to ask about all levels of schooling through college.)

- What were you brothers and sisters like?

- Where and when were your parents born? What did they look like? What were their occupations?

- Did your parents tell you how they met?

- Do you remember your grandparents? Do you recall any stories about them? What did they look like?

- Did you hear any stories about your great-grandparents? Did you ever meet your great-grandparents?

- When you were a child, who was the oldest person in your family?

- Did any relatives (other than your immediate family) live with you?

- Do you remember who your neighbors were when you were a child?

- Did your family have any traditions or celebrate any special holidays?

- Are there any items (stories, traditions, or physical items) that have been handed down through several generations of the family?

- When did you leave home? Where did you live?

- Did you join the military? If so, what branch of service were you in? What units were you a part of? Did you serve overseas?

- What occupations have you had? Did you have any special training?

- How did you meet your spouse?

- When and where did you get married? Did you go on a honeymoon? Where?

- When were your children born? Do you have any stories about the births?

- Do you know who in the family originally immigrated to this country? Where did they come from? Why did they leave their native land?

You can probably think of more questions that are likely to draw responses from your family. During the interview, stay flexible: Explore specific family events, share family legends, or ask for photographs that picture events that are being discussed. Also, if you want to see additional hints for conducting interviews, see "Recording Oral Histories: Tips and Topics" at www.familytreemaker.com/00000028.html

Looking for Love Letters, Laundry Receipts, and Other Important Documents

Those scraps from the past in the attics or basements of your family members' homes may be of genealogical significance to you now. For example, you may discover an old suitcase or cigar box full of documents like driver's licenses, war ration cards, and letters. These items may contain original signatures and other information that you can use to construct your ancestor's past.

When going through old family files, look for things that can serve as primary sources for facts that you want to verify. (For more on primary sources, see "Finding primary sources," earlier in this chapter.) Look for documents to verify addresses, occupations, church membership, and military service. Here is a list of some specific things you can look for:

- Family Bibles
- Legal documents (mortgages, titles, deeds)
- Insurance policies
- Wills
- Family letters
- Obituaries and newspaper articles
- Diaries
- Naturalization records
- Baptismal certificates and other church records
- Copies of vital records (birth, marriage, and death certificates; divorce decrees)
- Occupational or personnel records
- Membership cards

For a list of other items to look for around the home, see "Discovering Your Heritage 101 – The First Steps" (www.ancestry.com/home/howto/firststeps.htm) and "Finding Information at Home" (www.familytreemaker.com/00000027.html).

Dusting Off the Old Albums

So the saying goes: A picture is worth a thousand words. That is certainly true in genealogy. Photographs are among the most treasured documents for genealogists. Pictures show how your ancestors looked and what conditions they lived in. Sometimes, the flip side of the photo is more important than the picture itself. On the back, you may find crucial data like names, dates, and descriptions of places. Photographs are also useful as memory joggers for your family members. Pictures can help others recollect the past and bring up long-forgotten memories.

You may run into several different types of photographs in your research. Knowing when certain kinds of photographs were produced can help you associate a time frame with a picture. Here are some examples:

- **Daguerreotypes:** Daguerreotype photos were taken from 1839 to 1860. They required a long exposure time and were taken on silver-plated copper. You usually find them enclosed in a plastic or leather case, and the photographic image appears to change from a positive to a negative when tilted.

- **Ambrotypes:** Ambrotypes used a much shorter exposure time and were produced from 1858 to 1866. The image was made on thin glass and usually had a black backing.

- **Tintypes:** Tintypes were produced from 1858 to 1910. They were made on a metal sheet and the image was often coated with a varnish. You can usually find them in a paper cover.

- **Cartes-de-visite:** Cartes-de-visite were small paper prints mounted on a card. They were often bound together into a photo album. They were produced between 1858 and 1891.

- **Cabinet Cards:** Cabinet cards were larger versions of cartes-de-visite. They sometimes included dates on the borders of the cards. The pictures themselves were usually mounted on cardboard. They were manufactured primarily between 1865 and 1906.

- **Albumen Prints:** These were produced on a thin piece of paper that was coated with albumen and silver nitrate. They were usually mounted on cardboard. These prints were used between 1858 and 1910 and were the types of photographs found in cartes-de-visites and cabinet cards.

- **Stereographic Cards:** Stereographic cards were curved photographs that rendered a three-dimensional effect when used with a stereographic viewer. They were prevalent from 1850 to 1925.

- **Platinum Prints:** Platinum prints have a matte surface that appears embedded in the paper. The images were often highlighted with artistic chalk. They were produced mainly between 1880 and 1930.

> ✔ **Glass Plate Negatives:** Glass plate negatives were used between 1848 and 1930. They were made from light-sensitive silver bromide immersed in gelatin.

When dealing with photographs, keep in mind that they can be easily destroyed by too much light or humidity. For more information on preserving photographs, see "Preserving Your Treasured Family Documents" in Chapter 8. Also, some online resources can help you identify types of pictures. See the City Gallery site at `www.webcom.com/~cityg/` for 19th century photography information, and visit Photography as a Tool in Genealogy at `www.teleport.com/··fgriffin/photos.txt` for descriptions of several types of photographs.

Wandering through Birth, Death, Marriage, and Divorce Records

Vital records are one of the first set of primary sources typically used by genealogists (for more on primary sources see "Finding primary sources," earlier in this chapter). Vital records include birth, marriage, divorce, and death records and, for the most part, the originals are kept by local governments (although some governments have microfilmed them and stored them centrally). These records contain key information that can usually be relied upon as they were produced near the time that the event occurred and the information was provided by a witness to the actual event. (Outside the United States, vital records are often called civil registrations.)

Vital records are usually maintained in the county where the event occurred. Normally, you must contact the country clerk to receive a copy of a record. Some states centrally collect or microfilm their vital records, and they are available for public use at the state archives or library. You can find an online list of centralized vital record repositories in each of the states of the United States at the Where to Write for Vital Records site (`www.medaccess.com/states/`). For information on where to find vital record (and civil registration) information online, see "These Records Are Vital" in Chapter 6.

Birth records

Birth records are good primary sources for verifying, at a minimum, the date of birth, birthplace, and names of an individual's parents. Depending upon the information requirements for a birth certificate, you may also learn the birthplace of the parents, their ages, occupations, addresses at the time of

birth, whether the mother had given birth previously, date of marriage of the parents, and the names and ages of any previous children. Sometimes, instead of a birth certificate, you may find another record in the family's possession that verifies the existence of the birth record. For instance, instead of having a certified copy of a birth certificate, Matthew's grandmother had a Certificate of Record of Birth. This certificate attests to the fact that the county has a certificate of birth and notes its location. These certificates were used primarily before photocopiers became commonplace and it became easier to get a certified copy of the original record.

Birth records are less formal in older sources. Before modern record keeping, a simple handwritten entry in a book sufficed as an official record of an individual's birth. So, be very specific when citing a birth record in your genealogical notes. Include any numbers that you find on the record and where the record is located (including not only the physical location of the building, but also the book number and page number).

Marriage records

Marriage records come in several forms. Early marriage records may include:

- *Marriage bonds* (financial guarantees that a marriage was going to take place)
- *Marriage banns* (proclamations of the intent to marry someone in front of a church congregation)
- *Marriage licenses* (documents granting permission to marry)
- The actual *marriage record or certificate* (document certifying the union of two people)

These records contain, at a minimum, the groom's name, the bride's name, and the location where the ceremony took place. They may also contain occupation information, birthplaces of the bride and groom, parents' names and birthplaces, names of witnesses, and information on previous marriages.

One thing to be careful about when using marriage records: It's easy to confuse the date of the marriage with the date of the marriage bond, bann, or license. The latter records were often filed anywhere from days to several weeks before the actual marriage date. Also, do not assume that because you found a bond, bann, or license that a marriage actually took place. Some people had "cold feet" then as they do today.

Court records

Court cases and trials are not just a phenomenon of today's world. Your ancestor may have participated in the judicial system as a plaintiff, defendant, or witness. Some court records can provide a glimpse into the characters of your ancestors, whether they were frequently on trial for misbehavior or called as character witnesses. You can also find a lot of information on your ancestors if they were involved in land disputes, a common problem in some areas where land transferred hands often. Again, your ancestor may not have been directly involved in a dispute but may have been called as a witness. Another type of court record that may involve your ancestor are probate cases. Often, members of families contested wills or were called upon as executors or witnesses, and the resulting file of testimonies and ruling can be found in a probate record.

Marching to a Different Drummer: Military Records

While your ancestors may not have marched to a different drummer, at least one of them probably kept pace with a military beat at some point in life. Military records contain a variety of information; the two major types of records that you're likely to find are service and pension records. Draft or conscription records may also surface in your exploration.

Service records

Service records chronicle the military career of an individual. They often contain details about where your ancestors lived, when they enlisted or were *drafted* (conscripted), their ages, and their discharge dates. You may also find pay records (including muster records that state when your ancestors had to report to military units) and notes on any injuries that they sustained while serving in the military. Although most of the information contained in service records seems to be of little genealogical value, you can use these records to determine the unit in which your ancestor served. This information can lead you to pension records that do have genealogical importance. Also, service records can give you an appreciation of your ancestor's place within history — especially the dates and places where your ancestor fought or served as a member of the armed forces.

Pension records

Pensions were often granted to veterans who were disabled or who demonstrated financial need after service in a particular war or campaign; widows or orphans of veterans may also receive benefits. These records are valuable because, in order to receive pensions, your ancestors had to prove that they served in the military. Proof entailed a discharge certificate or the sworn testimony of the veteran and witnesses. Pieces of information that you can find in pension records include your ancestor's rank, period of service, unit, residence at the time of the pension application, age, marriage date, spouse's name, names of children, and the nature of the veteran's financial need or disability. If a widow submitted a pension application, you may also find records verifying her marriage to the veteran and death records (depending on when the veteran ancestor died).

Locating military records

Some military records (such as a discharge certificate or copy of orders) may turn up in your own home or the home of a relative. For other military records, you may need to visit a national archives or contact the appropriate military department. Here are some sites containing general information on military records:

- ✔ **Australia:** If you are interested in researching Australian military records see Australian Genealogy – Researching Armed Services Personnel (www.pcug.org.au/~mjsparke/mj_page1.html). Also, for unit histories, see Australian Army Regiments – Index of Web Sites (www.du.edu/~tomills/military/anzpac/aargxref.htm).

- ✔ **Austria:** You can find a list of the collections maintained in the Austrian State Archives War Archive (www.genealogy.com/gene/reg/AUT/krainf-e.htm).

- ✔ **Canada:** For a description of the military records that can be found in the Archives of Canada, see www.archives.ca/www/svcs/english/GenealogicalSources.html#Military Records and www.archives.ca/www/svcs/english/PersonnelRecords.html. To see regimental histories, see Canadian Army Regiments – Index of Web Sites (www.du.edu/~tomills/military/america/cargxref.htm).

- ✔ **Germany:** A few addresses for military archives in Germany are available at w3g.med.uni-giessen.de/gene/reg/SUD/sudet_ miarch.html and www.bawue.de/~hanacek/info/earchive.htm#CC

- ✔ **South Africa:** For unit histories, see South African Army Regiments – Index of Web Sites (www.du.edu/~tomills/military/africa/sargxref.htm).

- ✔ **United Kingdom:** In general, you can find military records at the Public Record Office that has a series of Family Fact Sheets on British military records (www.open.gov.uk/pro/famfacts.htm). You can also view a brief introduction to military records at midas.ac.uk/genuki/big/BritMilRecs.html. For regimental histories, see British Army Regiments – Index of Web Sites (www.du.edu/~tomills/military/uk/bargxref.htm).

- ✔ **United States:** The National Archives and Records Administration (www.nara.gov) houses several types of military records including service and pension records. You can also request information from the National Personnel Records Center (www.nara.gov/regional/stlouis.html) for more recent military records.

A useful guide to military records is "Military Service Records in the National Archives," General Information Leaflet 7, available from the National Archives and Records Administration, Room G-7, Seventh Street and Pennsylvania Avenue, NW, Washington, DC 20408.

Coming to Your Census

Finding genealogical records in the attics of your relatives' homes can take you only so far in the pursuit of your ancestors. Although vital records (see "Wandering through Birth, Death, Marriage, and Divorce Records," earlier in this chapter, for more details on vital records) can fill in some of the gaps, eventually you need a set of records that provides information on your ancestors that was taken at regular intervals — enter, census records.

United States Census schedules

Federal census records in the United States have been around since 1790. Censuses were conducted every ten years to count the population for a couple of reasons — to divide up the number of seats in the U.S. House of Representatives and to assess federal taxes. Although census collections are still done to this day, privacy restrictions prevent the release of any detailed census information on individuals for any year after 1920. Currently, you can find federal census data only for the census years 1790 to 1920.

Census records are valuable for you in that they can be used to take snapshots of your ancestors in ten-year increments. These snapshots allow you to track your ancestors as they moved from county to county, or state to state, and to identify the names of parents and siblings of your ancestors that you may not have previously known. Each census year contains a different amount of information, with more modern census returns (also called *schedules*) containing the most information.

The people who collected details on individuals were called *enumerators*. Traveling door to door, these census takers worked within an assigned district where they stopped at each residence to ask questions about the household. Being a census enumerator was not the most glamorous work. They were usually paid small amounts of money — usually barely enough to cover their expenses. Enumerators possessed differing levels of training and penmanship. These variations resulted in census returns that contained some readable information . . . and some illegible notes. Of course, on the plus side for genealogists, some enumerators went beyond the call of duty and made interesting notes on the families that they visited.

Using Soundex to search United States census records

For the censuses conducted from 1880 to 1920, you can use microfilmed indices organized under the Soundex system. The *Soundex* system is a method of indexing that takes names that are pronounced in a similar way but spelled differently and places them in groups. This indexing procedure allows you to find ancestors who may have changed the spelling of their name over the years. For example, you may find names like Helm, Helme, Holm, and Holme grouped together in the Soundex.

The Soundex code for a name consists of a letter and then three numbers. (Double letters count for only one number, and if your surname is short, you use zeros on the end to bring the total numbers to three.) To convert your surname to Soundex, use the first letter of your surname as the first letter of the Soundex code, and then substitute numbers for the next three consonants according to the following table. (For example, the Soundex code for the surname Helm is H450.)

1	B, P, F, V
2	C, S, K, G, J, Q, X, Z
3	D, T
4	L
5	M, N
6	R

Do the following to convert your surname to a Soundex code:

1. **Write down your surname on a piece of paper.**

   As an example, we'll convert the surname *Abell.*

2. **Keep the first letter of the surname and then cross out any remaining vowels (A, E, I, O, U) and the letters *W*, *Y*, and *H*.**

   If your surname begins with a vowel, keep the first vowel. If your surname does not begin with a vowel, cross out all of the vowels in the surname. So, in the surname *Abell,* we keep the letters *A*, *B*, *L*, and *L*.

3. **If the surname has double letters, cross out the second letter.**

   For example, the surname Abell has a double *L,* so we cross out the second *L,* which leaves us with the letters *A*, *B*, and *L*.

4. **Convert your letters to the Soundex code numbers according to the preceding chart.**

   We have the letters *A*, *B*, and *L* remaining. Because *A* is the first letter of the surname, it remains an *A*. The *B* converts to the number 1 and the *L* to the number 4. That leaves us with A14.

5. **Cross out any numbers that are the same side by side.**

   The remaining numbers of the Abell (A14) surname do not have the same numerical code next to each other. But it could happen with a name like Schaefer. Ordinarily, the name Schaefer would have the Soundex code of S216. However, because the *S* and the *C* both have the code of 2 and are side by side, you would eliminate the second 2 and come up with a Soundex code of S160.

6. **If you do not have three numbers remaining, fill in the rest with zeros.**

   Only two numbers remain in the Abell surname after I cross out the vowels and double letters. Because the Soundex system requires a total of three numbers to complete the code, I must fill in the remaining numerical spot with a zero. Thus, my result for Abell is A140.

Even though converting names to Soundex is really easy to do on paper (as you've just seen), we would be remiss if we didn't tell you about some online sites that offer free programs to do the conversions for you! Here are a few you may want to check out:

- ✔ **National Archives and Records Administration's Soundex Machine** (www.nara.gov/genealogy/soundex/soundex.html)
- ✔ **Surname to Soundex Code** (searches.rootsweb.com/cgi-bin/ Genea/soundex.sh)

> ✔ **Surname to Soundex Converter** (www.geocities.com/Heartland/
> Hills/3916/soundex.html)
>
> ✔ **Yet Another Soundex Converter** (rashoman.tjp.washington.edu/
> forms.soundex.formCGI.fcgi)

Lastly, we must warn you that Soundex is subject to human error. The indexing itself was done by humans, after all. Soundex codes were not always handled correctly or consistently by those who carried out the actual indexing. So it's possible that the person indexing made a coding error or failed to include some information. Therefore, if you're relatively certain that an ancestor should show up in a particular county in a census that uses Soundex, but the Soundex microfilm doesn't reflect that person, you may want to go through the census microfilm for that county anyway and look line-by-line for your ancestor.

Census records from other countries

The United States isn't the only country that has collected information on its population. Census counts have taken place in several countries throughout history. Here are examples of a few countries with census records.

Australia

Australia has taken a census every ten years since 1901. However, every return has been destroyed in accordance with law. There are other records that you can substitute for census returns in the form of convict returns and musters and post office directories. These returns are available for some states for the years 1788, 1792, 1796, 1800, 1801, 1805, 1806, 1811, 1814, 1816, 1817, 1818, 1819, 1820, 1821, 1822, 1823, 1825, 1826, and 1837. Some of these records can be found in the Mitchell Library in Sydney (www.slnsw.gov.au/ml/mitchell.htm), Archives Office of Tasmania (www.tased.edu.au/archives/), Latrobe Library in Melbourne, Public Records Office of Victoria, Battye Library in Perth (www.liswa.wa.gov.au/genbatt.html), and State Archives of Western Australia. For more information on locating census returns, see Censuses in Australian Colonies (www.users.on.net/proformat/census.html).

Austria

Austrian censuses were taken in the years 1857, 1869, 1880, 1890, 1900, and 1910. The first census that listed individuals by name was the 1869 Census. These returns include surname, sex, year of birth, place of birth, district, religion, marital status, language, occupation, literacy, mental and physical defects, residence, and whether the household had farm animals. For more information on Austrian censuses, see Austrian Census Returns 1869-1910 with Emphasis on Galicia (www.feefhs.org/ah/gal/jshea-ac.html) or Austrian Census for Galicia (www.feefhs.org/ah/gal/1880-gal.html).

Canada

Census returns are available for the years 1851, 1861, 1871, 1881, 1891, and 1901. The returns from 1851 to 1891 contain the individual's name, age, sex, province or country of birth, religion, race, occupation, marital status, and education. The returns for 1901 also include birth date, year of immigration, and address; for more information on data elements in the 1901 Census, see 1901 Census of Canada – Film Numbers (`www.geocities.com/Heartland/9332/census.htm`). These returns are stored at the National Archives of Canada (`www.archives.ca/MainMenu.html`). If you are looking for online information on specific census records, see the "Bob's Your Uncle, eh!" genealogy search engine (`indexes.mtrl.toronto.on.ca/genealogy/index.htf`). By selecting census from the drop-down box marked "Topic," you can see a variety of sites on census records including the 1753, 1921, 1935, and 1945 censuses of Newfoundland, French Canadian Heads of Households in the Province of Quebec in 1871, Index to the 1871 Census of Ontario, Index to the 1744 Quebec City Census, Nova Scotia Census Records, and the Toronto Census of 1837.

Denmark

The Danish Archives (`www.sa.dk/ra/uk/uk.htm`) has census returns for the years 1787, 1801, 1834, and 1840 (as well as other years up to 1916). The returns contain name, age, occupation, and relationship for each individual in the household. After 1845, census returns include information on the individual's place of birth. Census returns are available after they're 80 years old.

Germany

The German central government held censuses in 1871, 1880, 1885, 1890, 1895, 1900, 1905, 1910, 1919, 1925, 1933, and 1939. Unfortunately, these census returns do not contain much genealogical value because they were statistical in nature. For more information on the German census, see What About the German Census? (`www.qrz.com/gene/faqs/sgg.html#census`).

Ireland

Country-wide censuses have been conducted every ten years since 1821. Unfortunately, the census returns from 1821 to 1851 were largely destroyed in a fire at the Public Record Office in 1922. Fragments of these census returns are available at the National Archives of Ireland (an online searchable index of the 1851 County Antrim return is available at `www.genealogy.org/~liam/sea2.html`). The government destroyed the returns from 1861 and 1871. Returns for 1901 and 1911 still survive and are available at the National Archives of Ireland (`www.kst.dit.ie/nat-arch/index.html`). (Ireland suspended its law prohibiting the release of census returns for 100 years to make the 1901 and 1911 returns available to the public.) For more information on censuses in Ireland, see Census Records (`www.bess.tcd.ie/irlgen/census.htm`). If you are interested in Northern Ireland, see the Public Record Office of Northern Ireland site (`proni.nics.gov.uk/research/family/family.htm`).

Italy

The Italian State Archives (`homepage.interaccess.com/~arduinif/tools/arch001.htm`) contains national census for the years 1861, 1871, 1881, 1891, and 1901. For additional details on census records in Italy, see the Italian Genealogical Record page (`homepage.interaccess.com/~arduinif/tools/records.htm`).

Norway

The first census in Norway was conducted in 1769. A census by name was conducted for the first time in 1801, but was not repeated again until 1865. Each census after 1865 contained information such as name, sex, age, relationship to head of household, civil status, occupation; religion, and place of birth. For more information on Norwegian censuses, see Getting into the Norwegian Census (`www.isv.uit.no/seksjon/rhd/nhdc/michael02.htm`). An online searchable index of the 1801 Census of Norway is available (`www.uib.no/hi/1801page.html`). The 1900 Census of Norway (`teleslekt.nbr.no/teliss/e_index.html`) is also available online for a fee.

United Kingdom

Since 1801, censuses have been taken in the United Kingdom every ten years (except 1941). Most of the returns from 1801 to 1831 were statistical and did not contain names making them useless for genealogists. Beginning in 1841, the administration of the census became the responsibility of the Registrar General and the Superintendent Registrars who were responsible for recording civil registrations (vital records). This changed the focus of the census from the size of the population to details on individuals and families. The Public Records Office (`www.pro.gov.uk`) releases information in the census only after 100 years. You can find census returns for England and Wales at the Family Records Centre (`www.open.gov.uk/pro/frc.htm`) in London and for Scotland at the New Register House in Edinburgh. If you are not in either of those places, you can find copies of area returns at district libraries or Family History Centers.

Location, Location, Location: Land Records in Genealogical Research

In the past, ownership of land was used to measure the success of individuals. The more land that your ancestors possessed, the more powerful and wealthy they were. This concept often encouraged people to migrate to new countries in the search of land.

Land records may tell you where your ancestor lived prior to purchasing the land, spouse's name, and the names of children, grandchildren, parents, or siblings. However, to effectively use land records, you need to have a good idea of where your ancestors lived and possess a little background on the history of the areas in which they lived. Land records are especially useful for tracking the migration of families in the United States before the 1790 Census.

Most land records are maintained at the local level — in the town or county where the property was located. These records can come in multiple forms based upon the type of land record and the location in which it exists.

Land records in the United States

Your ancestors may have received land in the early United States in several different ways. Your ancestor may have purchased land or received a grant of land in the public domain — often called bounty lands — in exchange for military service or some other service for the country. Either way, the process probably started when your ancestor *petitioned* (or submitted an application) for the land. (It is possible that your ancestor laid claim to the land, rather than petitioning for it.)

If the application was approved, your ancestor was given a *warrant* — a certificate that allowed him or her to receive an amount of land. (Sometimes a warrant was called a *right*.) After your ancestor presented the warrant to a land office, an individual was appointed to make a *survey* — or detailed drawing and legal description of the boundaries — of the land. The land office then recorded your ancestor's name and information from the survey into a *tract book* (a book describing the lots within a township or other geographic area) and on a *plat map* (a map of lots within a tract).

After the land was recorded, your ancestors may have been required to meet certain conditions, such as living on the land for a certain period of time or making payments on the land. After they met the requirements, they were eligible for a *patent* — a document that conveyed title of the land to the new owner.

Land records for public domain land east of the Mississippi River are held by the Bureau of Land Management, Eastern States Land Office, 350 South Pickett Street, Alexandria, Virginia, and for the western states by the National Archives (www.nara.gov). For secondary land transactions (those made after the original grant of land), you probably need to contact the recorder of deeds for the county in which the land was held.

Here are some examples of sites with information on land records that you can find online:

- **Arkansas:** Arkansas Land Records – Interactive Search (`searches.rootsweb.com/cgi-bin/arkland/arkland.pl`)

- **Idaho:** Federal Land Records in Idaho (`www.usroots.com/cpadill/idahogs/fedland.htm`)

- **Illinois:** Illinois Public Domain Land Tract Sales (`www.sos.state.il.us:80/depts/archives/data_lan.html`)

- **Indiana:** Land Office Records at the Indiana State Archives (`www.ai.org/icpr/webfile/land/land_off.html`)

- **Louisiana:** Louisiana Land Records – Interactive Search (`searches.rootsweb.com/cgi-bin/laland/laland.pl`)

- **Oklahoma:** Federal Tract Books of Oklahoma Territory (`www.sirinet.net/~lgarris/swogs/tract.html`)

- **South Dakota:** Homesteading Records Information Page (`members.aol.com/gkrell/homestead/home.html`)

- **Tennessee:** An Introduction to the History of Tennessee's Confusing Land Laws (`funnelweb.utcc.utk.edu/~kizzer/genehist/research/landlaws.htm`)

- **Texas:** Texas General Land Office Archives (`www.glo.state.tx.us/central/arc/index.html`)

- **Virginia:** Introduction to Virginia Land History (`www.ultranet.com/~deeds/virg.htm`)

- **Wisconsin:** Wisconsin Land Records — Interactive Search (`searches.rootsweb.com/cgi-bin/wisconsin/wisconsin.pl`)

The topic of land records is so expansive, many books have been devoted to the subject. When you're ready to tackle land records in more depth, you may want to look at William Thorndale's "Land and Tax Records" in Szucs, Loretto Dennis and Sandra Hargreaves Luebking. *The Source: A Guidebook of American Genealogy.* Revised ed. Salt Lake City, UT: Ancestry, 1997.

Finding land records in other countries

Depending upon the country that you are researching you may find a number of ways that land transactions occurred. These links can assist you in figuring out how to research land records in a particular country:

> ✔ **Canada:** Land Records – Genealogical Sources in Canada
> (www.archives.ca/www/svcs/english/LandRecords.html)
>
> ✔ **England:** Land Records – Domesday Book and Beyond
> (www.rootsweb.com/~genclass/201/gen201_6.htm)
>
> ✔ **Ireland:** Land Records (www.bess.tcd.ie/irlgen/landrec.htm)

Visiting Libraries, Archives, and Historical Societies

Collecting additional information on the area where your ancestor lived may inspire you to search for information in public (and some private) libraries. Although local history sections are not generally targeted toward genealogists, the information you can find there is quite valuable. For example, public libraries often have city directories and phone books, past issues of newspapers (good for obituary hunting), and old map collections. Libraries may also have extensive collections of local history books that can give you a flavor of what life was like for your ancestor in that area. For a list of libraries with online catalogs see the webCATS site (www.lights.com/webcats/).

Archives are another place to find good information. They exist at several different levels (national, state, and local) and have different owners (public or private). Each archive will vary — some may have a large collection of certain types of documents, while others may just contain documents from a certain geographical area. To find archives see Repositories of Primary Sources (www.uidaho.edu/special-collections/Other.Repositories.html).

A third place to find additional information is at a historical society. Generally, historical societies have nice collections of maps, documents, and local history books pertaining to the area in which the society is located. Also, they are repositories for collections of papers of significant people who lived in the community. Often, you can find references to your ancestors in these collections, especially if the person whose personal documents are in the collection wrote a letter or transacted some business with your ancestor. Links to historical societies can be found on the Yahoo! site (www.yahoo.com/Arts/Humanities/History/Organizations/Historical_Societies/).

Discovering Family History Centers

You may be surprised to discover that your own hometown has a resource for local genealogical research! Sponsored by the Church of Jesus Christ of Latter-day Saints (LDS), over 2,500 Family History Centers worldwide provide support for genealogical research. The FamilySearch collection of CD-ROMs is among the important resources found in Family History Centers. They contain databases with the following information:

- ✔ **Ancestral File:** A database with over 29 million names available in family group sheets and pedigree charts.

- ✔ **International Genealogical Index:** A list of over 284 million individuals who are reflected in records collected by the LDS.

- ✔ **United States Social Security Death Index:** An index of those persons for whom Social Security death claims have been filed.

- ✔ **Military Index:** A list of United States soldiers killed in the Korean and Vietnam Wars.

- ✔ **Family History Library Catalog:** A catalog of over two million rolls of microfilm, one-half million pieces of microfiche, and 400,000 books and CD-ROMs available at the Family History Library in Salt Lake City.

Many other resources are available from Family History Centers, including their collection of microfilmed records and indices.

You need not be a member of the LDS church to use a Family History Center; the resources contained within them are available to everyone. Keep in mind that the workers at a Family History Center cannot research your genealogy for you, although they are willing to point you in the right direction. To find a family history center, see Where Is the Nearest Family History Center? at www.lds.org/Family_History/Where_is.html or consult your local telephone directory.

Chapter 2

Planning for Genealogical Success

• •

• •

*A*ll too often, we receive e-mail messages like this: "I'm looking for any information on Martha Looney. She was my great-great-grandmother. Please help me." Unfortunately, unless the individual in question is an ancestor of ours, we can do little to assist the person except to point them to resources that may help them. We receive so many of these messages each day that we can't reply to them all — so some of them never get answered. Our solution to this problem was to write this book!

Many times beginning genealogists don't know where to start because they're unsure of the normal research process, which is where we come in to help. This chapter covers some of the basic things to keep in mind when starting your research journey and offers some tips on what you can do when you hit "research bumps" along the way.

Introducing the Helm Online Family Tree Research Cycle

No book on research would be complete without having some sort of model to follow. We decided to create one just for online genealogists. We like to call our model — our version of the research process for online genealogists — the Helm Online Family Tree Research Cycle, for a lack of a better name. Figure 2-1 shows you the five phases of the cycle: planning, collecting, researching, consolidating, and distilling.

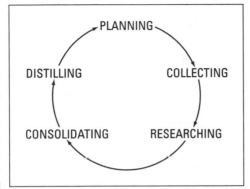

Figure 2-1:
The Helm
Online
Family Tree
Research
Cycle.

We liken the cycle to the steps you take to plant and sustain a tree:

- **Planning.** The first step in planting a tree is figuring out what kind of tree you want and deciding on a good place in your yard for the tree to grow. This step in the cycle is the *planning* phase. You want to select a family that you know enough about to begin a search and think about the resources you want to use to find the information you're looking for.

- **Collecting.** After you plan the location of the tree, you go to a nursery and pick out a suitable sapling and other materials that you need to ensure that the tree's roots take hold. The second phase of the cycle, *collecting,* is the same — you collect information on the family you're researching by conducting interviews and finding documents in attics, basements, and other home-front repositories.

- **Researching.** The next step is to actually plant the tree. You dig a hole, place the tree in it, and then cover the roots. Similarly, the *researching* phase of the cycle is spent digging for clues and finding information that can support your family tree.

- **Consolidating.** You've planted the tree and covered its roots. However, to make sure the tree grows, you mulch it and provide the nourishment it needs to survive. The *consolidating* phase of the cycle is the same in that you take the research you find and place it into your computer-based genealogical database or your filing system. These systems protect the research that you found by keeping it in a centralized location and provide an environment where you can see the "fruits" of your labor.

- **Distilling.** After your tree has taken root and begins to grow, you need to prune the old growth, allowing new growth to appear. Similarly, the *distilling* phase is where you use your computer-based genealogical database to generate reports showing the current state of your re-search. You can use these reports to "prune" from your database those individuals you've proven don't fit into your family lines — and perhaps find room for new genealogical growth by finding clues to other lines you need to follow up.

Divorce records

Divorce records are often overlooked by genealogists. Later generations may not be aware that an early ancestor was divorced, and the records recounting the event can be difficult to find. However, divorce records can be quite valuable. They can contain many important facts, including the age of the petitioners, birthplace, address, occupations, names and ages of children, property, and the grounds for the divorce.

Death records

Death records are excellent resources for verifying the date of death but are less reliable for other data elements like birth date and birthplace (these are often supplied by people who were not witnesses to the birth). However, information on the death record can point you in the right direction for records that can verify other events. More recent death records include the name of the individual, place of death, residence, parents' names, name of spouse, occupation, and cause of death. Early death records may only contain the date of death, cause, and residence.

Was Your Ancestor a Criminal? Using Civil and Court Records

There's good news — your ancestor need not have been a criminal for civil and court records to be useful in your genealogical research! Civil and court records may also contain information about your model-citizen ancestors — those fine, upstanding citizens who tended to make good witnesses.

Civil records

Generally, civil records include information on your ancestors' civic duties, and family members' interaction with local government. For example, several members of Matthew's branch of the Abell family held local posts in St. Mary's County, Maryland, including sheriff, inspector of tobacco, justice of the peace, and member of the legislature. Several civil records show when the Abells were sworn into office and some of the actions that they took within the community. Civil records are often found in local and state archives or libraries.

We think that using this model makes your research efforts a lot easier and more fulfilling. However, this model is merely a guide. Feel free to use whatever methods work best for you — as long as those methods make it possible for someone else to verify your research (through sources and so on).

Planning your research

You may hear it said that the Internet gives you the world at your fingertips. Discovering all the wonderful online resources that exist makes you feel like a kid in a candy store. You'll click around from site to site with wide eyes, amazed by what you're seeing, wanting to record everything for your genealogy — whether it relates to one of your family lines or not.

Because of the immense wealth of information available to you, putting together a research plan before going online is very important; it can save you a lot of time and frustration by keeping you focused. Tens of thousands of genealogical sites are on the Internet. If you don't have a good idea of what exactly you're looking for to fill in the blanks in your genealogy, you can get lost online. And getting lost is even easier when you see a name that looks familiar and start following its links, only to discover hours later (when you finally get around to pulling out the genealogical notes you already had) that you've been tracking the wrong person and family line!

Now that we've convinced you that you need a research plan, you're probably wondering what a research plan is. Basically, a *research plan* is a common-sense approach to looking for information about your ancestors online. A research plan entails knowing what you're looking for and what your priorities are for finding information.

If you're the kind of person who likes detailed organization (like lists and steps that you can follow to the tee), your research plan can be written on paper or kept on your computer. If you're the kind of person who knows exactly what you want and need at all times, and you have an excellent memory of where you leave off projects, your research plan can exist solely in your mind. In other words, your research plan can be as formal or informal as you like — as long as it helps you plot what you're looking for.

For example, say you're interested in finding some information on your great-grandmother. Here are some steps you can take to form a research plan:

1. **Write down what you know about the person you want to research.**

   Include details like the date and place of birth, marriage, and death, spouse's name, children's names, and any other details you think will help you distinguish your ancestor from other individuals.

2. **Conduct a survey of the appropriate links of a comprehensive genealogy site.**

   Take a trip out to sites like the Genealogy SiteFinder (www.genealogysitefinder.com) and look under the appropriate surname and geographic categories to see what kind of resources are available. (Chapters 3 and 4 go into online trips and searching for these types of information in more detail.) You may want to make a list of the sites you find on a sheet of paper or your word processor.

3. **Prioritize the resources that you want to use.**

   You may discover several different types of resources in your survey of a comprehensive site — resources like newsgroups, mailing lists, and World Wide Web sites. We recommend that you prioritize which resources you'll use first. You may want to visit a World Wide Web site prior to signing up for a mailing list, read a newsgroup for a while before posting to it, and so on. (For more on using these resources, take a look at Appendix A.)

4. **Schedule time to use the various resources you've identified.**

   Unfortunately, very few of us have time to conduct our research all at once, so it may be beneficial to schedule time to work on specific parts of your research. (Scheduling time is especially useful if you're paying by the hour for an Internet connection.)

Collecting useful information

After generating a research plan (see the preceding section, "Planning your research," for more information), you may need to fill in a few details like dates and locations of births, marriages, and deaths. You can collect this information through interviews with family members and by looking through family documents and photographs. (See Chapter 1 for tips on interviewing and using family documents and photographs.) You may also need to look up a few things in an atlas or gazetteer if you aren't sure where a certain location is. (Chapter 4 provides more information on online gazetteers.)

For a list of things that may be useful to collect, see Chapter 1. In the meantime, here are a few online resources that identify items to collect for your genealogy:

  ✔ **Ancestry Hometown Academy: Discovering Your Heritage — The First Steps** (www.ancestry.com/home/howto/firststeps.htm)

  ✔ **Family Tree Maker's Genealogy Site: A Trip Down Memory Lane** (www.familytreemaker.com/00000025.html)

  ✔ **Step-by-Step Guide to Finding Family Information** (www.familytreemaker.com/00000394.html)

Researching: Through the brick wall and beyond

Of course, researching your family history online is the topic of this entire book, so you'll be able to find the resources you need to do a great deal of your online research in these pages. However, a time will undoubtedly come when you run into what genealogists affectionately call the brick wall syndrome. The *brick wall syndrome* is when you think you've exhausted every possible way of finding your ancestor. Fortunately, a few people have posted some suggestions on how to get through a brick wall when you run into it. Check out these sites:

- ✔ **How to Get Past Genealogy Road Blocks** at www.firstct.com/fv/stone.html
- ✔ **When Your Family History Research Hits the Wall** at www.parkbooks.com/Html/res_guid.html

Using a database to consolidate your information

After you get rolling in your research, you often find so much information that you don't have enough time to put it all into your computer-based genealogical database. (A *genealogical database* is a software program that allows you to enter, organize, store, and use all sorts of genealogical information on your computer.) However, when possible, try to set aside some time to spend updating your database with the information you've recently gathered. This process of putting your information together in one central place, which we call *consolidating*, helps you gain a perspective on the work you've completed and provides a place for you to store all of those nuggets you'll need when you begin researching again. By storing your information in a database, you can always refer to your database for a quick answer the next time you try to remember where you found a reference to a marriage certificate for your great-great grandparents.

Distilling the information you've gathered

The final step in the cycle is distilling the information you've gathered into something you can use to find additional genealogical leads. Distillation can frequently be done by producing a report from your computer-based genealogical database. Most genealogical software programs produce reports for you in a variety of formats. For example, you can pull up a pedigree chart or an outline of descendants from information you've entered

in the database about each of your ancestors. You can use these reports to see what holes still exist in your research, and these missing pieces can then be added to the planning phase for your next research effort (starting the whole cycle over again).

Another advantage to genealogical reports is having the information readily available so that you can *toggle* back to look at the report while researching online, which will help you stay focused. (*Toggling* is flipping back and forth between open programs on your computer. For example, in Windows you press Alt+Tab to toggle.) Of course, if you prefer, printing copies of the reports and keeping them next to the computer while you're researching on the Internet serves the same purpose.

Too Many Ancestor Coals in the Research Fire

One last piece of advice: When you begin your research, take your time and don't get in a big hurry. Keep things simple and look for one piece of information at a time. If you try to do too much too fast, you run the risk of getting confused, having no online success, and getting frustrated with the Internet. This result isn't very encouraging and certainly doesn't make you feel like jumping back into your research, which would be a shame because you can find a lot of valuable research help online.

Chapter 3

What's in a Name?

*A*s a genealogist, you will probably start experiencing sleepless nights trying to figure out the maiden name of your great-great grandmother. Well, you may not have sleepless nights, but you may spend a significant amount of time thinking about and trying to find resources that will give you the answer to that crucial question. Although you're looking for information on a specific person, names are an important building block upon which your research depends. Often, a good research strategy is to look for information on a surname and then focus your research on particular individuals with that surname.

For example, when Matthew decided to go online for the first time, he didn't have a lot of information on his grandmother's family. He knew that her family was from Hardin County, Kentucky, but that was about all. For his first online search, he used her surname and found an e-mail address for another researcher living in Indiana. As it turned out, the researcher was related to his Kentucky branch and provided him with a lot of sources to further his research back several generations. Matthew then took that information and looked for specific information about his particular ancestors. While not everyone will have such good luck the first time, it is possible to achieve some research success just searching for surnames.

This chapter helps you with your first online search by covering the basics of a name search, presenting some good surname resource sites, and showing you how to combine several different Internet resources together to successfully find information on your family. If you need a refresher on how to use a World Wide Web browser prior to reading this chapter, take a look at Appendix A.

Selecting a Name to Begin Your Search

Selecting a name sounds easy, doesn't it? Just select your last name and you are off to the races. Unfortunately, depending on your surname, you may have quite a bit of trouble finding information that's relevant to your family. If your name is Smith or Jones, you may find thousands of sites with information on the surname, but not a bit of information that applies to your own family.

Try a unique name

The first time you begin researching online, try to begin with a surname that is, for lack of a better term, semi-unique. By this we mean a name that doesn't take up 10 pages in your local phone book, but is common enough that you can find some information on it the first time that you conduct a search. If you are really brave, you can begin with a very common surname, such as Smith or Jones, but you'll have to do a lot more groundwork up front. (For more on groundwork, see Chapter 1.)

Also, consider any variations in spelling that your chosen name may have. Often, you can find more information on the mainstream spelling of the surname than on one of its rarer variants. For example, if you are researching the surname Helme, you will have better luck finding information under the spellings Helm or Helms. If your family immigrated to the United States in the last two centuries, they may have "Americanized" their surname. Americanizing a name was often done so that the name could be easily pronounced in English, or sometimes the surname was simply misspelled and adopted by the family.

To find various spellings of the surname, you may need to dig through some family records or look at a site like Surnames: What's In A Name (`clanhuston.com/name/surnames.htm`).

Narrow your starting point

If you aren't sure how popular a surname is, try visiting a site like Hamrick Software's surname distribution site (`www.hamrick.com/names`).

At Hamrick's site, you can find the distribution of surnames in the United States based upon the 1850 Census, 1880 Census, 1920 Census, and phone books from 1990 to the present. All you have to do is enter your surname, select a year, and click on the Display button. The result is a new Web page containing a color map displaying the distribution of your surname.

For instance, Figure 3-1 shows a distribution map for the surname Abell in 1990. According to the map, in two states, only one out of every 1,000 individuals use this surname. In the remaining states, the name is even rarer. This gives you a good indication that the surname is somewhat unique. In contrast, during the same year, the surname Smith was held by at least one out of every 300 individuals in each state.

Looking at Figure 3-1, you may find it difficult to determine which two states have one out of 1,000 individuals using the surname Abell because of the way the colors show up as black, white, or shades of gray. If you visit Hamrick's site, the maps come up in color and are easier to read. (And just in case you're curious, the two states were Maryland and Kentucky.)

Keep in mind that Hamrick Software site is very popular, so you may want to access it at night when there may be fewer people visiting it.

A good reason to check out the distribution maps is that they can be used to identify potential geographic areas where you can look for your family later on in your research. This is especially true for maps generated from data from the 1850 and 1880 Census. For example, we generated another map on the Abell surname for the 1880 Census. We discovered that there were six states where the name appeared more frequently than in the rest of the country. If we hit a wall and can't find additional information online about a particular individual or the surname, we know that we can start looking at records in these states in the hopes of finding more clues about our particular branch of the family.

Figure 3-1:
A map of
the Abell
surname
distribution
in 1990 from
Hamrick
Software.

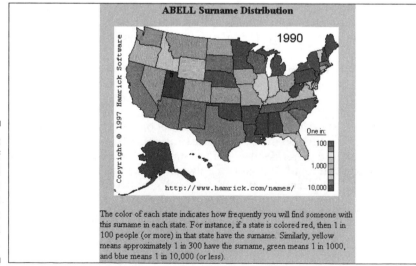

Use a name that you know about

In addition to picking a name that you're likely to have success researching, you want to use a surname that you know something about. If you have a family line where you know the names of your great-great grandparents, use that surname rather than a name where you only know your family line as far back as your grandparents. The more details that you know about those persons possessing the surname, the more successful your initial search is likely to be.

For example, Matthew used the unique surname Abell because he knew more about that side of his family. His grandmother once mentioned that her father was born in Kentucky in 1876. This gives him a point of reference for judging whether a site has any relevant information on his family. A site is relevant if it contains any information on Abells who were located in Kentucky prior to or around the year 1876. Try to use the same technique with your surname. For more information on how to extract genealogical information from your family to use in your research, see Chapter 1.

Select a grandparent's surname

Having trouble selecting a surname? Why not try the name of one of your grandparents? Using the surname of a grandparent can have several benefits. If you find some information on the surname but you aren't sure whether it's relevant to your family, you can check with a grandparent or other relatives to see whether they know any additional information that can help you. This may also spur interest in genealogy in other members of your family who can then assist you with some of your research burden or produce some family documents that you never knew existed.

With a name in hand, you're ready to see how much information is currently available on the Internet about that surname. Because this is your first step in a long journey to discover your family history, it is important to keep in mind that you want to begin slowly. *Don't try to examine every resource right from the start.* You are more likely to become overloaded with information if you try to find too many resources too quickly. Your best approach is to begin with a general survey of resources followed by a look at specific sites. And keep in mind that you can always bookmark all of the sites you see during your survey so that it's easier to return to them later when you're ready for more-in-depth researching. (Little rusty on how to set bookmarks on your Web browser? See Appendix A for a refresher.)

Looking at a Comprehensive Web Site

The best place to begin your survey of online resources on your chosen surname is at one of the comprehensive genealogical sites. By *comprehensive,* we mean that the site identifies a large number of other genealogical sites that contain information on a number of families, locations, or a variety of other subjects.

1. **Fire up your World Wide Web browser and go to the Genealogy Toolbox site located at** `genealogy.tbox.com`

   The Genealogy Toolbox is divided into three parts: Genealogy SiteFinder, Query Central, and the Journal of Online Genealogy. The Genealogy SiteFinder section profiles a variety of links to genealogical resources available on the Internet. Query Central allows researchers to post questions online for other individuals to answer. The Journal is a monthly online publication with articles on how to effectively re-search genealogy on the Internet.

   (If you have questions on using a browser, go to Appendix A.)

2. **Select Genealogy SiteFinder and choose the <u>Expanded Directory</u>.**

   Scroll down to the People category, and then select <u>Surnames</u>.

3. **Choose the first letter of the surname you're researching.**

   Matthew is looking for information on the surname Abell, so he chose <u>A</u> under the Surnames subcategory (Figure 3-2 shows the resulting page). Each link on the page includes a brief abstract of the contents of the site — which helps you determine whether the site is likely to contain information that is relevant to your family. If you are in doubt after reading the abstract, go ahead and visit the site. You may get lucky and find something of interest.

4. **If you find an interesting site, take a few minutes to explore it.**

   Remember that you are just doing a survey right now to give you an idea of how much information is out there on your selected surname — so don't stay out too long. If you don't find any sites to visit under the letter you selected in Step 3, don't get discouraged! It doesn't necessarily mean that there aren't any genealogical sites on your surname. It may mean that the maintainer of the Genealogy SiteFinder has not yet indexed the site to be included on the list. And even if it turns out that there isn't currently a site that focuses specifically on your selected surname, you still shouldn't give up. You may discover later on through other means that a lot of sites exist that contain information on your surname.

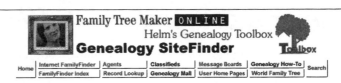

Figure 3-2:
The "A"
surnames
page of the
Genealogy
SiteFinder.

Finding the Site That Is Best for You

Your dream as an online genealogist is to find a site that contains all the information that you ever wanted to know about your family. Unfortunately, these sites will be few and far between (if they exist at all). Before you find the "golden site," you will discover a variety of other sites that vary greatly in the amount and quality of genealogical information. Knowing ahead of time what kinds of sites are out there and what common types of information you will encounter is useful.

Personal genealogical sites

Many of the sites that you encounter on the World Wide Web are personal genealogical sites. Individuals and families who have specific research interests establish these sites. You are likely to find information on the site maintainer's immediate family or on a particular branch of several different families, rather than on the surname as a whole. That doesn't mean that valuable information is not present on these sites — just that they have a more personal focus.

There's a wide variety of information found on personal genealogical sites. Some pages list only a few surnames that the maintainer is researching, while others contain extensive online genealogical databases and narratives. It all depends on the amount of research, time, and computer skills the maintainer possesses. Some common items that you see on most sites

include a list of surnames, an online genealogical database, Pedigree and Descendant charts (for information on these charts, see Chapter 8), family photographs, and the obligatory list of genealogical Internet links.

An example of a personal genealogical site from Australia is Andrea Johnson's Genealogy Page (http://www.geocities.com/Heartland/7031/). The site includes a Pedigree chart listing four generations of direct ancestors and an online genealogical database with 729 individuals. Each entry in the genealogical database is listed on a Family Group Sheet. (For descriptions of Pedigree charts and Family Group Sheets, see Chapter 8.) The Family Group Sheet shows the dates and places of birth, marriage, and death for the father, mother, and children. The site also has some narrative information on five of the maintainer's families (see Figure 3-3). Each narrative contains additional information on the family members who are on the Family Group Sheet and gives a broader overview of the history of the family than you may get through the database. The maintainer of the site also includes an e-mail address in case you have some questions or can contribute additional information.

Personal genealogical sites vary not only in content but also in presentation. Some sites are neatly constructed using soft backgrounds and aesthetically pleasing colors. Others sites, however, require you to bring out your sunglasses to tone down the fluorescent colors, or they use link colors that blend in with the background making it very difficult to navigate through the site. You should also be aware that a lot of personal sites use Javascripts, music players, and animated icons that can significantly increase your download times as they take a long time to load.

Figure 3-3:
A narrative on the McArdle family from Andrea Johnson's genealogy page.

My McArdle Family

Peter McArdle was born in 1834, at Moynalvy, Co.Meath, Ireland, the son of a farmer, Edward, and wife **Catherine (nee Kettlewell)**. He married **Elizabeth Kelly** (daughter of James & Margaret (nee Martin), 24 September 1859, at the Church of the Nativity, Moynalvy, Co.Meath. Two daughters, Catherine and Margaret, were born in Ireland, before the family emigrated to Australia, aboard the ship, "Hope". The "Hope" departed Liverpool on the 17th of March 1863, and arrived at Melbourne, Victoria, Australia on the 19th of June 1863. The family settled on a property as farmers, at Dead Horse (now Invermay), Ballarat, Victoria, Australia.

Nine more children were born into this family; Annie , Hannah , Bridget , Mary , Elizabeth , Edward , James , Peter , and John . A total of seven daughters, followed by four sons.

Peter died on the 11th of April 1908, from congestion of the lungs and decay, and was buried in the Ballarat Cemetery. After his death, Elizabeth moved to Brunswick, Victoria, to live with her daughter, Hannah, and died there on the 24th of April, 1928. She was buried at the Fawkner Cemetery with her sister, Catherine.

 Catherine Marcella McArdle (my Great Grandmother) the eldest daughter of Peter and Elizabeth (nee Kelly), was born about 1861, at Moynalvy,Co.Meath,Ireland. She grew up in the family home at Ballarat, and as a teenager, found employment as a housekeeper for a family who lived at Kew. She married **William James Short**

After you find a site containing information that is useful to you, it's a good idea to copy down the maintainer's name and e-mail address as soon as possible. It's also a good idea to contact the maintainer as soon as possible if you have any questions or want to exchange information. Personal genealogical sites have a way of disappearing without a trace as individuals frequently switch Internet providers.

One-name studies

If you're looking for a wide range of information on one particular surname, a one-name study site may be the place to look. These sites usually focus on researching one surname regardless of the geographic location where the surname appears. In other words, they welcome information about people with the surname worldwide. These sites are quite helpful because they contain all sorts of information about the surname, even if they don't have specific information about your branch of a family with that surname. Frequently, they have information on the variations in spelling, origins, history, and heraldry of the surname. One-name studies have some of the same resources you find in personal genealogical sites, including online genealogy databases and narratives.

Although one-name study sites welcome all surname information regardless of geographic location, the information presented at one-name study sites is often organized around geographic lines. For example, a one-name study site may categorize all the information about people with the surname by continent or country — such as Helms in the United States, England, Canada, Europe, and/or Africa. Or the site may be even more specific and categorize information by state, province, county, or parish. So, you are better off if you have a general idea of where your family originated or migrated. But if you don't know, browsing through the site may lead to some useful information.

The Iseli Family World Wide Web Site (`iseli.simplenet.com/`) is a one-name study site with an international focus. From the initial page (see Figure 3-4), you can choose to view the site in German, English, or French. (The site is scheduled to be available in Afrikaans soon and hopefully is by the time you're reading this!) The site is divided into several categories including variations in surname spelling, family branches, notable Iselis, family heraldry, and links to Iseli researchers' World Wide Web pages.

A notable portion of the Iseli site is the Iseli Millennium Project. This project seeks to produce a worldwide family genealogy to the year 2000 using the combined knowledge and research abilities of the users of the site.

The maintainers of one-name study sites welcome any information you have on the surname. These sites are often a good place to join research groups that can be instrumental in assisting your personal genealogical effort.

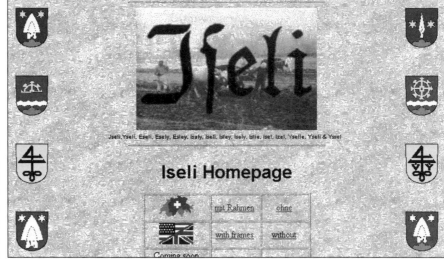

Figure 3-4:
The Iseli
Family
World Wide
Web Site
home page.

Genealogy Online Internet Directory in this book identifies some one-name study sites you may want to visit. Two sites that can help you determine if there are one-name study sites devoted to surnames you are researching are

- ✔ **Guild of One-Name Studies** (www.one-name.org)
- ✔ **SurnameWeb** (www.surnameweb.org)

Family associations and organizations

Family association sites are similar to one-name study sites in terms of content, but they usually have an organizational structure (such as a formal association, society, or club) backing them. The association may focus on the surname as a whole or just one branch of a family. The goals for the family association site may differ from those for a one-name study. The maintainers may be creating a family history in book form or a database of all individuals descended from a particular person. Some of the sites may require you to join the association before you can fully participate in their activities, but this is usually at a minimal cost or free.

The Wingfield Family Society site (www.wingfield.org/), shown in Figure 3-5, has several items that are common to family association sites. The site's contents include a family history, newsletter subscription details, membership form, reunion news, queries, mailing list information, and a directory of the society's members who are online.

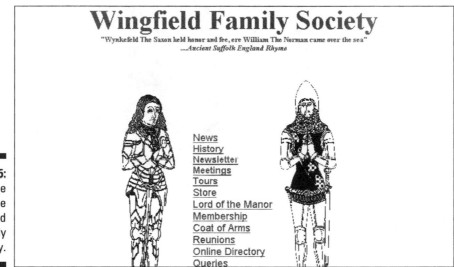

Figure 3-5:
The home
page of the
Wingfield
Family
Society.

Surnames connected to an event or place

A fourth place where you are likely to discover surnames is a site that has a collection of names connected with a particular event or geographic location. The level of information available on these sites varies greatly between sites and between surnames on the same site. Often the maintainers of such sites include more information on their personal research interests than other surnames, simply because they have more information on their own lines.

An example of a geographical site containing surname information is the Allegheny Regional Family History Society page at `www.swcp.com/~dhickman/arfhs.html` (shown in Figure 3-6). Although the focus of the site is on genealogical resources in the counties of northeast West Virginia, southwest Pennsylvania, western Maryland, and northwest Virginia, it has a section with online genealogical databases of families who lived in the region. You can also find a searchable surname list of the society's membership, census information, cemetery records, and articles on specific families in the region.

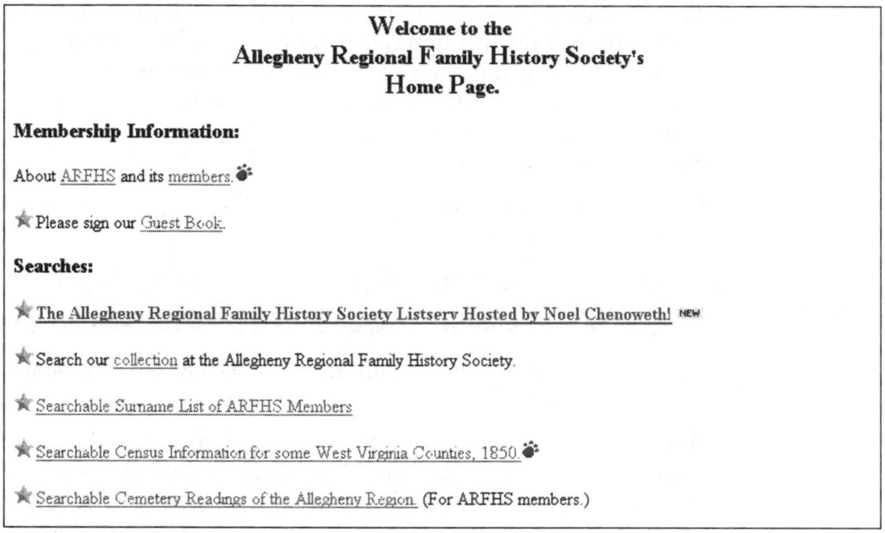

Welcome to the
Allegheny Regional Family History Society's
Home Page.

Membership Information:

About <u>ARFHS</u> and its <u>members</u>.

⭐ Please sign our <u>Guest Book</u>.

Searches:

⭐ <u>The Allegheny Regional Family History Society Listserv Hosted by Noel Chenoweth!</u> NEW

⭐ Search our <u>collection</u> at the Allegheny Regional Family History Society.

⭐ <u>Searchable Surname List of ARFHS Members</u>

⭐ <u>Searchable Census Information for some West Virginia Counties, 1850.</u>

⭐ <u>Searchable Cemetery Readings of the Allegheny Region.</u> (For ARFHS members.)

Figure 3-6:
The
Allegheny
Regional
Family
History
Society
home page.

Query for One: Seeking Answers to Your Surname Questions

Even if you can't find any surname-specific sites on your particular family, there is still hope! This hope comes in the form of queries. *Queries* are research questions that you post to a particular World Wide Web site, mailing list, or newsgroup, so that other researchers can help you solve your research problems. Often other researchers have information that they have not yet made available about a family, or they may have seen some information on your family even though it isn't a branch that they are actively researching.

Queries on the World Wide Web

One of the quickest ways of reaching a wide audience with your query is through a query site on the World Wide Web. (Appendix A has some information on the Web if you need help.) For an example of a query site, try the Query Central portion of the Genealogy Toolbox:

1. **With your Web browser, go to** `genealogy.tbox.com/query`

2. **Using the search engine at Query Central, do a quick search to see whether there are others who are researching your family lines and, if so, who they are and how to contact them.**

This particular query list at the Genealogy Toolbox includes a search engine that looks through queries posted on the site since October 1995. The index that the search engine uses is divided into quarters, so you will have to conduct a separate search for each quarter. You can change the quarter by using the drop-down menu next to the search engine submission form.

3. Return to the main Query Central page by using the Back button on your Web browser.

4. On the main Query Central page, choose <u>Add a Query</u>.

5. Type your query in the box, and then click the Submit button.

Be sure to include your e-mail address so that other researchers can reply to you directly.

Write your query according to the format specified by the site maintainer. Query lists can be found on a number of genealogical pages, and the format for posting queries often varies from site to site. Figure 3-7 provides an example of what the Genealogy Toolbox query list looks like.

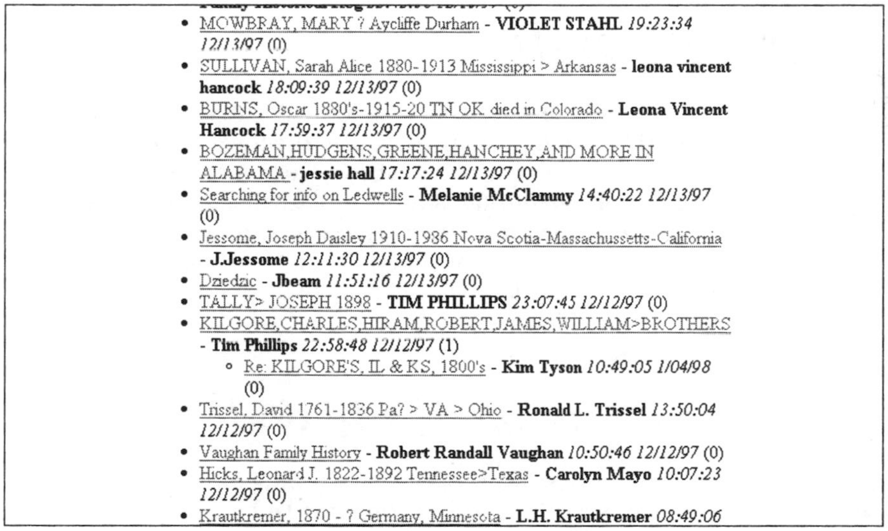

Figure 3-7:
A query
page
from the
Genealogy
Toolbox.

- MOWBRAY, MARY ? Aycliffe Durham - **VIOLET STAHL** *19:23:34 12/13/97* (0)
- SULLIVAN, Sarah Alice 1880-1913 Mississippi > Arkansas - **leona vincent hancock** *18:09:39 12/13/97* (0)
- BURNS, Oscar 1830's-1915-20 TN OK died in Colorado - **Leona Vincent Hancock** *17:59:37 12/13/97* (0)
- BOZEMAN,HUDGENS,GREENE,HANCHEY,AND MORE IN ALABAMA - **jessie hall** *17:17:24 12/13/97* (0)
- Searching for info on Ledwells - **Melanie McClammy** *14:40:22 12/13/97* (0)
- Jessome, Joseph Daisley 1910-1936 Nova Scotia-Massachussetts-California - **J.Jessome** *12:11:30 12/13/97* (0)
- Dziedzic - **Jbeam** *11:51:16 12/13/97* (0)
- TALLY> JOSEPH 1898 - **TIM PHILLIPS** *23:07:45 12/12/97* (0)
- KILGORE,CHARLES,HIRAM,ROBERT,JAMES,WILLIAM>BROTHERS - **Tim Phillips** *22:58:48 12/12/97* (1)
  - Re: KILGORE'S, IL & KS, 1800's - **Kim Tyson** *10:49:05 1/04/98* (0)
- Trissel, David 1761-1836 Pa? > VA > Ohio - **Ronald L. Trissel** *13:50:04 12/12/97* (0)
- Vaughan Family History - **Robert Randall Vaughan** *10:50:46 12/12/97* (0)
- Hicks, Leonard J. 1822-1892 Tennessee>Texas - **Carolyn Mayo** *10:07:23 12/12/97* (0)
- Krautkremer, 1870 - ? Germany, Minnesota - **L.H. Krautkremer** *08:49:06*

TIP

Keys to an effective query

Have you ever asked a question of thousands of strangers around the entire world? If you haven't, then you should be aware that this is exactly what you are doing when you post your first query.

A lot of genealogical sites on the Internet allow visitors to post questions *(queries)* about the people and places they are currently researching. Posting queries is a lot like calling the reference desk of your local library. Reference librarians can be a great help — if your questions contain enough detail for them to work with.

Keep these key things in mind when you are posting queries. First, make sure that your query is appropriate for the site. Several sites have specific requirements for queries, especially those sites that focus on specific geographical areas. Second, ensure that your query is formatted in a manner consistent with the site maintainer's instructions. Most of the query sites don't have an automated posting process, so the maintainer is probably posting all of the queries by hand. It helps them to have the query in a standard format and it helps those reading the query to quickly determine whether they can help the person. Here are some elements that you want to try to include in your query (as long as they are consistent with the site's format):

✔ **Type your surnames in all capital letters.** HELM is much easier to see than Helm when reading through thousands of queries.

✔ **Keep your query concise, but add some concrete information.** Dates of birth and death, specific locations where the person lived, and names of any spouses, parents, or children are concise but concrete. A good query example would be:

"HELM, George — I am looking for the parents of George Helm of Frederick County, Virginia (1723-1769). His wife was Dorothea and he had a son named George (who was a soldier in the American Revolution and later moved to Fentress County, Tennessee). George is buried in the German Reformed Cemetery in Winchester, Virginia. I can be contacted at mhelm@tbox.com or at the following mailing address. . ."

✔ **Your query should contain the basic elements that other researchers need to determine whether they can help you.** A good rule of thumb is that your query should, at a minimum, contain the answers to these questions:

Who. Who is the person you're looking for?

What. What specific information do you want about the person?

Where. Where did the person live? Where was the person born? Where did the person die?

When. When was the person born? When did the person die?

How. How can someone contact you? Include e-mail and postal mail addresses.

Mailing list queries

When you think of mailing lists you may have nightmares of the endless stream of "junk" mail that you receive every day as a result of some company selling your name to a mailing list. Well, fear no more. The type of mailing lists we are referring to deliver mail that you actually request. They also provide a means through which you can post queries and messages about your surnames and genealogical research in general.

Mailing lists are formed by groups of people who share common interests, whether those interests are in surnames, specific geographic areas, particular topics, or ethnic groups. The list consists of the e-mail addresses of each person who joins (or subscribes to) the group. When you want to send a message to the entire group, you send it to a single e-mail address that in turn forwards the message to everyone on the list. To join a mailing list, you send an e-mail to a designated address with a subscription message. You should then receive a confirmation e-mail letting you know that you are subscribed to the list and telling you where you need to send an e-mail if you want to send a message to everyone on the list.

So you know what a mailing list is, but how do you find one of interest to you? One way is to consult the comprehensive list of mailing lists found on the Genealogy Resources on the Internet site (`members.aol.com/gresinet/gen_mail.html`). The site breaks down the mailing lists into the categories of general, geographic/non-USA, software, United States, and surname.

Here's how you can find and join a mailing list for your surname.

1. **Point your Web browser to** `members.aol.com/gresinet/gen_mail.html` **and select the first letter of a surname that you are interested in.**

   The letters appear near the bottom of the page. We selected H̲ because we are looking for a mailing list on the surname Helm. A list of surnames with mailing lists pops up.

2. **Scroll through the list and choose a surname link from those listed on the page.**

   By scrolling through the list, you can see if your surname is represented. We scrolled through until we found our surname (see Figure 3-8) and clicked on that link. It took us to a page that had information on a mailing list pertaining to Helm.

   Note that several of the mailing lists include variations of the surname as part of the scope of their discussions—the Helm list includes 28 variants. So, even if the exact spelling of your surname does not appear in the list, it's a good idea to skim some of the surnames with similar spellings.

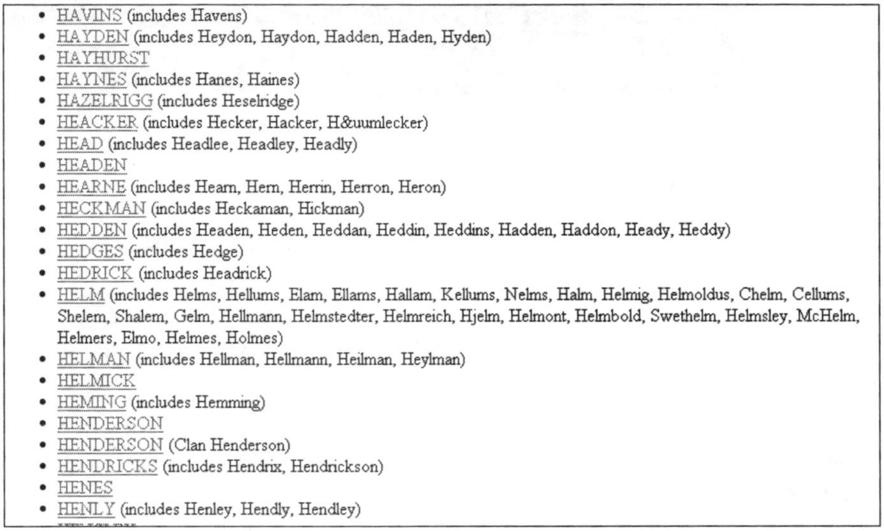

- HAVINS (includes Havens)
- HAYDEN (includes Heydon, Haydon, Hadden, Haden, Hyden)
- HAYHURST
- HAYNES (includes Hanes, Haines)
- HAZELRIGG (includes Heselridge)
- HEACKER (includes Hecker, Hacker, H&uumlecker)
- HEAD (includes Headlee, Headley, Headly)
- HEADEN
- HEARNE (includes Hearn, Hern, Herrin, Herron, Heron)
- HECKMAN (includes Heckaman, Hickman)
- HEDDEN (includes Headen, Heden, Heddan, Heddin, Heddins, Hadden, Haddon, Heady, Heddy)
- HEDGES (includes Hedge)
- HEDRICK (includes Headrick)
- HELM (includes Helms, Hellums, Elam, Ellams, Hallam, Kellums, Nelms, Halm, Helmig, Helmoldus, Chelm, Cellums, Shelem, Shalem, Gelm, Hellmann, Helmstedter, Helmreich, Hjelm, Helmont, Helmbold, Swethelm, Helmsley, McHelm, Helmers, Elmo, Helmes, Holmes)
- HELMAN (includes Hellman, Hellmann, Heilman, Heylman)
- HELMICK
- HEMING (includes Hemming)
- HENDERSON
- HENDERSON (Clan Henderson)
- HENDRICKS (includes Hendrix, Hendrickson)
- HENES
- HENLY (includes Henley, Hendly, Hendley)

Figure 3-8:
The surname mailing list page from Genealogy Resources on the Internet.

3. Follow the subscription instructions for your mailing list.

The instructions for the Helm mailing list told us to send an e-mail message with the word **subscribe** as the only text in the message body to one of two addresses.

The reason for including only the word **subscribe** is to accommodate automatic processing by a computer. When you send a message to join a mailing list, chances are it's processed automatically without human intervention. That is, a machine is automatically adding you to the mailing list when it reads the word subscribe in your message. If you add any other text, it doesn't know what to do with the message and you may not be added to the mailing list.

Typically, you can receive mailing lists in one of two ways. The first way, *mail mode,* simply sends you an e-mail message every time someone posts to the mailing list. While this practice is fine for small mailing lists, you probably don't want hundreds of messages coming in individually — unless you like to have lots of e-mail sitting in your inbox. To avoid this, try the second way of receiving the mailing list — *digest mode.* Digest mode groups several messages together and then sends them out as one large message. Instead of receiving 30 messages a day, you may receive only two messages with the text of 15 messages in each.

4. Start your e-mail program and subscribe to the mailing list.

We chose to subscribe to the digest mode of the Helm mailing list. To do this we started our e-mail program, created a new message with only the word subscribe in the body, and sent it off to the digest address — helm-d-request@rootsweb.com (see Figure 3-9). Within a couple of minutes, we received a confirmation message welcoming us to the mailing list.

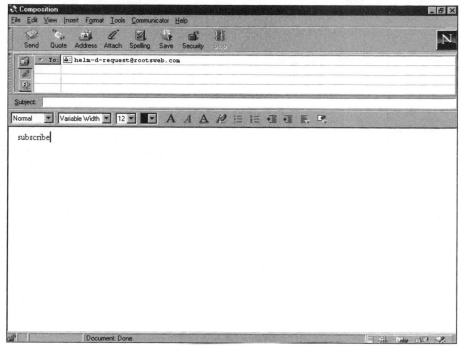

Figure 3-9:
An e-mail to
subscribe
to the Helm
surname
mailing list.

Within the text of the confirmation messages that most mailing lists
send is some valuable information that you want to hold on to for the
duration of time you subscribe to the list — such as how to
unsubscribe from the list, how to post messages to the list for others to
read, and whether there is a particular format required for posting
queries.

5. **Just read the messages without responding or posting your own**
messages for awhile. Begin posting your own queries and responses
to others' messages when you feel comfortable.

Reading messages but not posting your own messages is called *lurking*.
You may want to lurk on the mailing list to see what other messages
look like and to become familiar with the general culture of the list.
After you get a feel for the structure and attitude of the messages, jump
in and begin sending your own queries and messages!

Newsgroup queries

Another place where you can post queries is in a *newsgroup*. Newsgroups
are similar to mailing lists in that you use e-mail to send a message that
many people can read. The difference is that the message you send is not

e-mailed to everyone on a list. Instead it is posted to a news server, which in turn copies the message to other news servers. When someone wants to read a message on the newsgroup, they use a news reader program that connects them to a news server. In order to read newsgroups in this manner, your Internet service provider must receive a news feed in order for you to read a newsgroup, and you must configure your newsreader to pick up the feed.

Don't worry if you don't have access to a news feed through your Internet service provider. There are sites — such as DejaNews (www.dejanews.com) — that allow you to view and post to newsgroups over the World Wide Web. Also, you can receive posts from newsgroups through gatewayed mailing lists.

Gatewayed means that traffic from newsgroups is relayed to a mailing list and vice versa. You can find a list of the gatewayed newsgroups in the Genealogy Resources on the Internet Web site (members.aol.com/gresinet/gen_mail.html).

Newsgroup hierarchies

Newsgroups are categorized in *hierarchies*, where each hierarchy has a top-level label such as soc or alt. Most genealogical traffic flows through the soc hierarchy (although some traffic does come through the alt.genealogy newsgroup). Beneath the soc level is a second hierarchy, which is followed by a third level, and so on. The hierarchy of most interest is soc.genealogy. Currently there are 26 newsgroups under soc.genealogy. Seven of them deal directly with surnames. They are cleverly named:

- ✔ soc.genealogy.surnames.britain
- ✔ soc.genealogy.surnames.canada
- ✔ soc.genealogy.surnames.german
- ✔ soc.genealogy.surnames.global
- ✔ soc.genealogy.surnames.ireland
- ✔ soc.genealogy.surnames.misc
- ✔ soc.genealogy.surnames.usa

Learning the rules (formal and informal) for posting

Monitoring the newsgroup for a while (also called *lurking*) before posting a message is always a good idea. By lurking you get an idea of how the newsgroup works and what information is appropriate to post there. Believe us, a lot of people are out there who have used newsgroups for years and still post messages that are inappropriate for that particular newsgroup.

How do you find out what is appropriate to post? All newsgroups have *charters* that define the scope of the newsgroup. Some newsgroup *moderators* (people who help manage the newsgroup) frequently post the charters and tips on using newsgroups. Unfortunately, a lot of newsgroups don't have frequent posting of this information, so it may be difficult to tell whether a post is appropriate. Sometimes these discussions take on a life of their own and become distractions until the series of messages, called a *thread*, finally fizzles out. If you can't find the charter of the group, the safest thing to do is see what other people post (or you can consult the Usenet Newsgroup Charter Archive at `www.faqs.org/usenet/gsearch.html`). If you post an inappropriate message, hopefully someone will be kind enough to send you a simple reminder by e-mail (rather than *flame* you, or attack you online).

The `soc.genealogy.surnames` groups are moderated, which means that you can't post directly to them. When you send a message to a moderated newsgroup, it is first reviewed by an *automoderator*, a computer program that determines which of the surnames groups your message is posted in. Because a computer screens your message, formatting is very critical. The subject line of all queries requires a certain format, which you can find in the Frequently Asked Questions (FAQ) files located at `www.rootsweb.com/~surnames/`. Here are a few examples of acceptable subject lines:

```
Subject: HELM George / Dorothea; Frederick Co., VA,USA; 1723-
1769

Subject: HELM; VA,USA > TN,USA > IL,USA; 1723-

Subject: HELM; VA,USA>TN,USA>IL,USA; 1723-

Subject: HELM; anywhere; anytime

Subject: HELM Web Page; ENG / USA; 1723-
```

Be sure to include the correct abbreviations for the locations in your subject line. These codes will determine which newsgroup the automoderator places your message. You can find a list of the acceptable location codes on the Roots Surname List Country Abbreviations page (`www.rootsweb.com/roots-l/cabbrev1.html`). Also, be sure to place an e-mail address at the end of your query so that interested researchers can contact you directly.

You can search past posts to the `soc.genealogy.surnames` group on the World Wide Web. Go to the Web page at `searches.rootsweb.com/sgsurnames.html` (shown in Figure 3-10).

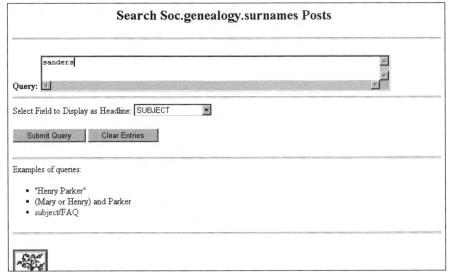

Figure 3-10:
The Search
Soc.
genealogy.
surnames
Posts page.

When you're at the Search Soc.genealogy.surnames Posts page, follow these steps:

1. **Using your Web browser, go to** searches.rootsweb.com/ sgsurnames.html

   (For more information on using a browser, see Appendix A.)

2. **Type the surname you are researching in the Query box.**

   Note that the Web site uses the words Query and Search interchangeably.

3. **Choose Subject in the Select Field To Display As Headline list box.**

   Subject is the first choice in the list box, so you don't actually have to click or choose if Subject is already showing.

4. **Click the Submit Query button.**

When you finish the preceding steps, a page called Operation Summary appears, showing you the results of your query on a specific surname. Notice that a line separates each record on the Operation Summary page. The last line of each record is labeled Select and includes a list of bracketed links that you can click to see different parts of the message in that record. To see the complete text of the message that was posted to the newsgroup, choose Full on the Select line.

Finding genealogy's most wanted

Every time you go into a post office, you see the Most Wanted pictures on the wall. In the genealogical world there is an online equivalent — Genealogy's Most Wanted located at www.citynet.net/mostwanted/.

Genealogy's Most Wanted lets you place a query about a specific person — that is, not just a surname, but an actual individual. The query can be no more than 70 words or so, so be sure it contains enough information for someone to work with. After you submit your query, it's placed in an alphabetical listing of surnames. The site contains over 14,600 listings presently.

You can also try to get your query listed as one of Genealogy Most Wanted's Top 11 Most Wanted (see Figure 3-11) at www.citynet.net/mostwanted/top11.html. This category lets you submit a query on a specific individual using between 200 and 500 words. You can include a photograph with a Top 11 query. Your query will remain on the Top 11 list for one month.

Make sure that you follow Genealogy Most Wanted's submission guidelines. They have two different sets of guidelines depending upon whether you are submitting a regular query or a Top 11 query.

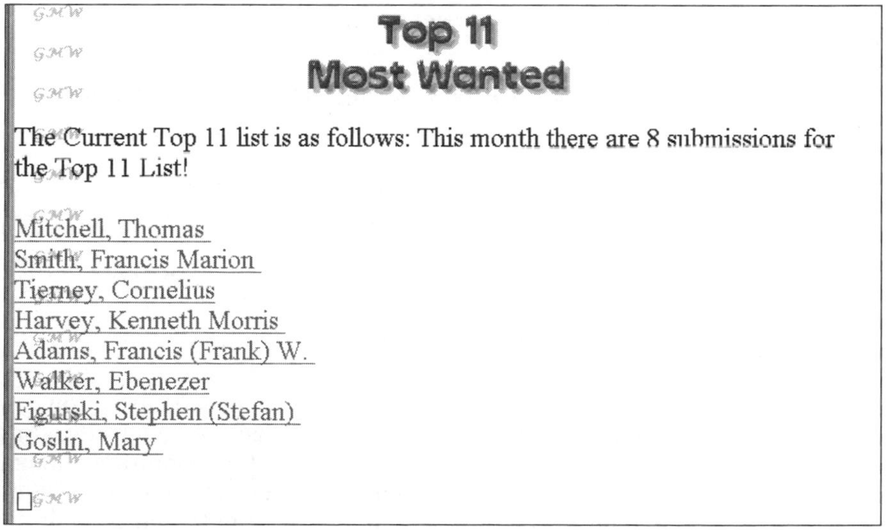

Figure 3-11: Genealogy's Top 11 Most Wanted.

Using E-Mail to Get Help

In "Query for One: Seeking Answers to Your Surname Questions," we discuss a couple of ways to research surnames through e-mail by using queries. E-mail can also be used to directly contact other researchers of your surname. You just need to know where to find them.

Identifying potential e-mail pals by using online directories to find everyone with the surname you're researching, getting their e-mail addresses, and then mass e-mailing all of them about your research and questions is a bad idea. While mass e-mailing everyone you can find with a particular surname will generate return mail for you, we can almost guarantee that the responses will be hateful and not helpful. Sticking with genealogical sites (like those we identify in a moment) when looking for other researchers who are interested in the same surnames as you is the better way to go about it.

The Roots Surname List

One of the oldest of the Internet genealogy resources is the Roots Surname List. The Roots Surname List (RSL) is simply a list of surnames (and their associated dates and locations) accompanied by contact information for the person who placed the surname on the list. So if you want to contact other submitters about particular surnames, all you have to do is look at the contact information and send them e-mail messages or letters in the mail detailing your interest in the surnames.

The format for the list looks like the following:

```
Helm 1723 now FrederickCo,VA>FentressCo, TN>FayetteCo,IL,USA mhelm
```

The line contains the surname, earliest date for which you have information on the surname, most recent date that you have for the surname, locations through which your family passed showing migration patterns (using a list of standard abbreviations), and a name tag for the submitter.

There is also a companion entry to every surname entry, called the *name tag*. This entry shows how to get into contact with the submitter. The name tag contains the submitter's name, e-mail address, and an optional mailing address. The following is a name tag that could be the companion to the preceding surname example:

```
mhelm Matthew Helm, mhelm@tbox.com, P.O. Box 76, Savoy, IL, 61874
```

You can submit surnames to the RSL through e-mail or with a form on the World Wide Web. Before submitting something for the first time, take a few minutes to read the RSL instructions (www.rootsweb.com/roots-l/ family.readme.html).

You have a couple of ways to conduct a search of the information on the RSL — which is a good thing, because there are currently over 350,000 surnames on the list.

✔ The first and easiest way is to search the RSL through the World Wide Web. You can do this by pointing your browser to www.rootsweb.com/ rootsweb/searches/rslsearch.html and filling in the surname and an optional location.

✔ The other way to search the RSL is through e-mail. You can search the RSL by sending an e-mail to a mail server located at server@genealogy.org. To check for the surname Abell on the RSL, you would send an e-mail message with the following text in the subject line: **find rsl abell.** If you found information on the Abell surname and wanted to contact a submitter listed as "mhelm," you would send the following text (in the subject line): **find rsl-addr mhelm.**

Surname-related e-mail resources

A number of resources are available that use e-mail as their primary communication tool. A list of these can be found at the Genealogy Resources on the Internet site at members.aol.com/johnf14246/gen_email.html. Among these resources are e-mail addresses of specific family associations, archives, and newsletters.

Using GenServ Information

One of the larger repositories of surname information on the Internet is the GenServ system. The GenServ system is a collection of GEDCOM files that are maintained on a central computer. (A GEDCOM file is produced when you export information from your genealogical database. For more information on GEDCOM, see Chapter 8.) You can request a variety of reports from the system. You submit requests through e-mail or over the World Wide Web, depending on the level of subscription that you purchase.

Currently the GenServ system contains information on almost 12 million surnames derived from over 9,000 GEDCOM files. The data maintained in the system comes from 48 different countries, making it a good place for international research. The cost of membership ranges from $6 to $12 a year, depending on your age and a few other factors. In addition to the monetary cost, there is a membership requirement that you submit your GEDCOM file — after all, that is how GenServ accumulates its data.

Among the reports that you can receive from the system are vital records, family information, ahnentafel, Descendant trees, and reports in the Henry number format. (For information on genealogical numbering formats like ahnentafel and Henry, see Chapter 8.)

GenCount report

The maintainers of GenServ give you an opportunity to see whether there's anything in their system of interest to you before you go through the membership process. You can do this by submitting a request for a GenCount report. This report provides you with an e-mail of the number of times that your selected surname appears in the GenServ system. To request a GenCount report, do this:

1. **Type the address** `www.genserv.com/gs3/samplecount.html` **into your Web browser. (Flip over to Appendix A for more on using browsers.)**

   The Submit Sample Searchcount Request to GenServ page appears. This page includes text boxes for you to enter the surname you are searching for and your e-mail address.

2. **Enter a surname and the e-mail address of where you want the report sent in the appropriate text boxes.**

   The surname you're searching for goes in the box called Enter SURNAME To Search For Here. Your e-mail address goes in the box Enter Your EMAIL ADDRESS Here.

3. **Click the Submit Request button.**

   A new page appears with the text `Sample Searchcount Request to GenServ Succeeded`.

Figure 3-12 shows the e-mail that we received when we requested a count of the Abell surname. As you can see, the system contains 2,090 entries for the surname — but this does not necessarily mean that there are 2,090 separate Abell individuals in the system. Some of these entries may be the same individual who appears in more than one GEDCOM file. You can request a GenCount report on an unlimited number of surnames, so take some time to request GenCounts for a few surnames to test the system.

```
Basic cost is only One Dollar a month for access, but first you must
send us a GEDCOM datafile of your own family.

For more information  about the datafile you may have received, please
send a GEDCOM file to the POSTAL address in the Geninfo file.  Please
read all the GenInfo file before sending questions.  If you wish the email
address or postal address of a subscriber to the system, then send a
GEDCOM datafile to the address in the GenInfo file.  We do not give
out subscriber addresses to non-subscribers.

The GenServ System has been operational on the Internet since 1991.  We hope
you will consider becoming a USER of the GenServ System. The GenServ
information is about 60,000 bytes long.

You may learn more about the system, see examples of reports available,
or get the GenServ information by accessing the GenServ homepage on WWW at

    URL   http://www.genserv.com/

Good luck to all.   Cliff Manis

================================================================================

The output of your GenCount request is:

    ***** 2090 entries found for name: "abell" *****

*-Cut-------------> End of all parts of this GenServ message <-------------Cut-*
```

Figure 3-12:
The results
of a
GenCount
request.

GenSample

If the GenCount report spurred your interest in the system, you may want
to take the next step and request a GenSample. GenSample sends you a list
of the individuals who have records in the GenServ system. The list looks
like this:

```
Abell, Aaron    76      Philips, Elizabe  A140    1810    ABELL
Abell, Abbot    953                        A140            ABELL
Abell, Abigail 12048 Lathrop, Barnaba  A140    1670    MUSA6HA
```

The first column lists the individual, followed by the individual's identification number in the system, spouse (if known), Soundex number (for information on Soundex, see Chapter 1), birth year, and database name.

You can receive a one-time-only GenSample by doing the following:

1. **Type the address** `www.Genserv.COM/gs3/samplesearch.html` **into
   your Web browser.**

   The Submit Sample Search Request to GenServ page appears. This page
   includes text boxes for you to enter the surname you're searching for
   and your e-mail address.

2. **Enter a surname and the e-mail address of where you want the
   report sent in the appropriate text boxes.**

   The surname you are searching for goes in the box Enter SURNAME To
   Search For Here. Your e-mail address goes in the box Enter Your EMAIL
   ADDRESS Here.

3. Click the Submit Request button.

A new page appears with the text `Sample Search Request to GenServ Succeeded.`

After you perform the preceding steps to submit your sample request, you begin receiving e-mail messages reflecting a list of the individuals with the selected surname in the format shown earlier. Depending upon how many individuals have that surname in the system, you can end up with over 100 e-mail messages (especially for names like Smith or Jones). When we submitted the Abell surname, we received eight e-mails.

If you decide to join the GenServ system, you will be able to request reports on the specific individuals that are listed in the GenSample. These reports may be requested through e-mail or on the World Wide Web. You can consult the GenServ documentation for details on how to properly request reports at `www.genserv.com/gs/gensdocs.htm`. Should you decide to join, you may also want to read about how to export a GEDCOM file from your database in Chapter 10.

Searching with Search Engines

If you can't find information anywhere else, or you want to find as much information as possible about a surname, then you are ready to use a search engine. With the amount of genealogical indices available (such as the comprehensive site mentioned earlier in "Looking at a Comprehensive Web Site"), we highly recommend that you exhaust those resources before using search engines because search engines can quickly overload you with information.

Search engines are programs that search huge indices of information generated by robots. *Robots* are programs that travel throughout the Internet and collect information on the sites and resources that they run across. You can access the information contained in search engines through an interface, usually through a form on a World Wide Web page.

A few genealogical search engines are available, and we recommend that you try those before you try the general search engines.

Comparing search engines

Several search engines are available when it comes time to conduct a large-scale search. The difference between them can be hard to tell. In terms of advanced search capabilities, some search engines have unique features; in terms of simple searches, they are, for the most part, basically the same with some small differences.

To find the differences among search engines on a simple search, we ran four basic searches on the search engines covered in the *Genealogy Online Internet Directory* to see how the results would vary. All these search engines support using a plus sign (+) to require keywords and quotation marks to look for exact phrase matches. In the following table, you can see the various numbers of hits that each search engine found when looking for a simple keyword (the surname McSwain with the M and the S in uppercase), two words where one was required (McSwain +Kentucky), two words where both were required (+McSwain +Kentucky), and an exact phrase (the name "William McSwain").

	AltaVista	Lycos	Infoseek	WebCrawler	Excite	HotBot
McSwain	2,122	170*	606	23	602	2,088
McSwain + Kentucky	479,142	10	41,720	9,660	124,830	191
+McSwain + Kentucky	141	10	3	2	28	191
"William McSwain"	11	1	1	0	14	13

*Lycos does not provide the total count for results on the search for the surname McSwain. However, there were at least 17 pages containing ten hits (or links) each.

GENDEX

GENDEX World Wide Web Genealogical Index (`www.gendex.com/gendex/`) was created to search the many online genealogical databases created through the GED2HTML program. (For more on the GED2HTML program, see the section on genealogical software utilities in the *Genealogy Online Internet Directory* in this book.) At press time, the database contained an index of over 5 million individuals in 1,800 databases.

1. **Type the address** `www.gendex.com/gendex/` **into your Web browser.**

   The GENDEX - - WWW Genealogical Index page appears.

2. **From the GENDEX - - WWW Genealogical Index page, click** <u>Access the Index</u>.

   Another page appears, with links to <u>surname index</u>, <u>site index</u>, and <u>site information</u>.

3. **Click <u>surname index</u>.**

   The GENDEX - - Index of Surnames page appears. This page includes text boxes labeled Enter A Prefix Of A Surname You Wish To Search For and Or, Enter A Surname And Search For Soundex-Equivalents.

4. **Enter the surname you are searching for in the text box titled Or, Enter A Surname And Search For Soundex-Equivalents. Then click the Submit button.**

   The Soundex page appears, showing a detailed breakdown of the surnames that meet your request. (For more information on Soundex, see Chapter 1.)

   We chose April's maiden name, Sanders. The Soundex page showed us the Soundex number for the name and a list of links to surnames with the number of instances of the surname in brackets following the link. For the surname Sanders, 2,808 entries are in the index. The results are listed in order of numbers of entries, rather than by the surname you entered. (For instance, if Sanders had not been the most frequently occurring surname for that Soundex code, it would not have appeared as the first link on the results page. Therefore, you may have to look through the entire results page to see whether your surname has an entry.)

5. **Click the appropriate link for your surname.**

   In our case, Sanders appears exactly as we want it on the page, so we click the <u>Sanders</u> link. The Surname page appears, with alphabetical ranges of given names for you to choose from. In our case, the page is called GENDEX - - Surname: SANDERS.

6. **Click the given name range for the individual you're looking for.**

   Clicking Sanders brought us to a second level index with a range of names. Each link is arranged alphabetically by the first name of the individual possessing the last name Sanders. We were looking for April's great-grandfather, John Sanders, and selected the link <u>Jemima / SANDERS/ - to - Kelli Elizabeth /SANDERS/</u>. After you select an age range from this index, a level 1 index of name ranges appears.

7. **Click a surname range on the Index level: 1 page.**

   We received a level 1 index including a number of John Sanders, so we could have chosen any one of five different links — depending on John's middle name. Because we thought that John's middle name was Duff, we selected <u>John /Sanders/ - to - John Fletcher /SANDERS/</u>. When you click a name range link, the Individuals page appears.

8. On the Individuals page, click the name of the individual you're searching for.

Figure 3-13 shows a list of individuals in the range from John Sanders to John Fletcher Sanders. Each surname is a link that takes you to the original database where the name appears. Also, to help you decide whether the person is who you're looking for, you can see the dates and places of that person's birth and death if those dates were included in the original database. After you are taken to the original database, you can return to the GENDEX page by clicking the Back button on your Web browser.

Keep in mind that GENDEX only indexes a small portion of the genealogical information available on the Internet. Also, use GENDEX when you are looking for information on a specific individual rather than researching a surname in general.

Internet FamilyFinder

The Internet FamilyFinder (www.familytreemaker.com/iffintro.html) by Brøderbund Software is a little more like traditional search engines. It uses robots to index sites on the Internet that have genealogical content. The Internet FamilyFinder search engine has a number of types of resources that can be searched at the same time. For example, at the time we visited the Internet FamilyFinder, you could search sites on the Internet, user home pages on Brøderbund's site, message boards, classified ads, and some of Brøderbund's genealogical CD-ROMs. Each of these types of sites are individually selectable — you can turn them off or on as you like.

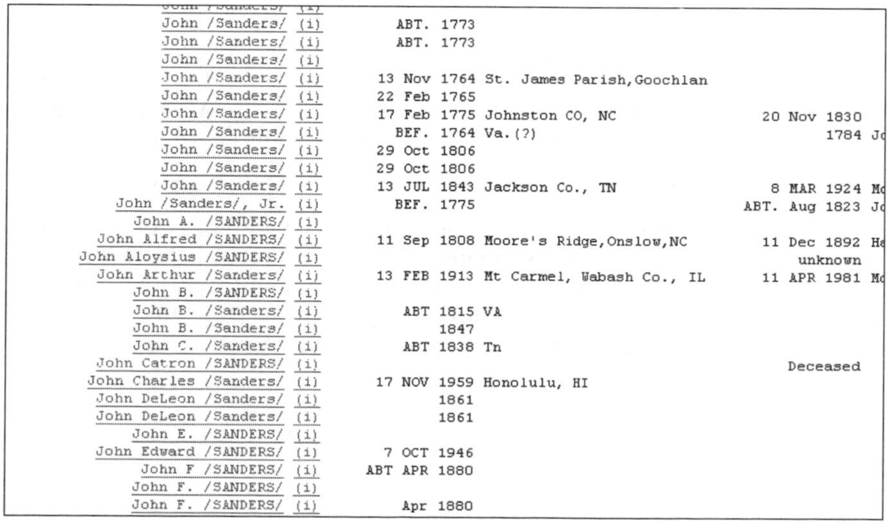

Figure 3-13:
A listing of individuals from the GENDEX index.

```
                  John /Sanders/  (i)
                  John /Sanders/  (i)      ABT. 1773
                  John /Sanders/  (i)      ABT. 1773
                  John /Sanders/  (i)
                  John /Sanders/  (i)      13 Nov 1764 St. James Parish,Goochlan
                  John /Sanders/  (i)      22 Feb 1765
                  John /Sanders/  (i)      17 Feb 1775 Johnston CO, NC        20 Nov 1830
                  John /Sanders/  (i)          BEF. 1764 Va.(?)                   1784 Jo
                  John /Sanders/  (i)      29 Oct 1806
                  John /Sanders/  (i)      29 Oct 1806
                  John /Sanders/  (i)      13 JUL 1843 Jackson Co., TN         8 MAR 1924 Mo
              John /Sanders/, Jr. (i)          BEF. 1775              ABT. Aug 1823 Jo
                John A. /SANDERS/  (i)
            John Alfred /SANDERS/  (i)      11 Sep 1808 Moore's Ridge,Onslow,NC 11 Dec 1892 He
          John Aloysius /SANDERS/  (i)                                           unknown
            John Arthur /Sanders/  (i)      13 FEB 1913 Mt Carmel, Wabash Co., IL 11 APR 1981 Mo
                John B. /SANDERS/  (i)
                John B. /Sanders/  (i)      ABT 1815 VA
                John B. /Sanders/  (i)          1847
                John C. /Sanders/  (i)      ABT 1838 Tn
           John Catron /SANDERS/  (i)                                          Deceased
          John Charles /Sanders/  (i)      17 NOV 1959 Honolulu, HI
           John DeLeon /Sanders/  (i)          1861
           John DeLeon /Sanders/  (i)          1861
                John E. /SANDERS/  (i)
           John Edward /SANDERS/  (i)       7 OCT 1946
                John F  /SANDERS/  (i)    ABT APR 1880
                John F. /SANDERS/  (i)
                John F. /SANDERS/  (i)         Apr 1880
```

To find information through the Internet FamilyFinder, follow these steps:

1. **Type the address** `www.familytreemaker.com/iffintro.html` **into your Web browser to go to the Internet FamilyFinder home page. (See Appendix A for details on using a browser.)**

   The page includes a list of options called Using the Internet FamilyFinder, located on the right side of the page.

2. **In the Using the Internet FamilyFinder list, click** <u>Try Internet FamilyFinder Now!</u>

   A new page appears with text boxes labeled Given Name, Middle, and Surname.

3. **Type the name of the individual you're researching into the Given Name, Middle, and Surname text boxes.**

   If you're looking for only general resources on a surname, just type the surname in the Surname text box.

   Because we were interested in finding information on the surname McSwain (which is April's grandfather's name), we typed **mcswain** in the Surname text box.

4. **Click the Search button.**

   The robot processes your request and shows you a page titled List of Matching Pages, which includes a table with five columns: Name, Date, Location, Found On, and Link. (Figure 3-14 shows an example of a list.)

Family Tree Maker `ONLINE`
Internet FamilyFinder

| Home | Internet FamilyFinder | Agents | Classifieds | Message Boards | Genealogy How-To | Search |
| | FamilyFinder Index | Record Lookup | Genealogy Mall | User Home Pages | World Family Tree | |

Searching for Mcswain, ...

List of Matching Pages:

[Next Page of Hits] [New Search]

Name	Date	Location	Found On	Link
Mcswain, Angela			Internet	**Linked Family Tree including Edith Slocumb** ... Mar 15 20:33:09 1996 I02192: **Angela McSwain** (8 Nov 1963 -) Angela ...
Mcswain, Joe			Internet	**Linked Family Tree including Edith Slocumb** ... BIRTH : 8 Nov 1963 Father: **Joe McSwain** Mother: Juanita Hancock ...
Mcswain, Joe			Internet	**Linked Family Tree including Edith Slocumb** ... Hancock _____ **Joe McSwain** _____ || |_____ ...

Figure 3-14:
A table of results from Brøderbund's Internet FamilyFinder.

The Name column is the full name of a person that the robot finds on the site. This can sometimes be misleading in that the robot doesn't always understand the structure of the Web page. For example, if you were to do a search on the surname Helm, you would find some interesting results. Several sites have a list of links to Web sites — in particular, Helm's Genealogy Toolbox. What the robot has done with several sites is combine the last word of the previous line in the list with the name Helm to form a name. On several sites, the last word of the previous line was the name of a state. So, the Internet FamilyFinder has an entry in the name field for Alabama Helm, Alaska Helm, and so on, for every state. The other important column is the Link column, which displays a link to the site where the name was found and provides a few lines for the site that puts the name in perspective. This helps you avoid going to sites that result from the robot not understanding how the Web page was constructed. If the robot finds more results than can be displayed on one screen, you can select Next Page of Hits to see more results.

5. Click a link in the Link column to go to a site.

You can return to the Internet FamilyFinder index by clicking on the Back button on your Web browser.

The Internet FamilyFinder robots are constantly searching more and more genealogical sites, so check back with it every once in a while to see if there's anything new. If you don't want to constantly come back to the Internet FamilyFinder, you can use an agent to notify you by e-mail when something new is found on your surname by the Internet FamilyFinder robots.

To use an Internet FamilyFinder Agent, follow these steps:

1. Point your browser to www.familytreemaker.com/ifaintro.html **and select Try Internet FamilyFinder Agents Now!**

2. Type in the full name or surname that you are interested in researching and select whether the agent should look for an exact match or a match that sounds like the name.

3. Choose where you want the agent to search (the Internet, user home pages, etc.), and click Create Task Now!

If you search a name or surname that is too general, you may receive a message that you should make your query more specific. This usually means that you need to add a first name or middle name. Don't worry about using specific names, because you can have up to 10 agents active at the same time.

General search engines

General search engines send out robots to catalog the Internet as a whole regardless of the content of the site. Therefore, on any given search you are likely to receive a lot of hits, only a few of which will hold any genealogical value (although sometimes you can get lucky and find some valuable information). We recommend the use of general search engines as a last resort for the beginning online genealogist — only when nothing else seems to work.

You can conduct several different types of searches with most search engines. It's always a good idea to look at the Help link for any search engine to see the most effective way to search. Also, they often have two search interfaces — a simple search and an advanced search. With the simple search, you normally just type in your query and hit the submit button. Advanced searches normally have a variety of options that you can use to refine your search. The best way to become familiar with using a search engine is to experiment on a couple of searches and see what kinds of results you get.

To try a search with the AltaVista search engine, follow these steps:

1. **Using your Web browser, head over to the AltaVista search engine at** www.altavista.digital.com **(For more on browsers, go to Appendix A.)**

2. **Select Search the Web for documents in any language, type your query into the box, and click the Search button.**

   Notice that you can select to search either documents on the World Wide Web or on Usenet newsgroups. Also, you can select documents in 25 specific languages, as well as "any language." To get a manageable number of hits (or results), consider limiting your search by using more than one word or using a couple of words in quotation marks so that Alta Vista looks for an exact match. For more information about search engines and how to control searches, see Appendix A and the *Genealogy Online Internet Directory*.

   We typed **sanders family genealogy** into the search engine and received 64,610 results (see Figure 3-15).

3. **Click on a link that interests you. You can click the Back button to return to the search engine results page.**

Keep in mind that the results of a search engine include every page the query exists. For example, if there's a genealogy site on the Sanders family that has 30 pages, then there are likely to be 30 entries in the search engine results all pointing to the same site (just different pages within the site). So, that is why you tend to get thousands of results with a simple query.

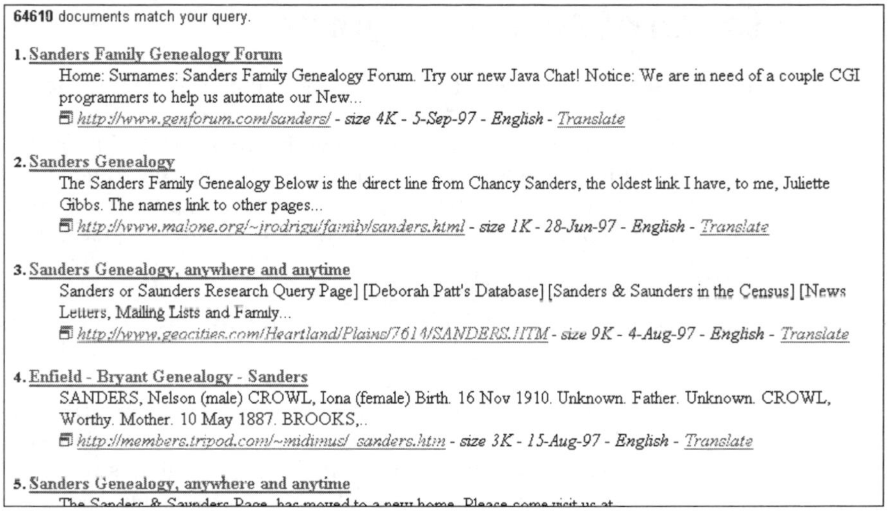

64610 documents match your query.

1. Sanders Family Genealogy Forum
   Home: Surnames: Sanders Family Genealogy Forum. Try our new Java Chat! Notice: We are in need of a couple CGI programmers to help us automate our New...
   http://www.genforum.com/sanders/ - *size 4K - 5-Sep-97 - English -* *Translate*

2. Sanders Genealogy
   The Sanders Family Genealogy Below is the direct line from Chancy Sanders, the oldest link I have, to me, Juliette Gibbs. The names link to other pages...
   http://www.malone.org/~jrodrigu/family/sanders.html - *size 1K - 28-Jun-97 - English -* *Translate*

3. Sanders Genealogy, anywhere and anytime
   Sanders or Saunders Research Query Page] [Deborah Patt's Database] [Sanders & Saunders in the Census] [News Letters, Mailing Lists and Family...
   http://www.geocities.com/Heartland/Plains/7614/SANDERS.HTM - *size 9K - 4-Aug-97 - English -* *Translate*

4. Enfield - Bryant Genealogy - Sanders
   SANDERS, Nelson (male) CROWL, Iona (female) Birth. 16 Nov 1910. Unknown. Father. Unknown. CROWL, Worthy. Mother. 10 May 1887. BROOKS,..
   http://members.tripod.com/~midimus/ sanders.htm - *size 3K - 15-Aug-97 - English -* *Translate*

5. Sanders Genealogy, anywhere and anytime
   The Sanders & Saunders Page, has moved to a new home. Please come visit us at

Figure 3-15:
Results of a
search
on the
AltaVista
search
engine.

If you're interested in conducting more complex searches using the search engines or just want to know more about them, we recommend you take a look through Appendix A along with the *Genealogy Online Internet Directory.* Also, you may want to pick up a copy of *World Wide Web Searching For Dummies,* 3rd Edition, from IDG Books Worldwide, Inc.

Verifying Your Information (Don't Believe Everything You Read!)

We have one last piece of advice for you when you are researching. Don't believe everything you read. Well, actually a pure genealogist would say, "Don't believe anything that you read." Either way, the point is the same — always verify any information that you find online with primary records (for more on primary records, see Chapter 1). The person who submitted the surname information must know that the information is true. If you can't prove it through a census record, vital record, or some other authoritative record, then the information simply may not be worth anything. However, just because you can't immediately prove it doesn't mean that you shouldn't hold on to the information. At some time in the future you may run across a record that does indeed prove the accuracy of the information.

Chapter 4

Locating Your Ancestors (Geographically Speaking)

*I*n your genealogical research, finding information only about your family's surnames isn't enough. To put together a truly comprehensive genealogy, you need to know things about where your ancestors lived and the times in which they lived. While you can get some of this information from other relatives and from documents that belonged to your ancestors, much of what you're looking for is available only in or from the actual areas where your ancestors lived. In this chapter, we examine some geographical resources that can help you develop the *where* and *when* in your genealogy.

Are We There Yet? (Researching Where "There" Was to Your Ancestors)

What did "there" mean for your ancestors? You have to answer this question to know where to look for genealogical information. These days, coming from a family that lived in the same general area for more than two or three generations is rather unique. If you're a member of such a family, you're a lucky person when it comes to genealogical research! However, if you're like the rest of us, you come from families that moved around at least every couple of generations, if not more often. Usually, finding out where all your ancestors lived — and when — presents a challenge. On the other hand, finding where your ancestors are from is one of the most rewarding challenges.

So how do you find out where your ancestors lived and the approximate time frames? By examining your notes from interviews with relatives and records you've collected so far, you can get a good idea of where your ancestors lived and when.

Using documents you already have in your possession

When attempting to geographically locate your ancestors, start by using any copies of records that you or someone else in the family has already collected. Your notes from interviews with family members, or from other resources you've found on your ancestors, will most likely contain some information about locations where the family lived and hopefully the approximate time frames.

Chances are you have at least some notes with general statements such as "Aunt Lola recalled stories about the old homestead in Fayette County, Kentucky." Of course, whether Aunt Lola recalled stories *firsthand* (those that she lived through or participated in) or her recollections were stories she heard from those before her will have an effect on the time frames for which you look for records in Fayette County. Either way, these stories give you a starting point.

Likewise, most public record documents that you've collected or someone else has given you — such as vital records, land records, military documents, and so on — provide at least two leads for you to use in tracking your family: the names of parents or witnesses to the event, and the date and place of the event (or at least the date and place of when and where the record was filed). Having this information can point you in the right direction of where to begin looking for records to substantiate what you believe to be true about your ancestors. Knowing a name to look for in a particular place and time gets you on your way to seeking other records.

If you have information about places where your ancestors lived, but not necessarily the time frame, you can still be reasonably successful tracking your ancestors based on the limited information you do have. Aids are available to help you approximate time frames, such as the Period Approximation Chart (www.netusa1.net/~hartmont/chart.htm). For example, say you've heard stories about your great-great-grandmother being born in Red River County, Texas but you don't know when she was born there. If you know approximately when she died and her age at death, you can use the Period Approximation Chart to calculate her approximate birth date. This chart helps you discover a time frame in which to look for records for her family in Red River County.

For additional information about using documents you already have and interviewing relatives to point you in the right direction, you may wish to check out Ancestry's Family History Academy: Discovering Your Heritage online course. Its page, called The First Steps (www.ancestry.com/home/howto/firststeps.htm), has lots of useful information about collecting memories and using home sources.

Taking a look at directories and newspapers

If you have a general idea of where your family lived at a particular time, but no conclusive proof, city and county directories and newspapers may be helpful. (Census records are quite helpful for this purpose, too. We discuss census records in Chapter 1 and Appendix C.) Directories and newspapers can help you confirm whether your ancestors indeed lived in a particular area and, in some cases, they can provide even more information than you expect.

Directories

Like telephone books of today, directories contained basic information about the persons who lived in particular areas, whether the areas were towns, cities, districts, or counties. Typically, the directory identified at least the head of the household and the location of the house. Some directories also included the names and ages of everyone in the household and occupations of any members of the household who were employed.

Unfortunately, there is no centralized resource on the Web containing transcriptions of directories or even an index to all directories that may exist on the Internet. But don't be discouraged. Some sites are available that can direct you to directories for particular geographic areas, but they are by no means universal. Three such examples are the Kansas State Historical Society Finding People site (www.ukans.edu/heritage/kshs/resource/findpeop.htm), the Ontario County Historical Society (www.rootsweb.com/~nyontari/onthist.htm), and San Francisco County Research Tips: City Directories (www.sfo.com/~timandpamwolf/sfdirect.htm).

Most sites like these are maintained by societies and associations that have made a commitment to post on the Web the contents of directories for their areas. Or at least they post a listing of what their libraries hold so that you know before you contact them whether they have something useful to you. We're sure that other societies and associations have similar directory information that we have yet to discover! To help you find out whether there

are similar projects for areas you are researching, we recommend you visit a comprehensive genealogical site. A comprehensive genealogical site helps you identify society and association Web pages, as well as those for local libraries and archives, that may make directories (or even indices of directories) available online. The Genealogy SiteFinder is one such comprehensive genealogical site that identifies these resources. You can find its Groups and Societies section at `www.familytreemaker.com/links/c/c-groups-and-societies.html`, and its Libraries and Archives section at `www.familytreemaker.com/links/c/c-libraries-and-archives.html`.

Newspapers

Unlike directories that list almost everyone in a community, newspapers are helpful only if your ancestors did something that was newsworthy — but you'd be surprised at what was considered newsworthy. Your ancestor didn't necessarily have to be a politician or a criminal to get his picture and story in the paper. Just like today, obituaries, birth and marriage announcements, public recordings of land transactions, advertisements, and gossip sections were all relatively common in newspapers of the past.

Finding copies online of those newspapers from the past is a challenge. Most of the newspaper sites that are currently online are for contemporary publications. Although you can read about wedding anniversaries and birthdays in England and Sweden today, you can't necessarily access online information about your ancestor's death in one of those countries in the 1800s. Many researchers are beginning to recognize the potential that the Web holds for making historical information from newspapers available worldwide. However, the commitment in resources prevents them from doing so as quickly as we'd like!

Here's what you're likely to find online pertaining to newspapers.

- ✔ **Indices:** A variety of sites serve as indices of newspapers that are available at particular libraries, archives, and universities. Most of these lists identify the names and date of the periodicals that are held in the newspaper or special collections. Some examples of index sites are:
  - The Newspapers at the National Library of Canada page (`www.nlc-bnc.ca/services/enews.htm`)
  - The Newspaper Collections at the State Library of Victoria, Australia (`www.slv.vic.gov.au/slv/newspapers/`)
  - North East Newspapers Held by the North East of Scotland Library Service (`www.aberdeenshire.gov.uk/ne_news.htm`)
  - The Online Newspaper Indexes Available in the Newspaper and Current Periodical Reading Room of the Library of Congress (`lcweb.loc.gov/rr/news/npindex2.html`)

✔ **Transcriptions:** A few sites contain actual transcriptions of newspaper articles, entire issues, and/or excerpts. Typically, the contents at these sites are limited to the topic and geographic interests of the person who transcribed the information and posted it for public access on the Web. A couple of examples are:

- Excerpts from Old Newspapers (`www.ida.net/users/dhanco/news.htm`) (See Figure 4-1.)

- The Knoxville Gazette (`www.ultranet.com/~smack/news.htm`)

✔ **Collectors' issues for sale:** Although they don't provide information directly from the newspaper online for you to use in your genealogical pursuits, sites are available to inform you about collectors' editions of newspapers and others can actually sell you copies of old newspapers. The latter generally market their newspapers as good gift ideas for birthdays and anniversaries. For the services to be really useful to you as a genealogist, you have to know a date and place of the event you want to document (and a newspaper name helps, too), as well as be willing to pay for a copy of that paper. Here are a couple of newspaper collector sites you may wish to check out.

- History Buff's Home Page by the Newspaper Collectors Society of America (`www.historybuff.com/`)

- Historic Newspaper Archives (`www.historicnewspaper.com/Index.html`)

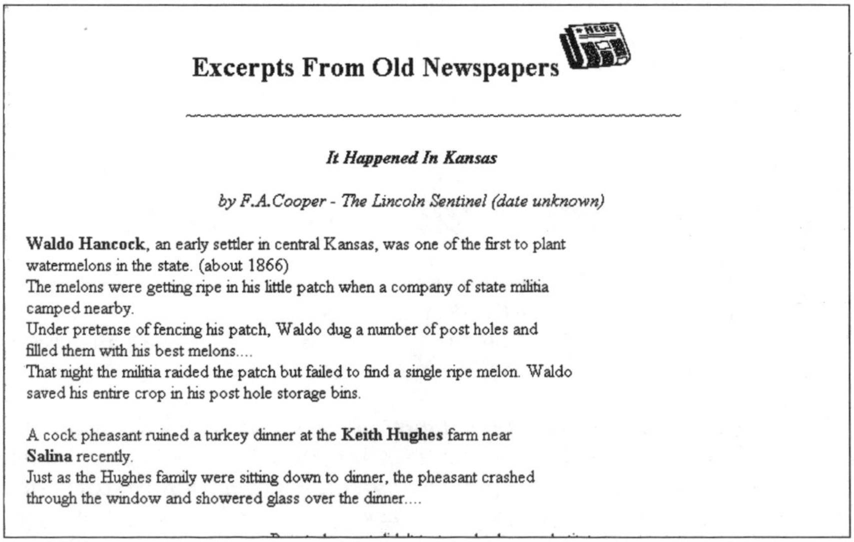

Figure 4-1:
The Excerpts from Old Newspapers site has transcriptions of articles and other information from newspapers.

Excerpts From Old Newspapers

It Happened In Kansas

by F.A.Cooper - The Lincoln Sentinel (date unknown)

Waldo Hancock, an early settler in central Kansas, was one of the first to plant watermelons in the state. (about 1866)
The melons were getting ripe in his little patch when a company of state militia camped nearby.
Under pretense of fencing his patch, Waldo dug a number of post holes and filled them with his best melons....
That night the militia raided the patch but failed to find a single ripe melon. Waldo saved his entire crop in his post hole storage bins.

A cock pheasant ruined a turkey dinner at the **Keith Hughes** farm near **Salina** recently.
Just as the Hughes family were sitting down to dinner, the pheasant crashed through the window and showered glass over the dinner....

✔ **Online newspaper projects:** As we state near the beginning of this section, a lot of people are beginning to recognize the important role newspapers play in recording history and the value of putting newspaper information on the Web. To this end, we've seen an increasing number of online projects to catalog or transcribe newspapers. Some of the projects are organized on a state level, and others are for cities or particular newspapers. The Web sites for these projects gives the purpose of the project, its current status, and how to find the newspapers if they've been transcribed or digitized and placed online. Here are a couple of examples of these sites.

• The Carson Appeal Newspaper Index (www.clan.lib.nv.us/docs/NSLA/ARCHIVES/appeal.htm)

• New England Old Newspaper Index Project of Maine (www.geocities.com/Heartland/Hills/1460/)

Now you know what you may find online in terms of newspapers, but how do you find these sites? We recommend that you use a trusty comprehensive genealogical site. (You've heard this before if you're reading this book section by section in order, right?) A comprehensive genealogical site helps you identify sites that contain information about newspapers and are maintained by newspapers, libraries and archives, societies and associations, and online newspaper projects. Most comprehensive sites have sites cross-indexed so that if a particular site fits in several of these categories, it appears in all of them. For example, the Carson Appeal Newspaper Index identified in the preceding list is an index for an actual newspaper (the *Carson Appeal*) and is part of a newspaper project for Nevada. Therefore, in Cyndi's List of Genealogy Sites on the Internet (an example of a comprehensive site, at www.CyndisList.com), it shows up under the categories of Newspapers (www.CyndisList.com/newspapr.htm) and Nevada (www.CyndisList.com/nv.htm).

Where Is Llandrindod, Anyway?

At some point during your research, you're bound to run across something that says an ancestor lived in a particular town or county but contains no details of where that town or county was — no state or province or other identifiers. How do you find out where that town or county was located?

A *gazetteer,* or geographical dictionary, provides information about places. By looking up the name of the town or county, you can narrow your search for your ancestor. The gazetteer identifies every known town or county by a particular name and provides varying information (depending on the gazetteer itself) about each of the towns or counties with that name. Typically, gazetteers provide at least the following for the town or county:

the state name and country. In the case of many contemporary gazetteers, they also provide the latitude and longitude of the place.

Using an online gazetteer is easy. All the online gazetteers are organized similarly and have query or search forms. Here's how to use one:

1. **Start your Web browser and head to the U.S. Geological Survey's Geographic Names Information System (GNIS) at** `mapping.usgs.gov/ www/gnis/` **(For information on using a browser, see Appendix A.)**

2. **Scroll down and then click the link titled <u>Query the GNIS Online Data Base</u>.**

   The list directly beneath the links tells you what you can expect to get from a query of the GNIS database. When you click the link, it takes you to the query form (see Figure 4-2).

3. **Enter any information that you have, tabbing or clicking between fields, and click the Send Query button at the bottom of the form when you are finished.**

   If you are not sure what a particular field is asking for, but you think you may want to enter something in it, click the Help link directly next to the field.

   If you know only the town name, enter the town name in the Feature Name field — leave all the other fields blank. For example, enter the name **Carson City** in the Feature Name field; then click the Send Query button.

≋USGS

Geographic Names Information System
Online Data Base Query Form

[General Instructions]

Feature Name: [ ] [Help]   Query Variant Name Also?: Yes ○ No ● [Help]

State Name: [ ] [Help]   County Name: [ ] [Help]

Feature Type: [ ] [Help]   Population Range: [ ] to [ ] [Help]

Elevation Range (feet): [ ] to [ ] [Help]   USGS 7.5' x 7.5' Map Name: [ ] [Help]

Does your Browser support Tables? Yes ● No ○ [Help]   Execute Query: [Send Query] or [Erase Query]

| GNIS Home Page | Mapping Information |

Figure 4-2: The query form for the U.S. Geological Survey's Geographic Names Information System (GNIS).

GNIS then executes a search of its database and returns the results to you in a list form. For **Carson City,** GNIS returns 11 records for you to review (see Figure 4-3). For each record, GNIS provides the feature name, state, county, type of feature (such as populated place, valley, cemetery, airport, lake, forest, and so on), latitude, longitude, and map information.

By adding the information you get from the online gazetteer to the other pieces of your puzzle, you can reduce the list of common place names to just those you think are plausible for your ancestors. By pinpointing where a place is, you can look for more records to prove that your ancestors really lived there.

For example, if your mother told you that your great-great-grandfather lived in a town called Carson City but didn't say where that Carson City was, you can use the information you just collected in the GNIS database query to narrow your search for places called Carson City.

From GNIS, you know there are 11 Carson City places in the United States. By reviewing the Feature Type field, you can eliminate all the Carson City places that aren't towns or populated places. (After all, it's not likely that your great-great-grandfather lived in a city hall, golf course, post office, church, city square, or station!) The process of elimination narrows your search down to five Carson City places on the GNIS list.

≋USGS

Geographic Names Information System Query Results

CARSON CITY

11 Feature records have been selected from GNIS.

Feature Name	St	County Name	Type	Latitude	Longitude	USGS 7.5' Map
Carson City Hall	CA	Los Angeles	building	334956N	1181543W	Torrance
Carson City	MI	Montcalm	civil	431042N	0845049W	Carson City
Carson City	MI	Montcalm	pop place	431037N	0845047W	Carson City
Carson City	MS	Greene	pop place	312202N	0883950W	Avera
Carson City	NV	Carson City (city)	civil	391005N	1194300W	New Empire
Carson City	NV	Carson City (city)	pop place	390950N	1194559W	Carson City
Carson City Golf Course	NV	Carson City (city)	locale	391018N	1194456W	New Empire
Carson City Post Office	NV	Carson City (city)	post office	391005N	1194552W	Carson City
Carson City Seventh Day Adventist School	NV	Carson City (city)	school	391127N	1194553W	Carson City
Carson City Square	NV	Carson City (city)	locale	391032N	1194425W	New Empire

Figure 4-3:
The results
of a GNIS
search on
the name
Carson City.

Using other facts you've collected about your great-great-grandfather (such as where he was born, where his kids were born, what kind of work he did, and so on), you may be able to determine the general area of the United States in which he lived. If you can, this narrows the list down even further. The remaining Carson City places are in Michigan, Mississippi, and Nevada — three states that aren't near each other. (However, it's important to note that if great-great-grandpa was a wanderer or had an occupation that required him to travel great distances, you may not be able to rule out any of the remaining three states with Carson City places in them.)

In addition to the GNIS database, some online gazetteers identify places in the United States and other countries. Here are some for you to check out:

- ✔ Australian Gazetteer (www.ke.com.au/cgi-bin/texhtml?form=AustGaz)

- ✔ Canada's Geographical Names (GeoNames.NRCan.gc.ca/english/Home.html)

- ✔ Ordnance Survey — Gazetteer of Place Names in Great Britain (www.campus.bt.com/CampusWorld/pub/OS/Gazetteer/index.html)

- ✔ U.S. Census Bureau's Gazetteer (www.census.gov/cgi-bin/gazetteer)

Most gazetteers are organized on a national level and provide information about all the places (towns, cities, counties, landmarks, and so on) within that country. However, there are exceptions to every rule. Some unique gazetteers list information about places within one state or province. One such example is the Kentucky Atlas and Gazetteer (www.uky.edu/KentuckyAtlas/). The Kentucky Atlas and Gazetteer has information about places within one state. For each place, it provides the name of the place, the type of place (civil division, school, cemetery, airport, and so on), source of information, *topoquad* (topographic map quadrangle that contains the feature), latitude, longitude, area (if applicable), population (if applicable), date of establishment, elevation, and a link to a map showing you where the place is.

Mapping Your Ancestor's Way

Maps can be an invaluable resource in your genealogical research. Not only do maps help you track your ancestors, but they also make a wonderful enhancement to your published genealogy by illustrating some of your findings.

Tracking the movements of your ancestors can be a lot of fun. Just reading about migrations in family histories, texts, and records is not the easiest way to understand where, why, and how your ancestors moved. Charting movements on maps makes visualizing the paths your ancestors took and obstacles they may have encountered easier. Maps also make the genealogy you put together more interesting for others to read because they enable the reader to see what you're talking about in your writings. Maps help tell your ancestors' stories, so to speak.

Different types of online sites have maps that may be useful in your genealogical research.

✔ **Images of Maps:** Several Web sites contain scanned or digitized images of historic maps. You can download or print copies of these maps, but they may not show you much in terms of how boundaries changed over time. Two such sites are Cartographic Images: Ancient, Early Medieval, Late Medieval, and Renaissance Maps (`www.iag.net/~jsiebold/carto.html`) and the Perry-Castañeda Library Map Collection at the University of Texas at Austin (`www.lib.utexas.edu/Libs/PCL/Map_collection/Map_collection.html`), which has maps for places all over the world.

✔ **Interactive Map Sites:** A few sites have interactive maps you can use to find and zoom in on areas. After you have the view you want of the location, you can print a copy of the map to keep with your genealogical records. Two such sites are MapQuest (`www.mapquest.com/`), which has interactive maps for too many countries to list here (including the United States, Canada, Germany, Italy, New Zealand, and the United Kingdom), and the U.K. Street Map Page (`www.streetmap.co.uk/`), which identifies streets in London or places in the United Kingdom. Interactive maps call up and can zoom in on locations. They are especially helpful when you're trying to pinpoint the location of a cemetery or town you plan to visit for your genealogical research, but they are limited in their historical helpfulness because they typically offer only current information about places. (If you'd like to see a complete list of the countries for which MapQuest has interactive atlases, you can click on the link next to the Country field of the interactive atlas site. Use the following instructions to get to the form.)

Here's how to use an interactive map site.

1. **Using your Web browser, go to MapQuest at** `www.mapquest.com` **(Flip over to Appendix A for more details on using a browser.)**

   MapQuest's main page comes up.

2. **Click the link that says <u>Interactive Atlas (Maps)</u>.**

   Clicking this link brings up the interactive atlas form you use to submit a search (see Figure 4-4).

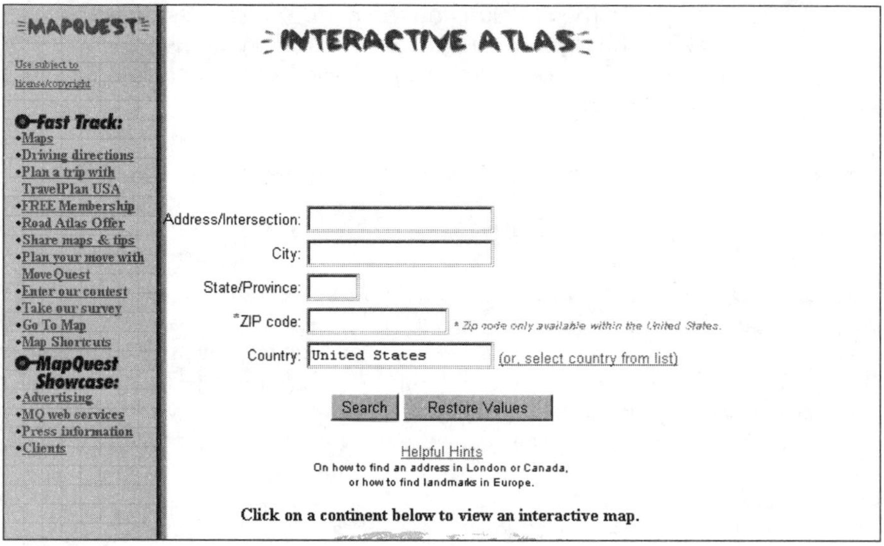

Figure 4-4:
You use
MapQuest's
Interactive
Atlas form
to look for
locations in
many
countries,
including
the United
States.

3. Enter any of the information you have into the form. Be sure to tab or click between the fields — if you hit the Enter key, MapQuest begins executing the search.

If you're merely looking for a town, you can skip entering information about an address/intersection, state, and zip code, but you need to specify the town and country. (Please note that MapQuest defaults to the United States. If you're looking for an address or town in a country other than the United States, you must make sure that the country is identified in the Country field.)

For example, say you're looking for an old family homestead at 1600 Pennsylvania Avenue in Washington, D.C. Enter **1600 Pennsylvania Avenue** in the Address/Intersection field, **Washington** in the City field, and **DC** (with no periods) in the State field. You don't necessarily need to enter the ZIP code, and you can leave the country set for the United States.

4. Click the Search button.

MapQuest then brings up a map of the requested place, if it can find it. If more than one town or street fits the description for the search, MapQuest prompts you to choose among all the matches. If MapQuest cannot find the requested place, it gives you a note stating this and a map for the closest place it could find that may match the place you requested.

In the search for 1600 Pennsylvania Avenue, MapQuest brings up a map of Washington, D.C. with a red star on the address requested. You can then use the map as it is or zoom in to see the surrounding area better by clicking on the Recenter Map and Zoom In dot at the bottom of the

TIP

map and then clicking on the map. You can also use the zoom buttons along the right-hand side of the map to gain perspective on where the place is located — you can choose from street level, to city, to regional, to national.

Crossing the line

Just as maps help you track your ancestors' movements and where they lived, they can also help you track when your ancestors didn't really move. Boundaries for towns, districts, and even states have changed over time. Additionally, for towns and counties to change names wasn't unheard of. Knowing whether your ancestors really moved or it just appeared they moved because of boundary- or town-name changes is important when you're trying to locate records for them.

To determine if a town or county changed names at some point, your best bet is to check a gazetteer or historical text on the area. (Gazetteers are discussed in the earlier section "Where Is Llandrindod, Anyway?") To find boundary changes can be a little more challenging, but resources are available to help you. For example, historical atlases illustrate land and boundary changes. You can also use online sites that have maps for the same areas over time, and a few sites deal specifically with boundary changes in particular locations. (A couple of examples are the Boundaries of the United States and the Several States (www.ac.wwu.edu/~stephan/48states.html) and the Counties of England, Scotland, and Wales prior to the 1974 Boundary Changes (midas.ac.uk/genuki/big/BRITAIN2.GIF). Or you can use software designed specifically to show you boundary changes over time and to help you find places that have disappeared altogether. One such program that tracks boundary changes in Europe is called Centennia Historical Atlas. You can find

information about it at its Web site (www.clockwk.com). Another such program for boundary changes in the United States is AniMap Plus (www.goldbug.com/AniMap.html), which is included on the CD-ROM accompanying this book. Here's a quick walk-through using the AniMap Plus demonstration to see how some counties have changed over time.

1. **Open the demonstration version of AniMap Plus that you installed from the CD-ROM that accompanies this book. (For installation instructions, see Appendix D.)**

   AniMap opens to a 1683 map that shows the 12 original counties of New York. All the counties are named in the upper left-hand corner of the map, abbreviations for each are explained in the County Codes box, and you can see the county boundaries themselves on the map.

2. **Double-click on Start Demo in the upper left-hand corner of the screen.**

3. **Click the NEXT button to advance to the next map of New York to see changes that took place between 1683 and 1686.**

   The box in the upper left-hand corner explains briefly changes that took place and which counties still existed in New York in 1686.

4. **You can advance through the maps in sequential order by clicking the NEXT button or you can skip to other years by double-clicking the years identified in the GO TO box.**

There's No Place Like Home — Using Local Resources

No doubt a time will come (possibly early in your research) when you need information that is maintained on a local level, say a copy of a record stored in a local courthouse, confirmation that an ancestor is buried in a particular cemetery, or even just a photo of the old homestead. So how can you find and get what you need?

Finding this information is easy if you live in or near the county where the information is maintained — you decide what it is you need, where it's stored, and then go and get a copy. Getting hold of locally held information isn't quite as easy if you live in another county, state, or country because, while you can determine what information you need and where it may be stored, finding out if the information is truly kept where you think it is and then getting a copy is another thing. Of course, if this situation weren't such a common occurrence for genealogists, you could just make a vacation out of it — travel to the location to finish researching there and get the copy you need while sightseeing along the way. But unfortunately, needing records from distant places is a common occurrence, and most of us can't afford to pack the bags and hit the road every time we need a record or other item from a place we don't live near, which is why it's nice to know resources are available to help.

From geographic-specific Web sites to local genealogical and historical societies to libraries with research services to individuals who are willing to do lookups in public records, a lot of resources are available to help you locate local documents and obtain a copy. Some resources are totally free, others may charge you a minimal fee for their time, and still others will bill you only for copying or other direct costs.

Geographic-specific Web sites

Geographic-specific Web sites are those pages that contain information specifically about a particular town, county, state, country, or other locality. They typically provide information about local resources, such as genealogical and historical societies, government agencies and courthouses, cemeteries, and civic organizations. Some sites have local histories and biographies of prominent residents online. Often they list and have links to other Web pages that have resources for the area. And sometimes they even have a place where you can post *queries* (or questions) about the area or families from there with the hopes that someone who reads your query will have some answers for you.

How can you find geographic-specific Web sites, you ask? Doing so is easy.

1. **Using your Web browser, go to the Genealogy Toolbox at** `genealogy.tbox.com` **(For more information on using a browser, see Appendix A.)**

2. **Select Genealogy SiteFinder.**

   Selecting Genealogy SiteFinder takes you to the Genealogy SiteFinder main page where you can choose whether to run a search on a location name or to look through the directory (see Figure 4-5).

3. **Scroll down the directory and click <u>Places</u>.**

   Clicking Places brings up a list of continents, countries, and states/provinces from which you can choose.

4. **Click the country or state/province of your choice.**

   This takes you to a page that lists all Internet sites pertaining to the country, state, or province you selected that are indexed in the Genealogy SiteFinder. Each entry includes a brief abstract of the site and a link to that site, so you can select the sites that sound promising.

The state and county pages making up the USGenWeb Project are good examples of geographic-specific Web sites that convey information about places in the United States. The USGenWeb Project is an all-volunteer, online effort to provide a central genealogical resource for information (records and reference materials) pertaining to counties within each state. (See the sidebar "Overview of the USGenWeb Project" in this chapter for more information.) There is also a WorldGenWeb project that attempts the same type of undertaking as USGenWeb, only on a global scale. For more information about WorldGenWeb, see the *Genealogy Online Internet Directory* in this book.

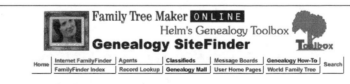

Figure 4-5:
Look for topics using a search engine or directory of subjects at the Genealogy SiteFinder.

Another good example of a geographic-specific Web site useful for genealogical research is the Genealogy Resource Page of the Hunter Valley in New South Wales, Australia (bhss.inia.net.au/patmay/). This site contains information about cemeteries, churches, court records, family history societies and libraries, and newspapers in the area. The site also identifies publications about New South Wales that may be of help in your genealogical research and provides some online family histories for some people from Hunter Valley.

And yet another example is the Newfoundland and Labrador Genealogy site (www.iosphere.net/~jholwell/cangene/nl.html), which identifies societies and associations, reference pages, personal pages by or pertaining to residents, historical and cultural entities, churches, archives, and museums in Newfoundland and Labrador, Canada. All these pages provide information about the traditional and online resources for the region, which can help you with your research. (*The Genealogy Online Internet Directory* also identifies some local geographic-specific resources on the Web.)

Genealogical and historical societies

Most genealogical and historical societies exist on a local level and attempt to preserve documents and history for the area in which they are located. Genealogical societies also have another purpose — to help their members research their ancestors whether they lived in the local area or elsewhere. (Granted, some surname-based genealogical societies, and even a couple of virtual societies, are an exception to this description of genealogical societies because they are not specific to one particular place.) Although historical societies don't have the second purpose of aiding members researching genealogy, they are typically quite helpful to genealogists anyway. Often, if you don't live in the area from which you need a record or information, you can contact a local genealogical or historical society to get help. Help varies from look-up services in books and documents the society maintains in its library to volunteers who will actually locate records for you and get copies to send you. Before you contact a local genealogical or historical society for help, be sure you know what services they offer.

Many local genealogical and historical societies have posted Web pages and identify exactly which services they offer to members and nonmembers online. To find a society in an area you're researching, try this:

1. **Using your Web browser, go to Genealogy Resources on the Internet: World Wide Web at** www-personal.umich.edu/~cgaunt/ gen_web.html **(For more information on using a browser, see Appendix A.)**

2. **Scroll down (if necessary) and select a link for "[Place Name] Resources" using the location where you are looking for an association or society as the place name.**

For example, if you are looking for a genealogical or historical society in Belgium, scroll down and click on the link for Belgium Resources. This action takes you to a page that identifies and links to all sorts of genealogical sites pertaining to Belgium.

3. **Look through the list of links to see if there are any associations or societies for the area you are looking. If so, click the link to visit the site.**

   Visit the group or society home page to see what services that group or society offers to members and nonmembers. If the group or society offers a service you need (lookup, obtaining copies of records, and so on), use whatever contact information the site provides to get in touch and request help.

GENEALOGY LINGO

Overview of the USGenWeb Project

The purpose of the USGenWeb Project is to provide a central genealogical resource for information (records and reference materials) pertaining to counties within each state. USGenWeb offers state-level pages for each of the states within the United States of America that have links to pages for each county, as well as links to other online resources about the state. At the county-level, the pages have links to resources about the county.

In addition to links to other Web sites with genealogical resources that are geographic-specific, most of the county-level pages have query sections, where you can post or read queries (or questions) about researching in that county. Some of the county-level pages offer other services in addition to the query section, such as a surname registry for anyone researching in the county and a look-up section that identifies people who are willing to look up information for others.

While some states have uniform-looking county pages with the same standard resources for each county, other states don't. The content and look of USGenWeb state and county pages varies tremendously from state to state.

In addition to state- and county-level pages under the USGenWeb Project, there are special projects that contain information that cross state- and county-lines. Some of these include:

- A project to collect and transcribe tombstone inscriptions so that genealogists can access the information online.

- An undertaking to transcribe all federal census data for the United States to make it available online.

- A project to gather military records and information about wars, transcribe the information, and make it available online.

The various pages and projects that make up the USGenWeb Project are designed and maintained by volunteers. If you're interested in becoming involved, visit the USGenWeb home page (www.usgenweb.org/).

Libraries and archives

Often, the holdings in local libraries and archives can be of great value to you — even if you can't visit the library or archive onsite to research. If the library or archive has an Internet site, go online to determine whether that library or archive has the book or document you need. (Most libraries and archives that have Web pages or other Internet sites make their card catalogs or another listing of their holdings available online.) After seeing if a library or archive has what you need, you can contact the library or archive to borrow the book or document (if they participate in an interlibrary loan program) or to get a copy of what you need (most libraries and archives have services to copy information for people at a minimal cost).

Try this to find online catalogs for libraries in a particular place.

1. **Using your Web browser, go to WebCats: Library Catalogues on the World Wide Web at** www.lights.com/webcats/ **(For more information on using a browser, see Appendix A.)**

2. **Select the link for the Geographical Index.**

   This brings up a Geographic Index of links sorted by area: Africa, Americas, Asia/Pacific Rim, and Europe/Middle East. The index also has links directly to some countries within those areas.

   For example, say you are looking for the national library of Australia to see if it has any books in its collection that would be helpful for your Australian research.

3. **Scroll down the Asia/Pacific Rim area, and click the link for Australia.**

   Clicking the link for Australia takes you to a page that lists known libraries and universities in Australia that have online catalogs.

4. **Browsing through the list, you can find that there is a national library. Click the link for the National Library of Australia.**

   This action takes you to the National Library's Catalogue. The main Web page for the Catalogue explains its purpose and collection, and provides specific information on how to search the site for particular publications or other works.

   From this point on, you would follow the site's instructions to search for it for books of interest and applicability to your particular research.

Professional researchers

Professional researchers are people who research your genealogy — or particular family lines — for a fee. If you're looking for someone to do all the research necessary to put together a complete family history, some do so.

If you're just looking for records in a particular area to substantiate claims in your genealogy, there are professional researchers who help by locating the records for you and getting you copies. Their services, rates, experience, and reputations vary, so you want to be careful when selecting a professional researcher to help you. Look for someone who has quite a bit of experience in the area in which you need help. Asking for references or a list of satisfied customers isn't out of the question (that way you know who you're dealing with prior to sending them money). Here's a list of questions you may want to ask when shopping around for a professional researcher.

- ✔ Is the professional researcher certified and, if so, by what organization?

- ✔ How many years experience does he/she have researching?

- ✔ What is his/her educational background?

- ✔ Does the researcher have any professional affiliations? In other words, does he/she belong to any professional genealogical organizations and, if so, which ones?

- ✔ What foreign languages does the researcher speak fluently?

- ✔ What records and resources does he/she have access to?

- ✔ What is the professional researcher's experience in the area where you need help? For example, if you need help interviewing distant relatives in a foreign country, has he/she conducted interviews in the past? Or if you need records pertaining to a particular ethnic or religious group, does he/she have experience researching those types of records?

- ✔ How does the researcher charge for his/her services — by the record, by the hour, or by the project? What methods of payment will he/she accept? What is the researcher's policy on refunds or dissatisfaction with his/her services?

- ✔ How many other projects is the researcher working on presently and what kinds of projects? How much time will he/she devote to your research project?

Finding professional researchers is as easy as finding geographic-specific sites, genealogical and historical societies, and libraries and archives in the preceding sections. Here's what you do.

1. **Using your Web browser, go to the Genealogy Toolbox at** genealogy.tbox.com **(For more information on using a browser, see Appendix A.)**

2. **Select Genealogy SiteFinder.**

   This takes you to the Genealogy SiteFinder main page where you can choose whether to run a search on a location name or to look through the directory.

3. **Scroll down the directory and click <u>Supplies and Services</u>.**

   Clicking on Supplies and Services brings up a list of types of supplies and services for which there are providers with Web sites.

4. **Click <u>Research Services</u>.**

   This takes you to a page that lists all Internet sites with information about the genealogical research services that are indexed in the Genealogy SiteFinder. Scroll through the list of sites to see which of the services may be restricted to particular geographic areas. Each entry includes a brief abstract of the site and a link to that site so it should be relatively easy to pick out researchers who restrict their services to particular areas.

5. **Identify those research services that work in the area you're interested in — or the services that aren't restricted at all geographically.**

   After figuring out which ones work in your area, visit the Web pages for those companies or people to see if their service is what you're looking for.

Planning Your Genealogy Travels by Using the Web

A wealth of other information is available to help you plan your travels — and it's all at your fingertips! You can surf the Web to check out hotels/motels, car rental places, airlines, local attractions, and a host of other things related to vacations. Two sites that provide links for all sorts of travel-related information are MapQuest (www.mapquest.com) and the Yahoo! Travel section (www.yahoo.com/Recreation/Travel/). Each has sections identifying transportation, lodging, dining, and a variety of other things you'll need while traveling. You can even use MapQuest (see "Mapping Your Ancestor's Way" earlier in this chapter) to plan your route if you're driving on your vacation in North America. Here's how:

1. **Using your World Wide Web browser, head over to MapQuest** (www.mapquest.com).

2. **Click the link for TripQuest.**

   This brings up the TripQuest page, which has two boxes for you to complete and some option dots under the boxes.

3. **In the first box, complete the four fields indicating where you are starting your journey.**

   The Select field allows you to use a pull-down menu with several options. You can have TripQuest use the address you specify as your

starting point or one of several other starting-point options (such as airports, bus stations, city halls, and court houses).

The Street Address field allows you to type in an actual street address. (This is the address TripQuest will use as your starting point if you indicate Use Address in the Select field.)

The City field is where you type in the city from which your journey will begin.

The State field is the state where you are beginning your trip.

4. **In the second box, complete the four fields indicating your destination (where you want to go).**

   The four destination fields are titled just like the starting fields and allow the same sort of information.

5. **Under Options: Route Type, click the appropriate button to indicate whether you want TripQuest to give you directions to go door-to-door or city-to-city.**

   If you need clarification on what the difference is between door-to-door and city-to-city, click on the What's the Difference link for an explanation.

6. **Under Options: Route Mapping, click the appropriate button to indicate whether you want an Overview Map with Text, a Turn-by-Turn Map with Text, or just the Text Only directions.**

7. **Click the Calculate Directions button.**

   TripQuest then determines the directions from your starting point to your destination. It provides you with the information.

   If TripQuest cannot determine a route for you, it provides an explanation and recommendations for you to try your TripQuest transaction again.

Part II
Finding the Elusive Records

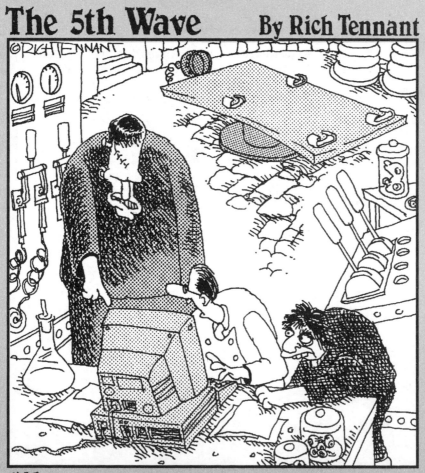

The 5th Wave   By Rich Tennant

"Hold your horses. It takes time to locate the ancestors for someone of your background."

In this part . . .

This part covers locating sites with hard-to-find information about groups of people and particular types of records — and figuring out how to use those sites effectively in your genealogical research. In here you find information about:

Researching African-American, American-Indian, and European ancestors

Sites relating to government records (such as census, vital records, immigration, land, military, and taxes) in several countries

Finding other miscellaneous records and information on various groups

Chapter 5
Ethnic Research

· ·

In This Chapter

▶ Discovering African ancestry

▶ Finding American-Indian sites

▶ Identifying Hispanic roots

▶ Researching European ethnic groups

· ·

*R*esearching a particular ethnic group can often be frustrating. Even though every ethnic group has records that are unique to it, the ethnic group may have been very mobile, making records hard to find. In some cases, records were destroyed during periods of war. Despite the difficulty in finding some of these records, ethnic research also can be very rewarding! By looking for records specific to ethnic groups, you get a clearer picture of your ancestor's part in history and find unique sources of information that can add color to your family story. This chapter examines some of the resources available online to assist you in finding ethnic-specific records.

Rather than repeat ourselves over and over again recommending this reference material, we thought it would be easier to tell you this up front. If you are looking for a good, reference resource that covers ethnic research, we recommend this book, which is available in print or on CD-ROM (as part of the Ancestry Reference Library): Szucs, Loretto Dennis and Sandra Hargreaves Luebking. *The Source: A Guidebook of American Genealogy*. Revised ed. Salt Lake City, UT: Ancestry, 1997. For information about its availability and contents, please visit www.ancestry.com.

African Ancestral Research

A common misconception is that tracing African ancestry is impossible. In the past decade or so, much has been done to dispel that perception. If your ancestors lived in the United States, you need to remember that, for the most part, you can use the same research techniques and the same records that genealogists of other ethnicities consult (census schedules, vital records, and other primary resources) back to 1870. Prior to 1870, your

research resources become more limited, depending upon whether your ancestor was a freedman or a slave. To make that determination, you may want to interview some of your relatives. They often possess oral traditions that can point you in the right direction.

If your ancestor was a slave, try consulting probate records of the slave owner (usually found in local courthouses), deed books (slave transactions were often recorded in deed books — also found in local courthouses), tax records, plantation records, and runaway slave records. These types of records can prove to be quite helpful because they identify persons by name.

Although your first inclination may be to turn to a slave schedule in the U.S. Census, you'll find that such schedules are less useful in your research because the *enumerators* who collected the census information did not record the names of slaves, nor did the government require them to do so. Please don't misunderstand us — that is not to say that slave schedules are a total waste of time! We just want to make sure you realize that the schedules are not going to provide you with verification by name that your ancestor is included in the record. Rather, you'll need to find other resources that name your ancestor specifically.

If your ancestors served in the American Civil War, they may have service and pension records. You can begin a search for service records in an index to Civil War records of the United States Colored Troops or, if your ancestor joined a state regiment, in an Adjutant General's report (an Adjutant General's report is a published account of the actions of military units from a particular state during a war; these are usually available at a library or archives). We discuss using the United States Colored Troops database later in this chapter.

Two other sources of records to keep in mind are those from the Freedman's Bureau and the Freedman's Savings and Trust. The Freedman's Bureau (its full name was the Bureau of Refugees, Freedmen and Abandoned Lands) was established in 1865 to assist ex-slaves after the American Civil War. The Freedman's Savings and Trust Company was also established in 1865 as a bank for ex-slaves. Several of its contributors were members of the United States Colored Troops during the war. Although the company failed in 1874, its records are now kept at the National Archives and Records Administration along with the records for the Freedman's Bureau. (The National Archives and Records Administration provides information about these records and their availability on microfilm at www.nara.gov/publications/microfilm/blackstudies/blackstd.html.)

For more information on using records to research your African ancestry, try the following:

✔ *Black Studies: A Select Catalog of National Archives Microfilm Publications.* Washington, DC: National Archives, 1984.

✔ Streets, David H. *Slave Genealogy: A Research Guide with Case Studies.* Bowie, MD: Heritage, 1986.

Mailing lists and newsgroups focusing on African research

Several key records are specific to African ancestral research, which means that you need to interact with other researchers. One place to start is the Afrigeneas mailing list. This mailing list focuses primarily on African genealogical research methods. On the World Wide Web page for the mailing list (at www.msstate.edu/Archives/History/afrigen/), you find the following:

- ✔ A set of frequently asked questions

- ✔ A newsletter

- ✔ Archived messages

- ✔ A link to a database of African-American surnames and their corresponding researchers

Here's how you subscribe to the Afrigeneas mailing list.

1. **Start your favorite e-mail program.**

   How you start your e-mail program depends on which e-mail program you use. Generally, you can begin the program by double-clicking on the program's icon or, in Windows 95, by executing the program from the Start button. If you're not sure how to start your e-mail program, see the documentation that came with the program. (You also can take a look at Appendix A for more information on e-mail.)

2. **Create a new e-mail message.**

   Usually you create a new e-mail message by clicking on an icon in your e-mail program's toolbar or by using a menu. If you don't know how to create a new e-mail message, consult the documentation that came with the program.

3. **Type** listserv@msstate.edu **in the TO: line.**

   Be sure that you type only **listserv@msstate.edu** in the TO: line. You subscribe to Afrigeneas at this listserv e-mail account. If you type anything more, your e-mail message will be kicked back to you as undeliverable and your attempt to subscribe will fail.

4. **Make sure that your e-mail address is in the FROM: line.**

   Some e-mail programs automatically fill in your e-mail address in the FROM: line. In that case, just make sure that it is correct. Otherwise, type in the e-mail address where you would like to receive postings to the Afrigeneas mailing list.

5. **In the body of the message type** subscribe afrigeneas [your First Name] [your Last Name].

    For example, if April is subscribing to the mailing list, she would type **subscribe afrigeneas April Helm** in the body of her message. Again, don't type anything more than this in the message or the automatic program that adds you to the mailing list gets confused and kicks out your attempt to subscribe.

6. **Send the e-mail message.**

    Your e-mail program probably has a Send button that will send the message when you click on it. If you don't see a Send button or command in one of the pull-down menus, consult your e-mail program documentation for details on sending a message.

Another resource to turn to when starting your research is the `soc.genealogy.african` newsgroup. This newsgroup focuses on research methods for genealogists interested in their African ancestry. To access the newsgroup, you need a newsgroup reader (for more on newsgroups, see Appendix A).

A third resource is the SLAVEINFO mailing list. This list is a forum for sharing genealogical data on slaves in the United States. To subscribe to the list, follow the same procedures given in the preceding numbered list, only send your subscribe message to `slaveinfo-l-request@rootsweb.com` with just the word "subscribe" in the body of the message.

Genealogical resource pages on the Web

A number of online resources are available to assist you in finding your African ancestry. One site that identifies several of these resources is Christine's Genealogy Website (see Figure 5-1) located at `ccharity.com/`. Here you'll find:

- A list of World Wide Web pages of interest to genealogists
- Transcriptions of records from the Freedman's Bureau (a government entity established to assist former slaves) arranged by state
- Lists of ex-slaves who emigrated to Liberia from 1820 to 1843
- Sites that contain transcribed wills that have slaves named or mentioned within them

For a brief list of resources that you can use offline, see the African American Genealogy page (`library.jmu.edu/library/guides/history/aageneal.htm`). This page covers resources such as:

- Bibliographies
- Primary sources

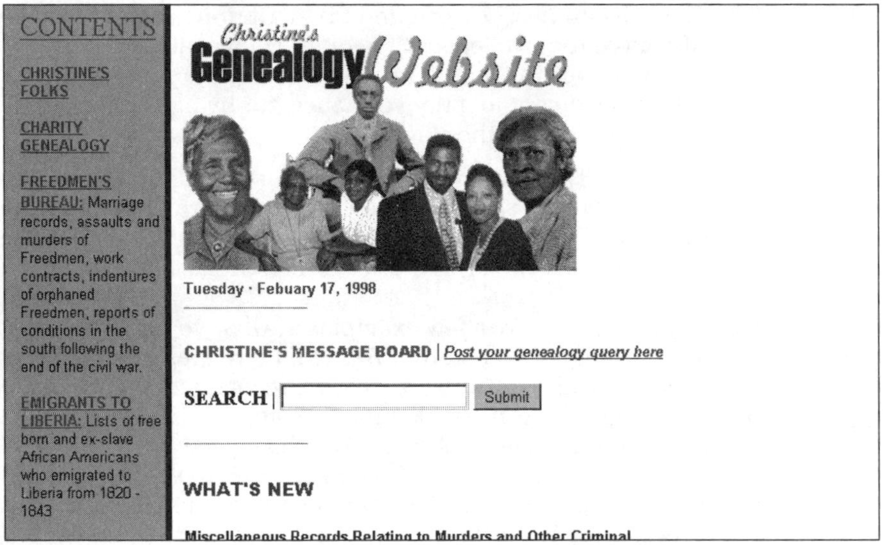

Figure 5-1: Christine's Genealogy Web site has several African-ancestry research resources.

- Biographical sources
- Diaries
- Cemetery sources
- Newspapers
- Electronic text sources

Transcribed records pertaining to ancestors with African roots

Many genealogists recognize the benefits of making transcribed and digitized records available for other researchers. However, limited resources prohibit most of these genealogists from being able to do so. A few Web sites have transcribed records that are unique to the study of African ancestry online. Here are some examples:

- **Cemetery Records:** For a transcribed list of an old slave cemetery in Denton County, Texas, see www.iglobal.net/mayhouse/Slavecem.html
- **Registers:** At a site called the Valley of the Shadow, you can view transcribed Registers of Free Blacks in Augusta County, Virginia (jefferson.village.virginia.edu/vshadow2/govdoc/govdoc.html#fb).

✔ **Slave Schedules:** You can find transcriptions of slave schedules at the African-American Census Schedules Online site at www.mindspring.com/~smothers/AACensus.htm. (Although these schedules do not identify your ancestor by name, they are useful if you know the name of the slave owner.)

✔ **Tax Lists:** The African American History and Genealogy Resources page (www.ilinks.net/~mcmaster/) includes transcriptions of the Charleston Free Negro Tax Lists of 1821 and 1822 and the Free People of Color in Charleston Directories of 1819, 1822, and 1840.

The preceding sites are a few examples of what you can find on the Internet in terms of transcribed records. To see if there are online records that pertain specifically to your research, we recommend you visit a comprehensive genealogical site and look under the appropriate category. For example, the Genealogy SiteFinder's African-American page (www.familytreemaker.com/links/c/c-people,ethnic-religious-groups,african-american.html) identifies resources for African-American research and its Records page (www.familytreemaker.com/links/c/c-records.html) identifies all sorts of records and indices for records that you can find online.

United States Colored Troops and other databases

Although only a few online databases currently focus on African ancestry, one that certainly deserves mention is the United States Colored Troops (USCT) database. The USCT is part of the Civil War Soldiers and Sailors System sponsored by the National Park Service (www.itd.nps.gov/cwss/usct.html). The database contains more than 230,000 names and 180 regimental histories of USCT units (see Figure 5-2).

To search the USCT database, try this:

1. **Point your World Wide Web browser to** www.itd.nps.gov/cwss/usct.html

   If you can't recall how to navigate your World Wide Web browser, see Appendix A.

2. **Click the button marked "Search USCT Data."**

   This button is located on the right side of the screen, near the bottom of the page. It will take you to another page where you can type in the name that you are researching.

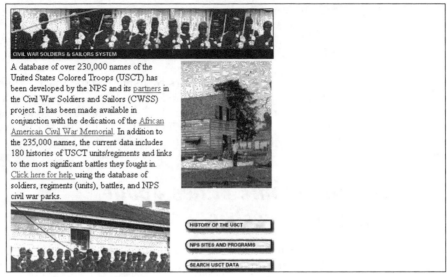

Figure 5-2:
The United
States
Colored
Troops
database
contains
information
on more
than
230,000
soldiers of
African
descent.

3. **Type a surname (using all capital letters) in the blank and then press the Enter key on your keyboard.**

   The blank is located next to the words "This is a searchable index. Enter search keywords:." For example, if April is searching for the surname "Sanders," she would type **SANDERS** in the blank, and then press Enter. The search engine looks through the database, picks up any matches to that surname, and then takes you to a page that shows the results of your search.

4. **Select a name by clicking on the appropriate name link on the results page.**

   The results page contains a list of names, the side on which the person fought during the war, and the unit of assignment. Click on the name to see the whole record on the soldier. For example, suppose that April is interested in learning about the soldier named Aaron Sanders. She would click on the link "Aaron Sanders," which would take her to another page that contains:

   - The first and last name of the soldier

   - Side on which the soldier fought during the war

   - Unit of assignment

   - Rank at enlistment

   - Rank at mustering out

- Company

- Aliases

- National Archives and Records Administration film number

After you identify potential ancestors by using the database, you can follow up by looking for the microfilm at the National Archives or ordering a copy of the actual military record. The USCT site explains how to find and get copies of the records on its page, "Where should you go to discover more information on Civil War soldiers?" (www.itd.nps.gov/cwss/cwss4.html).

Special ethnic pages about African ancestry

A number of World Wide Web sites include information on a particular subset of individuals of African ancestry. Here are some you may wish to visit:

- For information on persons of African ancestry in Mexico, see the brief article at the African Roots Stretch Deep into Mexico site (server.berkeley.edu/raza/work/story4.html).

- The African — Native Genealogy Homepage has details on the Estelusti, a tribe of Black Indians in Oklahoma (members.aol.com/angelaw859/index.html).

- You can find a brief article on the Free People of Color and Creoles at www.neworleansonline.com/sno21.htm

- Internet Nova Scotia has site called The African Presence that focuses on how Africans arrived in Nova Scotia (www.nstn.ca/bccns/).

To find additional sites with unique information about researching your African ancestry, we recommend you visit a comprehensive genealogical site and look under the appropriate category to review a list of links to such sites. (For a list of comprehensive genealogical sites, see the *Genealogy Online Internet Directory*.)

American-Indian Resources

Tracing your American-Indian heritage can be challenging. Your ancestor may have moved frequently and, most likely, few written records were kept. However, your task is not impossible. With a good research strategy, you may be able to narrow down your search area and find primary resources to unlock some of the mysteries of your ancestors.

One of the keys to your research is old family stories that have been passed down from generation to generation. So, interviewing your family members is a good way to find out what tribe your ancestor belonged to and the geographic area in which he lived. After you have this information, a trip to your local library is well worth the effort to find a history of the tribe and where it migrated throughout time. From this research you can then concentrate your search to a specific geographic area and have a much better chance of success in finding records of genealogical value.

Fortunately, the government of the United States did compile some records on American Indians. For example, you can find annual census lists of American Indians dating from 1885 to 1940 in the National Archives. You can also find probate and land records at the Federal level, especially for transactions occurring on reservations. For those who attended schools on reservations, you can also find school records in Federal repositories. Additionally, the Bureau of Indian Affairs has a vast collection of records on American Indians. (For more information about American Indian resources available from the National Archives and Records Administration, you may wish to visit `www.nara.gov/publications/microfilm/amerindians/indians.html`.)

You may also be able to find records on your ancestor in one of the many tribal associations in existence. (To find out how to contact one of the many tribes recognized in the United States, go to `www.indians.org/tribes/`.)

For more information on researching American-Indian records, see the following:

✔ Byers, Paula K., ed. _Native American Genealogical Sourcebook_. Detroit, MI.: Gale Research, 1995.

✔ Hill, Edward E. _Guide to Records in the National Archives of the United States Relating to American Indians_. Washington, DC: National Archives and Records Services Administration, 1981.

Where to begin looking for information about American Indians

For a general look at what Internet resources are available on American Indians, see the NativeWeb site (`www.nativeweb.org/`). NativeWeb has a resource center with hundreds of links to other Internet sites on native peoples around the world. Of particular interest to genealogists is its page on Tracing Your Roots (`www.nativeweb.org/pages/roots.phtml`).

If you have a question as to whether a tribe is officially recognized in the United States, you can visit the official list at the American Indian Tribal Directory (www.indians.org/tribes/). The list is categorized by tribe, state, and city/state.

To survey the types of records on American Indians available at the National Archives, see American Indians: A Select Catalog of NARA Microfilm Publications (www.nara.gov/publications/microfilm/amerindians/indians.html).

When you're ready to dive into research, you may want to join the INDIAN-ROOTS-L mailing list, which is devoted to discussing American-Indian research methods. You can subscribe to the list by taking the following steps:

1. **Start your favorite e-mail program.**

   The method of starting your e-mail program depends upon which e-mail program you use. Generally, you can begin the program by double-clicking the program's icon or, in Windows 95, by executing the program from the Start button. If you are not sure how to start your e-mail program, see the documentation that came with the program. (See Appendix A for more information on using e-mail.)

2. **Create a new e-mail message.**

   Usually you create a new e-mail message by clicking on an icon in your e-mail program's toolbar or by using a menu. If you don't know how to create a new e-mail message, consult the documentation that came with the program.

3. **Type** listserv@listserv.indiana.edu **in the TO: line.**

   Be sure that you type only listserv@listserv.indiana.edu in the TO: line. You subscribe to INDIAN-ROOTS-L at this listserv e-mail account. If you type anything more, your e-mail message will be kicked back to you as undeliverable and your attempt to subscribe will fail.

4. **Make sure that your e-mail address is in the FROM: line.**

   Some e-mail programs automatically fill in your e-mail address in the FROM: line. In that case, just make sure that it is correct. Otherwise, type in the e-mail address where you would like to receive postings to the INDIAN-ROOTS-L mailing list.

5. **In the body of the message type** SUB INDIAN-ROOTS-L [your first name] [your last name].

   For example, if April is subscribing to the mailing list, she would type only **SUB INDIAN-ROOTS-L april helm** in the body of her message. Notice that her first and last names are in all lowercase letters.

6. Send the e-mail message.

Your e-mail program probably has a Send button that sends the message when you click on it. If you don't see a Send button, consult your e-mail program documentation for details on sending a message.

For general information on how to begin researching American-Indian resources, see the article "How-To Guide for Native Americans" (members.aol.com/bbbenge/page12.html). A list of American-Indian sites on the Internet can be found on the Native American Genealogy page (members.aol.com/bbbenge/front.html). Another page that you may want to look at is Tawodi's American Indian Genealogy site (members.aol.com/tawodi/). It contains a how-to guide, a list of American-Indian texts online, and links to several tribal and American-Indian pages (see Figure 5-3).

Figure 5-3:
Tawodi's
American
Indian
Genealogy
site has a
how-to
guide and
links to
other
research
resources.

TAWODI'S
AMERICAN INDIAN GENEALOGY

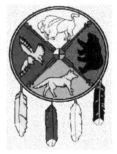

Researching Indian ancestry and heritage is a challenging and rewarding endeavor. It involves much more than finding great-great-grandparents on a census, or finally locating the Family Bible. Indian genealogy, like all genealogy, is much more than just names and dates--it is a study of the people, history, and culture of our ancestors. Whether you are trying to establish

American-Indian resource pages on the Web

Genealogists would have a much easier time researching American-Indian roots if some sites were dedicated to the genealogical research of specific tribes. If your ancestor's tribe passed through the state of Oklahoma, you may be in luck. Volunteers with the Oklahoma USGenWeb project (for more on USGenWeb, see Chapter 4) developed the Twin Territories site (www.rootsweb.com/~itgenweb/index.htm). The site contains a list of links to tribal genealogical pages including the following:

- ✔ Cherokee Nation Indian Territory (`www.usroots.com/itgenweb/itcherok/`)
- ✔ Cheyenne – Arapaho Lands Indian Territory (`www.geocities.com/Heartland/Hills/1263/itcheyarapindx.html`)
- ✔ Chickasaw Nation, Indian Territory 1837-1907 (`www.usroots.com/itgenweb/itchicka/`)
- ✔ Choctaw Nation, Indian Territory (`www.usroots.com/itgenweb/itchocta/`)
- ✔ Iowa Tribe of Oklahoma (`www.usroots.com/itgenweb/itiowa/`)
- ✔ Kiowa, Comanche, Apache Lands Indian Territory (`www.geocities.com/Heartland/Hills/1263/itcomancindx.html`)
- ✔ Muscogee (Creek) Nation of Oklahoma (`www.rootsweb.com/~itcreek/index.htm`)
- ✔ Potawatomi Nation (`tri.net/~kheidel/nativeamer/index.html`)
- ✔ Quapaw Agency Lands Indian Territory (`www.usroots.com/itgenweb/itquapaw/`)
- ✔ Sovereign Nation of the Kaw (`www.usroots.com/itgenweb/itkanza/`)

Transcribed American-Indian records

Many genealogists now recognize the benefits of making transcribed and digitized records available online for other researchers, but the realities of time and money prohibit most from being able to do so. A few Web sites have transcribed records that are unique to researching American-Indian roots, however. Here are some examples:

- ✔ The Chickasaw Historical Research Page (`www.flash.net/~kma/`) contains transcriptions of marriage records, a partial census roll of 1818, land sale records, court records, and treaty letters.
- ✔ 1851 Census of Cherokees East of the Mississippi (`members.aol.com/lredtail/siler.html`) has a transcription of the census including name, family number, age, and relationship to head of household.
- ✔ You can find several transcribed records at the South Dakota Native American Genealogy page (`www.geocities.com/Heartland/Plains/8430/`). These records include marriage lists, agency rolls, and links to cemetery records.

Again, these are a few examples of what you can find on the Internet in terms of transcribed records. To see if any online records pertain specifically to your research, visit a comprehensive genealogical site and look under the appropriate category. For example, the Genealogy SiteFinder's American-Indian page (`www.familytreemaker.com/links/c/c-people,ethnic-religious-groups,american-indian.html`) identifies

resources for research and its Records page (www.familytreemaker.com/links/c/c-records.html) identifies all sorts of records and indices for records that you can find online.

Hispanic Roots

A growing number of genealogists are researching their Hispanic roots (the dictionary defines Hispanic as relating to the people, language, and culture of Spain, Portugal, or Latin America). If you have Hispanic ancestors, you can use several different types of records to pursue your genealogy, depending upon when your ancestor immigrated.

If your ancestor immigrated in the 19th or 20th centuries, look for vital records, military records, photographs, passports, church records, passenger lists, naturalization papers, diaries, or other items that can give you an idea of the place of birth of your ancestor. For those ancestors who immigrated before the 19th century, you may want to consult the colonial records of Spain after you have exhausted any local records in the region where your ancestor lived.

For more information on researching Hispanic records see: Ryskamp, George R. *Hispanic Family History Research in the L.D.S. Family History Center.* Riverside, Calif.: Hispanic Family History Research, 1989.

Where to begin searching for genealogical information on Hispanic ancestors

If you are not sure where to begin your research, we recommend that you read messages posted to the soc.genealogy.hispanic newsgroup (for more information on newsgroups see Appendix A). Normally, a newsreader is required to read messages on the newsgroup; however, if you do not have a newsreader, you can read messages through a World Wide Web interface such as DejaNews (www.dejanews.com). If your interests lie in genealogy research in a specific country or ethnic subgroup, you may want to join one of the following mailing lists:

- **Cuba:** This mailing list is devoted to people who have a genealogical interest in Cuba. To subscribe to the mailing list, send a message to cuba-l-request@rootsweb.com with only the word "subscribe" in the body of the message.
- **Basque-L:** This list discusses Basque culture and periodically includes genealogical postings. To subscribe to the mailing list, send a message to listserv@cunyvm.cuny.edu with "SUBSCRIBE BASQUE-L [your first name] [your last name]" in the body of the message.

> ✔ **Spain:** This list is devoted to people who have a genealogical interest in Spain. To subscribe to the list, send a message to `spain-l-request@ rootsweb.com` with only the word "subscribe" in the body of the message.

Hispanic resource pages on the Web

We recommend you visit the Hispanic Genealogy page located at `ourworld.compuserve.com/homepages/alfred_sosa/`. This page is maintained by the CompuServe Hispanic Genealogy Section and contains information on how to get started, Hispanic organizations, Spanish heraldry, and a query page to post information about your ancestors. America Online also has a Hispanic forum (`users.aol.com/mrosado007/index.htm`). It includes a newsletter, surname list, and links to other Hispanic resources on the Internet. For a list of Hispanic resources by location, the Puerto Rican/ Hispanic Genealogical Society maintains a page of links to genealogical resources at `linkdirect.com/hispsoc/hispanic_links.htm` (see Figure 5-4). For resources specific to a country or area, see the following sites:

> ✔ **Argentina WorldGenWeb** (`www.geocities.com/Heartland/Plains/ 6909/argentina.html`)
>
> ✔ **Basque Genealogy Homepage** (`www.concentric.net/~Fybarra/`)
>
> ✔ **Cuban Genealogy Resources** (`ourworld.compuserve.com/ homepages/ee/`)
>
> ✔ **Genealogía de Venezuela** (`www.geocities.com/Heartland/Ranch/ 2443/`)
>
> ✔ **Genealogical Research in South America** (`www.saqnet.co.uk/ users/hrhenly/latinam1.html`)
>
> ✔ **Genealogy in Costa Rica** (`www.nortronica.com/genealogy/`)
>
> ✔ **Mexican GenWeb Project** (`www.rootsweb.com/~mexwgw/`)
>
> ✔ **Peru — The WorldGenWeb Project** (`www.rootsweb.com/~perwgw/`)
>
> ✔ **Puerto Rican Research** (`www.familytreemaker.com/ 00000382.html`)
>
> ✔ **Dominican Research** (`www.familytreemaker.com/00000366.html`)
>
> ✔ **Cuban Research** (`www.familytreemaker.com/00000365.html`)

Transcribed records for Hispanic ancestors

Although many genealogists recognize the benefits of posting transcribed and digitized records online, relatively few sites actually have them — primarily because of the time and cost involved to transcribe or digitize the

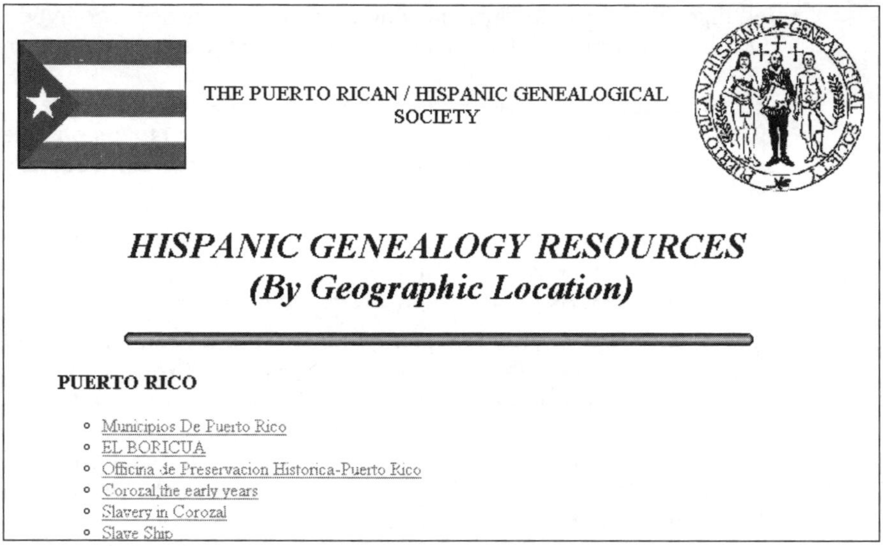

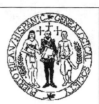

THE PUERTO RICAN / HISPANIC GENEALOGICAL
SOCIETY

Figure 5-4:
A
categorized
listing of
Hispanic
resources
on the
Puerto
Rican/
Hispanic
Genealogical
Society.

HISPANIC GENEALOGY RESOURCES
(By Geographic Location)

PUERTO RICO

- Municipios De Puerto Rico
- EL BORICUA
- Officina de Preservacion Historica-Puerto Rico
- Corozal,the early years
- Slavery in Corozal
- Slave Ship

records. However, that is not to say that there aren't any sites with transcribed records! Here are a few examples:

✔ You can view transcribed records from the 1757, 1780, 1791, 1823, and 1860 censuses of the village of Guerrero in Mexico (along with baptismal records) at `members.aol.com/gallegjj/viejo.html`

✔ Selected Parish Registers from Uruguay and Argentina are available at `www.saqnet.co.uk/users/hrhenly/latinam1.html`

✔ A list of slaves in Bayamon, Puerto Rico is found at `ponce.inter.edu/proyecto/in/hchg1010/inventar.html`

Because this is just a sampling of the transcribed records that are available online, we recommend that you visit a comprehensive genealogical site if you are interested in learning whether other sites pertain more specifically to your research. For example, you can choose from a long list of ethnic groups at the Genealogy SiteFinder's Ethnic/Religious Groups page (`www.familytreemaker.com/links/c/c-people,ethnic-religious-groups.html`) to look for resources specific to a group you are researching.

Lost in Europe

If one or more of your ancestors came from Europe, consult information on one of the continent's many ethnic groups. Your level of genealogical success with European ethnic records depends greatly on the history of the group. Ancestors from places that weathered several wars and border

changes may have fewer surviving records than those who lived in a more stable environment. Here is a sampling of European ethnic research sites:

- **German Genealogy Pages:** The German Genealogy Pages (`www.genealogy.com/gene/faqs/sgg.html`) focus on research of German, Austrian, Swiss, Alsatian, Luxemburger, and Eastern European genealogy.

- **Francetres:** This site (`www.cam.org/~beaur/gen/welcome.html`) focuses on genealogy of French-speaking groups including French Canadians, Acadians, Cajuns, Belgians, and Swiss.

- **Federation of East European Family History Societies (FEEFHS):** If you are looking for research guides for Eastern Europe, this is a good place to start. The Federation's pages (`feefhs.org/`) have information on the Albanian, Armenian, Austrian, Belarusian, Bohemian, Bulgarian, Carpatho-Rusyn, Croatian, Czech, Danish, Finnish, Galician, German, Hutterite, Hungarian, Latvian, Lithuanian, Polish, Moravian, Pomeranian, Romanian, Russian, Silesian, Slavic, Slavonian, Slovak, Slovenian, Transylvanian, Ukrainian, and Volhynian ethnic groups.

- **IRLGEN: Tracing Your Irish Ancestors:** IRLGEN (`www.bess.tcd.ie/irlgen/genweb2.htm`) has guides on sources of genealogical information in Ireland, a list of county heritage centers, and useful addresses.

- **Italian Genealogy Homepage:** The Homepage (`www.italgen.com/`) covers many topics including medieval genealogy, tips for researching in Italy, records repositories, common surnames, and history (see Figure 5-5).

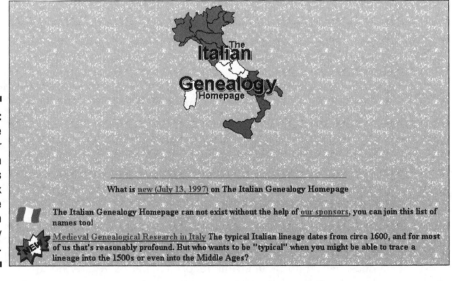

Figure 5-5:
If you are looking for your Italian ancestors take a look at the Italian Genealogy Homepage.

What is new (July 13, 1997) on The Italian Genealogy Homepage

The Italian Genealogy Homepage can not exist without the help of our sponsors, you can join this list of names too!

Medieval Genealogical Research in Italy The typical Italian lineage dates from circa 1600, and for most of us that's reasonably profound. But who wants to be "typical" when you might be able to trace a lineage into the 1500s or even into the Middle Ages?

✔ **Nordic Notes on the Net:** Nordic Notes on the Net (nordicnotes.com/) includes information on the Danish, Finnish, Icelandic, Norwegian, and Swedish ethnic groups.

✔ **UK and Ireland Genealogical Information Service (GENUKI):** GENUKI (midas.ac.uk/genuki/) includes details on English, Irish, Scottish, Welsh, Channel Islanders, and Manx ethnic groups.

The following sites, which are available at Family Tree Maker Online, provide background information and lists of print resources pertaining to immigration to the United States by the ethnic group indicated:

✔ **Greek Research** (www.familytreemaker.com/00000372.html)

✔ **Hungarian Research** (www.familytreemaker.com/00000373.html)

✔ **Polish Research** (www.familytreemaker.com/00000381.html)

✔ **Russian Research** (www.familytreemaker.com/00000383.html)

✔ **Spanish Research** (www.familytreemaker.com/00000385.html)

To find information on European ethnic groups, your best bet is to consult a comprehensive genealogy site. Here is an example of such a search:

1. **With your World Wide Web browser, go to the Genealogy Resources on the Internet site at** users.aol.com/johnf14246/internet.html

   In the first paragraph of the site, you see a list of resources including "Mailing Lists, USENET Newsgroups, anonymous File Transfer Protocol (FTP), Gopher, World Wide Web, Telnet, and E-Mail."

2. **Select the link marked <u>World Wide Web</u>.**

   This link takes you to an alphabetic listing of categories of genealogical World Wide Web sites.

3. **Click on a geographic/ethnicity.**

   We are interested in finding information on individuals of Dutch ancestry, so we chose the link entitled "Dutch Resources." This brings up a page with a list of Dutch-related links.

4. **Choose a link from the list that interests you.**

Asian Resources

If your ancestors came from Asia or the Pacific Rim, you'll want to look for information on one of the continent's many ethnic groups. Of course, your success finding records will depend greatly on the history of the group and

its record-keeping procedures. Currently, there is little genealogical information online pertaining to these areas and peoples. Here is a sampling of Asian and Pacific Rim resources that you can find:

- ✔ **Vietnamese Research** (www.familytreemaker.com/00000387.html)
- ✔ **Genealogy in Non-Western Civilizations (India, China, Japan, the Arab World, and Jewish)** (win-www.uia.ac.be/u/pavp/gengen.html#nwest)
- ✔ **Genealogical Gleanings (genealogies of the rulers of India, Burma, Cambodia, Thailand, Fiji, Tonga, Hawaii, and Malaysia)** (www.uq.net.au/~zzhsoszy/index.html)
- ✔ **Chinese Surnames** (www.geocities.com/Tokyo/3919/)
- ✔ **Chinese Surname Queries** (www.ziplink.net/~rey/ch/queries/)
- ✔ **Chinese Research** (www.familytreemaker.com/00000364.html)
- ✔ **Ancestors from the former Dutch East Indies** (ourworld.compuserve.com/homepages/paulvanV/eastindi.htm)
- ✔ **Japan WorldGenWeb Project** (www.rootsweb.com/~jpnwgw/)
- ✔ **Japanese Research** (www.familytreemaker.com/00000376.html)
- ✔ **Philippines Genealogy Web Project** (www.geocities.com/Heartland/Ranch/9121/)
- ✔ **Filipino Research** (www.familytreemaker.com/00000369.html)
- ✔ **British Ancestors in India** (www.ozemail.com.au/~clday/)
- ✔ **Asian Indian Research** (www.familytreemaker.com/00000361.html)
- ✔ **Korean Research** (www.familytreemaker.com/00000377.html)

Chapter 6
Government Records

Governments are bureaucratic institutions no matter where you live. Fortunately, you can cash in on some of the information that they have meticulously kept for hundreds of years. Records at all levels of government are immensely valuable to genealogists. During the four years that we lived in the Washington, D.C. area, we tried to take full advantage of government resources like the National Archives. In fact, we had a regularly scheduled night each week for research. Unfortunately, when we moved back to the Midwest, we gave up a great deal of our ability to conveniently conduct research on government records. So, we looked for ways to research them from the comfort of our own home — online. But finding primary records online can often be a problem.

Although the use of scanners enables people to scan original documents and put them online, and it's true that sites are emerging with transcribed information, finding actual records online is still rare. Instead, what you find are resources that will help you identify the types and locations of primary records so that you are prepared when you write, e-mail, or call to request copies of the records or go to a library or archive to make your own copies. Many Internet sites contain background information and even searchable indexes. This chapter identifies some of the Internet resources that will help you find the keys to government treasure chests of genealogical information.

Counting on the Census

One of the most valuable tools to a genealogist is census records. Many countries count and gather information about their populations periodically. However, most countries did not begin conducting nationwide censuses regularly until the 19th century. Nevertheless, census records are valuable for tying a person to a place and for discovering relationships between individuals. For example, let's say that you have a great-great-great grandfather named Nimrod Sanders. You're not sure who his father was, but you do know that he was born in North Carolina. By using a census index, you may be able to find a Nimrod Sanders in a North Carolina census index who is listed as a child of someone else. If the age of Nimrod, the location, and names of siblings fit, then you may have found one more generation to add to your genealogy.

Often, a census includes information such as a person's age, sex, occupation, birthplace, and relationship to the head of the household. Sometimes, the *enumerators* (the people who conducted the census) added comments to the census record, such as a comment on the physical condition of an individual, that may give you further insight into the person's life. For additional information about the value and format of censuses, see Chapter 1.

Getting the lowdown on censuses

Several Web sites provide background information about census records in particular countries. They explain what years the census records cover, how the censuses were conducted, and information they contain of value to genealogists. Also, they give you the details on where you can find and obtain copies of these census records. Here is a list of general census information sites from various countries around the world:

- **Australia:** Censuses in Australian Colonies (www.users.on.net/proformat/census.html)

- **Canada:** National Archives of Canada (www.archives.ca/www/GenealogicalSources.html#Census Records)

- **England, Scotland, and Wales:** Genuki Census Information (midas.ac.uk/genuki/big/eng/census.html)

- **Ireland:** Sources of Genealogical Information in Ireland (www.bess.tcd.ie/irlgen/census.htm)

- **Norway:** Norway Online Information Service (www.norway.org/ancestor.htm#Cens)

- **United States:** National Archives and Records Administration (www.nara.gov/genealogy/microcen.html)

For a summary of the contents of each United States census return, and advice on how to use the censuses, turn to the "Finding Treasures in the U.S. Federal Census" article on the Treasure Maps site located at `www.firstct.com/fv/uscensus.html`. Also, if you run into abbreviations that you don't understand, take a look at Genealogy Record Service's "Census and Soundex Relationship Abbreviations" page at `biz.ipa.net/genrecord/abbreviations.htm`

Finding your ancestors in census records

Imagine that you are ready to begin looking for your ancestors in census records. You hop in the car and drive to the nearest library, archives, or Family History Center. Upon arrival, you find the microfilm roll for the area where you believe your ancestors lived. You then go into a dimly lit room, insert the microfilm into the reader, and begin your search. After a couple hours of rolling the microfilm, the back pain begins to set in, the cramping of the hands becomes more severe, and the handwritten census documents become blurry as your eyes strain from reading each entry line by line. You come to the end of the roll and still have not found your elusive ancestor. At this point you begin to wonder if there's a better way.

Fortunately, a better way does exist for a lot of census records — census indices. *Census indices* contain a listing of the people who are included in particular census records, along with references indicating where you can find the actual census record. Traditionally, they come in book form — but now some individuals have taken the time to transcribe some of these indices and place them online or on CD-ROM.

Although there are no central World Wide Web sites that contain indices for all census records (at least not yet), some sites contain partial listings of census indices. These sites may contain indices for several states over several years, one index for one census year, or something in between. But, of course, your question is how do you find these online indices?

One place to start is at a comprehensive genealogy site. These sites typically include links to census records under a geographical heading. Genealogy SiteFinder (`www.familytreemaker.com/links`) and Cyndi's List of Genealogy Sites on the Internet (`www.CyndisList.com`) are a couple of good sites for finding things by location.

For example, say you want to find an Alan McSwain who lived in Ontario sometime around 1870. Your first step would be to find out whether a census was taken in or around 1870. To do so, follow these steps:

1. **Fire up your World Wide Web browser and go to Cyndi's List of Genealogy Sites on the Internet at** www.CyndisList.com

   The home page of Cyndi's List has a category index toward the bottom of the page.

   (For more information on using a Web browser, take a look at Appendix A.)

2. **Scroll down to the category called Canada Index. Select Ontario from the table of Canadian provinces listed on the page.**

   Selecting Ontario takes you to another page called Canada – Ontario. There you find a category index at the top of the page in smaller print. Among several other categories, you see Canada GenWeb Project, General Resource Sites, and Government & Cities.

3. **Select Records: Census, Cemeteries, Land, Obituaries, Personal, Taxes and Vital from this category index.**

   This takes you further down the page where you find a list of links to Canadian records on the Internet. Start scanning for records near 1870 — there are some sites with information on the 1871 Census.

4. **Choose the link <u>1871 Ontario Census Index</u>.**

   The link takes you to a portion of the National Archives of Canada site that features a searchable index of the 1871 Census (see Figure 6-1).

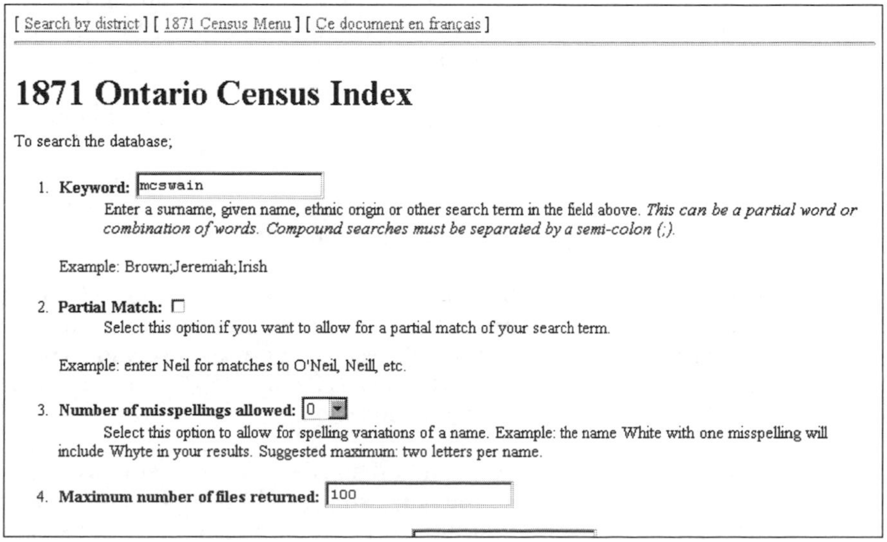

[<u>Search by district</u>] [<u>1871 Census Menu</u>] [<u>Ce document en français</u>]

1871 Ontario Census Index

To search the database;

1. **Keyword:** mcswain
      Enter a surname, given name, ethnic origin or other search term in the field above. *This can be a partial word or combination of words. Compound searches must be separated by a semi-colon (;).*

   Example: Brown;Jeremiah;Irish

2. **Partial Match:** ☐
      Select this option if you want to allow for a partial match of your search term.

   Example: enter Neil for matches to O'Neil, Neill, etc.

3. **Number of misspellings allowed:** 0 ▾
      Select this option to allow for spelling variations of a name. Example: the name White with one misspelling will include Whyte in your results. Suggested maximum: two letters per name.

4. **Maximum number of files returned:** 100

Figure 6-1:
The search page for the 1871 Ontario Census Index.

5. **In the box next to Keyword, type** mcswain **or another name that interests you, and then click Submit.**

   A search on the McSwain name yields two results: Alan McSwain and Mary McSwain.

6. **Click on the link for Alan McSwain to see his entry in the transcribed census record.**

   The link takes you to the entry in the record for Alan McSwain. From the record, you can see that there also are two other entries for individuals with the surname McSwnm. These individuals may quite possibly be related to Alan as they have similar surnames and are from Scotland — as is Alan.

This same search strategy works for a census index for any country. If you can't find an index for the census you're looking for in a comprehensive site, try using one of the large Internet search engines such as Lycos (www.lycos.com) or AltaVista (www.altavista.digital.com). (For more on using search engines, check out Appendix A.)

If you find one of your ancestors in a census index, make sure you write down the county, township, house number, and page in which you find the ancestor. Then you can make a specific request for a copy of the census record, reducing the amount of time it takes to have it sent to you (and reducing the frustration levels of those pulling records for you), or of course, you can always try to find the record and make a copy of it for yourself at your local library, archives, or Family History Center.

Remember that the objective of a census index is only to let you know who was included in the census return and where the record is located. Also, keep in mind that indices that are transcribed may have omissions and typographical errors. When in doubt, you can always check the official index to the census.

Finding individuals in the United States census

Census indices are a very important resource for finding individuals in the United States census. Similar to the way you find census indices for any other country (see the preceding section "Finding your ancestors in census records"), you can use comprehensive genealogy sites to find links to indices for individual states. These indices come in a variety of forms and have varying amounts of information. However, there's one additional resource that researchers can use to find individuals in United States records — the FamilyFinder Index.

The FamilyFinder Index (www.familytreemaker.com/ffitop.html) is produced by Brøderbund Software. The Index contains over 153 million names from census records, marriage records, Social Security, death

records, and family trees contained on CD-ROMs manufactured by the company. You can use the Index to do a preliminary search for individuals in census records from 1790 to 1880 online. The Index provides the name of an individual, estimated date, location, and the name of the CD-ROM where the name appears. Here's an example:

1. **Point your World Wide Web browser to the FamilyFinder Index at** `www.familytreemaker.com/ffitop.html`

   You see a page with a gray button marked Search Expert. (The button has a picture of a book and a detective on it.)

   (Check out Appendix A for more on using a browser.)

2. **Click the Search Expert button.**

   This leads you to a page with the word Name with a field next to it, followed by a button marked Search Now.

3. **Type a name that interests you in the field and click the Search Now button.**

   We're interested in finding census records that contain one of Matthew's ancestors, Uriah Helm. So, we type **Helm, Uriah** in the field. This generates a search results page.

4. **Review the results page for the estimated date and location of the selected individual.**

   In our case, we see only one entry for Uriah Helm. The entry indicates that a Uriah Helm is present in 1860 in Illinois and is located on Census CD 318 (see Figure 6-2).

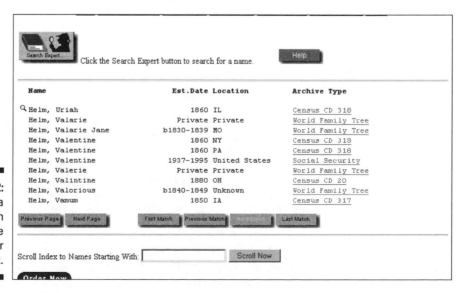

Figure 6-2: Results of a search on the FamilyFinder Index.

Click the Search Expert button to search for a name.   Help

Name	Est.Date	Location	Archive Type
Helm, Uriah	1860	IL	Census CD 318
Helm, Valarie	Private	Private	World Family Tree
Helm, Valarie Jane	b1830-1839	MO	World Family Tree
Helm, Valentine	1860	NY	Census CD 318
Helm, Valentine	1860	PA	Census CD 318
Helm, Valentine	1937-1995	United States	Social Security
Helm, Valerie	Private	Private	World Family Tree
Helm, Valintine	1880	OH	Census CD 20
Helm, Valorious	b1840-1849	Unknown	World Family Tree
Helm, Varnum	1850	IA	Census CD 317

Previous Page   Next Page   First Match   Previous Match   Next Match   Last Match

Scroll Index to Names Starting With: [   ]   Scroll Now

Order Now

After you know whether the FamilyFinder Index identifies entries that pertain to your ancestor, you can decide what route to take to get the documentation. You have a couple of options: You can purchase the FamilyFinder CD-ROMs from Brøderbund so that you have your own copy of the CD-ROM census record where Uriah Helm's name showed up or you can go through the regular means to obtain a copy of the actual census record (from microfilm) at an archives or Family History Center.

Using a transcribed online census

As an online genealogist, what you really want is access to all the census records on Aunt Bettie with the click of a mouse. Unfortunately, the genealogy world is not quite there yet. Some efforts are currently underway to transcribe census records for use online. Some of these transcriptions have only a portion of the entire census, while others have the complete census return for a certain area.

As with any transcribed record, you should always verify your findings with the original record. Often, census records are difficult to read due to their age, the quality of the handwriting, and so on — so, mistakes do occur in the transcription process. But, these records are better than having nothing at all!

Finding transcribed records on the Internet is very similar to finding census indices. We recommend that you first try one of the comprehensive genealogical sites under a geographical category. (For example, if you're looking for someone in the 1801 Norwegian census, you can look under the Norway category on the comprehensive site.) For a list of comprehensive sites, see the *Genealogy Online Internet Directory* in this book. To see a step-by-step walk-through of a search using a comprehensive site, see the "Finding your ancestors in census records" section earlier in this chapter.

Census records in the United States have always been a mainstay of genealogists. So most of the transcribed censuses that you will see on the Internet come from the United States (although that doesn't mean that censuses from other countries are not online — as you will see later in this section). Until recently, these censuses have not been transcribed in any systematic fashion. (However, a new project undertaken by the USGenWeb group is trying to change this. See `www.usgenweb.org/census/census.htm` for details.) Individuals simply transcribed those censuses that they were interested in or that were associated with a geographical area they were researching. This fact does not diminish the importance of these efforts; it only explains why you may see a census record for one county, but not for the county right next to it. A site that attempts to list all of the census transcription efforts is the Census Online site at `www.census-online.com/links/index.html`. Here's an example of a search on the site:

1. **Using your World Wide Web browser, head to the Census Online site at** www.census-online.com/links/index.html

   You see a page with a list of states for which census transcriptions are available.

   (If you're wanting more information on using a browser, flip over to Appendix A.)

2. **Select a state for your search.**

   For our example, we're interested in finding census information on an Isaac Metcalf who lived in Baylor County, Texas around 1880, so we selected Texas.

3. **At the top of the screen is a list of counties for the state. Click on a county.**

   We selected Baylor County.

4. **From the list of links for the county, select one that interests you.**

   We chose the 1880 Federal Census link, which takes us to a page of transcribed census entries where we can scroll down to an individual named Isaac Metcalf.

   In the event that you chose to look at another state or link to another census-related site within Texas, you may have to perform additional steps to find the information you are looking for.

The most plentiful type of transcribed census records you're likely to encounter is what we refer to as the *plain text census*, which is a Web page or a text file that is simply a transcription of the actual census record. That is, it does not contain any kind of search function. You have to skim the page to find the person you're looking for. The 1870 Census for Penn Township, Stark County, Illinois (members.aol.com/ZCyberCat/private/ castleton.html) is an example of this type of census return (see Figure 6-3). For each individual, the record includes the house number of the household, last name, first name, age, sex, race, occupation, real estate value, personal property value, and birthplace. This site is also typical of smaller census sites in that it focuses on the records on one county (actually, one township in one county).

Some sites have collections of several census returns for a specific geographic area (over an extended period of time). A good example of this is the Censuses of Gloucester and South Warwickshire 1851-91 site in England (www.silk.net/personal/gordonb/cotswold.htm). Here you can find several transcribed census returns for most of the subdivisions, with some having transcribed returns for all five censuses during the time period. Each record has at least the last name, first name, age, and occupation for the individuals identified in the census.

NUMBER	LAST NAME	FIRST NAME	AGE	SEX	RACE	OCCUPATION	REAL ESTATE	PERSONAL PROPERTY	BIRTHPLACE
75	COGLAN	DANIEL	56	M	W	LABORER			OH
	COGLAN	AMY	54	F	W	KEEPING HOUSE			OH
76	SNARE	JOHN P	75	M	W	FARMER	18375	3275	MD
	SNARE	NANCY	57	F	W	KEEPING HOUSE			PA
	SNARE	R.S. SCOTT	23	M	W	FARMER		800	PA
	SNARE	EDWIN	21	M	W	FARMER		300	IL
	SNARE	ALBERT	19	M	W	FARMER		100	IL
77	MCCLOUGHLIN	JAMES	68	M	W	FARMER	4000	230	IRELAND
	MCCLOUGHLIN	ELIZABETH	66	F	W	KEEPING HOUSE			IRELAND
	REAGAN	WILLIAM	21	M	W	FARMER		300	MI
78	LATON	WILLIAM	21	M	W	FARMER		500	OH
	LATON	MATILDA M	24	F	W	KEEPING HOUSE			IL
	LATON	IDA F	13	F	W				IL
	LATON	CARRIE E.	11	F	W				IL
	LATON	REUBEN A	9	M	W				IL

Figure 6-3: A section of the 1870 United States Census for Penn Township, Stark County, Illinois.

If you're interested in seeing an example of the use of a simple search engine to display census records, visit the 1891 Antigonish Census of Nova Scotia (www.ced.tuns.ca/~parkerb/antigonish_search.html). To use this searchable database, type in the surname you're researching and click on the Search for Surname button. If the surname you're looking for isn't in the database, you won't receive any results. If it is in the database, you'll see a page with the number of family members, including last names, first names, sex, ages, relationship to head of household, and occupation of each individual.

Another site that has a simple search engine to display census records is the Census of Norway. The Census of Norway used a nationwide approach for the 1801 census (www.uib.no/hi/1801page.html). At this site you can search for individuals who lived in each parish in Norway as of February 1, 1801. The site has a search engine that can be used with a farm name, first name, or surname. You can also read a handy article on the naming practices of Norway to assist you.

If you're looking for a little more elaborate search engine, point your browser to the Danish Demographic Database at ddd.sa.dk/ddd2.htm. This Danish Demographic Database is a joint project of the Danish Data Archives, Danish Emigration Archives, and Centre of Microfilming at the Danish State Archives. It contains partial census records from 1787 to 1911 — not all of the paper records have been computerized. You can search for particular individuals online (using searches by parish, district, county, birthplace, place name, family/household number, name, age, occupation, position in household, and year of census). But remember the one catch to using this search engine: You must register with the service before you can download information. The service is free of charge.

The future for census information

Many genealogists are no longer satisfied with using transcribed information. After all, even if you find useful information, you have to take a second step to confirm the information through a copy of the primary record. In response to this demand, a few companies are now developing electronic versions of census records that you can use on your personal computer. While these resources have not yet made it online, they're becoming available on CD-ROM.

One of these companies is Country Publishers, which produces the Census View CD-ROMs. The company has samples of its work available online at www.galstar.com/~censusvu/ (see Figure 6-4). At the time of the printing of this book, Country Publishers has digitized some of the census returns for Alabama, Arkansas, Georgia, Illinois, Indiana, Kentucky, Missouri, North Carolina, Oklahoma, South Carolina, Tennessee, and Texas.

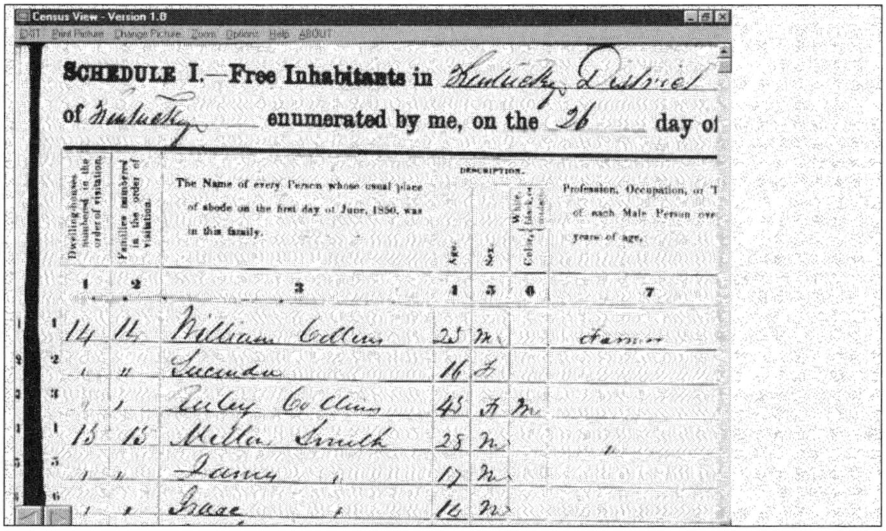

Figure 6-4:
Census
View
CD-ROM
site by
Country
Publishers.

Also, Brøderbund Software has released its first CD-ROM with scanned images of census microfilm records. The six CD-ROM set covers the 1850 Federal Census for the State of Virginia. The set includes not only the scanned images, but a searchable index as well that guides you to the appropriate records.

These Records Are Vital

Sometimes it seems that with every major event in our lives comes a government record. One is generated when we're born, get married (as well as get divorced), have a child, and pass on. Vital records (also called *civil registrations*) are the collective name for these types of records. Traditionally, these records were kept at the local level. States and countries have only recently made an effort to collect and centralize their holdings of vital records. In a similar manner, the record holders have just recently begun to expand the number of vital-record indices available online. You are likely to encounter three types of vital record sites: general information sites, vital record indices, and transcribed vital records.

Vital record information sites

If you are looking for information on how to order vital records within the United States, you have a few sites to choose from. The most comprehensive site is probably MedAccess Corporation with information from the National Center for Health Statistics entitled "Where to Write for Vital Records" (www.medaccess.com/states/). A page for each state lists the type of record, its cost, address to send requests, and additional remarks, such as the time period during which records were kept and who to make the check payable to (see Figure 6-5). You also can find information on obtaining vital records for foreign or high-sea births and deaths of United States citizens.

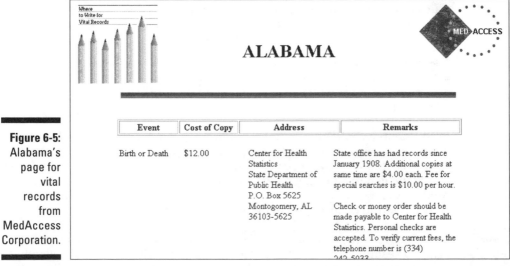

Figure 6-5: Alabama's page for vital records from MedAccess Corporation.

ALABAMA

Event	Cost of Copy	Address	Remarks
Birth or Death	$12.00	Center for Health Statistics State Department of Public Health P.O. Box 5625 Montgomery, AL 36103-5625	State office has had records since January 1908. Additional copies at same time are $4.00 each. Fee for special searches is $10.00 per hour. Check or money order should be made payable to Center for Health Statistics. Personal checks are accepted. To verify current fees, the telephone number is (334) 242-5033.

Although the MedAccess site does not contain any online indices or records, it's a good way to become familiar with where each state houses its vital records. Later on, as you locate records on more ancestors, you will probably want to use this site as a quick reference for getting mailing addresses for your many records requests.

For those of you looking for civil registrations (vital records) outside of the United States, here are some helpful sites:

- ✔ **Australia:** For Australian records, you can find an article on purchasing certificates from the General Registrar's offices at `www.cohsoft.com.au/afhc/certs.html`

- ✔ **Canada:** For a list of addresses to request copies of civil registrations in Canada, see the National Archives of Canada page on Records of Births, Marriages, and Deaths at `www.archives.ca/www/BMDRecords.html`

- ✔ **Denmark:** For background on and the contents of vital records in Denmark and Greenland, see the Civil Registration System in Denmark site at `http://www.cpr.dk/cprsysuk.htm`

- ✔ **England:** A Guide to Civil Registration in Great Britain can be found at `www.personal.u-net.com/~gmcro/st_caths.htm`. The Guide contains details on the history of civil registrations and has a focus on record repositories in Manchester.

- ✔ **Ireland:** Information on Irish civil registrations and their microfilm indices can be found in an article entitled "Irish Civil Registration" on the Irish genealogy home page at `www.bess.tcd.ie/roots/civilreg.htm`

- ✔ **Poland:** You can find a sample letter for requesting civil registration records from the Polish Civil Registration Office at `www.man.poznan.pl/~bielecki/cro.htm`

- ✔ **Scotland:** If you are interested in Scottish records, look at the Organization of Civil Registration in Scotland page at `www.open.gov.uk/gros/regscot.htm`, which is maintained by the General Register Office for Scotland.

If the country you're researching isn't in the preceding list, try looking at one of the comprehensive genealogy sites (a list of these is provided in the *Genealogy Online Internet Directory* within this book) or conduct a search on one of the general Internet search engines like Lycos (`www.lycos.com`) or AltaVista (`www.altavista.digital.com`) to see if a similar site with vital records for the country you're interested in exists.

Don't overlook these information sites just because they don't contain primary resources. You still need to use more traditional ways of collecting records because very few transcribed or digitized records exist online. Also,

even if you find a transcribed record online, you may want to order a copy of the original record to place in your filing system — in which case, you will need addresses from these sites.

Vital record indices

Vital record indices serve much the same purpose as census indices: They point to the locations of original records. You can use indices to confirm that an ancestor's vital records are available prior to submitting a request for the record. And knowing the exact location of the record can often make retrieval of the record a lot easier.

The easiest way to find vital record (and civil registration) indices on the Internet is to search along geographical lines. Suppose that you're looking for registrations in British Columbia — you want to look under the appropriate category. As an example, here's a step-by-step search for civil registrations using the Genealogy SiteFinder:

1. **Point your World Wide Web browser to the Genealogy SiteFinder site at** www.familytreemaker.com/links

   The home page for the Genealogy SiteFinder contains a subject directory of links on the site.

   (See Appendix A for how-to information on using a browser.)

2. **Click the <u>Places</u> category in the subject directory.**

   You see a list of links to continents and countries.

3. **Scroll down to the country that interests you and select the appropriate link.**

   In our case we're looking for civil registrations in British Columbia, so we scroll down to the Canada entry and select the link to British Columbia.

4. **Click a link to go to a site featuring civil registrations (vital records).**

   We select <u>Vital Events Indexes</u> off the British Columbia page, which takes us to a site maintained by the British Columbia Archives containing indices to marriage and death registrations. Depending upon the site you select, you may need to go through additional steps to find the information you're looking for.

The site mentioned in the preceding steps has a query page for the marriage index that allows you to search for the groom's surname, groom's given name, bride's surname, bride's given name, year or year range for the marriage, month, day, event place, registration number, British Columbia Archives microfilm number, or GSU microfilm number (see Figure 6-6). The

results of the search provide you with the bride's name and groom's name, event date, event place, registration number, British Columbia Archives microfilm number, and GSU microfilm number. This information can then be used to order a copy of the appropriate original document.

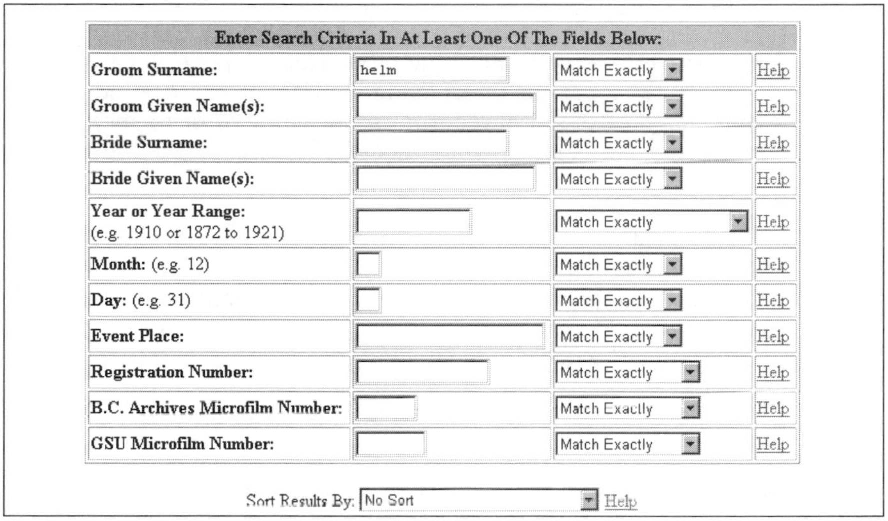

Enter Search Criteria In At Least One Of The Fields Below:			
Groom Surname:	helm	Match Exactly	Help
Groom Given Name(s):		Match Exactly	Help
Bride Surname:		Match Exactly	Help
Bride Given Name(s):		Match Exactly	Help
Year or Year Range: (e.g. 1910 or 1872 to 1921)		Match Exactly	Help
Month: (e.g. 12)		Match Exactly	Help
Day: (e.g. 31)		Match Exactly	Help
Event Place:		Match Exactly	Help
Registration Number:		Match Exactly	Help
B.C. Archives Microfilm Number:		Match Exactly	Help
GSU Microfilm Number:		Match Exactly	Help

Sort Results By: No Sort   Help

Figure 6-6:
Search form for the British Columbia Archives Marriage Index.

Another approach to finding vital statistics (civil registrations) is to go to the USGenWeb (www.usgenweb.org) or WorldGenWeb (www.worldgenweb.org/) page for the appropriate state or country. For example, we want to find a death certificate on Matthew's great-grandfather, William Henry Abell (of Larue County, Kentucky). To do this, we go through the following steps:

1. **Using your browser, go to the USGenWeb site located at** www.usgenweb.org

   You see a page with a large table with two columns on it. The left column is labeled Links for The USGenWeb Project.

   (See Appendix A for more details on using browsers.)

2. **Select the <u>Text-Only</u> link under the heading Links to States.**

   This link takes you to a page with a list of states and the URLs associated with each state page.

3. **Click on a state that interests you.**

   In our case, we select Kentucky because we're looking for someone who died in the state of Kentucky.

Also, as a shortcut, you can always get to any USGenWeb state page by typing www.usgenweb.org/ and the two letter postal code for the state. For example, for Kentucky, we can type www.usgenweb.org/ky

4. At the USGenWeb state page for the state that you chose, look for a link to vital records information or research links.

We chose the link Kentucky Research Helps and Links off the Kentucky USGenWeb page because the description said that it included links to Vital Stats.

5. Follow links on the pages to find vital records information.

In our case, we scroll down to the section marked Kentucky Vital Statistics Records and click on the link labeled Kentucky Vital Records, which takes us to the Kentucky Vital Records Index page maintained by the University of Kentucky.

6. Scroll down to the appropriate section and type in the name you want to search. Then click Submit Query.

Sticking with our example, we go to the section Kentucky Death Index for 1911-1986 and type in **Abell, William H**.

7. Scan the results of your query.

In our case, the results page contains two individuals named William H. Abell. One died in Larue County, the other in Jefferson County. The location seems right for the William from Larue County. We check the death date, September 7, 1955, and the age, 82, both of which are consistent with what we've heard from interviews with family members. The database also supplies us with the record volume number and certificate number, which we can use to find an actual copy of the certificate.

Transcribed vital records

If you aren't lucky enough to have a copy of your great-grandfather's marriage certificate, you need a way to discover the information contained within the document. The best method to find this information is to order a copy of the certificate from the appropriate government source. (For more information on this strategy, see "Vital record information sites" earlier in this chapter.) But before you spend the money to get a copy, see if the record is really of interest to you — which is where transcribed vital records come in handy.

Transcribed records can come in several forms. A researcher may have transcribed a series of records of a particular county or a state may have established a database of records. Either way, these sites can be helpful in determining if the record you're looking for will be useful.

A good place to begin searching for transcribed vital records is a comprehensive genealogy site. For example, the following is a step-by-step search for a transcribed record for a Jacob Gardner, who was married in Indiana around 1850.

1. **Using your World Wide Web browser, go to** `users.aol.com/ johnf14246/internet.html`

   You go to the Genealogy Resources on the Internet site. In the first paragraph, note the list of resources including Mailing Lists, USENET Newsgroups, anonymous File Transfer Protocol (FTP), Gopher, World Wide Web, Telnet, and E-Mail.

2. **Select the link marked World Wide Web.**

   This link takes you to an alphabetic listing of categories of genealogical World Wide Web sites.

3. **Click on a geographic location where you believe a transcribed vital record may be located.**

   We're looking for a record in the state of Indiana, so we choose the Indiana Resources link.

4. **Choose a link from the list that contains transcribed vital records.**

   In our case, the Marriage Index – through 1850 link looks promising. We click on the link and go to the page maintained by the Indiana State Library.

5. **If you selected a link other than the one we chose, follow the directions on the site to access the transcribed records. For our search, click on the part of the alphabet corresponding to the first letter of either the bride or groom's surname.**

   We're looking for Jacob Gardner, so we choose the link marked E – F – G, which loads a page with six boxes. These boxes ask you to type in the name of the bride or groom, their spouse, county, and date.

6. **Type in the surname of either the bride or groom and then click the Search button.**

   We typed in the surname **Gardner** and first name **Jacob** for the groom. We left the rest blank because we didn't know the spouse's name or the actual date of the marriage.

7. **Examine the results to see if the record is useful to you.**

   The results page gives us one marriage record of Jacob Gardner and Harriet Simmons married in Jefferson County, Indiana, on November 2, 1848. Using some groundwork that we already have on the family, we then check to make sure that this information is consistent with what we already know about Jacob.

The future of online vital records

You can see the future of online vital record searches in the General Register Office for Scotland Internet Service (www.open. gov.uk/gros/regscot.htm). By the time this book is published, the Service will provide World Wide Web access to a fully searchable index of:

✔ Births/baptisms and banns/marriages from Old Parish Registers dating from 1553 to 1854

✔ Births, marriages, and deaths from the Statutory Index from 1855 to 1897 (along with selected census records)

The index will include nearly 30 million names, and users will be able to order extracts of the records online using a credit card.

Other places that you may be able to find transcribed vital records include:

✔ USGenWeb (www.usgenweb.org) and WorldGenWeb (www.worldgenweb.org) local pages

✔ Sites for state, local, and national archives (which can be located through comprehensive genealogy sites such as those listed in our *Genealogy Online Internet Directory* section)

✔ General Internet search engines (also found in our *Genealogy Online Internet Directory* section)

Investigating Immigration and Naturalization Records

You may have heard the old stories about your great-great grandparents who left their homeland in search of a new life. Some of these stories may include details about where they were born and how they arrived at their new home. Although these are great stories, as a genealogist you want to be able to verify information in the stories with documentation.

Often the document you're looking for is an immigration or naturalization record. *Immigration records* are documents that show when a person moved into a particular country to reside; *naturalization records* are documents showing that a person became a citizen of a particular country without having been born in that country. Sometimes these documents can be

difficult to find, especially if you don't know where to begin looking. Unless you have some evidence in your attic or have a reliable family account of the immigration, you may need a record or something else to point you in the right direction. One useful set of records are census records (for more on census records see "Counting on the Census" earlier in this chapter). Depending on the year your ancestors immigrated, census records may contain the location of birth and tell you the year of immigration and the year of naturalization of your immigrant ancestor.

Emigration records — documents that reflect when a person moved out of a particular country to take up residence elsewhere — are also useful to researchers. These records are found in the country your ancestor left and can often help when you're unable to find immigration or naturalization records in the new country.

Locating immigration, emigration, and naturalization records online can be difficult. The common types of records that genealogists use to locate immigrants — passenger lists, immigration papers, emigration records — are just now becoming available on the Internet. A good starting point for determining an ancestor's homeland is to look at census records (for more on census records see "Counting on the Census" earlier in this chapter). Some census records indicate where the individual was born, when he/she immigrated, and the date of naturalization. Because a great deal of early immigration and naturalization processing was done at the local level, census records may give you an indication of the location to look for immigration records.

Here are some examples of online records:

- **Emigration Records:** Norwegian Migration Database (www.sffarkiv.no/database/dbutbase.htm)
- **Immigration/Naturalization Records:** McLean County, Illinois Immigration Records (www.mclean.gov/cc/imgrecs/imgrecs.html)
- **Passenger Lists:** Mayflower Passenger List (members.aol.com/calebj/alphabet.html)

Comprehensive genealogical sites are a good place to begin looking for online records sources (see the *Genealogy Online Internet Directory* for a list of comprehensive genealogy sites). When looking at comprehensive genealogy sites, you're likely to find these types of records categorized under immigration, naturalization, passenger lists, or by geographical area.

As an example, suppose that you have a family legend that Martin Saunders immigrated to America on a ship called Planter sometime in the first part of the 17th century. The following steps show how to search for a passenger list to confirm the legend.

1. **Start your World Wide Web browser and go to** www.CyndisList.com

   The home page of Cyndi's List has a category index toward the bottom of the page.

   (See Appendix A for more information on using browsers.)

2. **Select the category of Ships, Passenger Lists & Immigration.**

   The page that comes up next shows a category index at the top that includes items like Famous & Historical Ships, General Reference Sources, and Immigration and Naturalization.

3. **Click on the link <u>Ship, Passenger & Crew Lists</u>.**

   The screen displays a list of links to passenger lists.

4. **Scroll down to the section called Specific Ships, Localities or Topics.**

   We're looking for a ship called Planter that arrived in America in the first half of the 17th century.

5. **Select the <u>Passenger List: Planter 1635</u> link.**

   The link brings up a page with a list of passengers for the ship. Scrolling down the page, we find a Martin Saunders, age 40, from Suffolk on board the ship.

Another source of links to immigration and naturalization sites can be found on the Emigration/Ship Lists and Resources page of a personal genealogy site called Addie's Genealogy Home Page (www.geocities.com/Heartland/5978/Emigration.html). At the time of this writing, the page contains links to 123 sites on the World Wide Web with immigration and passenger list content.

If you're looking for some background information on immigration and naturalization within the United States, take a look at the National Archives and Records Administration page on Naturalization Records at www.nara.gov/genealogy/natural.html and Everton Publishers' Handy Tips on Immigration and Passenger Lists at rro.everton.com/help/Immigration_contents.html-ssi. For Canadian immigration records, see the National Archives of Canada pages on immigration records (www.archives.ca/www/ImmigrationRecords.html) and on citizenship (www.archives.ca/www/GenealogicalSources.html#Citizenship Records).

Land Lovers

Land records are some of the most plentiful sources of information on your ancestors. Although a census occurred only once every ten years, land transactions may have taken place two or three times a year, depending upon how much land your ancestor possessed. These records don't always

contain a great deal of demographic information, but they do place your ancestor in a time and location, and sometimes in a historical context as well. For example, you may discover that your ancestors were granted military bounty lands. This discovery may tell you where and when your ancestors acquired the land, as well as what war they fought in. You may also find out how litigious your ancestors were by the number of lawsuits they filed or had filed against them as a result of land claims.

Getting a foundation in the history of land records prior to conducting a lot of research is probably a good idea. Here are some sites with general information on land records:

- ✔ **Canada:** Land Records in Ontario (`wwnet.com/~treesrch/ontland.html`)

- ✔ **Ireland:** Irish Genealogy Home Page (`www.bess.tcd.ie/irlgen/landrec.htm`)

- ✔ **United States:** Land Records Reference (`www.ultranet.com/~deeds/landref.htm`)

Of course, these are just a few examples of some sites with background information about land transactions in those particular countries. To see if a similar site exists for a country you're interested in, or if you're looking for any kind of land record, we recommend you take an online trip over to a comprehensive genealogical site and look under that location, as well as look under a directory heading or category for land records (if there is one). Here is an example search:

1. **Using your Web browser, go to the Genealogy Toolbox at** `genealogy.tbox.com` **(For more information on using a browser, see Appendix A.)**

2. **Select Genealogy SiteFinder.**

   This takes you the Genealogy SiteFinder main page where you can choose whether to run a search on a location name or to look through the directory.

3. **Click on the <u>Places</u> category in the directory.**

   You see a list of links to continents and countries.

4. **Scroll down to the country and/or state that interests you and select the appropriate link.**

   For the sake of an example, say you're looking for land records that pertain to the state of Illinois. Scroll to the United States section and click the Illinois link.

SiteFinder brings up a list of links to known online resources for the state of Illinois. Among these are two that look promising. The Illinois Land Records page at `www.museum.state.il.us/exhibits/il-gis/puranim.html` and the Illinois Public Domain Land Tract Sales Database at `www.sos.state.il.us/depts/archives/data_lan.html`.

5. **Click on a link to go to one of the sites that looks like it has information to meet your needs.**

   Click the link for the <u>Illinois Public Domain Land Tract Sales Database</u>. The database contains records of more than 500,000 first-time land sales of public domain land between 1815 and 1880. Each entry includes the purchaser's name, date, number of acres, price per acre, county code, township, section, range, volume and page number of entry, and sale type. The database is searchable by name, date, type, acres, price, county (using county codes), and a free-form compound search.

In addition to using a comprehensive genealogical site to identify land records, you may want to check out geographical-related resources such as the USGenWeb project (`www.usgenweb.org`) or the WorldGenWeb project (`www.worldgenweb.org`). They break down resources by location (country, state, and/or county depending on which you use — USGenWeb or WorldGenWeb). For more information about USGenWeb, see Chapter 4 or the *Genealogy Online Internet Directory* included with this book. (For more information about WorldGenWeb, see the Directory as well.) Of course, if your attempts to find land records and information through comprehensive sites and geographical-related sites don't prove as fruitful as you'd like, you can always turn to a search engine like AltaVista (`www.altavista.digital.com`). (See Appendix A for more on using search engines.)

Military Tales

You've probably heard the family stories about how your great-great grandfather fought in a particular war. Or you may have a weapon that he used or uniform that he wore. Either way, you probably want to find more information about the part that he played in history.

Military records come in various forms, such as unit rosters, muster records, service records, and pension applications. You can piece together quite a story for a family history book when you use military records along with other resources, such as regimental histories. For example, one of Matthew's ancestors, George Helm, served in the American Revolution. His pension record shows that he served in Captain Shepherd's company of Colonel Rawlings' Rifle regiment in the Maryland line from 1776 to 1779, and

that he was taken as a prisoner of war for seven weeks at Fort Washington. To find out just what George was doing, we can check a regimental history, or pick up a history book that discusses the campaigns in the vicinity of Fort Washington. Although Matthew could have relied on George's account alone — he lucked out finding George's testimony of his activities over the three year period in a pension record — he confirmed these details in a history book, being the genealogist that he is. Matthew thought it a good idea to verify that George's memory had not failed him — after all, George was giving testimony almost 50 years after the war.

Online military records appear in several different forms, depending upon which country and when the individual served. Here are just a few online resources describing military records:

- **Australia:** Australian Archives Fact Sheet page on military service (www.aa.gov.au/AA_WWW/FactSheets/FS63.html)

- **Canada:** Military and Civilian Personnel Records page on the National Archives of Canada site (www.archives.ca/www/PersonnelRecords.html)

- **United Kingdom:** Public Records Office leaflets (midas.ac.uk/genuki/big/#MilitaryRecords)

- **United States:** National Archives and Records Administration's page on military service records (www.nara.gov/publicatoins/microfilm/military/) and the National Personnel Records Center (www.nara.gov/regional/mpr.html)

As we mention at the beginning of this section, military records can come in various forms. Here are examples of the online version of these types:

- **Casualty Lists:** Canadian Books of Remembrance (schoolnet2.carleton.ca/books/remember.htm)

- **Cemetery Records:** Confederate Graves at Brice's Crossroads (www.mindspring.com/~hawkmoon/totbccem.htm)

- **Military Census:** Cumberland, Providence County, Rhode Island 1777 Military Census (ftp://ftp.rootsweb.com/pub/usgenweb/ri/providen/military/militry1.txt)

- **Muster/Recruitment Records:** National Archives of Canada, Canadian Expeditionary Force Database (www.archives.ca/db/cef/index.html)

- **Pension Records:** 1835 Federal Pension List for Virginia (www.rootsweb.com/~usgenweb/va/vapensio.htm)

- **Regimental Histories:** Duke of Cornwall's Light Infantry (www.digiserve.com/msyoung/dcli.htm)

✔ **Service Records:** United States Colored Troops (USCT) Database (www.itd.nps.gov/cwss/usct.html)

✔ **Unit Rosters:** Ohio Historical Society Military Rosters Searchable Database (www.ohiohistory.org/resource/database/rosters.html)

If you're looking for military records for countries outside of the United States, your best bet is to consult one of the comprehensive genealogy sites or conduct a search using a general Internet search engine (sites for both of these types can be found in the *Genealogy Online Internet Directory*). The following is an example of a search using one of the general search engines, AltaVista:

1. **Go to the AltaVista search engine at** www.altavista.digital.com

2. **Select "Search [the Web] for documents in [any language]," type your query into the box, and click on the "search" button.**

   We're interested in finding a regimental history of the Royal Welsh Fusilier Regiment that was assigned to America during the American Revolution. We type in **welsh fusiliers**, a simple query that results in 27,346 documents.

3. **Click on a link that interests you. You can click on the Back button to return to the search engine results page.**

   We select the first link, <u>No Title</u>. (We don't know the title of the document; however, the search engine's site description gave us information which helped us determine if this was something we're interested in.) The link takes us to The Royal Welch Fusiliers in America home page — a page for the re-enactment company.

4. **Look for a link to regimental history.**

   In our case, the page has a link to a brief history regiment.

For those researching United States military units, you may want to consult the Military Records for Genealogy site (www.sky.net/~mreed/military/military.htm). This site, part of the USGenWeb project, has links to the various other sites all over the United States that contain some form of military records. The sites are categorized by major war.

For example, suppose that we want to find out what unit Matthew's great-great grandfather, Uriah Helm, served in during the American Civil War. We know that he lived in Fayette County, Illinois just before the war began, so we're looking for muster or service records for Illinois units. Here is an example of how to complete the search for Uriah:

1. **Open your browser and type in the URL to the Military Records for Genealogy site at** www.sky.net/~mreed/military/military.htm

   The page contains links to each major war involving the United States including the American Revolution, War of 1812, Mexican-American War, American Civil War, Indian Wars, Spanish-American War, World War I, World War II, Korean War, and Vietnam War.

2. **Click on the link for the war that interests you.**

   We're looking for American Civil War records, so we click on the link marked Civil War. This loads a page with links to each state with records related to the war.

3. **Select a state to research.**

   Uriah lived in Illinois just before the war, so we select Illinois.

4. **Choose a link for the resource you're looking for.**

   Fortunately, the first link on the list is a database of Illinois Civil War veterans maintained by the Illinois State Archives, which is the link we selected.

5. **Follow the instructions on the page to find your ancestor.**

   In our case, we select the link to search the database. A page loads providing you with space to type in the name of your ancestor. We type in **helm, uriah** and receive a results page indicating that Uriah Helm of Wheatland Township fought in Company G, 7th Cavalry. Consulting an atlas, we confirm that Wheatland Township is in Fayette County. We can use this information to order copies of service records for Uriah from the National Archives.

Most online military sites cover one specific war or historical period. In fact, a great deal of the available military sites are on the American Civil War. If you're unable to find information on the particular war or unit in a comprehensive genealogy site or general Internet search engine, you may want to try a search on the Yahoo! site (www.yahoo.com) under the appropriate country or historical heading.

Taxation with Notation

Some of the oldest records available for research are tax records. Tax records come in a variety of forms, including property, inheritance, and church taxation records. Most of the early tax records that you encounter were most likely collected at a local level (that is, at the county or parish level). However, many local tax records have since been turned over to state or county archives. Some of these archives now make tax records available

on microfilm, as do Family History Centers. (If you have a Family History Center in your area, you may be able to save yourself a trip, call, or letter to the state archives by checking with the Family History Center to see if they have copies of tax records on hand for the area in which you're interested.) And a few maintainers of tax records — including archives and Family History Centers — have started to make information about their holdings available online. Generally, what you find online are either indices or transcriptions of these microfilm records.

Here are just a few examples of the types of online resources you'll find pertaining to tax records:

- ✔ **General Information:** Tax Records as a Source for Local and Family History (`ftp://sable.ox.ac.uk/pub/users/malcolm/genealogy/pro/ri056.txt`)
- ✔ **Tax List:** Persons Who Paid Hearth Tax in the Parish of Raphoe in County Donegal, Ireland in the Year 1665 (`skysurf.co.nz/~hugh/raphoe.txt`)
- ✔ **Transcribed Tax Record Book:** Woodruff County, Arkansas 1867 Tax Records (`pages.prodigy.com/stevenbutts/1867.htm`)

To identify sites that contain tax records for countries other than the United States, we recommend you visit a comprehensive genealogical site or the appropriate WorldGenWeb site (`www.worldgenweb.com`). For more information about WorldGenWeb, see the *Genealogy Online Internet Directory*.

If you're locating records in the United States, try a USGenWeb site for the state or county. Here's what to do:

1. **Go to the USGenWeb site at** `www.usgenweb.org`

    You see a page with a large table with two columns on it. The left column is labeled Links for The USGenWeb Project.

2. **Select the <u>Text-Only</u> link under the heading Links to States.**

    This link takes you to a page with a list of states and the URLs associated with each state page.

3. **Click on a state that interests you.**

    In our case, we select Pennsylvania because we're looking for tax records in Lancaster County. Also, as a shortcut, you can always get to any USGenWeb state page by typing `www.usgenweb.org/` and the two letter postal code for the state. For example, for Pennsylvania, we could type `www.usgenweb.org/pa`

4. From the USGenWeb state page (for the state that you chose), find a link to vital records information or research links.

On the Pennsylvania counties page we select the link to Lancaster County. We then click on the link <u>Courthouse</u>, which leads us to another link called <u>Tax and Census Lists</u>. This link takes us to a third page with a listing of tax lists for the county.

Chapter 7

Records Off the Beaten Path

● ●

In This Chapter

▶ Seeking out information through religious group records

▶ Finding information through fraternal orders

▶ Using medical files in your research

▶ Picture this: Using photographs as a research aid

▶ Checking out genealogy and adoption records

● ●

A lot of people who are familiar with genealogy know to use census records, vital records, tax lists, and wills to find information on their ancestors. These records tend to take a snapshot of the life of an individual at a particular point in time. But as a genealogist, you want to know more than just when your ancestors paid their taxes — you want to know something about them as people.

For example, one time when April was looking through some pictures, she came across a photograph of her great-great grandfather. He was dressed in a uniform with a sash and sword and was holding a hat with a plume in it. As far as April knew, her great-great grandfather had not been in the military, so she decided to dig for some information about the uniform. Although part of the picture was blurry, she could make out three crosses on the uniform. One was on his sleeve, the second on the buckle of his belt, and the third was a different kind of cross that was attached to his sash. April suspected that the symbols were Masonic. She visited a few Masonic sites on the World Wide Web and found that the crosses indicated that her great-great grandfather had been a member of the Order of the Temple within the Masonic organization. Of course, she would never have known that he was a member of the organization had she depended solely upon the usual group of records used by genealogists.

This chapter looks at some examples of unique or hard-to-find records that can be quite useful in family history research. These records include those kept by religious groups and fraternal orders, medical files, photographs, and adoption records.

Religious Group Records

In the past, several countries required attendance at church services or the payment of taxes to an ecclesiastical authority. While our ancestors may not have appreciated these laws at the time, the records that were kept to ensure their compliance can benefit you as a genealogist. For those places where there were no such laws in effect, there are a variety of records that were kept by church authorities or congregations that you can use to develop a sketch of the everyday life of your ancestor.

Some of the common records you encounter include baptismal records, parish registers, marriage lists, meeting minutes, and congregation photographs. Each type of record may include several different bits of information. For instance, a baptismal record may include the date of baptism, date of birth, parents' names, and location where the parents lived.

Several sites provide general information and links to all sorts of resources that pertain to specific religions and sects. Here are a few examples:

- ✔ **Anabaptists:** Hall of Church History — The Anabaptists (www.gty.org/~phil/anabapt.htm) has an introduction to the beliefs of the Anabaptists and links to Anabaptist resources on the Internet.

- ✔ **Catholic:** Catholic Archives of Texas (www.onr.com/user/cat/) includes a description of the databases, original records, rare books and periodicals, and old photographs available at the archives.

- ✔ **Huguenot:** Huguenot Resources — Olive Tree Genealogy (www.rootsweb.com/~ote/hugres.htm) lists books and societies available to those researching French Protestants that fled to Switzerland, Germany, England, America, and South Africa.

- ✔ **Hutterite:** Hutterite Genealogy HomePage (feefhs.org/hut/frg-hut.html) gives an introduction and links to resources for the sect found in Austria, Bohemia, Moravia, Slovakia, Hungary, Romania, Canada, the United States, and the Ukraine.

- ✔ **Lutheran:** Lutheran Roots Genealogy Exchange (www.aal.org/lutheran_roots/) has a registry of researchers looking for information about Lutheran ancestors and a message board where you can post questions specifically about your research.

- ✔ **Jewish:** JewishGen (www.jewishgen.org) has information about the JewishGen organization and frequently asked questions about Jewish genealogy, as well as indices of other Internet resources including searchable databases, special interest groups, and JewishGen family home pages.

- ✔ **Mennonite:** Mennonite Research Corner (`www.ristenbatt.com/genealogy/mennonit.htm`) features general information about Mennonites and a collection of online resources for researchers.

- ✔ **Methodist:** Methodist Archives and Research Centre (`rylibweb.man.ac.uk/data1/dg/text/method.html`) contains information on its collections and a guide on using the archives for family history research (under "Guides and Catalogues").

- ✔ **Moravian Church:** The Moravian Church (`www.moravian.org/`) home page includes information on one of the oldest Protestant denominations. You can also find links to various Moravian resources on the Internet here.

- ✔ **Quaker:** The Quaker Corner (`www.rootsweb.com/~quakers`) contains a query board, a list of research resources, and links to other Quaker pages on the World Wide Web (see Figure 7-1).

- ✔ **United Church of Canada Archives:** The United Church Archives (`vicu.utoronto.ca/archives/archives.htm`) has information on the holdings of the archives and a page on genealogical research. The archives contain records for the Presbyterian Church in Canada, Methodist Church (Canada), Congregational Union of Canada, Local Union Churches, and the Evangelical United Brethren Church.

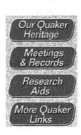
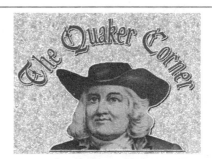

◆ **QUAKER-ROOTS DISCUSSION GROUP** SUBSCRIBE NOW!
◆ Visit the NEW QUAKER-ROOTS ARCHIVES
◆ Visit the QUAKER QUERIES MESSAGE BOARD
◆ Post a QUAKER QUERY
◆ **RESEARCH RESOURCES FOR QUAKER GENEALOGY**
Book Publishers, Family Research Groups & Newsletters, Mailing Lists, News Groups, On-Line Resources, Publications, Quaker Books, Records & Libraries

Figure 7-1:
The Quaker
Corner
home page.

A few church organizations have online descriptions of the holdings in their archives. You can see an example of this at the "What is a Family History Center?" page (www.lds.org/Family_History/What_is.html). This site, maintained by the Church of Jesus Christ of Latter-day Saints, explains what a family history center is, the resources you find there, and how to use those resources for your research. (If you're curious about the resources found in Family History Centers, see Chapter 1.) Likewise, the Center for Mennonite Brethren Studies in Fresno, California (www.fresno.edu/cmbs/geneal.htm) and the Catholic Archives of Texas (www.onr.com/user/cat/) each identifies the specific resources available at their locations, including databases, original records, rare books and periodicals, and old photographs.

Of course, at some point you'll want to find sites with indices or actual records online. Finding religious records on the Internet can be quite challenging. We recommend that you start by using one of the larger comprehensive genealogy sites listed in the *Genealogy Online Internet Directory* found in this book, some of the specialty religious sites as mentioned previously, or by looking at sites that are referenced on personal genealogy pages. To find religious sites, try this:

1. **Open your World Wide Web browser and go to the Genealogy Toolbox at** genealogy.tbox.com

   If you need a refresher on operating a World Wide Web browser, see Appendix A.

2. **Select the link marked <u>Genealogy SiteFinder</u>.**

3. **Under Genealogy SiteFinder you find several categories. Select the category <u>People</u> and then select <u>Ethnic/Religious Groups</u>.**

4. **Under Ethnic/Religious Groups, select the religious group that interests you.**

   For example, we were interested in finding out information on Quakers, so we selected the <u>Quakers</u> link.

5. **Select a link off of the Quakers page, which takes you to another site on the World Wide Web.**

   After you select a religious group, you see links to sites on the Web about that group. You may want to read the abstracts to determine whether the site may contain the information you're looking for.

If you're curious about what types of information for religious groups is available on the Internet, here are a few examples:

✔ **Baptism/Marriage Records:** The Cochin Churchbook (www.telebyte.nl/dessa/cochin.htm). This is an online index of marriages and baptisms from 1751 to 1804 in the Dutch Church of Cochin, India.

✔ **Cemetery Records:** Quaker Burying Ground, Morris, New York (www.rootsweb.com/~nyotsego/morbga.htm). This site provides information collected from Quaker gravestones in Morris, New York, including the person's name, date of birth and death, age, and whether there is information about anyone else contained on the same tombstone. (See Figure 7-2.)

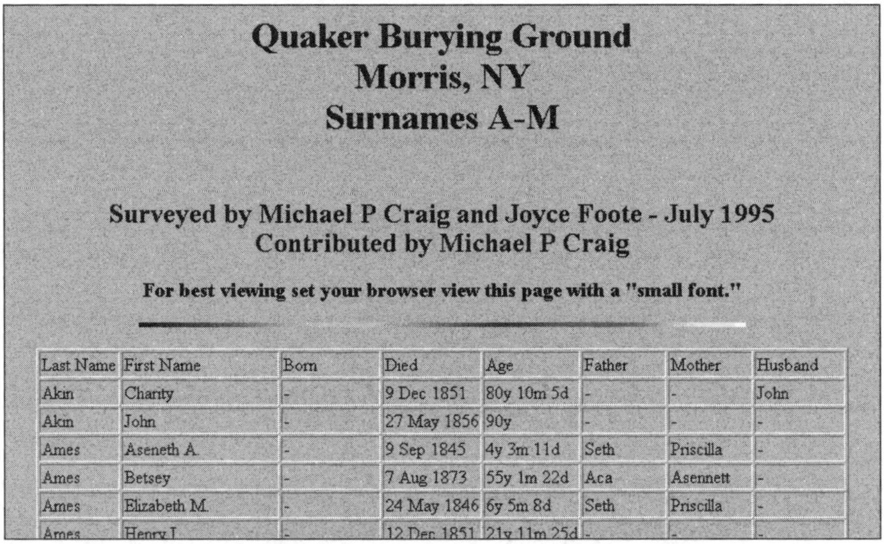

Figure 7-2:
The Quaker Burying Ground table provides information taken from gravestones in Morris, New York.

Quaker Burying Ground
Morris, NY
Surnames A-M

**Surveyed by Michael P Craig and Joyce Foote - July 1995
Contributed by Michael P Craig**

For best viewing set your browser view this page with a "small font."

Last Name	First Name	Born	Died	Age	Father	Mother	Husband
Akin	Charity	-	9 Dec 1851	80y 10m 5d	-	-	John
Akin	John	-	27 May 1856	90y	-	-	-
Ames	Aseneth A	-	9 Sep 1845	4y 3m 11d	Seth	Priscilla	-
Ames	Betsey	-	7 Aug 1873	55y 1m 22d	Aca	Asennett	-
Ames	Elizabeth M	-	24 May 1846	6y 5m 8d	Seth	Priscilla	-
Ames	Henry L	-	12 Dec 1851	21y 11m 25d	-	-	-

✔ **Family Registers:** Consolidated Index of the Church Family Registers (www.mbnet.mb.ca/~mhc/allindxf.htm). This is an index of family registers, which you can sort by husband's name or wife's maiden name, for the 1843 Bergthaler Mennonite Church (Russia) and the 1878, 1887, and 1907 Chortitzer Mennonite Church (Manitoba).

✔ **Parish Directory:** Holy Trinity Church, Boston, Massachusetts (www.eskimo.com/~mvreid/htc.html). The Holy Trinity Church site has an 1895 parish directory that is searchable, an ongoing project to identify and post information about church members who served in the Civil War, and a list of those church members who served in World War I.

Fraternal Orders

Were any of your ancestors members of fraternal orders or service clubs? A lot of them are out there, and chances are, you have at least one ancestor who was a member of an order or club. Although most of the more

commonly known organizations are for men, there are affiliated organizations for women, too. Here are a few general information sites on fraternal orders and service clubs:

- **DeMolay:** DeMolay International (`www.DeMolay.org/`)
- **Eagles:** Fraternal Order of Eagles (`members.aol.com/w9439/page2.html`)
- **Elks:** Benevolent Protective Order of the Elks (`www.elks.org/`)
- **Freemasonry:** e-m@son (`www.freemasonry.org/`) and A Page About Freemasonry (`web.mit.edu/dryfoo/www/Masons/index.html`)
- **Job's Daughters:** International Order of Job's Daughters (`www.iojd.org/`)
- **Kiwanis International:** Kiwanis International (`www.kiwanis.org/`)
- **Knights of Columbus:** Knights of Columbus (`www.kofc-supreme-council.org/`)
- **Lions Clubs:** LionNet (`www.lionnet.com/`)
- **Moose:** Moose International (`www.mooseintl.org/`)
- **Odd Fellows:** Independent Order of Odd Fellows (`128.125.109.137/IOOF.html`)
- **Optimist International:** Optimist International (`www.optimist.org/`)
- **Order of the Eastern Star:** Grand Chapter Order of the Eastern Star (`www.indianamasons.org/easternstar.htm`)
- **Rainbow for Girls:** International Order of the Rainbow for Girls (`www.iorg.org/`)
- **Rebekahs:** Rebekahs (`128.125.109.137/IOOF/Rebekahs.html`)
- **Rotary International:** Rotary International (`www.rotary.org/`)
- **Shriners:** The Shrine of North America home page (`shriners.com/`)

Most of the online sites related to fraternal orders provide historical information about the clubs and current membership rules. While the sites may not provide you with actual records (membership lists and meeting minutes), they do give you an overview of what the club is about and an idea of what your ancestor did as a member. The sites also provide you with the names and addresses of local chapters so you can contact them to see if they have original resources available for public use or if they will send you copies of anything pertaining to your ancestor.

An important thing to note is that having information about a fraternal order does not necessarily make a particular site the organization's official site. This is particularly true for international organizations. You may find Web

pages for different chapters of a particular club in several different countries, and while each site may have some general club information in common, they are likely to have varying types of information specific to that chapter of the organization.

If you're looking for sites containing information on fraternal organizations, you may want to try some of the comprehensive genealogy sites. If you can't find sufficient information there, try one of the general Internet search engines. A list of both types of sites can be found in the *Genealogy Online Internet Directory* of this book. To find information on fraternal orders through a general Internet search engine, try this:

1. **Open your World Wide Web browser and go to the AltaVista search engine page at** `www.altavista.digital.com` **(or you can substitute the address of your favorite search engine).**

   For more information on using a browser and search engines, check out Appendix A.

2. **Type the name of a fraternal organization in the search box and then click the Search button.**

   Make sure that the search option is marked The Web in the sentence above your search box — that is, the sentence should read Search The Web For Documents In Any Language. We were interested in finding information about the Knights of Columbus, so we put that phrase in the search box.

3. **Select a link that interests you from the search results page.**

   After clicking the Search button, you see a page with the results of your search. Each result has the title of the site and a brief abstract taken directly from the page. You can use these to determine whether the site contains information that you are interested in before visiting it.

Medical Files

A few years ago, we read in a local newspaper about a physician who was studying a certain rare disorder. This doctor had a hunch that all the individuals who had the disorder were descended from the same ancestor. After conducting some genealogical research, the physician was able to trace every person having the disorder back to one family in Maryland. While the genealogical research did not result in an immediate cure for the disorder, it did explain how the disorder spread throughout the United States.

Helping people learn more about hereditary diseases to which they may be predisposed is one of the ways medical files can enhance genealogy. Knowing that others before you have had a certain disease can help diagnosis in the present. The other way medical files are useful to genealogists is that they provide interesting information about your ancestors and give you an idea of what they endured.

Currently, online resources pertaining to medical information are limited to sites discussing death certificates and why using medical files in genealogy is important. Death certificates are useful because most provide primary and secondary causes of death. For more information about vital records and information of interest to genealogists, review Chapters 1 and 6.

Here are a couple of sites you can visit if you are interested in reading more about using medical records in your genealogy. The Family Links Medical Genealogy (www.familylinks.com/medgen/) site has several articles about using medical files in genealogy (see Figure 7-3). Also, you can find a few articles on researching medical history on the Family Tree Maker Online site (www.familytreemaker.com/issue6.html).

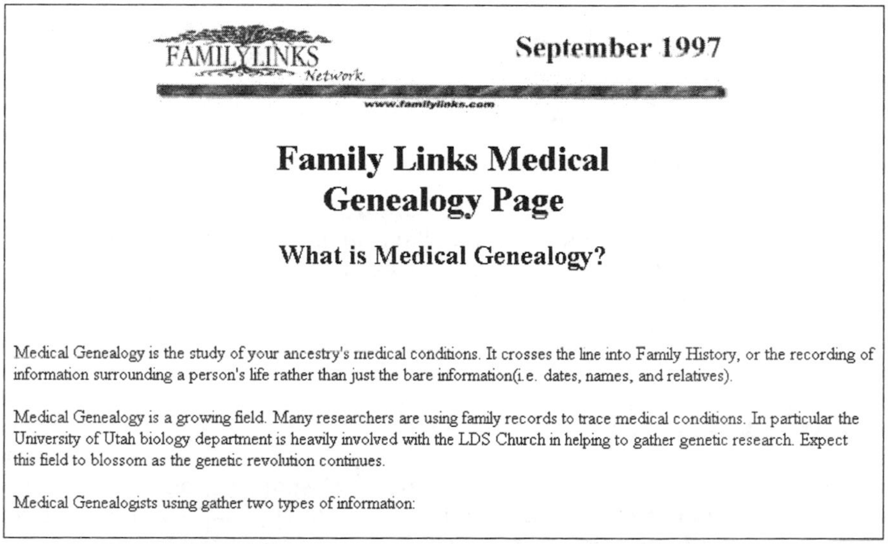

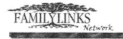

September 1997

FAMILYLINKS *Network.*

www.familylinks.com

Family Links Medical Genealogy Page

What is Medical Genealogy?

Medical Genealogy is the study of your ancestry's medical conditions. It crosses the line into Family History, or the recording of information surrounding a person's life rather than just the bare information(i.e. dates, names, and relatives).

Medical Genealogy is a growing field. Many researchers are using family records to trace medical conditions. In particular the University of Utah biology department is heavily involved with the LDS Church in helping to gather genetic research. Expect this field to blossom as the genetic revolution continues.

Medical Genealogists using gather two types of information:

Figure 7-3: Family Links Medical Genealogy page.

A Photo Is Worth a Thousand Words

In Chapter 1, we discuss the value of photographs in your genealogical research (if you don't want to look back to Chapter 1 — well, we'll just say that we think they are very valuable). But a lot of us don't have photographs

of our family beyond two or three generations, though it sure would be great to find at least an electronic copy of a picture of our great-great grandfather. Actually, that a picture of your great-great grandfather exists is quite possible. Another researcher may have it posted on a personal site or the photograph may be part of a collection belonging to a certain organization. You may also be interested in pictures of places where your ancestors lived. Being able to describe how a certain town, estate, or farm looked at the time your ancestor lived there adds color to your family history.

You can find various types of photographic sites on the Internet that can assist you with your research. These types include sites that explain the photographic process and the many types of photographs that have been used throughout history, sites that contain collections of photographs from a certain geographic area or time period in history, and pages that contain photographs of the ancestors of a particular family. Here are some examples:

- ✔ **General Information:** City Gallery (www.webcom.com/cityg) has a brief explanation of the types of photography used during the 19th century, a photography query page, and a gallery of photographs from one studio of the period (see Figure 7-4).

- ✔ **Photograph Collections:** Images of the American West (www.treasurenet.com/images/americanwest/), Images of the Civil War (www.treasurenet.com/images/civilwar/), and American Memory: Photographs, Prints and Drawings (lcweb2.loc.gov/ammem/phcoll.new.html) all contain several digitized photographs.

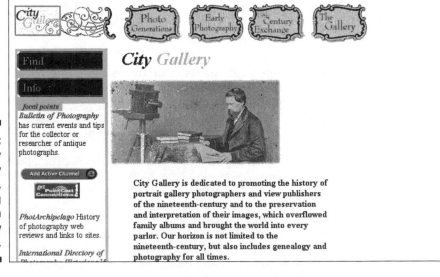

Figure 7-4:
The City Gallery Web site, specializing in 19th century photography.

✔ **Photograph Identification:** Fallen Leaves Lost Genealogy Photos (`www.surnames.com/Organizations/agcig/leaves.htm`) has a collection of photographs with a little more genealogical focus. Designed and maintained by the Arizona Genealogy Computer Interest Group, this site posts old photos that have been donated to the group with the hopes that someone will recognize the people in them and be able to claim them. Information about the photos is posted as well, including any names written on them, the photographer's name, approximate time frame in which the picture was taken, and anything pertaining to where the photos were taken or found (see Figure 7-5).

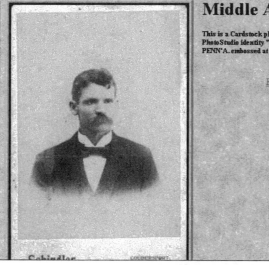
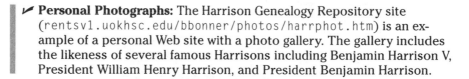

Middle Aged Man

This is a Cardstock photo with no information on the back. The front has the Photo Studio identity "Schindler" with the address "COUDERSPORT PENN'A. embossed at the bottom.

Return to AGCIG Photo Page

Figure 7-5: A photograph of an unidentified man from the Fallen Leaves Lost Genealogy Photos site.

✔ **Personal Photographs:** The Harrison Genealogy Repository site (`rentsv1.uokhsc.edu/bbonner/photos/harrphot.htm`) is an example of a personal Web site with a photo gallery. The gallery includes the likeness of several famous Harrisons including Benjamin Harrison V, President William Henry Harrison, and President Benjamin Harrison.

To find photographic sites, you may want to visit one of the comprehensive genealogy sites or general Internet search engines mentioned in the *Genealogy Online Internet Directory* here in this book. If you're interested in finding photographic collections, try this:

1. Fire up your World Wide Web browser and go to Cyndi's List of Genealogy Sites on the Internet located at `www.CyndisList.com` **(See Appendix A if you have any questions on using a browser.)**

The home page of Cyndi's List has a category index toward the bottom of the page.

2. **Scroll down to the category called Photographs & Memories.**

   Selecting Photographs & Memories takes you to another page with a list of links to sites on the World Wide Web.

3. **Select a link off of the Photographs & Memories page that interests you.**

Adoption Records

A lot of genealogists are interested in adoption records, including those who were adopted themselves, who gave up children for adoption, and those who have ancestors who were adopted.

If you fall into the first two groups (a genealogist who was adopted or gave up a child for adoption), there are some online resources that may help you. Most of the sites are intended to help individuals find members of their birth family. The online resources include registries, reference materials, advice and discussion groups, and information on legislation pertaining to adoption. Registries allow you to post information about yourself and your adoption with the hopes that a member of your birth family will see the posting and contact you. (Likewise, if you are the birth parent of an adoptee, you can post a message with the hopes that the adoptee sees it and responds.)

Unfortunately, what you won't find online are sites that contain actual adoption records — generally, for legal reasons. Rather, you need to rely on registries and other resources that point you toward more substantial information about adoption. If you have a successful reunion with your birth parent(s) through registering with an online site, then hopefully you can obtain information about their parents, grandparents, and so on so that you know where to begin your genealogical pursuit of that family line.

Here are some online sites that have adoption registries, reference materials, advice and discussions, and/or legislative information.

- ✔ **Adoptees Internet Mailing List** (www.webreflection.com/aiml/)
- ✔ **CANADopt** (nebula.on.ca/canadopt/)
- ✔ **AdoptioNetwork** (www.adoption.org/)
- ✔ **Reclaiming My Roots Registry Database** (www.geocities.com/Heartland/Hills/2638/database.html)

If you fall into the group of genealogists interested in adoption records (those who had ancestors who were adopted), you may have a more difficult time finding information. We have yet to discover any sites specifically designed to aid in research for adopted ancestors. In fact, you may have to rely on the regular genealogical resources — particularly query pages and discussion groups — and the kindness and knowledge of other researchers to find information about your adopted ancestors.

If you're searching for general types of adoption resources, using a general Internet directory like Yahoo! may be the best course of action. To find resources using Yahoo!, try this:

1. **Open your World Wide Web browser and go to Yahoo! at**
   `www.yahoo.com`

   If you need a refresher on operating a World Wide Web browser, see Appendix A.

2. **Select <u>Society And Culture</u>, and then <u>Families</u>.**

   A second way to find items in Yahoo! exists that may be a lot quicker. You can place a search term in the box near the top of the screen and have Yahoo! search for the topic. For example, you can type **Adoption** in the blank and then click the Search button, which produces a results page that has links to take you directly to the appropriate page in Yahoo! containing adoption links.

3. **Under the Families category, select the link marked <u>Adoption@</u>.**

   This takes you directly to the adoption page — even though it's a couple of levels down in the directory's hierarchy.

4. **Choose a link to another subdirectory in Yahoo! or a link to an Internet site containing information of interest to you.**

   Most of the links in Yahoo! have brief descriptions following them to give you an idea of what kind of information is on the site. An example of a Yahoo! page is found in Figure 7-6.

- <u>Adoptee Resources</u> *(24)* NEW!
- <u>Announcements</u> *(6)*
- <u>Birth Parents</u> *(4)*
- <u>Books</u>@
- <u>China</u> *(10)*
- <u>Foster Parenting</u>@
- <u>Lesbian, Gay and Bisexual Resources</u>@

- <u>Magazines</u> *(2)*
- <u>Organizations</u> *(30)*
- <u>Orphanages</u>@
- <u>Placement Agencies</u>@
- <u>Products and Services</u>@
- <u>Regional</u> *(14)* NEW!
- <u>Seeking to Adopt</u> *(40)*
- <u>Usenet</u> *(3)*

- <u>AdoptionSearch</u> 👓✓
- <u>International Adoption and Child Abduction</u> 👓✓ - detailed information from the US Department of State's Office of Childrens Issues.

- <u>Adoption Advocates</u> ▸REVIEW◂ - provides online and printed publications on federal and state adoption rules, legislation, and financial assistance/subsidy resources.
- <u>Adoption Agency Guide</u> - start here when looking for a good adoption agency. Make sure your agency is qualified and ethical.
- <u>Adoption Connection</u> - links to adoption information; some state statutes on line.
- <u>Adoption Counselor .com</u> - find an adoption counselor to help you in your adoption.
- <u>Adoption Information and Online Support</u> - info/support, including getting started, books, magazines, professional articles, personal stories by adoptive family, birth family, adoptee.
- <u>Adoption Jigsaw Tasmania, Inc.</u> - is an association for the natural parents, adoptees, adoptive parents, relatives, friends and other people interested in the effects of adoption and fostering.

Figure 7-6:
The Yahoo! adoption subdirectory.

Part III
Maximizing
Research Resources

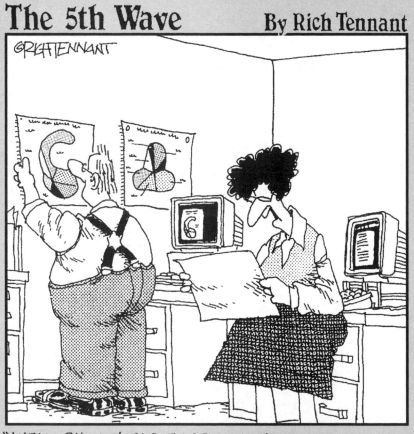

The 5th Wave — By Rich Tennant

"WELL, SHOOT! THIS EGGPLANT CHART IS JUST AS CONFUSING AS THE BUTTERNUT SQUASH CHART AND THE GOURD CHART. CAN'T YOU JUST MAKE A PIE CHART LIKE EVERYONE ELSE?"

In this part . . .

Find out how to maximize your online research by effectively using as many available resources as possible. The chapters in this part cover everything from using genealogical software to organizing your notes and data to sharing information with others to coordinating research efforts to designing your own genealogical Web page. Along the way, you also find out a little history about GEDCOM and the best way respect others' privacy and copyrights.

Chapter 8

Keeping Your Ancestors in Line: Organizing and Presenting Your Findings

In This Chapter

▶ Constructing a record-keeping system

▶ Getting started with genealogical software

▶ Producing genealogical reports

▶ Selecting accessories for your computer

*A*fter you collect all this great genealogical data, it doesn't do you much good if you can't find any of it when you need it. You don't want to run all over your house trying to pull together all the scraps of paper — notes from your research at the library in your desk, letters from relatives in your mail-to-be-sorted basket, photocopies of some Pedigree charts mixed in with your magazines. You may forget where you placed a particular document and miss something important because your documents aren't organized and all kept together in a centralized location.

This chapter examines ways of organizing and preserving genealogical data. We cover traditional storing methods and preservation techniques, computer systems and hardware, and genealogical software. We also examine some of the more common forms, charts, and reports.

Getting a Firm Foundation in Traditional Methods of Genealogical Organization

No finer tradition exists in genealogy than collecting tons of paper and photographs. Up until now, you've probably used whatever means possible to take notes while talking with relatives about your ancestors or looking up

information in the local library — from notebook paper, to receipts you have in your pocket or purse, to sticky notes. You may have used your camera to take pictures of the headstones in the cemetery where some of your ancestors are buried or the old family homestead that is now abandoned and barely standing. And you've probably collected some original source documents — like the certified copy of your mother's birth certificate grandma gave you, the family Bible from Aunt Lola, and the old photograph of your great-great-grandfather as a child that you found while digging through the attic. Now what are you supposed to do with all these things? Organize those documents!

Even if you decide to use genealogical software to track your research progress, you'll always have paper records and photographs you want to keep. The following sections contain some tips to help you become well organized (genealogically, anyway).

Establishing good organizational skills

You've probably already discovered that taking notes on little scraps of paper works adequately at first, but the more notes you take, the harder time you have sorting through them and making sense of the information on each. To avoid this situation, establish some good note-taking and organizational skills early on by being consistent in how you take notes. Write the date, time, and place that you research and the names of the family members you interview at the top of your notes. This information can help you later on when you return to your notes to look for a particular fact or when you are trying to make sense out of conflicting information.

You want your notes on particular events, persons, books, and so forth to be as detailed as possible — including who, what, where, when, why, and how. And most important, always cite the source of your information (with the following guidelines in mind)!

- ✔ **Person:** Include that person's full name, relationship to you (if any), the information, contact data (address, phone number, e-mail address), and the date and time you and this person spoke or communicated.

- ✔ **Record:** Pvclude the name or type of record, record number, book number (if applicable), the name and location of the record-keeping agency, and any other pertinent information.

- ✔ **Book or magazine**: Include all bibliographic information.

- ✔ **Microfilm or microfiche:** Include all bibliographic information and make a note at the end as to the form of the document.

> ✔ **Web site or other Internet resource:** Include the name of the copy-right-holder for the site (or name of the site's creator and maintainer if no copyright notice appears on it), name of the site, address or uniform resource locator (URL) of the site, the date the information was posted or copyrighted, and any notes with traditional contact information for the site's copyright-holder or creator.

If you need some help, be sure to check out this resource: Mills, Elizabeth Shown. *Evidence: Citation and Analysis for the Family Historian.* Baltimore, MD: Genealogical Publishing Company, 1997.

Understanding genealogical charts and forms

Many charts and forms are available that can help you organize your research efforts, as well as aid in your record keeping. Some examples include Pedigree charts that show the relationships between family members, descendant charts that list every person who descends from a particular ancestor, and census forms that look like the actual census records for particular years. Some of these charts and forms are available from companies such as Everton Publishers (www.everton.com). The sooner you become familiar with the most common types of charts and how to read them, the sooner you can interpret a lot of the information you receive from other genealogists. Chapter 1 examines some of these charts and forms in greater detail, and we discuss some forms you can generate using your computer in the section "Sharing Your Genealogical Success with Others" later in this chapter.

Assigning unique numbers to your family

If you have ancestors who share the same name, or when you get to the point where you have collected a lot of information on several generations of ancestors, you may have trouble distinguishing one person from another. To avoid confusion and the problems that can arise from it, you may want to use a commonly accepted numbering system to keep everyone straight.

One well-known numbering system is called *ahnentafel*, which means "ancestor" (Ahnen) and "table" (Tafel) in German. You may also hear ahnentafel referred to as the *Sosa-Stradonitz System* of numbering, as it was first used by a Spanish genealogist named Jerome de Sosa in 1676 and popularized in 1896 by Stephan Kekule von Stradonitz. Ahnentafel is a method of numbering that shows a mathematical relationship between parents and children. Ahnentafel numbering follows this progression:

1. The child is assigned a particular number: y

2. **The father of that child is assigned the number that is double the child's number: 2y**

3. **The mother of that child is assigned a number that is double the child's number plus one: 2y + 1**

4. **The father's father is assigned the number that is double the father's number: 2(2y)**

   And the father's mother is assigned the number that is double the father's number plus one: 2(2y) + 1

5. **The mother's father is assigned a number that is double the mother's number: 2(2y + 1)**

   And the mother's mother is assigned a number that is double the mother's number plus one: 2(2y + 1) + 1

6. **And so forth through the ancestors.**

The mathematical relationship works the same way going backwards through the generations — a child's number is one-half the father's number and one-half (minus any remainder) the mother's number.

In a list form, the ahnentafel for April's grandfather would look like this (and see Figure 8-1 for a chart):

1 John Duff Sanders, b. 10 Mar 1914 in Benjamin, Knox Co., TX; d. 15 Mar 1996 in Seymour, Baylor Co., TX; ma. 24 Dec 1939 in Sherman, Grayson Co., TX.

2 John Sanders, b. 19 Oct 1872 in Cotton Plant, Tippah Co., MS; d. 2 Mar 1962 in Morton, Cochran Co.; TX, ma. 28 Sep 1902 in Boxelder, Red River Co., TX.

3 Nannie Elizabeth Clifton, b. 1 Apr 1878 in Okolona, MS; d. 27 Apr 1936 in Morton, Cochran Co., TX.

4 Harris Sanders, b. 27 Mar 1824 in Montgomery Co., NC; d. 21 Feb 1917 in Tippah Co., MS; ma. June 26, 1853.

5 Emeline Crump, b. 20 Oct 1836; d. 21 Feb 1920 in Tippah Co., MS.

6 William Clifton, b. 5 Mar 1845 in SC; d. 9 Feb 1923 in Boxelder, Red River Co., TX; ma. 5 Nov 1872 in Birmingham, AL.

7 Martha Jane Looney, b. 8 Mar 1844; d. Boxelder, Red River Co., TX.

John Duff Sanders' number is equal to one, because he's the base individual for the ahnentafel. His father (John Sanders) is number two (because 2 x 1 = 2), and his mother (Nannie Elizabeth Clifton) is three (2 x 1 + 1 = 3). His father's father (Harris Sanders) is four (2 x 2 = 4) and his father's mother (Emeline Crump) is five (2 x 2 + 1 = 5). John Sanders' number (2) is one-half his father's number (4 ÷ 2 = 2), or one-half minus any remainder of his mother's number (5 ÷ 2 = 2.5; 2.5 minus remainder of .5 = 2) — well, you get the idea.

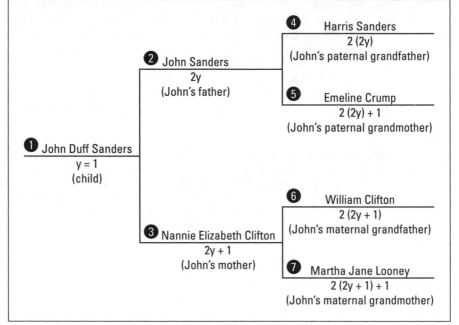

Figure 8-1. An illustration of the ahnentafel numbering system as applied to an ancestor (Pedigree) chart.

As you can imagine, after a while you begin to tire from all these calculations — especially if you are doing them for ten or eleven generations of people. So, if your genealogy software supports it, we highly recommend that you run an ahnentafel report from it — saving you a lot of time and trouble. (We discuss software packages and some of their capabilities in the *Genealogy Online Internet Directory* of this book.)

Some people confuse ahnentafel with *tiny tafel,* which is a compact way to show the relationships within a family database. Tiny tafel provides only the Soundex code for a surname, and the dates and locations where that surname may be found according to the database. (For more on Soundex codes and how they are determined, check out Chapter 1.) Tiny tafels are often used by computer programs to match the same individual in two different genealogy databases. The following example shows a tiny tafel:

C413	1845	1936	Clifton\South Carolina/Cochran Co. TX
C651	1836	1920	Crump/Mississippi
L500	1844		Looney/Red River Co. TX
S536	1824	1996	Sanders\Montgomery Co. NC/Baylor Co. TX

The *Henry System* is another well-known numbering system. This system assigns a particular number to the progenitor, or furthest-back ancestor about whom you know in a particular family line, and then assigns each of

his children a number in sequence that combines his number with the numbers one, two, three, and so forth through nine. (If the progenitor had more than nine children, the tenth child is assigned an "X," the eleventh an "A," the twelfth a "B," and so on.) Then the children's children are assigned the progenitor's number, plus the number of a parent (who is the progenitor's child), plus a number in sequence. For example, if progenitor number one (1) had 12 children, then his children would be 11, 12, 13, . . . 1X, and 1A. Child 11's children would be assigned the numbers 111, 112, 113, and so forth.

For example, suppose that one of your ancestors, John Jones, had 12 children. The names of these children were Joseph, Ann, Mary, Jacob, Arthur, Charles, James, Maria, Esther, Harriett, Thomas, and Sophia. Joseph had one child named Gertrude and Thomas had three children named Lawrence, Joshua, and David. Under the standard Henry system the children's children are numbered like this:

1	John Jones		
	11	Joseph Jones	
		111	Gertrude Jones
	12	Ann Jones	
	13	Mary Jones	
	14	Jacob Jones	
	15	Arthur Jones	
	16	Charles Jones	
	17	James Jones	
	18	Maria Jones	
	19	Esther Jones	
	1X	Harriett Jones	
	1A	Thomas Jones	
		11A1	Lawrence Jones
		11A2	Joshua Jones
		11A3	David Jones
	1B	Sophia Jones	

Several modifications have been made to the Henry System. One modification uses periods between the double-digit Henry numbers; instead of the first three children being 11, 12 and 13, they are 1.1, 1.2, and 1.3. Another modification numbers the children born after the ninth child in a different manner; instead of numbering the children 1X, 1A, and 1B, they are 1(10), 1(11), 1(12).

By no means are these systems the only genealogical numbering systems in existence. Ahnentafel and Henry are just two of the easier systems to learn. Several others have been designed to display genealogies in book form. If you are curious about some of these systems, take a look at `www.genealogy.org/~st-clair/numbers/` where you can find descriptions of each of the major numbering systems.

If you decide to use a numbering system, you can place the corresponding unique number for each individual on the file that you set up for them in your paper record-keeping system, as well as in your genealogical software.

Making copies of source documents

You don't want to carry original records with you when you're out and about researching. The chances of misplacing or forgetting a document are too great to risk! You have a few options. Write down the basic information from the records, make photocopies of those that you must have with you for your research, or scan the documents and store them on your laptop or notebook computer. (We talk more about using computers for your notes later in this chapter in the "Storing and Organizing Information with Your Computer" section.) Then use your notes and copies out in the field. Place the original documents in the safest place you can think of — a lockbox, fireproof file cabinet or safe, or safe-deposit box.

Deciding on a method for storage

Now you must decide how to store those papers. A filing system is in order! If you already have a file cabinet with some available room in it and some folders, then you're all set. If you don't have a file cabinet, think about getting one or some other container for filing. You can use almost anything in which you can stand some files on end — a magazine rack, a crate, or a file-storage box. Next, you need some file folders. If you're like us, you may want brand-spanking new, clean folders, but even recycling those older folders where you used to keep your tax records and receipts works after you slap some new labels on them. If you prefer, you can bypass this kind of filing system and go directly to storing your documents in three-ring binders (which we discuss in the next section).

Try preparing a folder for each relative and ancestor. Start with folders for each of your children (if you have children, that is) and work your way backward. In each folder, keep charts and forms, copies of original records, notes, and any correspondence that relates to that person. You may have some records that overlap people — for example, a marriage certificate for you and your spouse. In such cases, make two copies of that record and keep one copy in each person's folder, or make a note in one folder concerning the location of the record in the other folder. You can do the same if you

have a record that overlaps more than two people. If, for example, you have a census record that reflects information about five people in a family, you can either keep a copy in each person's folder or make notes in each folder as to where the copy of the census return is. Because most of the papers that you're keeping in these files are copies or working notes, we recommend investing the money in a good three-ring hole punch so you can have each piece of paper ready to move to a three-ring binder in a moment's notice.

Preparing notebooks for on-site use

Unless you use a laptop or notebook computer that has your genealogical software and all the information you've collected stored on it, you need a way to take information about your ancestors with you when you go on-site to research. Obviously, you can't cart your file cabinet with you, and you may look a little strange dragging a crate full of files into the local library (not to mention that carrying all your folders with you in a crate, or even a book-bag, may get a little heavy). So what should you do? We recommend using three-ring binders. You can transfer the notes and records that you normally keep in your files to the binders when you're going to be researching. This system allows you to take only those records and notes you know you need and permits you to place new notes (taken on loose-leaf paper) directly with information about a particular person. (Of course, if you keep all your documents in three-ring binders all the time, you won't need to transfer the documents to and from your filing system at home. You can just grab the appropriate binder you need and go.)

Preserving Your Treasured Family Documents

Time is going to take its toll on every document in your possession. The longer you want your records and pictures to last, the better care you need to take of them now. The following sections discuss some tips for preserving your family treasures so that you can pass them down to future generations in the best shape possible.

Storing vital records under the right conditions

Place birth certificates, marriage licenses, and other records between acid-free paper in albums. Keep these albums in a dark, dry, and temperature-consistent place. Ideally, store these documents in a place that is 65 to 70

degrees Fahrenheit year-round, with a relative humidity of less than 50 percent. You may consider placing these albums in a steel file cabinet. Also, try to avoid using ink, staples, paper clips, glue, and tape around your documents (unless you use a product designed for document repair).

For your precious documents (original birth certificates and family papers), rent a safe-deposit box or find another form of off-site storage. Of course, one of the best methods of preservation is to make an electronic copy of your document with a scanner.

Protecting your photographs

Fight the urge to put all your photos of every ancestor on display, because light can damage them over time. Keep your most-prized pictures in a dark, dry, and temperature-consistent place. If you use a photo album for storage, make sure that it has acid-free paper or chemically safe plastic pockets, and that you affix the pictures to the pages using a safe adhesive. Other storage options include acid-free storage boxes and steel file cabinets. Store the photographs in a place around 65 to 70 degrees Fahrenheit year-round, with a relative humidity of less than 50 percent. Avoid prolonged exposure of photographs to direct sunlight and fluorescent lights. And, by all means, have negatives made of those rare family photos and store them in envelopes (the kind without gumming or glue!) that are clearly marked.

You can preserve photographs a couple of other ways. First, you can convert photographs of an earlier time to a newer and safer kind of film. A local photograph shop that specializes in preservation can do this for you. Because color photographs fade more quickly than their black and white counterparts, you may want to make black and white negatives of your color photographs. Also, as with documents, you can always preserve your photographs electronically by scanning them in to your computer or by having a Photo CD made by your photographic developer.

Check out some Web sites to provide you with more detailed tips on preserving your family treasures. Here are two of them:

- ✔ "Weekly Tips on Preservation and Photo Organizing" by Thomas Davis at www.geocities.com/Heartland/2878/preserve.html
- ✔ "Just Black and White's Tips for Preserving Your Photographs and Documents" by David Mishkin at www.maine.com/photos/tip.htm

Additionally, these sites list some mail-order sources of products if you don't know where you can get chemically safe storage products (albums, paper, boxes, adhesives, and so forth) for your photos and records.

Even though you want to preserve everything to the best of your ability, don't be afraid to pull out your albums to show to visiting relatives and friends if you want to do so. On the other hand, don't be embarrassed to ask these guests to use caution when looking through your albums. Depending on the age and rarity of some of your documents, you may even want to ask guests to wear latex gloves when handling the albums so that the oil from their hands doesn't get all over your treasures. Upon realizing how important these treasures are to you, most guests won't mind using caution.

Storing and Organizing Information with Your Computer

Now that you have your paper records and photographs in order, it's time to put your computer to work storing and manipulating your family history. Although some genealogists argue otherwise, a computer may be your best friend when it comes to storing, organizing, and publishing your genealogical information.

You can use your computer to house genealogical software that can store information on thousands of individuals, access CD-ROMs containing indices to valuable genealogical records, scan images to preserve your family heritage, and share information with researchers throughout the world via the Internet.

Several software programs enable you to track your ancestors easily and successfully. You can store facts and stories about them, place scanned photographs of them with their biographical information, and generate numerous reports at the click of a button. Some even allow you to store audio and video recordings with the software. (This capability is especially wonderful if you want to put together a multimedia presentation on your genealogy to share at a reunion or conference!)

Most of the genealogical software programs available from major software companies often have many features and system requirements in common. Look closely at the specific system requirements on the box of the software that you choose to ensure that you make the most out of your computer and software.

In general, the following is what we recommend as minimum requirements for your computer system to adequately run most genealogical software. However, keep in mind that if you want to add additional accessories to your computer to assist your genealogical effort (such as scanners, software, and so forth), or if you want to store electronic images, you may need to have a higher end system — that is, a faster microprocessor, more random access memory (RAM), and larger hard drive space.

If you have an IBM or compatible personal computer, you need:

- ✔ At least a 486 processor (most software manufacturers strongly recommend a Pentium)
- ✔ Windows 95 (or Windows 3.1 in the enhanced mode)
- ✔ A CD-ROM drive
- ✔ 16 megabytes of free hard-disk space
- ✔ 16 megabytes of RAM
- ✔ VGA display with at least 16 colors
- ✔ A Microsoft-compatible mouse

If you have a Macintosh computer, you need:

- ✔ A Power PC processor
- ✔ System 7.1.2 or higher
- ✔ A CD-ROM drive
- ✔ 15 megabytes of free hard-disk space
- ✔ 16 megabytes of RAM

Finding a Research Mate (Of the Software Variety)

You probably thought that you already found that perfect research mate — that special person you drag to every library, cemetery, and courthouse where you need to research, right? Wrong! The research mate we're referring to comes in a little box, with CD-ROMs or floppy disks, and you load it on your computer and then let it perform all sorts of amazing tasks for you.

Several software programs are available for storing and manipulating your genealogical information. They all have some standard features in common; in general, most serve as databases for family facts and stories, have reporting functions where you can generate already completed charts and forms, and have export capabilities so that you can share your data with others. Each software program has a few unique things that make it stand out from the others, such as the capability to take information out of the software and generate online reports at the click of a button. Here is a list of the things you want to watch for when looking at and evaluating different software packages:

✔ **How easy is the software to use?** Is it graphically friendly so that you can see how and where to enter particular facts about an ancestor?

✔ **Does the software generate the reports that you need?** For instance, if you are partial to family group sheets, does this software support them?

✔ **Does the software allow you to export and/or import a GEDCOM file?** GEDCOM is a file format that is widely used for genealogical research. For more information about GEDCOM, see the sidebar titled, "GEDCOM: The genealogist's standard," later in this chapter.

✔ **How many names can this software hold?** You want to make sure that the software you use can hold an adequate number of names (and the accompanying data) to accommodate all your ancestors about whom you have information. Keep in mind that your genealogy will continue to grow over time.

✔ **Can your current computer system support this software?** If the requirements of the software cause your computer to crash every time you use it, you won't get very far in your genealogical research.

✔ **Does this software provide fields to cite your sources and keep notes?** Including information about the sources you've used to gather your data — with the actual facts if possible — is a sound genealogical practice. For more information about the importance of citing sources and how to do so, take a look at Chapter 10.

Entering Information into Family Tree Maker for Windows

To help you get a better idea of how software can help you organize your records and research, and to help you figure out what features to look for in particular software packages, we show you one example of a genealogical software package that is available and how to use it.

One of the more popular software programs is Family Tree Maker for Windows from Brøderbund Software. You can load a basic version of the software onto your computer from the CD-ROM accompanying this book. (For installation instructions, see Appendix D.)

When you first open Family Tree Maker for Windows, you see a blank Family Page with the cursor already set in the *Husband* field. This page is the starting point for inserting information about yourself and your family. If the first person for whom you are entering information is a female, tab down to the *Wife* field to begin. Figure 8-2 shows a Family Page within Family Tree Maker For Windows.

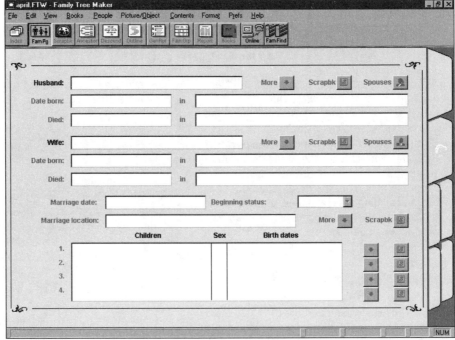

Figure 8-2:
A blank
family page
in Family
Tree Maker
for
Windows.

Completing the Family Page

You may find it easiest to enter information about yourself, your spouse, and children, then work backward through your parents, grandparents, great-grandparents, and so forth. After you complete your direct lines back as far as you can, come back and enter Family Page information about siblings, nieces and nephews, cousins, and other relatives. Always enter as much information as you have available for each of the fields on the Family Pages. This may save you from having to come back to complete the page later on. Follow these steps to fill in the Family Page:

1. Enter your name.

Using the appropriate field (*Husband* or *Wife*) based on your gender or family role, enter your name in this order: first name, middle name, last name. Even if you are unmarried, use one of these two fields for your own information and just leave the spouse field blank.

After you enter your name, Family Tree Maker for Windows automatically creates a Family Page for your parents. When you need to enter more detailed information about your parents, you can click the appropriate tab on the right-hand side of the screen to get to their Family Page.

GENEALOGY LINGO

GEDCOM: The genealogist's standard

As you have probably already discovered, genealogy is full of acronyms. One such acronym that you hear and see in writing over and over again is *GEDCOM* (GEnealogical Data COMmunication). Over the past ten years, GEDCOM has become the standard for individuals and software manufacturers for exporting and importing information from genealogical databases. Simply put, GEDCOM is a file format intended to make data transferable between different software programs so that people can share their family information easily.

The Church of Jesus Christ of Latter-day Saints first developed and introduced GEDCOM in 1987. The first two versions of GEDCOM were released for public discussion only and not meant to serve as the standard. With the introduction of Version 5.x and later, GEDCOM was accepted as the standard.

Having a standard for formatting files is beneficial to you as a researcher because it enables you to share the information you've collected with others who are interested in some or all of your ancestors. It also enables you to import GEDCOM files from these same and other researchers who have information about family lines and ancestors in whom you are interested. And you don't even have to use the same software as the other researchers! You can use Reunion for Macintosh, and someone with whom you want to share information can use Family Tree Maker for Windows, yet having GEDCOM as the standard in both software programs enables each of you to create and exchange GEDCOM files.

To convert the data in your genealogical database to a GEDCOM file, follow the instructions provided in your software manual or under the program's Help menu. You can create the GEDCOM file relatively easily; most software guides you through the process with a series of prompts or text (or dialog, if you prefer) boxes. The most difficult thing about the process is finding out what software your fellow researcher uses so that you can make sure your software generates a customized file for that other software.

In addition to creating GEDCOM files to exchange one-on-one with other researchers, you can generate GEDCOM files to submit to larger cooperatives that make the data from many GEDCOM files available to thousands of researchers worldwide via the World Wide Web and e-mail. One such cooperative effort, GenServ, has grown incredibly since its inception in 1989. (For more information about GenServ, see Chapter 3.) You can also convert your GEDCOM file to HTML so that you can place the data directly on the World Wide Web for others to access. Software utilities are available (such as GED2HTML) that make it a snap for you to convert your GEDCOM file to HTML. (For more information on generating Web pages using GED2HTML, see Chapter 11.)

2. **Enter your date of birth in the *Date born* field, and enter your place of birth in the *in* field.**

   Press the Tab key to move among the fields on the page. Notice that some fields (*Date born*, *Died*, and *Location*s for each) are disabled when you first begin. As soon as you type in your name, these fields become active so that you can enter information in them.

In the *Date born* field, enter your birth date, including month, day, and full four-digit year. The software has a default format for dates, so you can use the date spelled out (January 15, 1965) or abbreviated with numerals (01/15/1965). The system automatically converts the date to the spelled out format (January 15, 1965) unless you change the default format.

Note: Uh-oh. Some people will say we just gave you wrong instructions about the way to enter dates! Diehard genealogists and former military personnel will tell you that the order should be day, month, then year instead (for example, 15 January 1965) — another perfectly acceptable method for dating, and one that is quite often international. Even though we're likely to get a lashing for saying this, over the past couple of years we've seen both methods (month, day, year and day, month, year) used just about equally, so we recommend you use whichever one feels most comfortable to you.

If you inadvertently use only two numerals for the year, the software prompts you to use a four-digit year. For example, if you enter 01/15/65 into a *Died* field, a dialog box appears, asking you to choose a complete year for the date — 1965, 1865, 1765, and so forth. Additionally, if you aren't sure about the exact date of an event, Family Tree Maker for Windows allows you to use abbreviations for "circa" or "about." However, the software automatically defaults to "Abt" in the field upon your entering one of the codes. For example, if you enter cir. 01/15/1965, the software converts it to "Abt January 15, 1965." (Again, if you prefer "Cir" to "Abt," you can change the default settings.)

Tab to the next field and enter your place of birth. Always include as much information as possible in every field, including the town, county or parish, and state of your birth. If you want, you can also include the country.

3. **Enter information about your spouse. If you don't have any spouse information to enter, go to Step 5.**

   Enter your spouse's name in the appropriate *Husband* or *Wife* field. After the date and place of birth fields are active, tab down and enter your spouse's information in the *Date born* and *in* fields just like you did for yourself.

   After you enter your spouse's name, Family Tree Maker for Windows automatically creates a Family Page for the spouse's parents. When you need to enter more detailed information about your in-laws, you can click the appropriate tab on the right-hand side of the screen to get to their Family Page.

4. **Enter your marriage information in the *Marriage date*, *Beginning status*, and *Marriage location* fields.**

   Like the birth and death fields, the *Marriage date* and *Marriage location* fields are disabled until you have names entered in both the *Husband* and *Wife* fields. After the fields become active and you finish entering

the basic information about you and your spouse, tab down to the *Marriage date* field and enter the date of your wedding. In the *Marriage location* field, enter the town, county/parish, and state where you were married. If you want, you can also include the country. If, for some reason, the *Beginning status* field reflects the wrong status for you after you complete the date and place fields for marriage, use the pull-down menu to change the status. For example, if the status field still shows that you are single after you enter your marriage date and place, you can use the pull-down menu to change the status field to married.

The *Beginning status* field reflects the relationship status between the persons whose information is contained in the *Husband* and *Wife* fields. The *Beginning status* field starts out reflecting Single, until both fields have information, and then it assumes Married. If the *Beginning status* field reflects the wrong status for the relationship of the two people, use the pull-down menu to change the status. Your choices are Single, Married, Friends, Partners, Private, Unknown, and Other. Also, the *Beginning status* field controls titles for some of the other fields on the Family Page. If you select that the relationship status of the two people is Friends or Partners, Family Tree Maker for Windows automatically changes *Husband* and *Wife* to Friend or Partner and *Marriage date* and *Marriage location* to *Meeting date* and *Meeting location*.

5. **Enter information about your children (if applicable) in the table at the bottom of the page. The information includes names of Children, Sex, and Birth Dates. If you don't have any children information to enter, skip this step.**

When you are recording information about your children, the software can be a little deceiving. At first glance, it appears you can enter information only up to four children, but this is not the case. To get to a fifth or subsequent child field, press Enter after recording the previous child's date of birth; the software brings up a fifth or subsequent line for you to use. (You can also use the scroll bar to get to additional lines — the scroll bar will appear when you enter the fourth child.)

For each child, enter the child's full name, sex, and date of birth in the appropriate columns. After you enter a child's information, Family Tree Maker for Windows automatically creates a Family Page for that child. When you're ready to enter more detailed information about your children (such as their places of birth, marriage information, and so forth), click the appropriate child's tab on the right-hand side of the screen to get to his or her Family Page. Or you can use the View pull-down menu to find the Index of Individuals from which you can choose the child by name.

As you're entering information about people, we encourage you to cite your sources of the data. Most genealogical software programs, including Family Tree Maker for Windows, allow you to enter source information. For specific instructions on how to do so in your particular software, see the help file or user's manual that came with the software.

One other feature of Family Tree Maker for Windows you should know about tries to help you enter name and location information (you may have already encountered this feature in your first Family Page). Sometimes this feature saves you time, but if what you want to enter has a subtle difference from what you entered before, this feature can frustrate you. As soon as the software recognizes that you're repeating characters in the same order as in a previous field, a dialog box appears with the name or location so that you can just press Enter to automatically populate that field with the information. For example, say you have several ancestors who were born in Larue County, Kentucky. After you type "Larue County, Kentucky" or "Larue Co., Kentucky" for one ancestor, anytime you begin typing it for additional ancestors, the software recognizes it and prompts you to populate the field with the same phrase.

Another feature is that all the fields have instructional boxes that pop up after the mouse's pointer has been on the field for a couple of seconds (see Figure 8-3). The instructional boxes are very helpful if you aren't sure exactly what information to include in the field.

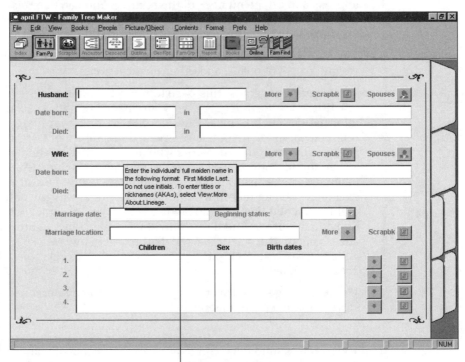

Figure 8-3:
An example of an instructional box.

If you keep your pointer on a field, an instructional box pops up to guide you.

Working with the supplemental pages

On the Family Page are some icons that you haven't yet explored in your Family Page creation. Next to the *Husband*, *Wife*, and *Marriage location* fields are two to three icons that lead to the supplemental pages for information about these people or events.

The *More* icon takes you to a section where you can select pages with forms for recording particular types of information about your relatives, including Facts, Address, Medical, Lineage, and Notes. The following list explains how to use each page:

- ✔ **The Facts page:** Use this page to hold up to 13 facts about an ancestor. The page includes two fields for each fact — a *Date (optional)* field and a *Comment/Location* field. Use these fields to record information such as the places (and dates) of an ancestor's burial and christening, or even where your ancestor lived in particular census years.

- ✔ **The Address page:** Use this page to enter the current or last-known address and phone number of the relative. You can use this information in another feature of the software to generate letters or address labels for those with whom you correspond via mail.

- ✔ **The Medical page:** Use this page to enter the individual's height, weight, cause of death, and other medical notes.

- ✔ **The Lineage page:** Use this page to record a number of items, such as any titles (Dr., Rev., Jr., Sr., Col.) your ancestors had, "also known as" information (such as nicknames or aliases), and your filing system reference number. Also, you can record the nature of this person's relationship with the ancestors who are identified as the person's father and mother, as well as select whether to include the relationship in any trees or kinship reports you generate using the software. For example, you can record whether the individual was the natural-born child, stepchild, foster child, and so on, of the ancestor identified as the individual's father. And if the individual was an illegitimate child of the ancestor, you can select to exclude them from any trees or reports by checking the box next to the phrase "Exclude this relationship from Trees and Kinship."

- ✔ **The Notes page:** Use this blank page to record any personal notes and stories about a particular ancestor.

The *Scrapbook* icon takes you to a section where you can link your software to photographs, sound files, and movies about this particular ancestor that you've stored on your computer. To insert an object, choose Insert from the Picture/Object menu and follow the instructional boxes.

If your ancestor was married more than once, click the *Spouses* icon to include information about the additional spouses. You can create "new" spouses and record other spousal information, as well as designate which spouse should be the "preferred" one for your database.

Entering information for your other ancestors

After entering all the information you have for your first person (most likely yourself), use the tabs that run down the right-hand side of the screen to go to the Family Page for your parents and enter all the information you have about them. After you're done with them, use the tabs to get to the Family Pages for your grandparents and so on as you progress backward through your ancestors.

Sharing Your Genealogical Success with Others

After you organize all your paper documents and enter as much information as possible into your genealogical software, you can share with others what you've gathered and organized, or generate notes to take with you on research trips. (If you haven't organized your information yet, use the earlier sections in this chapter to help you.) The time has come to report on your findings, so to speak.

Your genealogical software can help you by generating printed reports reflecting the information you collected and entered. Most genealogical software packages have several standard reports or charts in common, including a Pedigree chart (also called an Ancestor chart), Descendant chart, Outline of descendants, Family Group Sheet, and Kinship report.

First we examine the different types of reports. Then we walk you through how to generate them using Family Tree Maker for Windows. (For more information about entering information into and using Family Tree Maker for Windows, please review the preceding section, "Entering Information into Family Tree Maker for Windows.")

Pedigree (or Ancestor) charts

Family Tree Maker for Windows calls its Pedigree chart an Ancestor chart. Going across a page horizontally, it identifies a primary person including that person's name, date and place of birth, date and place of marriage, and

date and place of death. The chart uses lines to show the relationship to the person's father and mother, then each of their parents, then their parents, and so on until the chart runs off the page. See Figure 8-4 for an example of a Pedigree chart generated using Family Tree Maker for Windows.

Descendant charts

A Descendant chart contains information about an ancestor and spouse (or spouses if there's more than one), their children and their spouses, grand-children and spouses, and on down the family line. A Descendant chart is usually formatted from top to bottom (vertically) on a page, rather than running across the page as a Pedigree (Ancestor) chart does. See Figure 8-5 for an example of a Descendant chart generated using Family Tree Maker for Windows.

Outline reports

A family Outline is a list of the descendants of a particular ancestor. The first numbered line contains the name (and sometimes the years for birth and death) of the primary ancestor. The next line shows a spouse, followed by

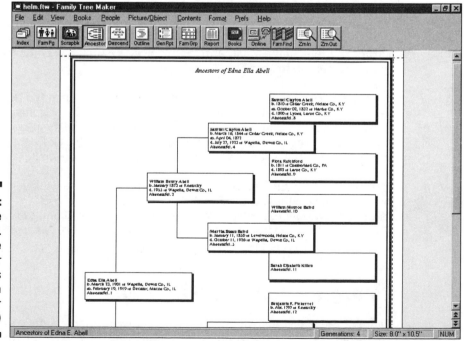

Figure 8-4:
A Pedigree chart. (Family Tree Maker for Windows calls this an Ancestor chart.)

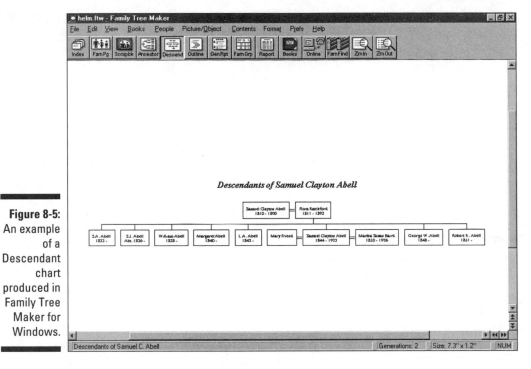

Figure 8-5:
An example
of a
Descendant
chart
produced in
Family Tree
Maker for
Windows.

the next numbered line that contains the name of the ancestor and spouse's first child. If that child is married and has children, the child's spouse follows, as do the names and information on each of the child and spouse's children. See Figure 8-6 for an example of an Outline report generated using Family Tree Maker for Windows.

Family Group Sheets

A Family Group Sheet is a summary of vital information about a particular family. At the top of the page, the Group Sheet shows the *Husband*, followed by the *Wife* and any children of the couple, and shows biographical information (such as dates and places of birth, marriage, and death). However, information on the children's spouses and children is not included on this Family Group Sheet; you can generate a separate Family Group Sheet for each child's family (if applicable). See Figure 8-7 for an example of a Family Group Sheet generated using Family Tree Maker for Windows.

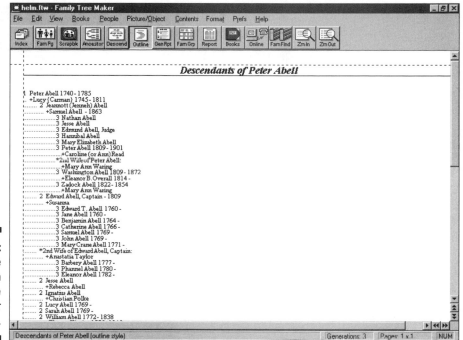

Figure 8-6:
An Outline
report in
Family Tree
Maker for
Windows.

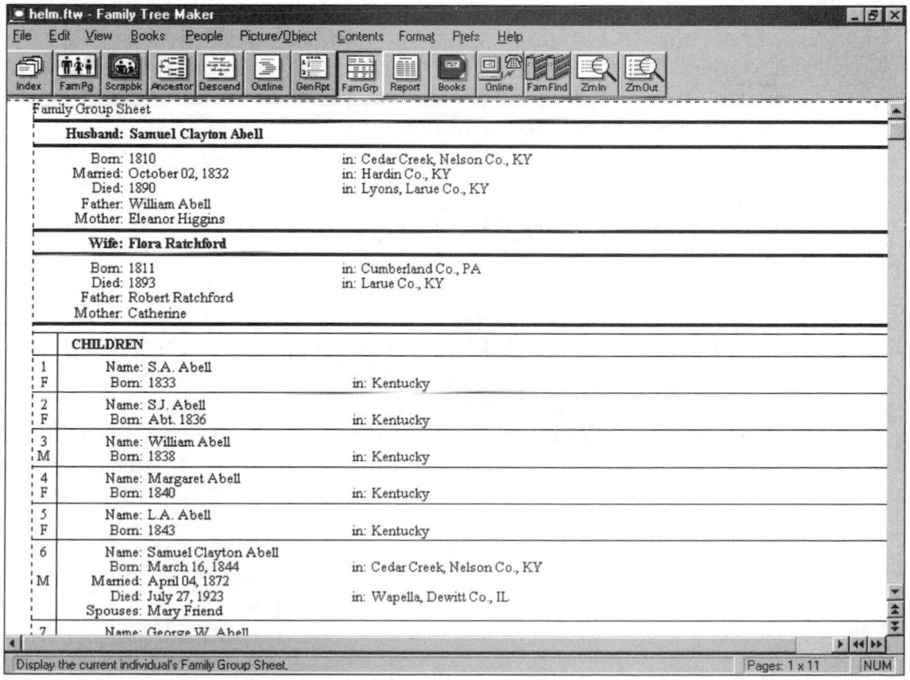

Figure 8-7:
A Family
Group
Sheet from
Family Tree
Maker for
Windows.

Kinship reports

A Kinship report is a list of family members and how they relate directly to one particular ancestor. This report includes the name of the family member, the person's relationship to the primary ancestor, and the Civil and Canon Codes reflecting the degree of relationship between the two people. See Figure 8-8 for an example of a Kinship report generated using Family Tree Maker for Windows.

Civil and Canon Codes explain the bloodline relationship in legal terms — in other words, they identify how many *degrees of separation* (or steps) are between two people who are related by blood. Civil law counts each step between two relatives as a degree, so two people who are cousins have a degree of separation equal to four, which is the total of two steps between one cousin and the common grandparent and two steps between the other cousin and the common grandparent. Canon law counts only the number of steps from the nearest common ancestor of both relatives, so the degree of separation between two cousins is two. The grandparent is two steps separated from each of the cousins.

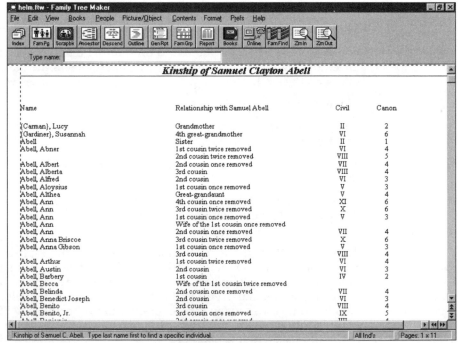

Figure 8-8:
An example of a Kinship report in Family Tree Maker for Windows.

Generating Charts/Reports Using Family Tree Maker for Windows

See the "Completing the Family Page" section earlier in this chapter for the details on how to fill out a Family Page entry for each of your ancestors. When you have Family Pages in Family Tree Maker for Windows for your ancestors, follow these steps to create any of the five charts/reports that we discuss in the preceding paragraphs.

1. **Open Family Tree Maker for Windows.**

   Usually, you can open your software by double-clicking the icon for that program or by going to the Programs menu from the Start button (in Windows 95) and selecting the particular program.

2. **Under the View pull-down menu, select the Index of Individuals.**

   This action brings up a box that lists all the individuals entered in your database in alphabetical order.

3. **Scroll through the index and select the person for whom you want to generate a chart/report by double-clicking on the name or highlighting the name and clicking the OK button.**

   This takes you to the Family Page for the person you've selected.

   For example, if Matthew wanted to produce a Pedigree chart for his ancestor Samuel Abell, he highlights Samuel Abell in the index then clicks on the OK button.

4. **Place your cursor in the person's name field.**

   Move your cursor into the *Husband*, *Wife*, or *Children* fields to select the exact person on whom you want to generate a chart/report.

   Matthew places the cursor in the *Husband* field, which reflects the name Samuel Abell.

5. **Click the appropriate button in the button bar at the top of the Family Tree Maker for Windows screen, or choose View⇨ [Type of tree or report].**

   There are buttons in the button bar for Ancestor charts, Descendant (Descend.) charts, Outlines, and Family Group Sheets (Fam. Grp.). Or if you're using the pull-down menu, the charts/reports appear as Ancestor Tree, Descendant Tree, Outline Descendant Tree, Kinship, and Family Group Sheet. (You can generate other reports using Family Tree Maker for Windows, but these are the most common types and the five we've discussed in this chapter.)

   Family Tree Maker for Windows generates the requested chart/report for the person you've selected.

For an example of producing a chart on Samuel Abell, Matthew clicks the button that says Ancestor or uses the View pull-down menu to select Ancestor Tree. Then Family Tree Maker for Windows automatically generates a Pedigree chart for Samuel Abell. (To see what this Pedigree chart looks like, refer back to Figure 8-4.)

6. **Look at the chart on the screen, copy it to your word processor to save, or print it out to share with others.**

   For more information about moving reports into your word processor, see Chapter 10.

Formatting and customizing charts/reports

Keep in mind that you can control exactly what to include in each of these charts or reports — from telling Family Tree Maker for Windows how many generations to include, to excluding particular ancestors, to changing the types of information to include, to customizing the appearance (borders and fonts). Here are some quick references to help you when manipulating the content of these reports in Family Tree Maker for Windows:

- To control the number of generations included on the chart or report: Choose Contents⇨# of Generations to Show.
- To change the format: Choose Format⇨Tree Format.
- To change boxes, lines, and borders: Choose Format⇨Box, Line, & Border Styles.
- To change the fonts: Choose Format⇨Text Font, Style, & Size.

It's important to note that other genealogical software programs allow you to manipulate your charts/reports in a similar manner.

Hammers, Screwdrivers, and Other Hardware: Is Your Computer Equipped?

As you grow more accustomed to using the information you store in your computer, you may want to consider other hardware and equipment that you may need or want to add to your system to enhance your genealogy research and the reports you generate. You may want to start including electronic images of some of the photographs and original documents that you have in your paper filing system. You may think about adding audio of your grandmother reminiscing, or video of your grandchild greeting people at the family reunion. As you find additional documents, you may want to

add images of them to your main database as well. So what kind of computer hardware or other equipment do you need in order to include images and other enhancements with your genealogical information?

You need to consider four pieces of equipment when you prepare to enhance your genealogy with audio and video — sound cards, video-capture boards, scanners, and digital cameras.

Sound cards

A sound card is an internal device that comes standard on most computers today. It allows you to hear any audio that comes on software (particularly games) or audio files that you download off the Internet. In most cases, the card also allows you to record your own audio from your stereo, radio, video camera, or microphone. However, you must have software that supports recordings. If your sound card is capable of recording and you have adequate software, you simply plug the sound source into the microphone jack or sound-in jack on the back of your computer, set your software to record, and go for it. After you make the recording, you can import it into your genealogical software if the genealogical software supports audio.

Video-capture boards

Similar to a sound card, a video-capture board enables you to grab images from your video camera. You can use moving images or still pictures, depending on your video-capture board and the accompanying software. Video-capture boards don't usually come standard with computers. They have varying system requirements depending on the manufacturer and the software that is included. Be sure that your computer system can handle a particular video-capture board and software before making your purchase.

Scanners

Scanners have become one of the most popular computer peripherals for genealogists. Everyone wants to include some family photos with their genealogy or preserve precious documents electronically. And with the cost of scanners decreasing and bundled software allowing you to use a scanner as a scanner, fax machine, and copier, it is not unrealistic to think about adding a scanner to your equipment collection.

A variety of scanners are available. The most common types are snapshot, sheetfed, and flatbed. Also, you can still find a few hand-held scanners around. You can find color scanners and scanners that capture images only in black and white. The system requirements for scanners vary greatly, so

read the packaging of the scanner you are considering very carefully. Additionally, each scanner requires software to make the scanner work, so carefully read over the system requirements and capabilities of the software as well. Here is a quick rundown of the major types of scanners:

- ✔ **Snapshot scanners** are perfect for creating electronic images of photographs that measure 5 x 7 inches or smaller because snapshot scanners are made to work primarily with that size of photograph. Snapshot scanners are compact and come in external and internal varieties. You feed the photograph into the scanner, and then the scanner captures an image before sending the photo back out. Some snapshot scanners have a removable top that you can use as a hand-held scanner in order to capture images larger than 5 x 7 inches.

- ✔ **Sheetfed scanners** are typically a little wider than a regular sheet of paper (8.5 inches across). They are still rather compact, as far as scanners go, but they are all external. You feed the photograph or document into the feeder on the scanner, and the scanner captures an image as the document goes through. Like some snapshot scanners, some sheetfed scanners have a removable top that you can use as a hand-held scanner in order to capture images larger than 8.5 inches across.

- ✔ **Flatbed scanners** are usually large and bulky. They are not portable in the least because they must lie on a flat surface for you to use them. You lift the top of the scanner and place your document or photograph on the bed of the scanner, close the lid, and tell the scanner (through your software) to capture the image.

- ✔ **Hand-held scanners** used to be readily available and quite popular because of their relatively low cost. The trend seems to be to replace hand-held scanners with snapshot and sheetfed scanners with removable tops that can be hand-held. Hand-held scanners are external and compact. They are the perfect size to carry with you when you go on-site for your genealogical research. You scan photos and other objects by holding the scanner and slowly moving it over the object while holding down a button. Although hand-held scanners are convenient, the quality of scanned image that you get depends greatly upon how steady your hand is, how good the lighting is where you are scanning, and the original size of the document.

Digital cameras

Digital cameras are one of the newest technologies to capture genealogists' interest. Being able to take all your photographs with a camera that downloads directly to your computer where they can be easily imported into your genealogical database is definitely exciting! Depending upon the model, you either store the digital pictures within the memory of the camera or on a $3^1/_2$-inch disk. With the models that store the images internally, you must

take the extra step to download the images to your computer through a serial cable. For the models that save to a floppy disk, you can simply insert the disk into your computer and copy the files to your database.

As with every other computer peripheral, if you are considering purchasing a digital camera, carefully read the package and software requirements to make sure that your computer system can support the equipment.

Traveling with Your Genealogical Tools

Whether going to a family reunion, traveling a couple hundred miles to research in a particular county or province, or giving a presentation at a conference, chances are you may eventually want to take your show on the road. If you are just testing the waters to see whether it's worth your time and money to buy a computer for genealogical purposes, you may want to consider getting a laptop or notebook computer instead of a desktop system. Portable computers give you the flexibility to take your genealogical database with you wherever you go, as well as some presentation possibilities that desktop systems don't allow because of their size.

Portable databases

As you get more involved in genealogy and begin to take research trips, you may find it useful to have your database with you. Of course, you can always print out the contents of your database, but who wants to carry around thousands of pages? One alternative is to carry a notebook computer with you. Notebooks have become very popular in the past year, especially because they have become more affordable and more powerful. Most notebooks have capabilities similar to their desktop counterparts, but in a more convenient package.

Another group of research assistants are gaining prominence on the market — palmtops. Palmtops are hand-sized computers that can contain some of the same programs housed on desktop computers. Some of the first generation palmtops run on a scaled-down version of Microsoft Windows (called Windows CE) and have special versions of software designed to run on the smaller machines. The newer palmtops have more storage capacity and, therefore, fewer limitations. But even if you have a first generation palmtop, you can still use it to take electronic notes and view small genealogical reports.

Storage on the run

If you already own a desktop system and aren't in the market to buy a notebook or palmtop, don't worry! You have other means for transporting your data and reports without spending the money on another whole computer.

Your database may grow too large to fit on a regular 3$\frac{1}{2}$-inch floppy disk. However, other disks exist, such as CD-ROMs or Zip disks, that hold a lot more data and can easily accommodate your genealogical database. Buying a CD-ROM writer or Zip disk is a lot cheaper than buying a laptop computer. Of course, the drawback to using a disk to transport your data is that you need a computer on the other end that can handle the disk and information contained on it. So before you take a CD-ROM with all your family information to that reunion at Aunt Lola's, make sure that Aunt Lola's computer has a CD-ROM drive and any necessary software to play back the contents of your disk.

One other portability issue is having a means for getting information from a computer source away from home to your computer. Most public libraries and Family History Centers have genealogical information on computer that you can access. You can use a 3$\frac{1}{2}$-inch floppy disk to download information you find on computers and CD-ROMs at these research facilities. Popping a floppy disk into the computer at the library to download a few lines of information about an ancestor is sure a lot easier than hand-writing everything and a lot cheaper than paying for each individual printout!

Chapter 9

Coordinating Your Attack: Getting Help from Other Researchers

• •

• •

*O*ne way to think of genealogical research is as a long journey. You may begin the journey by yourself, but before long, you discover that the journey goes a lot faster when someone else is along with you. In your genealogical journey, these travel partners may come in the form of a single individual researching the same family as yourself, a research group searching for several branches of a family, or a genealogical society that coordinates the efforts of several individuals researching different families.

In the next few pages we explore ways of finding (and keeping) research partners, as well as ways that research groups and genealogical societies can help you meet your research goals.

Putting All Your Eggs in One Basket: Relying Only on Your Research

The old saying is that you shouldn't put all your eggs in one basket. This saying applies to genealogical research — don't try to do all the research yourself. As you will discover, there are an awful lot of people out there researching, and it would be a shame for you not to take advantage of the work they have done and vice versa.

We can't emphasize enough the benefits of sharing genealogical data. Sharing is the foundation on which the genealogical community is built. For example, when Matthew began researching his genealogy, he went to the

National Archives, Library of Congress, and several regional libraries and archives. Along the way, he found a few books that mentioned some of his ancestors in passing and was able to discover some original records that helped him piece together some things. When he shared his information online, he then discovered how many people were working on his surname. During the month following the posting of his Web site, he received messages from 40 other Helm researchers — one of whom lived in Slovenia! While not all of these researchers were working on Matthew's specific branch (only two of the 40 were directly related), he received valuable information on some of the areas that other researchers were working on. Matthew may never have discovered that some of these researchers existed had he not taken the first step to share his information.

By knowing what other researchers are pursuing, you can coordinate with them to share not only information you've collected, but also to work together toward your common goal. Maybe you live closer to a source for court records relating to your ancestor than a distant cousin with whom you are communicating online, but the cousin lives near a family grave site that you'd like to have a photo of. Rather than duplicating efforts to collect the court records and photographs, you can make arrangements for each of you to get the desired items that are closest to you and then exchange copies of them over the Internet or through traditional mail.

The Shotgun Approach

So you should coordinate and share your research with others. Now you're probably wondering how you find individuals to share your information with. Well, you could start going through telephone books and calling everyone with the surname that you are researching. But given how some people feel about telemarketers, we obviously don't recommend this as a strategy.

Similar to this telemarketing strategy is sending mass e-mails to anyone you find with your surname through one of the online white pages sites. We refer to this mass e-mail strategy as the *shotgun approach*. While you may find one or two people who answer you in a positive way, a lot of people may find your unsolicited e-mail irritating. Instead of bearing the wrath of hundreds of people, go to a site focusing on genealogy to find the names of those researchers interested in your surname — the better way to go about it.

Also, please note that we aren't saying that e-mail directories don't have a function in genealogy (see Appendix A for details on how to use an e-mail directory). E-mail directories can be a good place to find an e-mail address that you have lost, an address of a relative who will be interested in your e-mail, or to see the distribution of your surname in the United States and throughout the world (see Figure 9-1).

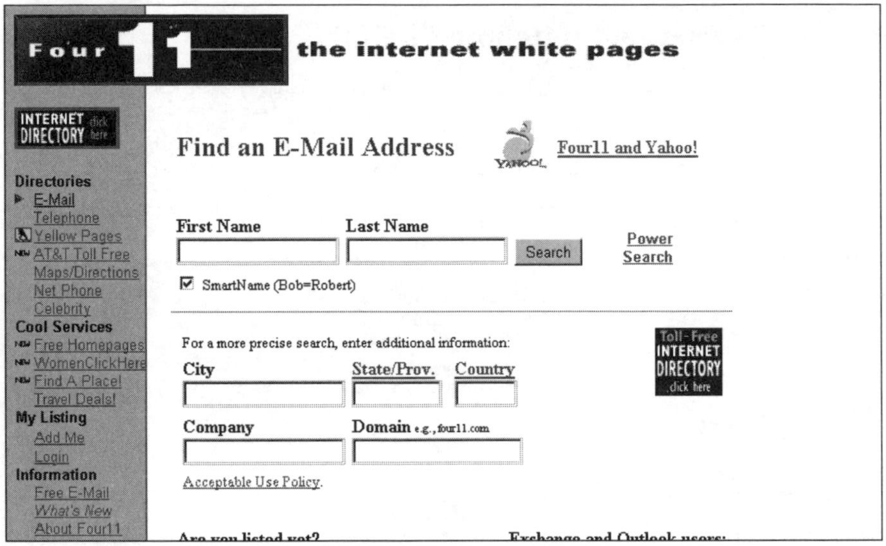

Figure 9-1:
Here's an example of an online e-mail directory (Four11).

Making Friends (And Keeping Them) Online

Probably the best place to begin your search for others doing similar research is the Roots Surname List (see Figure 9-2). The Roots Surname List (www.rootsweb.com/rootsweb/searches/#rsl) is one of the oldest genealogy resources on the Internet and consists of a list of individuals, the surnames they're researching, and the geographic locations where those surnames are found. (For more on using the Roots Surname List, see Chapter 3.) Other places to find fellow researchers include query pages on the World Wide Web, newsgroups, and mailing lists (if you need a refresher on using these or other surname resources, you can find more information in Chapter 3 and Appendix A). After you've identified some potential online friends, send them e-mail messages introducing yourself and briefly explain your purpose for contacting them and the ancestors you are researching (see the following tips).

Before we send you out to contact several people, it's only fair to give you a few pieces of advice:

✔ When sending messages to the maintainers of Web sites, make sure that the maintainer can use or respond to information on the surname that you're researching. Sometimes maintainers keep information on their

Surnames matching "helm"

New entries are marked by a +, modified entries by a *, and expiring entries by an x. Clicking on the highlighted code words will give the name and address of the researcher who submitted the surname. (If no names are listed below this line, then none were found.)

```
Helm          ----  1188 RUS>SWE>DNK>DEU>FRA hhelm
Helm          1089  1652 DEU>FRA>ENG>SCT>IRL hhelm
Helm          1422  1789 SCT>IRL>RI>MA>CT,USA hhelm
Helm          1641  1780 SCT>BRB>NY>NJ>PA,USA hhelm
Helm          1650   now ENG>VI>KY,USA pips
Helm          1660  1996 ENG>FrederickCo,VA>SelbyCo,KY>Guernsey,OH>IN>IL dregen
Helm          1663  1810 NY>NJ>PA>VA>KY,USA hhelm
Helm          1680  1925 SCT>IRL>NY>NJ>PA,USA hhelm
Helm          1715  1715 NLD>ZAF lesleyr
Helm          1726   now PA>MD>KY>IN,USA pips
Helm          1735  1782 Niederbronn-les-Bains,ELS,FRA philippe
Helm          1735  1855 PA>DE>VA>KY>TN,USA hhelm
Helm          1741  1818 DEU>BedfordCo,VA>BotetourtCo,VA,USA lpc
Helm          1745  1880 PA>VA>NC>SC>GA,USA hhelm
Helm          1750   now RandolphCo,IN,USA xtd
Helm          1759  1930 PA>UT,USA wll
Helm          1760   now MEC,DEU>Clayton/Buchanan,IA,USA braunh
Helm          1760  1859 ENG?>VA>KY,USA mahendon
Helm          1780   now VA,USA oracoons
Helm          1790  1900 PRU>WillCo,IL,USA tcash
Helm          1790  1951 DEU>LancasterCo,PA>ArmstrongCo,PA,USA mjgent
```

Figure 9-2: Entries for the surname "Helm" on the Roots Surname List (RSL).

sites for other people. If so, they usually have separate contact addresses for those individuals. Other sites may be general in nature where the maintainer has information on several surnames that they personally do not research. Usually these maintainers will have a notice on their site stating that they do not entertain research questions.

✔ Make your messages brief and to the point. E-mail messages that run five or six pages can overload some people. If the person you're sending the message to is interested in your information, you can send a more detailed message at a future date.

✔ Ensure that your message has enough detail for the recipients to decide whether the information relates to their research. Include names, dates, and places as appropriate.

✔ Use net etiquette, or *netiquette,* when creating your messages. Remember, e-mail can be an impersonal medium. While you may mean one thing, someone who doesn't know you may mistakenly misinterpret your message. (For more on netiquette, see the sidebar "Netiquette: Communicating politely on the Internet.")

If you're needing more information on using e-mail, refer to Appendix A.

Netiquette: Communicating politely on the Internet

Part of becoming a member of the online genealogy community is learning to communicate effectively and politely on the Internet. Online communication is often hampered by the fact that you can't see the people with whom you are corresponding – and you can't hear the intonation of their voices to determine what emotions they're expressing. To avoid misunderstandings, follow some simple guidelines — called *netiquette* — when authoring messages.

- Don't send any message that you wouldn't want posted on a bulletin board at work. You should expect that every e-mail you send is potentially public.

- Make sure that you don't violate any copyright laws by sending large portions of written/published works through e-mail. For more information on copyrights, see Chapter 11.

- If you receive a *flame* (a heated message usually sent to provoke a response), try your best to ignore it. Usually no good comes from responding to a flame.

- Be careful when responding to messages. Instead of replying to an individual, you may be replying to an entire group of people. Checking the To: line before hitting the send button is always a good idea.

- Use mixed case when writing e-mail messages. ALL UPPERCASE LETTERS INDICATES SHOUTING! The exception to this is when you are sending a query and you place your surnames in all uppercase letters, such as George HELM.

- If you are participating in a mailing list or newsgroup and you are replying with a message that is only of interest to one person, consider sending that person a message individually rather than e-mailing the list as a whole.

- When joking, use smileys, type **<grins>**, or **<g>**. A *smiley* is an *emoticon* that looks like **:-)**. (Turn the book on its right side if you can't see the face.) *Emoticons* are graphics created by combinations of keys on the keyboard to express an emotion within an e-mail. Here are a few emoticons that you may run into:

:-)   Happy, smiling

;-)   Wink, ironic

:->   Sarcastic

8-)   Wearing glasses

:-(Sad, unhappy

:-<   Disappointed

:-o   Frightened, surprised

:-()   Mustache

Forming Research Groups

If your relatives are tired of hearing about your genealogy research trips or the information that you found out on great-uncle William, but you'd like to have someone to share your triumphs with, you may be ready to join a research group. *Research groups* are any number of people who coordinate their research and share resources to achieve success. These groups may conduct research based on a surname, family branch, or geographic location. Individuals who live geographically close to each other may make up a research group, or the group may consist of people who have never personally met each other. Research groups may have a variety of goals and may have a formal or informal structure. They are quite flexible organizationally and depend entirely upon the membership of the group.

A good example of an informal research group is one that Matthew discovered shortly after he posted his first Web page. An individual who was researching one of his surnames on the East Coast of the United States contacted him. After exchanging a couple of e-mails, Matthew learned that this individual was part of a small research group studying the origins of several different branches of the Helm surname. Each member of the group contributes the results of his or her personal research and provides any information that he or she has found, which may be of use to other members of the group. As a whole, the group has sponsored research by professional genealogists in other countries. Several more researchers have joined the group just recently (as more researchers are discovered on the Internet), and everyone communicates regularly through e-mail.

You find an example of a more formal approach to research groups at the Dawson Family History Project page (web.globalserve.net/~dawson/index.htm). The mission of this group is to become the definitive source for all genealogical and historical information chronicling the Dawson family from the days of William the Conqueror to the present. The site is constructed to help Dawson researchers collaborate with each other and is divided into three principal areas: researchers, reunions and family associations, and library. The reunions and family associations section contains, as you would expect, address and contact information on associations and reunions. The library has a bibliography of works on the surname. Central to the site, however, is the researchers area. Here you can see the members of each of the nine research groups that are arranged geographically. There is a group for Australia, Canada, Northern Ireland, Scotland, Wales, England, New Zealand, Republic of Ireland, and the United States. Under each research group, you find the names of researchers (including e-mail addresses), date ranges they are interested in, provinces, states, or counties of research, and their Web addresses (see Figure 9-3).

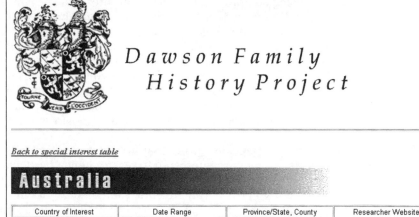

Figure 9-3:
A list of the
Australian
research
group at the
Dawson
Family
History
Project site.

Back to special interest table

Australia

Country of Interest	Date Range	Province/State, County	Researcher Website
Anderson, Robyn	1830-present	Victoria, Fitzroy	
Holt, John Forster or Holt, John Forster	c1825 - now		
McCarthy, Jenney	c1831		

To find research groups, your best bet is to visit a comprehensive genealogical Web site or a site that specializes in surnames, such as SurnameWeb (www.surnameweb.org). Here is an example of finding a surname on the site:

1. **After you're online and you've started your World Wide Web browser, go to the SurnameWeb site located at** www.surnameweb.org

   Scroll down to the middle of the page until you see a link to <u>Search the Surname Registry</u> (For a refresher on using a browser, see Appendix A.)

2. **Select the <u>Search the Surname Registry</u> link.**

   After the page loads, you see a column on the left with letters of the alphabet under the word Search.

3. **Choose a letter of the alphabet that is the first letter of the surname you're researching.**

   For example, say the surname you are interested in begins with the letter *P*. Find the link to the letter <u>P</u> and click it. This action brings up a Web page with a range of letters like *Pa-Pd, Pe-Pg, Ph-Pn,* and *Po-Pz.*

4. **Click a link for the appropriate letter range.**

   We want to find sites relating to the surname *Pollard,* so we choose the link with the range *Po-Pz,* which loads a page with a list of links of surnames with entries on the site.

5. **Select a surname from the list of surname links.**

   We choose the link for the Pollard surname, which presents us with two links to sites on the surname.

In addition to using comprehensive genealogy sites and specialized surname sites, there are other ways to identify possible research groups. One way to find research groups pertaining to surnames is to visit a one-name studies index. You can find a list of one-name studies sites at the Guild of One-Name Studies page (www.one-name.org) or the Association of One-Name Studies (server.mediasoft.net/ScottC/aons.htm). Another way is to look to existing larger groups that may have specific research components, such as genealogical societies. (The following section "Becoming a Solid Member of (Genealogical) Society" goes into more detail on genealogical societies.)

If you can't find an established group that fits your interests, why not start one online yourself? If you're interested in researching a particular topic, the chances are very good that others out there are interested as well. Maybe the time's come for you to coordinate efforts and begin working with others toward your common research goals. Starting a research group online can be relatively easy — just set up a Web page to serve as the central resource for anyone researching a particular topic, area, or family. (See Chapters 11 and 13 for details on how to design your own Web page.) Soon (hopefully!) others will come to visit your site, and you can begin to coordinate with them.

Becoming a Solid Member of (Genealogical) Society

Genealogical societies can be great places to learn research methods and to coordinate your research. Several different types of societies exist. They range from the more traditional geographical or surname-based societies to new "cyber-societies" (societies that exist only on the Internet) that are redefining the way that people think about genealogical societies.

Geographical societies

Chapter 4 introduces geographical-based *genealogical societies* as groups that can help you discover resources in a particular area in which your ancestors lived or as groups in your hometown that can help you discover how to research effectively. However, local genealogical societies can provide another service to their members. Often these societies will coordinate local research efforts of the members in the form of projects. To locate geographical societies, consult a comprehensive genealogy site (in the *Genealogy Online Internet Directory*) or the site of a genealogical society federation like the Federation of Genealogical Societies (www.fgs.org), Federation of Family History Societies (www.vellum.demon.co.uk/genuki/FFHS/), and the Federation of East European Family History Societies (www.feefhs.org/).

These projects can take many forms. For example, the Illinois State Genealogical Society (`www.tbox.com/isgs`) is working on several projects including creating a database of county marriage records, updating a list of Illinois pioneers, and forming a list of all cemeteries within the state (see Figure 9-4).

Figure 9-4:
The Illinois
State
Genealogical
Society
cemetery
location
project.

	ILLINOIS STATE GENEALOGICAL SOCIETY		
	CEMETERY LOCATION PROJECT		
Counties Reported to ISGS:	**Goals of this project are:**	**Counties not reported:**	**Counties not reported**
Bureau	1. to identify and locate every cemetery in Illinois. This includes those that have been abandoned, moved, no longer in use, and presently used. The cemeteries are located by county, township name and number, range, and section.	Adams	
Carroll		Alexander	Macoupin
Cass		Bond	Madison
Champaign		Boone	Marshall
Cook		Brown	Mason
DeKalb		Calhoun	Massac
DuPage	2. to indicate whether or not a cemetery has been published and the availability of the cemetery records. The information is not complete. A lot of counties are not represented.	Christian	McDonough
Edgar		Clark	McHenry
Effingham		Clay	McLean
Fayette		Clinton	Menard
Jefferson		Coles	Mercer
Kankakee	TO ADD A CEMETERY:	Crawford	Monroe
Kendall		Cumberland	Montgomery
Knox	If you wish to contribute to this project, please complete the form below and submit. You do not have to do your whole county! Just enter the cemeteries that you know! Please make	DeWitt	Moultrie
Lee		Douglas	Peoria
		Edwards	Perry
		Ford	Pike
		Franklin	Pope
		Fulton	Pulaski

Apart from the official projects of genealogical societies, there are also projects that smaller groups of members can begin. For example, you may belong to a county genealogical society and decide to join with a few members to write a history on the pioneers of a particular township within the county. If each member of the team shares the fruits of his or her research, you can cover three or four times more ground than you could by yourself.

Family and surname associations

Family associations also frequently sponsor projects that coordinate the efforts of several researchers. These projects may focus on the family or surname in a specific geographic area or point in time, or they may attempt to collect information about every individual possessing the surname throughout time and then place them in a shared database.

You can find family and surname associations through comprehensive genealogy sites (listed in the *Genealogy Online Internet Directory*), a general Internet search engine (also listed in the *Genealogy Online Internet Directory*), or through a site specializing in associations. One directory that focuses on associations is the Genealogical Websites of Societies and CIGS (www.genealogy.org/~gwsc/). Here is a sample search on the site:

1. **Start your World Wide Web browser and go to** www.genealogy.org/~gwsc/

   The page contains links to several types of associations.

2. **Choose the link <u>Family and Surname Associations</u>.**

   A new page loads with a number of links to association Web pages arranged alphabetically.

3. **Scroll down the page until you find a link that interests you.**

   You can use the buttons marked End, Home, and Top to navigate through the page.

If a family or surname association is not currently working on a project that interests you, by all means suggest a project that does (as long as the project is relevant to the association as a whole).

Chapter 10
Sharing Your Wealth Online

A fter you hit a certain point in your research, you may want to find ways of sharing the valuable information you have discovered — after all, sharing information is one of the foundations of the genealogical community. Often when you share information, you get a lot of information in return from other researchers. For example, shortly after we began the Helm/Helms Family Research page, several other Helm researchers throughout the world contacted us. We discovered that several Helm lines existed that we did not even know about. Plus, we received valuable information on our own line from references that other researchers discovered during their research.

In this chapter, we focus on methods that you can use to share information (except for placing your information on the World Wide Web, which we cover in Chapter 11) and ways to let other researchers know that you have information to share.

Why Would Anyone Want Your Stuff?

"Why would anyone want my stuff?" seems like a logical first question when you stop and think about making available the many tidbits and treasures you've collected. Who would want a copy of that old, ratty-looking photograph you have of great-great-grandma as a girl sitting in a pile of dirt on an Illinois farm? Nobody else wanted it in the first place, and that is probably how you ended up with it, right? The picture has sentimental value only to you. Wrong! A good possibility is that some of great-great-grandma's other descendants are out there looking for information about her. They, too, would love to see a picture of her when she was a little girl — even better, they'd love to have their own electronic copy of that picture!

As you develop more and more online contact with other genealogists, you may find a lot of people who are interested in exchanging information. Some may be interested in your research findings because you share common ancestors, and others may be interested because they are researching in the same geographical area where your ancestors were from. Aren't these the reasons that you're interested in seeing other researchers' stuff? Sharing your information is likely to encourage others to share theirs with you. Exchanging information with others may enable you to fill in some gaps in your own research efforts. Even if the research findings you receive from others don't directly answer questions about your ancestors, they may give you clues about where to find more information to fill in the blanks.

Also, just because you don't have your genealogy traced back to the Middle Ages doesn't mean that the information you have isn't valuable. While you need to be careful about sharing information on living persons, you should feel free to share any facts that you do know about ancestors you know are deceased. Just as you may not know your genealogy any further than your great-grandfather, someone else may be in the same boat — and with the same person! Meeting up with that fellow researcher can lead to a mutual research relationship that can produce a lot more information in a shorter amount of time.

Spreading the Word on What You Have

So you're at the point where you recognize the value in sharing your genealogical information online. If you're not, please reread the preceding section — we certainly thought our arguments for sharing online were convincing! Now, you ask, how do you begin letting people know what you have? Well, the first thing to do is come up with a marketing plan for your information — much like a business does when it decides to sell a product.

Masterminding a surname marketing plan

A *surname marketing plan* is simply a checklist of places and people to contact to effectively let the right individuals know about the information you have to contribute to the genealogy community. As you devise your plan, ask yourself the following questions:

- **What surname sites are interested in my information?** To find surname sites, see Chapter 3.
- **Which geographical sites are interested in my information?** For geographical sites, see Chapter 4.

> ✔ **What association sites (both family and geographical) are interested in my information?** See Chapters 3 and 4 for association sites.
>
> ✔ **Which general sites (such as query sites and GEDCOM collections) are interested in my information?** See Chapters 3 and 4 for some general sites.

Keep in mind that you want to use all available Internet resources to let people know about your information, including mailing lists and newsgroups, in addition to targeting Web sites.

For example, April has information on a McSwain family. She knows that they lived in Madison, Estill, Jessamine, and Nicholas counties in Kentucky. To let people know that she has information on the family, she first looked for a one-name study page on the surname McSwain, personal pages that have connections to the McSwain family, and any mailing lists dedicated to discussing the family. She also tried to find sites for each county in Kentucky that the McSwains were found in. Then she searched for family societies or county genealogical or historical societies in Kentucky that look for information on their past inhabitants. Finally, she looked for general query sites and GEDCOM repositories that may accept her information.

Contacting your target audience

After you write down the names and addresses of sites you want to target, you need to begin notifying them. You probably want to create a brief but detailed e-mail message to make your announcement. When submitting your message, look at the format required by each resource you're contacting. For example, the `soc.genealogy.surnames` newsgroups have a specific format for subject lines (for examples, see Chapter 3). Some *query sites* (places where you can post genealogical questions to get help from other researchers) also have specific formats, so you may need to modify your message for each of these sites. (For more information about query sites and posting queries, see Chapter 3.)

Here is a sample message to give you some ideas:

```
MCSWAIN, 1810-1910, KY, USA
I have information on the family of William McSwain of
Kentucky. William was born in 1802, married Elizabeth Hisle
in March 1827, and had the following children: Thomas,
Mary, Joseph, Sarah, Susan, Margaret, Elizabeth, Nancy, and
James.
```

Most people understand that you're willing to share information on the family if you post something to a site, so you probably don't need to say that within your message. Remember, people are more likely to read your message if it's short, to the point, and contains enough information for the readers to determine that you have information that can help them (or that they have information that can assist you).

Exporting Your Information

Suppose you contact some others who are interested in your information. What's the best way to share your information with them? Certainly, one way is to type everything up, print it out, and send it to them (of course, because we promote electronic methods of conducting genealogy, we don't really encourage you to do that). Or, you can use your genealogy database to export a file that the recipients can then import into their databases and run as many reports as they want from it — and save a few trees in the process.

GEDCOM files

Most genealogical databases subscribe to a common standard for exporting their information called *Genealogical Data Communication,* or GEDCOM. (Beware that some genealogical databases deviate from the standard a little — making things more confusing.) A GEDCOM file is a text file that contains your genealogical information with a set of tags that tells the genealogical database importing the information where to place it within its structure. For a little history and more information about GEDCOM, please see Chapter 8. Figure 10-1 shows an example of a GEDCOM file.

So why is GEDCOM important? It saves a lot of time and energy in the process of sharing information. The next time someone asks you to send them some information, you can export your genealogy data into a GEDCOM file to send to them rather than having to type it up or save your entire database.

We can show you how easy it can be to make a GEDCOM using Family Tree Maker for Windows, which is on the CD-ROM that accompanies this book. (For installation instructions, see Appendix D.) To export information from Family Tree Maker for Windows to GEDCOM, try this:

1. **Open Family Tree Maker for Windows.**

   Usually, you can open your software by double-clicking the icon for that program or by going to the Programs menu from the Start button (in Windows 95) and selecting the particular program.

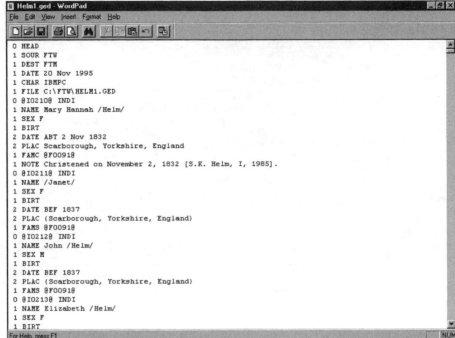

```
Helm1.ged - WordPad                                    _ □ ×
File  Edit  View  Insert  Format  Help

0 HEAD
1 SOUR FTW
1 DEST FTM
1 DATE 20 Nov 1995
1 CHAR IBMPC
1 FILE C:\FTW\HELM1.GED
0 @I0210@ INDI
1 NAME Mary Hannah /Helm/
1 SEX F
1 BIRT
2 DATE ABT 2 Nov 1832
2 PLAC Scarborough, Yorkshire, England
1 FAMC @F00910
1 NOTE Christened on November 2, 1832 [S.K. Helm, I, 1985].
0 @I0211@ INDI
1 NAME /Janet/
1 SEX F
1 BIRT
2 DATE BEF 1837
2 PLAC (Scarborough, Yorkshire, England)
1 FAMS @F00910
0 @I0212@ INDI
1 NAME John /Helm/
1 SEX M
1 BIRT
2 DATE BEF 1837
2 PLAC (Scarborough, Yorkshire, England)
1 FAMS @F00910
0 @I0213@ INDI
1 NAME Elizabeth /Helm/
1 SEX F
1 BIRT

For Help, press F1                                     NUM
```

Figure 10-1:
A typical
GEDCOM
file
displayed in
WordPad.

2. **Use the default database that comes up, or choose Open Family File from the File menu to choose another database.**

3. **After the database for which you want to create a GEDCOM is open, choose File⇨Copy/Export Family File.**

   The New Family File dialog box appears. This dialog box allows you to pick a name for the file and choose the format to save the file in (GEDCOM).

4. **Type the new name for your GEDCOM file in the *File name* field, move your cursor to the *Save as type* field and select GEDCOM (*.GED) as the format, and then click the Save button.**

   The Export to GEDCOM dialog box appears, as shown in Figure 10-2. This dialog box lets you choose to set up the GEDCOM in a specific format.

5. **In the *Destination* field, choose the destination software program to which you want to export the file.**

   If you don't know which program the other person with whom you're sharing the GEDCOM uses, leave the setting on its default of Family Tree Maker for Windows.

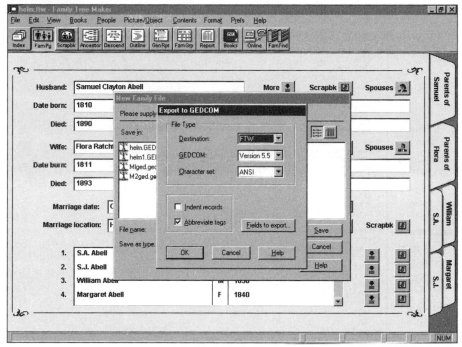

Figure 10-2:
The Export
to GEDCOM
dialog box
in Family
Tree Maker
for
Windows.

6. In the *GEDCOM* field, choose the version of GEDCOM to which you're exporting.

Most genealogical software is compatible with the most recent version of GEDCOM, so you're usually safe to keep the default setting. If you know that the person to whom you are sending your GEDCOM is using older software that supports an older version of GEDCOM, you have the opportunity here to change the output settings to accommodate that person.

7. In the *Character set* field, choose ANSI (which is the default).

8. If you have a preference for how the GEDCOM output is formatted, check or uncheck the *Indent records* and *Abbreviate tags* check boxes.

You can select to have the GEDCOM output indent records rather than writing all the coded lines in a straight list, flushed left in the file (see Figure 10-1 for an example of the flush-left GEDCOM). Indenting the records makes it a little easier to read through the GEDCOM when you open it in a word processor; Family Tree Maker indents lines based on the number code for the line. For example, all 1s would be flush left, 2s would be indented once, and 3s would be indented twice.

Likewise, you can select to have the GEDCOM tags abbreviated rather than written in their entirety. For example, the tags "Header" would be "Head" and "Address" would be "Addr."

9. **Click the *Fields to export* button to select which fields to export into your GEDCOM output file, if you want to export only selected fields.**

   The default settings do not include all the fields of information that are possible in a GEDCOM, so it's important that you tell the software to include particular fields or all fields if there are certain notes or other information you want included.

10. **After you complete all the required boxes and are satisfied with the options that you have selected, click the OK button.**

    When you click the OK button, a bar appears across the screen showing the percentage complete of the export and with the words "Exporting Individuals" listed above it.

After the file is exported to your hard drive, you can open it in a word processor (such as WordPad) and review it to ensure that the information is formatted the way you wanted it. Also, reviewing it in a word processor is a good idea so that you can ensure you've included no information on living persons and manually edit it if you need to do so. After you're satisfied with the file, you can cut and paste it into an e-mail message or send it as an attachment using your e-mail program.

Reports

GEDCOM is great when you have two individuals who have genealogical software that supports the standard. But what about all the people who are new to genealogy and have not made an investment in software yet? How do you send them information that they can use? One way is to generate reports through your genealogical software and export them into your favorite word processing or spreadsheet application, and then print copies to mail or attach copies to e-mail messages.

Chapter 8 gives step-by-step instructions for entering all your detailed family information into the Family Tree Maker for Windows genealogical software. You need to have the information entered into some type of genealogical software before you can export it to a word-processing program. The process for exporting a report should be similar for most genealogical software that you may choose. The following steps show you specifically how to export a report from Family Tree Maker for Windows to a word-processing program:

1. **Open Family Tree Maker for Windows.**

   Usually, you can open your software by double-clicking the icon for that program or by going to the Programs menu from the Start button (in Windows 95) and selecting the particular program. If you are not sure how to open your word processor, consult the user's manual that came with the software.

2. From the View menu, choose the Index of Individuals.

This action brings up a box that lists all the individuals entered in your database in alphabetical order.

3. Scroll through the index and select the person for whom you want to generate a chart/report by double-clicking on the name or highlighting the name and clicking the OK button.

This action takes you to the Family Page for the person you've selected.

For example, if Matthew wants to generate a report for his ancestor Samuel Abell IV, he highlights his name in the index and clicks the OK button.

4. Place your cursor in the person's name field.

Move your cursor into the *Husband, Wife,* or *Children* fields to select the exact person on whom you want to generate a chart/report.

Matthew would move the cursor into the name field for Samuel Abell IV.

5. Click the appropriate button for the chart/report you want (in the button bar at the top of the Family Tree Maker for Windows screen), or choose View⇨[Type of tree or report].

There are buttons in the button bar for Ancestor charts, Descendant (Descend.) charts, Outlines, and Family Group Sheets (Fam. Grp.). Or if you're using the pull-down menu, the charts/reports appear as Ancestor Tree, Descendant Tree, Outline Descendant Tree, Kinship, and Family Group Sheet. (You can generate other reports using Family Tree Maker for Windows, but these are the most common types and the five we've discussed in this chapter.)

Family Tree Maker for Windows generates the requested chart/report for the person you've selected.

For our example, if Matthew wishes to generate an Outline of Samuel Abell's descendants, he clicks the Outline button or uses the View menu to choose an Outline Descendant Tree. Family Tree Maker for Windows then generates an Outline chart/report that Matthew sees pop up on the screen.

6. Choose Edit⇨Copy Outline Descendant Tree.

This places a copy of the report on the Windows Clipboard, allowing you to paste it into any Windows application that supports cutting and pasting information.

Matthew copies the Outline Descendant Tree (or Outline chart/report, if you prefer) to the Clipboard by following step 6.

7. Open WordPad (or any other word processor), and choose Edit⇨Paste.

This action places the outline descendant report into your word processor. You can now edit the report just as if you had typed the report into the word processor itself (see Figure 10-3).

After pasting the Samuel Abell Outline chart/report in WordPad, Matthew can review and edit it there to ensure that it has all of the information he wishes to include when sharing it with others. He can also double-check to ensure that it doesn't include any information on living persons.

When you have your Outline report in a word-processor file, you can activate your favorite e-mail program and send the word-processor file to the individual who is requesting information. If the report is long, you can include it with your e-mail as an attachment. If the report is short, you can simply cut and paste it into the text of your e-mail message.

If You Post It, They Will Come

Instead of sending information to several different individuals, consider placing your information at a site where people can access it at their convenience. One option is to post your information on a World Wide Web site (see Chapter 11 for more information). But you have some other options if you're not ready to take the Web designing plunge.

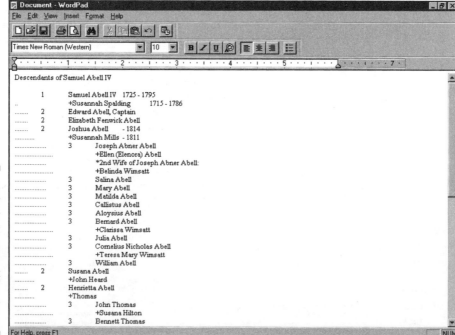

Figure 10-3: A Family Tree Maker for Windows Outline report inserted into WordPad.

One option is to find others who are working on your same surnames or geographical areas and who already have Web pages, and ask them to post your information on their sites. Don't be offended if they decline — often Internet accounts have specific storage limits and they may not have room for your information.

A second option is to submit your information to a general site that collects GEDCOM files. The GenServ system is one of the oldest GEDCOM repositories on the Internet. (For more on GenServ, see Chapter 3.) You can find a newer collection of GEDCOM files on the commercial site maintained by Ancestry, Inc. (www.ancestry.com/home/tree.htm). Ancestry maintains the World Tree, which is a searchable database of GEDCOM files submitted by genealogists throughout — you got it — the world.

You can submit your GEDCOM file by e-mail to gedcom@ancestry.com. After receiving your GEDCOM file, Ancestry indexes it and makes it available for other genealogists to download (see Figure 10-4).

If you use one of the genealogical software programs by larger manufacturers (software companies), you have a third option, which is really a variation of the first option (creating a Web page). You can submit reports directly to the Internet by taking advantage of space offered by the software company. Versions 3.4 and later of Family Tree Maker for Windows offer this option and allow you to submit reports directly to its World Wide Web site for users of the software.

Although the basic edition of Family Tree Maker for Windows which accompanies this book on CD-ROM does not offer the capability to upload reports from the software to Family Tree Maker for Windows' Web site, we thought

Figure 10-4:
Ancestry's
World Tree
collection
of GEDCOM
files.

Ancestry World Tree

Currently contains 2,624,654 million individuals and growing

Contribute your Family Tree

Field	Search	Matches
Last Name	**ABELL**	139

139 Combined Matches

Name	Sex	Birth	Death	Burial	Parents	Marriages	Original File
Ann Minerva Abell	Female	22 Feb 1822	11 Nov 1869 West Albany, New York		Parents	Marriage 1	Download original file
Zula Belvy ABELL	Female		1963 Austin, Travis Co, Tx	Squaw Creek Cemetery, Glen Rose, Tx	Parents	Marriage 1	Download original file
Ann Minerva Abell	Female	22 Feb 1822	11 Nov 1869 West Albany, New York		Parents	Marriage 1	Download original file
Joshua ABELL	Male				Parents	Marriage 1	Download original file
Sarah ABELL	Female				Parents	Marriage 1	Download original file
Ann Minerva	Female	22 Feb 1822	11 Nov 1869 West Albany, New		Parents	Marriage 1	Download original

you'd like to see how the process works anyway. So we walk through it here. Chapter 8 gives detailed instructions for entering all your family information into the Family Tree Maker for Windows genealogical software. When you have plenty of genealogical information entered into Family Tree Maker for Windows, follow these steps to export any reports you generate to the Web site:

1. **Open Family Tree Maker for Windows.**

   Usually, you can open your software by double-clicking the icon for that program or by going to the Program menu from the Start button (in Windows 95) and selecting the particular program.

2. **From the View menu, choose the Index of Individuals.**

   This action brings up a box that lists all the individuals entered in your database in alphabetical order.

3. **Scroll through the index and select the person for whom you want to generate a chart/report by double-clicking on the name or highlighting the name and clicking the OK button.**

   This takes you to the Family Page for the person you've selected.

4. **Place your cursor in the person's name field.**

   Move your cursor into the *Husband, Wife,* or *Children* fields to select the exact person on whom you want to generate a chart/report.

5. **Click the appropriate button for the chart/report you want (in the button bar at the top of the Family Tree Maker for Windows screen), or choose View⇨[Type of tree or report].**

   There are buttons in the button bar for Ancestor charts, Descendant (Descend.) charts, Outlines, and Family Group Sheets (Fam. Grp.). Or if you're using the pull-down menu, the charts/reports appear as Ancestor Tree, Descendant Tree, Outline Descendant Tree, Kinship, and Family Group Sheet. (You can generate other reports using *Family Tree Maker for Windows,* but these are the most common types and the five we've discussed in this chapter.)

   Family Tree Maker for Windows generates the requested chart/report for the person you've selected.

6. **Choose File⇨Publish Report on the Internet.**

   A dialog box appears, thanking you for sharing your information with others on the Internet and reminding you to make sure that you have already established an online connection.

7. **If you've already established your online connection, click the OK button.**

   Your Internet connection automatically takes you to the Family Tree Maker site, which recognizes that you're uploading a report. A dialog box appears, explaining that Family Tree Maker is preparing your home

page and copying your report to it. The dialog box also asks if you'd like to submit the entire contents of your database.

8. **Click the No button unless you want to share the entire contents of your database (every name that you've entered and information on each individual) and you are absolutely positive that your database does not contain information about living persons.**

After successfully uploading your data, Family Tree Maker lets you know and tells you within how many minutes your home page containing the report will be available online. When that amount of time has passed, you can follow the online or user's manual instructions from Family Tree Maker for Windows to go and view your user home page and online reports. Figure 10-5 shows an example of the resulting report posted on the Web.

Citing Your Sources

We can't stress enough the importance of citing your sources when sharing information online. Including references reflecting where you obtained information is just as important when you're sharing information online as it is when you're recording these references while researching. Not only does referencing provide the other person with leads to possible additional information, but it also provides you a place to return to and double-check your facts if someone challenges the information. Sometimes you may find that after exchanging information with another researcher, you both notice

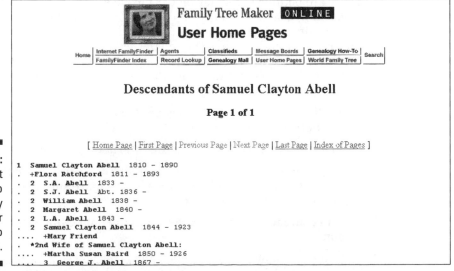

Figure 10-5:
A report posted to the Family Tree Maker Online Web site.

that you have conflicting information about a particular ancestor. Knowing where to turn to double-check the facts and hopefully find out whose information is correct can save you a lot of time and embarrassment.

See Chapter 8 for a discussion on the importance of citing sources. Here are some ways to cite online sources of information:

> ✔ **E-mail messages:** Matthew Helm, [<mhelm@tbox.com> or P.O. Box 76, Savoy, Illinois 61874]. "Looking for George Helm," Message to April Helm, 12 January 1998. [Message cites vital records in Helm's possession.]

> ✔ **Newsgroups:** Matthew Helm, [<mhelm@tbox.com> or P.O. Box 76, Savoy, Illinois 61874]. "Computing in Genealogy" in soc.genealogy.computing, 12 January 1998.

> ✔ **World Wide Web sites:** Matthew Helm, [<mhelm@tbox.com> or P.O. Box 76, Savoy, Illinois 61874]. "Helm's Genealogy Toolbox." < genealogy.tbox.com> January 1998. [This site contains numerous links to other genealogical resources on the Internet. On January 12, located and checked links on Abell family, found two that were promising.] (Of course, with a note like the preceding one in brackets, you would expect that your next two citations are the two Web sites that looked promising, and for each you would provide notes stating exactly what you did or did not find.)

While most genealogical software programs now allow you to store source information and citations along with your data, many still do not export the source information automatically. For that reason, double-check any reports or GEDCOMs you generate to see whether your source information is included before sharing them with other researchers. If the information is not included, be sure to let the others know where you got your data in some other format (either in your e-mail message to them or in a word-processor file).

Mandatory Lecture on Privacy

We couldn't sleep at night if we didn't give you the mandatory lecture on maintaining the privacy of living individuals when sharing your genealogical information. So, here it goes.

In the rush to get genealogical information out on the Internet, people sometimes forget that portions of the information in their databases, and thus in their GEDCOM files, are considered private. Horror stories exist of social security numbers from living individuals ending up in GEDCOM files available on the Internet, and from people who didn't know they were

illegitimate children and found out through an online database, and so forth. Private detectives and other people who are searching for information on living persons frequently use genealogical databases to track people. For these reasons, some states and countries have made it illegal to share information about living persons on the Internet without first getting each person's permission to do so. To avoid an invasion of privacy and any legal problems that could arise from your sharing information, you should always clean out (exclude) any information on living individuals from your GEDCOM file before giving it to anyone.

More and more genealogists are now aware of the privacy implications of online genealogy. As a result, some have designed programs to clean out information on living individuals from GEDCOM files. One such piece of freeware, GEDClean, is available on the CD-ROM that accompanies this book, (as well as from members.aol.com/tomraynor2/gedclean.htm.) Even if you use software to clean a file, make sure you double-check the data contained to ensure that the software catches everything and that you don't share any information on living people.

Chapter 11

From Your Computer to the World

In This Chapter

▶ Finding a home for your home page

▶ Getting to know and coding HTML

▶ Using genealogical software utilities

▶ Enhancing your Web pages with photographs

*Y*ou have your genealogical database loaded with information about your relatives and ancestors, and you've shared data with others via e-mail. Now you're ready to take on the really fun part of genealogy online — posting your own Web page! Here we explore where you can post a simple page and how to do so. This chapter gives you just the basics on creating a Web page.

We feel we need to warn you up front — if you are looking for detailed information about beginning and advanced programming in HTML, you may be disappointed. Genealogy is the focus of this book — not HTML programming. This chapter covers the very basics and gets you started. For more information about HTML, we recommend you check out these other *...For Dummies* books (all published by IDG Books Worldwide, Inc.): *Dummies 101: Creating Web Pages*, by Kim Kommando; *The Internet For Dummies*, 5th Edition, by John Levine, Carol Baroudi, and Margaret Levine Young; and *HTML For Dummies*, 3rd Edition, by Ed Tittel and Steve James.

Home Sweet Home

Before you can begin building your home page, you need to find a home (or a host, if you prefer) for it. While you can design your home page on your own computer using a word processor, and you can store the original there, others won't be able to see it unless your computer connects directly to the Internet. Most computers aren't, so you'll have to find a host Web server for your home page.

Commercial Internet service providers

If you subscribe to a commercial Internet service provider (also called an ISP) like America Online, CompuServe, or a local provider, you may already have a home for your Web page — whether you realize it or not. Most commercial ISPs include in their memberships a specific space allocation for user home pages. Check your membership agreement to see if you have space allocated, and follow the ISP's instructions for getting your Web page (after you've created it) from your computer to their server. (If you didn't keep a copy of your membership agreement, don't fret! Most ISPs have an informational Web page that you can get to from your ISP's main page; the informational page goes over membership benefits.) You may as well take advantage of this service if you're already paying for it. If, by chance, your particular membership level doesn't include Web space, but the ISP has other membership levels that do, hold off on bumping up your membership level! You can take advantage of some free Web-hosting services available that may save you money. Keep reading. . . .

Free home pages

Several Web sites give you free space for your home page provided you agree to their rules and restrictions. We can safely bet that you won't have any problems using one of these freebies, as the terms (such as no pornography, nudity, or explicit language allowed) are genealogist-friendly. Using that picture of Uncle Bob in his birthday suit on New Year's Eve would be in poor taste, anyway. So leaving out the photo altogether is a small price to pay for free Web space!

If you go the free Web space route, remember that the companies that provide the space must have a way to pay their bills. Often, they can make space available free to individuals by charging advertisers for banners and other advertisements. In such cases, the Web hosts reserve the right to require that you leave any such advertisements that they place on your home page there. If you don't like the idea of an advertisement on your home page, or you have strong objections to one of the companies that advertises with the site that gives you free space, it's in your best interest to look for a for-cost Web space for your home page.

For a list of places where you can get a free Web page, check out Yahoo! Free for All Pages (www.yahoo.com/Computers_and_Internet/Internet/World_Wide_Web/Searching_the_Web/Indices_to_Web_Documents/Free_for_All_Pages/). Of course, there's not enough room in this book for us to provide information about each of these companies or services (after all, this is a book about genealogy — not Web pages). So we'll focus on just three.

Tripod

`www.tripod.com/planet/membership`

Tripod provides 5MB of free space and access to its HomePage Builder utility, which helps you design and post your page. You also get chat-room access, an online guest book for your page, and a free e-mail account that forwards messages automatically to the e-mail address you specify when you register for Tripod's free services.

To join Tripod, you must complete the online form that you find at their Internet address, or URL (Uniform Resource Locator). The information that Tripod asks for in the registration form includes your full name, address and country, e-mail address, gender, and birth date. (If you would like to know more about why Tripod collects all this information and how they use it, please see Tripod's Privacy Vow at `www.tripod.com/planet/membership/signup/privacy.html`.) Tripod also asks you how you learned of its services, and you must pick a member name that you would like to use online at Tripod. After you submit the registration form, Tripod e-mails you a password to access the system and some basic instructions. (Remember to write down your password and store it in a safe place for future use!) You then return to the Tripod site and follow the online instructions for creating a Web page. (Creating a Web page is covered in the "Do You Speak HTML?" section later in this chapter.)

Angelfire

`www.angelfire.com/register.shtml`

Angelfire provides 200K of free space and a free e-mail account that forwards messages automatically to the e-mail address you specify when you register for Angelfire's free services.

To join Angelfire, you must complete the online form that you find at their site. The registration form requires your full name, address and country, gender, age, and e-mail address. Within a few seconds of submitting the registration form, Angelfire e-mails you a password to access the system and some basic instructions. You then return to the site and follow the online instructions for creating a Web page. (Creating a Web page is covered in the "Do You Speak HTML?" section.)

GeoCities

`www.geocities.com/join/freehp.html`

GeoCities provides 6MB of free space and a free e-mail account, as well as access to the GeoCities File Manager from which you can choose programs to help you create and update your Web page. (Or you can choose to submit your own custom-made page using GeoCities' EZ File Upload Utility or File Transfer Protocol.)

Joining GeoCities is a little more difficult than registering at the other two example sites, so follow these steps:

1. **Choose Family⇨Heartland⇨Join this Neighborhood.**

   You must choose a GeoCities neighborhood. This choice is pretty easy, as most genealogical pages are in the Heartland neighborhood. The system then tells you to look for a vacancy in one of Heartland's suburbs.

2. **Click on a suburb that interests you.**

   You get to roam through the blocks of the neighborhood looking for the little picture of a house with a label *Vacant*.

3. **When you find a vacancy, click on the house number.**

   You now see the New Member Application. Select the services that interest you — Free Personal Home Page Program or GeoPlus (paid-for membership that gives you Web space plus other benefits for a minimal monthly fee).

4. **Unless you want the GeoPlus service, choose the Free Personal Home Page Program.**

   GeoCities then gives you a form to complete. You need to provide your full name, address, country, e-mail address, gender, date of birth, the name you want to go by on GeoCities, and the theme of your page. (If you would like to know more about why GeoCities collects all this information and how they use it, please see GeoCities Statement on Privacy at www.geocities.com/members/info/privacy.html.) The form also asks if you want the free e-mail account to go with your home page and if you want to receive various e-mail promotions about products and services. Lastly, the *optional* section of the application asks for information including your highest level of education completed, household income, marital status, occupation, and interests.

5. **Check your information and click Submit.**

   After you submit the registration form, GeoCities gives you a welcome message with some general instructions, and e-mails you a password to access the system. Remember to record your password and keep it in a safe place!

   The e-mail message also includes some more detailed instructions and informs you of some restrictions. You can then return to the URL identified in the e-mail message and follow the online instructions for creating a Web page, or create your own Web page and return later to upload it. (Creating a Web page is covered in the "Do You Speak HTML?" section later in this chapter.)

User pages from software companies

Some software companies also offer free sites. A few of the genealogical software manufacturers allow users of that software to upload Web pages to their servers. One such example is *Family Tree Maker*. If you use *Family Tree Maker* (versions 3.4 or 4.0 for Windows or 3.02 for Power Macintosh), you can create a user home page using the software and upload it to the *Family Tree Maker* site. Chapter 10 explores posting information from *Family Tree Maker* directly to free user-Web pages and walks you through the process.

Do You Speak HTML?

HyperText Markup Language (or HTML) is the language of the World Wide Web. HTML is a code in which text documents are written so Web browsers can read and interpret those documents, converting them into graphical images and text you can see through the browser. HTML is a relatively easy language to learn, and many genealogists who post Web pages are self-taught. If you prefer not to read about it and teach yourself by experimenting, however, classes and some other resources are available to teach you HTML or code documents for you. (Chapter 13 provides information about classes and addresses to some online resources that help you design a Web page.)

For more information about the World Wide Web and Web browsers, take a look at Appendix A.

Here are a couple of things to remember about HTML.

- ✔ You write HTML as a text document using a text editor, HTML editor, or word processor, and save it as a text document (with the filename extension of .htm).
- ✔ You use a World Wide Web browser to interpret HTML documents as graphical and text pages on the Internet.

What does HTML look like?

To get an idea of what HTML looks like — both as the text document and the converted graphical image — take a look at a Web page and its underlying code. Figure 11-1 shows the low-graphic version of the Journal of Online Genealogy (www.onlinegenealogy.com/current/default1.htm). Notice that there is one graphical figure at the top (the Journal's banner), text reflecting the month and issue, and then links to articles with descriptions following.

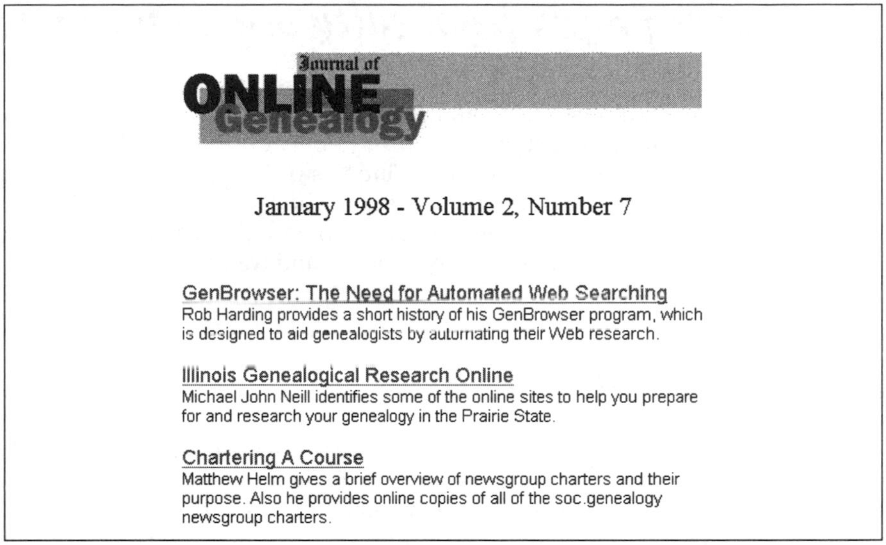

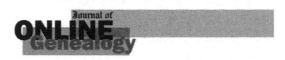

January 1998 - Volume 2, Number 7

GenBrowser: The Need for Automated Web Searching
Rob Harding provides a short history of his GenBrowser program, which is designed to aid genealogists by automating their Web research.

Illinois Genealogical Research Online
Michael John Neill identifies some of the online sites to help you prepare for and research your genealogy in the Prairie State.

Chartering A Course
Matthew Helm gives a brief overview of newsgroup charters and their purpose. Also he provides online copies of all of the soc.genealogy newsgroup charters.

Figure 11-1:
The low-graphics version of the Journal of Online Genealogy.

Figure 11-2 shows what the Journal's HTML codes (also called tags) look like. Notice that the tags are placed within angle brackets ⟨ ⟩. These tags tell the browser how to interpret the text that follows and whether or not to actually show that text on the Web page. Just as you need to tell the browser when to begin interpreting text in a certain manner, you need to tell it when to stop as well. This ending command consists of an open bracket, a front slash, the tag word, and a close bracket, like this </[word]>.

For example, in the line

```
<TITLE>Journal of Online Genealogy -- Low Graphic Edition
</TITLE>
```

The ⟨TITLE⟩ tag tells the browser where to begin treating text as a title and ⟨/TITLE⟩ tells it where to end that treatment. Think of HTML tags as on and off commands where ⟨ ⟩ indicates *on* and ⟨/ ⟩ indicates *off*.

```
<HTML>
<HEAD>
<TITLE>Journal of Online Genealogy - Low Graphic Edition
</TITLE>
</HEAD>


<BODY BGCOLOR="#FFFFFF">

<CENTER>
<IMG SRC = "../images/jogl.jpg" WIDTH = 468 HEIGHT = 96></CENTER>
<P><BR>

<CENTER><FONT SIZE = 5>January 1998 - Volume 2, Number 7</FONT></CENTER><P><BR>

<A HREF = "com0051.htm"><FONT SIZE = "4" FACE = "Arial,Helvetica,Geneva">GenBrowser: The Need
for Automated Web Searching</FONT></A><BR><FONT SIZE = "3" FACE = "Arial,Helvetica,Geneva">Rob
Harding provides a short history of his GenBrowser program, which is designed to aid
genealogists by automating their Web research.</FONT>
<P>

<A HREF = "onl0171.htm"><FONT SIZE = "4" FACE = "Arial,Helvetica,Geneva">Illinois Genealogical
Research Online</FONT></A><BR><FONT SIZE = "3" FACE = "Arial,Helvetica,Geneva">Michael John
Neill identifies some of the online sites to help you prepare for and research your genealogy in
the Prairie State.</FONT>
<P>

<A HREF = "../news/new0101.htm"><FONT SIZE = "4" FACE = "Arial,Helvetica,Geneva">Chartering A
Course</FONT></A><BR><FONT SIZE = "3" FACE = "Arial,Helvetica,Geneva">Matthew Helm gives a brief
overview of newsgroup charters and their purpose.  Also he provides online copies of all of the
soc.genealogy newsgroup charters.</FONT>
<P>
```

Figure 11-2:
The HTML
file
underlying
the Journal
of Online
Genealogy's
low-graphic
Web page.

Some basic tags for writing your own HTML

Figure 11-2 shows you what the tags look like and begins to explain how the tags work, but what are the tags themselves? HTML involves too many tags to do justice here when the main point is to create and post a basic genealogical Web page. We concentrate just on a few basic HTML tags and their meanings in this chapter.

If you're interested in more advanced HTML programming, take a look at Chapter 13. For an even more detailed read, check out *HTML For Dummies,* 3rd Edition, *MORE HTML For Dummies,* 2nd Edition, and *HTML 4 For Dummies,* published by IDG Books Worldwide, Inc.

Take a look at Table 11-1 for some basic tags and their functions. For each of the tags identified the off, or ending, command would be the same word in brackets preceded by a / (slash symbol). (We explore a few exceptions to the off rule after this list.) You must turn off tags in the reverse order that you turned them on. For example, if you use the tags <HTML><HEAD> then you would close them with </HEAD></HTML>.

Table 11-1		Tag, You're It!
Tag	**What It Means**	**What It Tells the Browser**
<HTML>	HTML	This text document is written in HTML and should be interpreted as such.
<HEAD>	Head element	The following text is the header of the document. (This is where you put the title and any descriptive information.)
<TITLE>	Title	The following text is the title of the Web page. (It should appear in the title bar at the very top of your browser.)
<BODY>	Body	The body or main part of the document. (Here, you put all pertinent information you want to appear on your Web page.)
<H1>	Heading	Denotes a heading for the page or section, and the size that it should be. (Headings come in six levels: <H1>, <H2>, <H3>, <H4>, <H5>, and <H6>. H1 is the largest print and H6 is the smallest.)
<CENTER>	Center	Center the following text on the page or within a table-cell or column.
<B>	Bold	Bold the following text.
<I>	Italicize	Italicize the following text.
<U>	Underline	Underline the following text.
<A HREF = " ">	A hypertext reference	The following text is a link to another page/site and should take people there when they click on it. (The URL for the other site goes in the quotation marks; the off command for this code is simply </A>.)
<FONT COLOR = " ">	Font color	The following text should be a particular color. (The color, written in either code or plain English, goes in the quotation marks. The off command is </FONT>.)
<FONT SIZE = " ">	Font size	The following text should be a particular size. (The size goes in the quotation marks. The off command is </FONT>.)
<FONT FACE = " ">	Font face	The following text should be printed in a particular font or typeface. (The font or typeface name goes in the quotation marks. The off command is </FONT>.)

Tag	What It Means	What It Tells the Browser
`<OL>`	Ordered list	The following is going to be a numbered list. (Use this code with `<LI>`, identified in Table 11-2. The off command is `</OL>`.)
`<UL>`	Unordered list	The following is going to be a bulleted list. (Use this code with `<LI>`, identified in Table 11-2. The off command is `</UL>`.)

You don't necessarily have to close all HTML tags. Table 11-2 shows codes that are exceptions to the off rule. You don't have to use a `</>` code to tell the browser when to stop interpreting something.

Table 11-2	Closing-Tag Exceptions	
Tag	**What It Means**	**What It Tells the Browser**
`<P>`	Paragraph break	Skip a line and begin a new paragraph.
` `	Line break	End a line here, then go to the next line to begin the next command or line of text.
`<LI>`	List item	This is a new item to identify on its own line in a list.
`<IMG SRC = " ">`	Image source	Pick up a graphical image from a URL to insert here. (The URL or address of the graphical file goes between the quotation marks.)
`<HR>`	Horizontal rule	Put a horizontal line across the page here to divide up the page.
`<BODY BGCOLOR = " ">`	Body background color	The background color of the body of the document should be a particular color. (The code for the color goes in the quotation marks.)
`<ALINK COLOR = " ">`	Active link color	Color each link on the page a certain color until it is visited by people who load the page into their browsers. (The color, written in either code or plain English, goes in the quotation marks.)
`<VLINK COLOR = " ">`	Visited link color	This is the color that each link on the page becomes after the person has clicked through to the link and then returns to the page. (The color, written in either code or plain English, goes in the quotation marks.)

You probably noticed that we use all uppercase letters in our coding, but *that is* just our own preference. You can use lowercase, uppercase, or a combination of both when programming in HTML. We prefer all uppercase because it makes it a lot easier to identify where the codes are when you need to go in and edit an HTML document. In other words, using all upper-case for the codes helps offset the commands so they're easier to find and change or fix. We also like to skip lines between commands so that it's easier to look through the HTML document and see how it's coded.

Writing some HTML

Using the basic codes we've provided in the preceding section, you can design and write a simple but functional Web page. Try this:

1. **Open your simple word processor (such as WordPad if you're using Windows 95 or Write if you use Windows 3.1, SimpleText on a Mac).**

   Usually, you can open your software by double-clicking the icon for that program or by choosing Start⇨Programs (in Windows 95) and then selecting the particular program. If you aren't sure how to open your word processor, consult the user's manual that came with the software.

2. **Begin by identifying that your document is going to be an HTML file. You do this by typing** `<HTML>` **on the first text line.**

3. **Identify your head element by typing** `<HEAD>` **on the next line.**

   Personally, we would probably skip a line and put the `<HEAD>` code on the third line so that it's easier to see where the command begins. But it's your choice whether to put it on the second or third line. World Wide Web browsers don't recognize the skipped lines in the text documents; thus your Web page will be interpreted the same whether you skip lines between codes or not.

   Remember, the head element contains the title and descriptive informa-tion about your HTML document that is going to be hidden behind the Web page.

4. **Give your Web page a title by typing** `<TITLE>Leapin' Lizard's Genealogy Page</TITLE>` **on the next line.**

   Of course, you don't really have to use "Leapin' Lizard's Genealogy Page" if you don't care to do so. Put whatever title you like on the page — just make sure the title reflects the Web page's content or purpose.

   Remember that the title appears in the top part (title bar) of your Web browser. The title doesn't actually appear on the Web page.

5. **Turn off your head element by typing** `</HEAD>` **because you're ready to begin the body of your HTML document.**

6. **Indicate that the body of your document is beginning. Do this by typing** `<BODY>` **on the next line. (If you plan to have background color, skip this step and go to Step 7.)**

   The body of the document is going to contain any graphics and textual information you want to share with visitors to your Web page.

7. **If you're going to use background color, type** `<BODY BGCOLOR = "White">` **on the next line.**

   Of course, you don't have to use white for your background color. You can use any color you choose as long as browsers recognize it universally. (Be sure to include the quotation marks!) We identify in Chapter 13 some Web sites that have links to many pages with colors, backgrounds, and graphics that you can download and use.

8. **If you set a background color and want to set the link colors, now is the time to do so. Type** `ALINK = "Blue"` **and** `VLINK = "Gray"` **inside the** `<BODY BGCOLOR>` **tag.**

   What you end up with is

   `<BODY BGCOLOR = "White" ALINK = "Blue" VLINK = "Gray">`

   The preceding code tells the browsers that visit your page to make all active links blue until the links are visited (clicked on). When someone visits a link, the browser should make the link gray when the visitor returns to your page.

9. **Set up the headline for your page. On the next line, type** `<H1><FONT COLOR = "Green"><CENTER>Leapin' Lizard's Genealogy Page </CENTER></FONT></H1>`

   Again, you don't have to use "Leapin' Lizard's Genealogy Page" if you have another headline that describes what you're putting on your sample Web page.

   Notice that we turned off the codes for the headline in an order opposite from when we turned them on. We turned off the centering code, then font color, and then the headline size.

10. **Add some text to your page.**

    Make some up! Simply type in the text using any of the codes listed earlier that you want to try. Be sure to indicate any paragraph breaks by typing `<P>` at the end of the paragraph.

11. **Type** `<UL>` **on the next open line to start an unordered list of the surnames you're researching.**

    This step creates a bulleted list that identifies names you're researching. Identifying the surnames you're working on helps people who visit your home page to know right away whether your information is likely to be relevant to them and/or whether they will have any information that may interest you.

12. **Add each surname to your list, preceding each one with** ⟨LI⟩ **and putting each on its own line.**

    List three or four surnames for this example. On your real page, identify as many of the surnames you're researching that you can.

13. **When you finish your list, turn off the list by typing** ⟨/UL⟩ **on the next line.**

Whew! Now that wasn't so hard now, was it? You now have a page with a heading, body text, a list, and maybe some background color. Are you ready for more? Then, continue! Now you can try adding some links to your page.

1. **Type in some text telling people who visit the page what is next — something like** Here are some of my favorite links. **will do.**

2. **Start another unordered list by typing** ⟨UL⟩

3. **For your first link. Type**

   ```
   <LI><A HREF = "http://www.onlinegenealogy.com"> Journal
   of Online Genealogy</A> - a free ezine with articles
   about genealogy on the Internet.
   ```

   Notice that you put the URL for the Journal in the quotation marks that follow the ⟨A HREF = command and you used only ⟨/A⟩ to turn off the link.

4. **For your next link, type**

   ```
   <LI><A HREF = "http://www.idg.com/books/index.html"> IDG
   ...For Dummies books</A> - publishers of this cool
   new book, <I>Genealogy Online For Dummies</I>
   ```

   Notice that using the proper name of a book allows you to try using the italicize command ⟨I⟩.

5. **When you finish your list, turn it off by typing** ⟨/UL⟩ **on the next line.**

6. **Indicate that the body of your HTML document is ending by typing** ⟨/BODY⟩ **in the next line.**

7. **Tell the Web browsers that your HTML document is ending by typing** ⟨/HTML⟩ **on the last line.**

8. **Save your document in text format, giving it an HTML extension (.htm). Save it to your hard drive or a floppy disk.**

   If you're not sure how to save your file in the text document format, you need to review the user's manual that came with your word-processing software. Typically you can use the Save As function under the File pull-down menu. When the dialog box comes up, it has a field that allows you to change the format to a text document. Then all you have to do is

type in what you want to name the document and put an .htm file extension on it. For example, we'll save this exercise as "leapin1.htm" on our hard drive.

When it comes time to make your real home page, you may save it to your hard drive, and then upload it to the Web server that will host your page. While you may be able to save your page directly to the Web server, be sure to keep a backup copy of the file on your own machine or a floppy disk so you have it should you need it.

Congratulations — You have just written an HTML document! Figure 11-3 shows you what your document should sort of look like.

Figure 11-3:
This shows you what Leapin' Lizard's HTML document looks like in the word processor where it was created.

```
<HTML>
<HEAD>
<TITLE>Leapin' Lizard's Genealogy Page</TITLE>
</HEAD>

<BODY>
<BODY BGCOLOR = "White" ALINK COLOR = "Blue" VLINK COLOR = "Gray">

<H1><CENTER>Leapin' Lizard's Genealogy Page</CENTER></H1><P>

My name is Leapin' Lizard and my passion is genealogy.  I just started researching my family
lines last year, but I have already collected quite a bit of information that I am willing to
share with anyone who is interested.<P>

The surnames I am researching include<BR>
<UL>
<LI>Lizard
<LI>Newt
<LI>Salamander
</UL>

Here are links to some of my favorite Web sites.
<UL>
<LI><A HREF = "http://www.onlinegenealogy.com/">Journal of Online Genealogy</A> - a free ezine
with articles about genealogy on the Internet
<LI><A HREF = "http://www.idg.com/books/index.html">IDG ...For Dummies books</A> - publishers of
this cool new book, <I>Genealogy Online For Dummies</I>
</UL>

</BODY>
</HTML>
```

Want to see what the page looks like through a browser's eyes? Try this:

1. Open up your World Wide Web browser.

Usually you can open the browser by double-clicking its icon or using the Start menu (in Windows 95) to get to your programs. You do not necessarily have to be online to look at your Web page, so don't worry about going through all the steps for signing onto your Internet service provider account. Just open the browser.

2. Use your browser's Open Page command to open the document.

Most browsers have an Open Page command under the File pull-down menu. Clicking on Open Page brings up a dialog box asking you which file you want to open. Type the name of the file where you saved your HTML document (or use the browse feature to search for your document) and hit Enter or click the OK button.

Figure 11-4 shows you what the Leapin' Lizard page we created looks like.

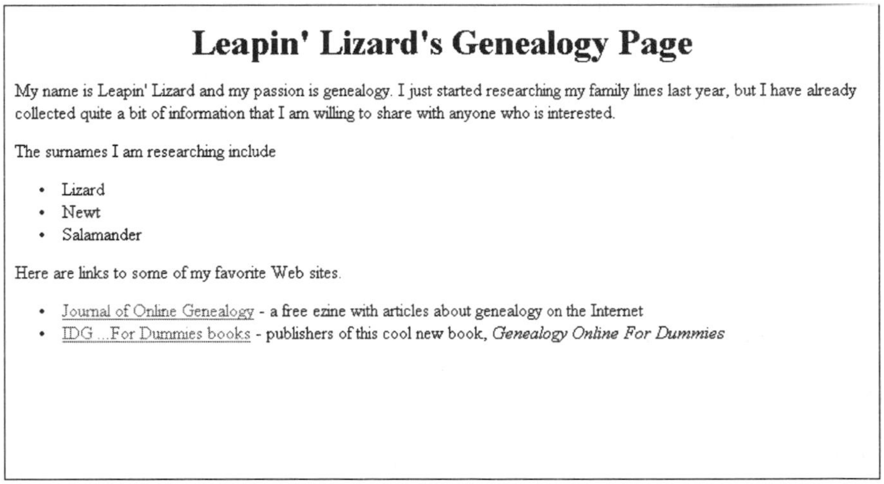

Figure 11-4:
The Leapin' Lizard's Genealogy Page that we created using basic HTML codes.

Leapin' Lizard's Genealogy Page

My name is Leapin' Lizard and my passion is genealogy. I just started researching my family lines last year, but I have already collected quite a bit of information that I am willing to share with anyone who is interested.

The surnames I am researching include

- Lizard
- Newt
- Salamander

Here are links to some of my favorite Web sites.

- Journal of Online Genealogy - a free ezine with articles about genealogy on the Internet
- IDG ...For Dummies books - publishers of this cool new book, *Genealogy Online For Dummies*

Using an HTML editor

An HTML editor is a program that walks you through HTML programming so that you don't have to learn all the codes and remember to turn them on and off. Some editors take text that you've already written in your word processor to work with, while others have you type the text directly into the editor. To tell the editor which part of the HTML document particular text should be, the editor allows you to click on an icon or pull-down menu option and then applies the necessary codes.

The CD-ROM that accompanies this book has a couple of HTML editors on it that you can experiment with.

✔ HTML Web Weaver Lite (for Macintosh)

✔ HomeSite and HotDog (for PCs)

Using tutorials or online HTML editors

Some of the sites that host Web pages for free have online HTML editors and tutorials that you can use (also for free) if you sign up for a Web page with them. The tutorials and editors walk you through designing your Web page, prompting you to pick things you want on your page and save your page at appropriate times. Then they write the actual HTML tags for your page. Each of the three hosts of free Web pages that we explored in the "Home Sweet Home" section earlier in this chapter has a basic editor. Here's more information about their services.

Tripod

Tripod has a Quickpage Builder that gives you templates to choose from in designing your home page with them. You pick a layout, create your title and headline, and pick a color scheme. You can choose to have images on your page, enter the text you want included, have a list of links and/or a counter on your page, and select whether or not to include your contact information.

Angelfire

Angelfire's Basic Editor feature lets you pick the colors and any background pattern for your page, enter a headline and pick a font size for it, choose a base font for regular text on your page, and enter a URL for an image if you want one on your page. Basic Editor also allows you to put on your page a list of items, links to other sites, free-standing text (where you can put in some of your own HTML codes if you choose to do so), and a counter.

GeoCities

The GeoCities Basic Editor allows you to title your home page, put an icon on it, add some text and links, use horizontal rules to separate sections, and provide your e-mail address so people can contact you.

In addition to the basic editors, most Web hosts give you the option to write your own HTML documents and upload them to their servers. Some even have advanced editors or special programs for uploading documents. To use any of the HTML editors and tutorials that your Web host provides, follow the instructions you received when you signed up for a home page with that host.

A Little Help from Some Genealogical Software Utilities

After learning to write a little HTML or to use HTML editors to code documents for you, you're ready to design your home page. To do this, you need to decide exactly what your home page will contain. In Chapter 10, we look at sharing GEDCOM data online via means other than the World Wide Web. Of course, you'd probably like to share your GEDCOM on your own home page. To that end, we look at getting your GEDCOM ready for sharing on the Web and how to format it without having to go line by line converting your GEDCOM to HTML manually. For more information about GEDCOM, see Chapter 8.

First and foremost, you want to make sure that your GEDCOM file is ready to share with others. By this, we mean that it is free from any information that could land you in the doghouse with any of your relatives — close or distant! (For more about the reasons for ensuring your GEDCOM has no information about living individuals, head over to Chapter 10. You can also take a look at this chapter's sidebars "Privacy" and "Copyrights.")

Some genealogical software programs in which you store your data allow you to indicate whether you want information on each relative included in reports and GEDCOMs. Other programs don't allow you to do this. You can imagine what a hassle it is to sort through a GEDCOM line by line, deleting information on living relatives if you have a couple of thousand individuals (or more!) in your database. To alleviate having to do this task, a genealogist developed a helpful little program called GEDClean.

GEDClean is a freeware utility that searches through your GEDCOM file and remove any information about living persons for you. The utility then saves the cleaned GEDCOM for you to use with other genealogical utilities designed to help you put your information on the Web. We include GEDClean on the CD-ROM at the back of this book. Here's how to use it:

1. **Install and open the GEDClean program by following the instructions in Appendix D.**

   Upon opening GEDClean, a yellow window pops up that has the three steps for GEDClean on it.

2. **Click on Step 1: Select the name of your GEDCOM file.**

   You should see a dialog box asking you to specify the GEDCOM you want to use with GEDClean.

3. **Choose the GEDCOM file you created in Chapter 10 or another GEDCOM that you have readily available. Click OK.**

   This step brings you back to the yellow window, and the name and directory path of your GEDCOM should appear under Step 1.

4. **Click on Step 2: Select individuals to exclude from your GEDCOM file.**

   You should see a dialog box that asks what you want to do to exclude living individuals from your GEDCOM. You can use an existing file that identifies all living persons whose data is in your GEDCOM. You can have GEDClean scan your GEDCOM looking for anyone with a specific note that indicates they are alive. Or you can have GEDClean scan your entire GEDCOM and look for anyone who may possibly be alive.

   Unless you have an existing file that states who should be excluded, or you've somehow marked your GEDCOM file to reflect living individuals, you should choose option three and have GEDClean scan the whole GEDCOM looking for people who may be alive.

5. **Click Option 3: Analyze GEDCOM⇨OK.**

   For each person that GEDClean finds with no vital information (primarily birth date or death date), you get a yellow window asking what you want to do with that person. This window is called *Unknown Status*.

6. **If GEDClean prompts you with an Unknown Status window, type either** living **(details will be excluded in the cleaned GEDCOM) or** not living **(details will be included).**

   Be forewarned that if you have a lot of people in your database and thus in your GEDCOM, the process of responding to each window for Unknown Status can be a little time-consuming. However, making sure that you exclude information on any living relatives is well worth the effort!

7. **Click on Step 3: Clean the GEDCOM file.**

   GEDClean runs through the GEDCOM and removes information on those people you have indicated as alive. The utility then saves your original GEDCOM under a new name (with the extension .old) and saves the cleaned GEDCOM under your original GEDCOM's name.

8. **Choose File⇨Exit to exit GEDClean.**

When you have a GEDCOM that is free of information about all living persons, you're ready to prepare your GEDCOM to be placed on the Web. You can choose from several programs to help you convert your GEDCOM to HTML so that you can place it on the World Wide Web. (A few of these programs are identified in the *Genealogy Online Internet Directory* in this book, and their Web addresses are provided if you want to check them out.) GED2HTML may be the most commonly known GEDCOM-to-HTML converter available, and guess what? We've included it on the CD-ROM that accompanies this book. Here is how to use it with your cleaned up GEDCOM.

1. **Open the GED2HTML program, which appears on the CD-ROM that accompanies this book.**

   Follow the instructions in Appendix D for installing and opening GED2HTML. Upon opening, GED2HTML gives you a dialog box asking for you to enter the location of your GEDCOM file (you can browse if you can't remember the path name for the GEDCOM), and two fields for entering options.

2. **Type the path for your GEDCOM file (for example c:\my documents\helm.ged). Click OK.**

   GED2HTML then runs a program using your GEDCOM file. You can watch it going through the file in a black window that it brings up. After it's done, close the window by pressing Enter.

   GED2HTML saves the output HTML files in a folder appropriately called HTML in the same directory where the GED2HTML program is.

3. **Press Enter to get rid of the program window.**

   This action brings you back to the yellow window, and the name and directory path of your GEDCOM should appear under Step 1.

4. **Open your World Wide Web browser.**

   Usually you can open the browser by double-clicking its icon or by using the Start menu (in Windows 95) to get to your programs.

5. **Use your browser's Open Page command to open any of the HTML output files to look at.**

   Most browsers have an Open Page command under the File pull-down menu. When you click on Open Page, it brings up a dialog box asking you which file you want to open. Use the browse feature to go to the directory where GED2HTML put your HTML output. Select an HTML document to look at.

   After seeing what your output looks like and reviewing it to make sure it doesn't contain any information that shouldn't be posted, you are ready to add it to your Web page (or link to it as its own Web page).

6. **Following any instructions from your Web host, upload your GED2HTML files to the Web server where your home page is kept. Put any links to those files on your home page so you can share your GEDCOM information online.**

   For example, GED2HTML saved an HTML-coded index of all of the people in your GEDCOM to a file called persons.html. After uploading or copying this file to your Web host's server, you can use a link command <A HREF = "[directory path]/persons.html"> from your main home page to this index of persons to share it on the Web.

Privacy

Sometimes, we genealogists get so caught up in dealing with the records of deceased persons that we forget that much of the information we've collected and put in our databases pertains to living individuals. In our haste to share our information with others online, we create our GEDCOMs and reports, and then ship them off to recipients without thinking twice about whether we may be offending someone or invading their privacy by including information about them. We need to be more careful!

Why shouldn't you include everything you know about your relatives?

✔ By doing so, you may be invading someone's right to privacy. Your relatives may not want you sharing personal information about them with others, and they may not have given you permission to do so.

✔ Genealogists are not the only people who visit genealogical Internet sites where information gets posted. For example, private detectives are known to lurk about, watching for information that may help their cases. Estranged spouses may visit sites looking for a way to track down their former partners. Also, people with less-than-honorable intentions may visit a genealogical Web site looking for potential scams or abuse victims. And some information, such as your mother's maiden name, may help the unscrupulous carry out fraud.

Your safest bet when sharing genealogical information is to include only data that pertains to people who have long been deceased — unless you have written consent from living persons to share information about them. By *long been deceased*, we're talking more than 25 years.

Uncle Ed for All to See: Displaying Your Photos Online

While the content of genealogical Web pages with lots of textual information about ancestors or geographic areas may be very helpful, all-text pages are not going to attract and hold peoples' attention. We get tired of sorting through and reading narratives, don't you? We really like to see things that personalize a Web page and are fun to look at. Like graphics and icons, photographs are ideal for this purpose. A couple of nice-looking, strategically placed photos of ancestors make a site feel like a home.

If you have some photographs that have been scanned and saved as .jpg or .gif images, you can post them on your Web page. Just make sure that a copy of the .jpg or .gif file is uploaded to your Web host's server in a directory you can point to with HTML codes on your home page. By using the `<IMG SRC = " ">` code, you can tell browsers where to go to pick up that image/photograph for visitors to your home page to see. (Be sure to type the file name for that image exactly as it appears on your hard drive or other resource!)

Copyrights

Copyright is the controlling right a person or corporation has over the duplication and/or distribution of a work that the person or corporation created. While facts themselves cannot be copyrighted, works in which facts are contained can be. Although the fact that your grandma was born on January 1, 1900 cannot be copyrighted by anyone, a report that contains this information and was created by Aunt Lola may be. So you need to be extremely careful to cite Aunt Lola as the source of this information when using her report in your genealogy.

With regard to copyright and the Internet, just because you found some information on a Web site (or other Internet resource) does not mean that it is not copyrighted. If the Web page contains original material along with facts, it is copyrighted to the person who created it — regardless of whether or not the page has a copyright notice on it!

To protect yourself from infringing on someone's copyright and possibly ending up in a legal battle, you should:

✔ *Never* copy another person's Web page, e-mail, or other Internet creation (such as graphics) without his or her written consent.

✔ *Never* assume that a resource is not copyrighted.

✔ *Never* print an article, story, report, or other material to share with your family, friends, genealogical or historical society, class, or anyone else without the creator's written consent.

✔ *Always* cite sources of the information in your genealogy and on your Web page.

✔ *Always* link to other Web pages rather than copying their content on your own Web page.

✔ *Always* be careful.

If you don't understand what copyright is or you have questions about it, you should check out a couple of valuable Web pages. Brad Templeton wrote both (and holds the copyright to them!). The pages are:

✔ An Introduction to Copyright (www.clari.net/brad/copyright.html)

✔ 10 Big Myths about Copyright Explained (www.clari.net/brad/copymyths.html)

Just as you want to be careful about posting factual information about living relatives, be careful about posting photographs of living persons. If you want to use an image that has such people in it, you need to be sure to get their permission before doing so. Some people are very sensitive (and rightly so) about having their picture posted on the Web for the world to see. Also use common sense and taste in picking out the pictures on your page. While a photo of little Susie at age 3 wearing a lampshade and dancing around in a tutu may be cute, a photo of Uncle Ed at age 63 doing the same thing may not be so endearing!

The Genealogy Online For Dummies Internet Directory

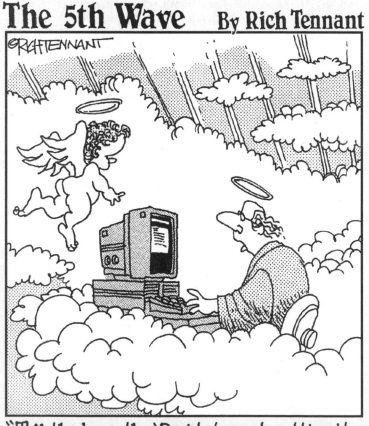

The 5th Wave By Rich Tennant

"Tell the boss the 'Begets' aren't cutting it. The people are demanding online access."

In this directory . . .

Look no further for an overview of the types of sites you can find online. This directory lists (along with some descriptive narratives on why such sites are useful to you) actual sites and abstracts of what you find at each site. Examples of comprehensive genealogical sites and search engines are provided, as well as resources that are surname-related, government sponsored, geographic-specific, or commercial in nature. More specifically, this directory has information to help you find

✔ Comprehensive genealogical Web sites

✔ Booksellers and publishers

✔ Software information

✔ Surname-related Web pages

✔ Professional researchers

✔ Hard-to-find records

✔ Search engines

The Genealogy Online For Dummies Internet Directory

● ●

*N*ow here's the part you've been waiting for: a directory of World Wide Web sites on several genealogical topics. Narrowing each section down to just a few sites was difficult because there are so many thousands of genealogical sites from which to choose. We hope you like the ones we settled on and find them useful. For each site, we provide the name of the site, the URL (Web address), and a brief description of what you can find there. Also, the mini icons (micons, as we like to call 'em) tell you at first glance what kinds of resources the site offers. Here's a list of the micons and what each one means:

Queries: At this site you can post genealogical questions pertaining to surnames, geographic locations, or research in general.

Online database: This site includes an online database of genealogical information. By online database, we mean a collection of data that may include any of the following: everything known about families or surnames, indexes, and other such collections of information.

Online records: Here you find transcribed and/or digitized records with genealogical value. The information at this site is either a transcription from actual records (such as vital records, military personnel files, census returns, and so on) or a digitized (scanned) copy of actual records.

FAQs: This site includes a section with Frequently Asked Questions and their answers about a particular aspect of genealogical research.

Searchable: This site has a search engine you can use to look for keywords and/or surnames.

Index: This site includes a section listing genealogical resources (including other genealogical sites, types of records, and information from actual records).

GEDCOM: This software supports GEDCOM, the standard for sharing data between genealogical programs.

Post to Web: This software enables you to take information from the database and post it directly to the World Wide Web.

D-4 Micons

On the CD: A version of this software is included on the CD-ROM that accompanies this book.

Book: This software has features that allow you to put together your own genealogical book containing charts, forms, photographs, and reports that you generate using the data you've entered into that software.

Online ordering: Here you can place orders for genealogical books or supplies online.

Multimedia: This software supports the use of photographs, sound, or video in your genealogy.

Download: You can download software at the URL indicated.

Charge for Services: The maintainer of the page charges for some services at this site or described at this site.

Booksellers and Publishers

Sometimes finding a specific book about a particular surname, geographic location, or event in history can be difficult. After all, not all local bookstores or libraries have the best collections of genealogical books and supplies. In fact, most of the bookstores we've been to carry between three and ten titles on genealogy, and that's about it. (Well, hopefully they've added this book to their shelves, bringing the grand total to between four and eleven!)

When you're unable to find that certain book you're looking for in the local bookstore or library, online bookstores and publishers come in handy. These online resources identify books (and other products) that they publish and/or sell, and most of them tell you how you can order from them. (Even if you can't order online from them, their Web sites tell you how you can order by mail or phone.) Following is a list of some online bookstores and publishers that specialize in genealogy-related materials. If you want to see a more extensive listing of genealogy bookstores, we recommend you visit a comprehensive genealogy Web site. (See the next section for more information about comprehensive sites.)

AGLL Genealogical Services

www.agll.com/

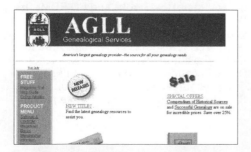

Visit the American Genealogical Lending Library (AGLL) for a variety of genealogical merchandise: AGLL Genealogical Services publishes Heritage Quest magazine, as well as retails books, charts and forms, maps, CD-ROMs, software, and other genealogical products. AGLL's Web site includes information about new titles that it has for sale, as well as special offers, online articles, and help guides.

Ancestry HomeTown

www.ancestry.com

A must-see site for online researchers: Ancestry Inc. is best known as the publisher of *The Source: A Guidebook of American Genealogy,* and the two magazines *Ancestry* and *Genealogical Computing.* Its Web site, Ancestry HomeTown, has information about books and electronic products that are available for purchase. It also has several value-added resources for genealogists, including searchable databases like the online Social Security Death Index and the World Tree, as well as informational columns by well-known genealogists. While a decent number of Ancestry's online services are free, some of their online services are restricted to subscribers. The Web site provides detailed information about what's restricted to subscribers and how to subscribe.

Everton Publishers

www.everton.com

Helpful information on getting started: Everton Publishers publishes the popular *Everton's Genealogical Helper* magazine, as well as genealogical books and research aids. Their Web site provides detailed information about *Everton's Genealogical Helper* and has a section called Everton's Secure On-Line Shopping

D-6   Booksellers and Publishers

where you search for books, CD-ROMs, software, and other products available for purchase from Everton Publishers. Their Web site also has informational sections about beginning your genealogical research, U.S. and international resources, and genealogical workshops that are being offered.

Frontier Press Bookstore

www.doit.com/frontier/frontier.cgi

Look here for a special genealogical book: Frontier Press Bookstore specializes in providing genealogical and historical books, CD-ROMs, and audio tapes. The Frontier Web site has an online catalog that you can browse by subject, as well as listings of new publications that are available and a bargain basement where you can find special deals.

Genealogical Publishing Company

www.genealogical.com/

The first place to look for formally published genealogies: Genealogical Publishing Company is a large publisher of genealogical books. Its Web site provides a catalog of books that are published by and available from Genealogical Publishing Company, as well as a listing of releases on CD-ROM. Although you cannot yet order online from Genealogical Publishing Company, you can print an order form at its Web site, complete it, and mail or fax it to the company. Or you can order by phone.

Global Genealogy Supply

www.globalgenealogy.com/main.htm

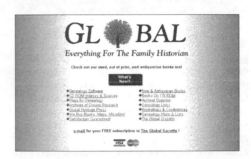

All things genealogical: Global Genealogy Supply is a retailer of all things genealogical and is based in Canada. They offer books, software, CD-ROMs, maps, microfilm, and archival supplies (items for preservation of documents and photos). In 1997, Global Heritage Press was formed as the publishing arm of Global Genealogy Supply and has now begun printing genealogical and historical books. Global Genealogy Supply's Web site provides information about its publishing house, available books and products (along with their prices), workshops and conferences, and hints for researching. The Web site also has a free online newsletter for genealogical research in Canada, called *The Global Gazette.*

Heritage Books, Inc.

www.heritagebooks.com/

$

Check out this site for an online archives: Heritage Books, Inc. publishes genealogical and historical books and CD-ROMs. Its Web site has an online archives to which you can subscribe, as well as some free resources. It also has general information about the company, online book and CD-ROM catalogs, and a list of links to other resources you may be looking for that Heritage does not carry (like photo

restoration, out-of-print books, and software). You can't order from Heritage Books online, but the site provides detailed instructions about how to order by mail, fax, phone, and e-mail.

The Institute of Heraldric and Genealogical Studies Family History Bookshop

www.cs.ncl.ac.uk/genuki/IHGS/
   Catalogue.html

Genealogical books and supplies that are British in nature: The Institute of Heraldric and Genealogical Studies Family History Bookshop is physically located in England. It has books that are geographic-specific in nature (covering England, Scotland, Wales, and Ireland), as well as heraldic titles and books specifically for beginners to genealogy as well as for advanced researchers. Its Web site includes a list of publications and their prices that are available from the Family History Bookshop. The Bookshop also offers research aids including maps, charts, and pamphlets, along with visual-aid kits to use in teaching others about genealogy.

Comprehensive Sites

A comprehensive genealogical site is one that identifies a large number of other genealogical sites, which contain information on surnames, families, locations, or a variety of other subjects. Most of the comprehensive sites have the names and URLs indexed in some manner — usually the sites are broken down into categories. Some people refer to these comprehensive sites as large genealogical *indices* or *listings*.

Most comprehensive sites are relatively easy to navigate because they categorize their links to other genealogical sites. As long as you know the topic you're looking for, you can glance through the listing and see if anything is available. For example, if you are looking for American Revolution-ary War records for the state of Massa-chusetts, you can visit a comprehensive site and look in its sections pertaining to the American Revolution, military records, and the state of Massachusetts.

Some of the comprehensive sites make searching even easier through the use of a search engine! Rather than having to look through the index of topics at the comprehensive site and then review the list of other sites that pertain to that topic, you can enter a keyword into a form and let the search engine do the work for you. Typically, the search engine returns the results in the form of a list of possible matches to your keyword, and you can pick from that abbreviated list any sites you wish to visit.

Here are a few of the comprehensive genealogical sites you can find online, along with descriptions of their features.

Genealogy SiteFinder

www.genealogysitefinder.com

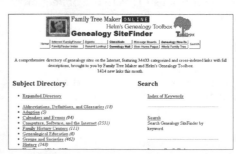

D-8 Comprehensive Sites

Let the search engine identify sites for you: Genealogy SiteFinder is a cooperative effort between the Genealogy Toolbox and Family Tree Maker (FTM) Online. It merges the content of the Toolbox with the technology available from FTM. SiteFinder identifies over 34,000 categorized and cross-indexed online genealogical sites, providing each site's name and a brief abstract of what it offers. The main directory of SiteFinder has 25 standard subjects from which you can choose. While the directory is easy to navigate, a search engine is available if you prefer not to use a directory structure to look for sites. To use the search engine, you enter a keyword (or more) and let the engine search SiteFinder's entries for you.

Genealogy Home Page

www.genhomepage.com

Visit the site that was the first of its kind: Created and maintained by Stephen Wood, Genealogy Home Page was the very first of the comprehensive genealogical sites. It classifies Internet genealogical sites in 13 areas, including Genealogy Help and Guides, Internet Guides and Genealogy Home Pages, and Upcoming Genealogy Events. Two unique aspects to Genealogy Home Page are the FTP site and "What's New" sections. The Genealogy Anonymous FTP Site is a collection of downloadable freeware, shareware, archived ROOTS-L files, and other FTP files. And in the sections called "What's New" and "What's Really New in WWW Genealogy Pages," you can find frequently updated lists of new sites on the Web or sites that are newly listed in the Genealogy Home Page.

RAND Genealogy Club

www.rand.org:80/personal/Genea/

Club members give advice on genealogical research: The RAND Genealogy Club site identifies resources that the club members find useful in their own online genealogical research. Links to the resources are broken down into categories, including reference information; historical information; regional, ethnic, and religious groups; computer and Internet; and miscellaneous. Each of these categories includes a list of subcategories. Also, the RAND Genealogy Club provides a list of highly recommended links and links to surnames, family trees, and queries.

Genealogy Resources on the Internet

www-personal.umich.edu/~cgaunt/ gen_int1.html

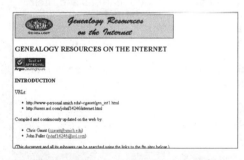

Visit here to identify sites by type of resource: Christine Gaunt and John Fuller work together to bring you Genealogy Resources on the Internet. This comprehensive site identifies online resources by type of resource. It includes sections on mailing lists, USENET newsgroups, anonymous FTP, Gopher, World Wide Web, Telnet, and e-mail. The World Wide Web resources are sorted by various topics including geographic-specific, ethnic, and descriptive. Several of the sections not only identify and link to resources, but also explain in detail what the resource is and how to use it.

Cyndi's List of Genealogy Sites on the Internet

www.CyndisList.com/

Site will send you e-mail when it's updated: Cyndi's List of Genealogy Sites on the Internet, which was created and is maintained by Cyndi Howells and is sponsored by Sierra, provides links to more than 27,000 sites of interest to genealogists. The links are categorized and cross-referenced in more than 70 categories. Cyndi's List has a personal feel — and a mailing list you can sign up for to receive notices about updates and changes to the site.

Elusive Records

Some unique records and resources can be of great value to you in your genealogical pursuits. Some records pertain to a particular group of people; others are commonly-thought of records that are just hard to find because of past disasters (fire, war, and government changes). Here are some examples of sites that fit the bill.

Adoptee and Genealogy Page

www.mtjeff.com/~bodenst/page3.html

Stop by to see resources available for those researching adoptions: Part of Carrie's Crazy Quilt Web site, the Adoptee and Genealogy Page identifies online resources for persons researching their adoptions and the genealogies of their birth parents.

Adoptee Searcher's Handbook

www.login.net/inverc/search.htm

Visit this site for all sorts of adoption information: This is a how-to site that explains the where and how of researching adoptions. It identifies resources that are available online to help in your research, including general adoption Web sites, registries and support groups, searchable databases, church archives, and libraries and newspapers. It also provides information about provincial law in Canada pertaining to adoption records.

Bible Archives, The

www.islandnet.com/~anna/tba.html

Transcribed records from family Bibles: The purpose of The Bible Archives is to serve as a collection and sharing point for any records contained in genealogists' family Bibles. You can submit information that you've found in a family Bible that has been passed along to you, along with some basic facts about the records you're reporting on, and Anna Buxton will place the information on the Internet for others to access. Or you can download a copy of the Archives (via FTP) to see the information that others have submitted.

Cemeteries in and around Gunning Shire, New South Wales

www.pcug.org.au/~gchallin/cemeteries/
  top.htm

Transcribed inscriptions from gravestones in Gunning Shire: Graeme Challinor has visited and catalogued the graves and memorials at cemeteries in and around Gunning Shire in New South Wales, Australia. For each cemetery that he visited, he includes the exact coordinates (longitude and latitude), the size of the cemetery, miscellaneous information about the cemetery or its surroundings, an area diagram, and transcriptions of the inscriptions on every gravestone in the cemetery. In all, he provides information on 16 cemeteries.

D-10 Ethnic Records

Convicts Transported Arriving New South Wales in 1788, 1790 and 1791

www.ozemail.com.au/~jsnelson/
    convict3.html

Lists of convicts sent from England to Australia: John Snelson's site has lists of English convicts who were sent to Australia in 1788, 1790, and 1791. A little bit of background information is provided for each of the lists, including the ships involved, numbers of convicts and others on board, and source of the information. The lists are in alphabetical order by surname, which makes looking through them easy and quick.

Family Links Medical Genealogy Page

www.familylinks.com/medgen/
    index.htm

Look here to find out why to use medical information in your genealogy: Family Links provides articles explaining what medical genealogy is and why it is beneficial to include medical facts in your genealogical research.

Ghosts of the Gold Rush

www.gold-rush.org/ghost-01.htm

A fun site for history of the Gold Rush and information on some people involved: This is a fun and interesting site for everyone — even those without ancestors who were part of the Klondike Gold Rush! In addition to a chapter-by-chapter history of the Gold Rush (appropriately called the Klondike Gold Rush) and stories about "Klondike stampeders," this site has a searchable database of information about individuals involved in the Gold Rush. The Pan for Gold Database contains information from many sources

and was put together by the Dawson City Museum. You can search by surname or part of a name, and the database provides a list of resources about individuals who have that name. The list identifies the source of the information, tags each of the columns of information provided, and then includes a transcription of the original information. Some of the entries have codes attached to them to indicate file sources, microfilm numbers, mining claims, and some census information including ethnicity, occupation, social status and religion.

Illinois State Archives: Chicago City Council Proceedings Files, 1833-1871

www.sos.state.il.us/depts/archives/
    data_chi.html

Index of council files: The Illinois State Archives, in conjunction with the University of Illinois at Chicago, provide an online index of the more than 35,000 files that document the Chicago City Council Proceedings between 1833 and 1871. These files, which were thought to have been lost in the Great Fire in 1871 until they were rediscovered in 1983, contain the working papers and documents of the city council. You can search this index by subject term or by date. For each record identified in the index, there is a file title, calendar and/or fiscal year for the file, file number, and filing month and date. If you find the index for a file in which you are interested, you can then use the control number to write to the Illinois Regional Archives Depository to get a copy.

Ethnic Records

If your ancestors were members of a particular ethnic group, you want to find online sites that have records and

information pertaining specifically to that group. Although not as prevalent as surname-related and geographic-specific Web sites, some ethnic resources are now available to help you. Here are a few sites geared toward particular ethnic groups.

Afrigeneas

www.msstate.edu/Archives/History/ afrigen/

A must-see site for African ancestry research: The Afrigeneas Web site is closely associated and complements the Afrigeneas mailing list, which was created as a place to discuss family history research and promote genealogy, particularly as it pertains to African ancestry. The Web site has a helpful Frequently Asked Questions (FAQs) section, an online newsletter with articles of interest to all genealogists, and surnames-related sections.

American Indian Tribal Directory

www.indians.org./tribes/

Look here to see which tribes are officially recognized by the U.S. government: The American Indian Tribal Directory lists all the tribes of American Indians recognized by the United States government. You can search the list by tribe, state, or city and state. The directory is downloadable, as well.

Christine's Genealogy Website

ccharity.com/

Here you'll find links to lots of resources on African-American research: Christine's Genealogy Website is a collection of online resources for African-American

genealogical research. You can read through the index of online resources, or you can search the site using keywords or names.

National Archives and Records Administration: American Indians

www.nara.gov/publications/microfilm/ amerindians/indians.html

Federal resources on American Indians: Here, the National Archives and Records Administration (NARA) provides an online copy of "American Indians: A Select Catalog of NARA Microfilm Publications." It identifies records and other resources that are available from NARA pertaining to American Indians. NARA provides background information about each of the government agencies for which it holds records, as well as gives detailed information about each of the types of records that are available on microfilm for the agencies. Some of the agencies include the Bureau of Indian Affairs, the Geological Survey, and the Fish and Wildlife Service. Some of the records include various correspondence, field reports, orders and circulars, fiscal records, special censuses, records relating to treaties, territorial papers, appointment papers, court cases, and military records. The site also explains how and where you can get copies of the microfilms of these records.

National Archives and Records Administration: Black Studies

www.nara.gov/publications/microfilm/ blackstudies/blackstd.html

Federal resources on African-Americans: This is an online copy of the National Archives and Records Administration (NARA) guide called "Black Studies: A Select Catalog of NARA Microfilm Publications." It identifies records and other resources that are available from NARA pertaining to African-Americans. NARA provides background information about

D-12 Ethnic Records

each of the government agencies for which it holds records, as well as gives detailed information about each of the types of records that are available on microfilm for the agencies. Some of the agencies include the Congress, General Accounting Office, Department of State, and the Bureau of Refugees, Freedmen, and Abandoned Lands. Some of the records include various correspondence, military service records, reports of operations, reports about abandoned and confiscated lands, personnel records, labor contracts, school reports, census records, and public health records. The site also explains how and where you can get copies of the microfilms of these records.

National Park Service: U.S. Colored Troops (USCT) Database

www.itd.nps.gov/cwss/usct.html

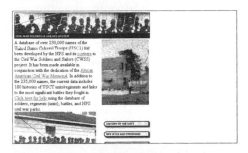

A fabulous site for anyone interested in African-Americans who served in the American Civil War: This is a well-designed and very interesting site that contains a searchable database of more than 230,000 names of the United States Colored Troops (USCT). The database was developed by the National Park Service (NPS) and its partners in the Civil War Soldiers and Sailors (CWSS) project. To search the database, click on the "Search USCT Data" button to get to the search page, then type in the last name of

the soldier for whom you are looking for information. The database then produces a list of everyone who had that last name and served in one of the U.S. Colored Troops. You can click on any of the people on the list for more detailed information, including full name, side of the Civil War on which the soldier fought, unit and company (if available), rank entering and upon discharge, aliases (also known as *names*), and the microfilm information for the military records in the National Archives and Records Administration.

NativeWeb

www.nativeweb.org/

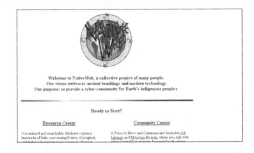

Check out this site for information about aborigines worldwide: NativeWeb is a cooperative effort to provide a community on the Internet for aboriginal or native persons of the world. The site is broken down into three main sections: a resource center, communications center, and news and announcement list. A Tracing Your Roots section is in the resource center, which provides helpful advice for genealogical research and a list of online resources to aid in your research.

Family Associations

Sometimes it is difficult to distinguish between one-name studies and family association sites because their content is usually similar (see One-Name Studies, later in this directory). However, there is an underlying organization for every family association page that is missing from one-name studies. Formal family associations may focus on a surname as a whole or on a particular branch and, as a result, the association's Web site will focus on the same. Similarly, projects that the family association is undertaking (such as writing a book or putting together a comprehensive database of information from all members) may carry over to the Web site. The most distinguishable characteristic is that the Web site may require that you be member of the family association before you can fully participate at the site or access some of the information online.

Harrington Genealogy Association

www.genealogy.org/~bryce/ harrgene.html

A site to visit if you're researching the surname Harrington: The Harrington Genealogy Association's Web site provides information about all its resources and membership. The Association focuses on collecting data on all Harringtons and those with variant surnames, and it has a collective database made up of GEDCOM files. The main communication tools are the HarrGene mailing list and bulletin board, where you can participate in discussions or post queries about any Harrington family. Also included are sections identifying current researchers, ongoing projects, and some of the Harrington branches worldwide.

MacDermot Clan Homepage

www.macdermot.com/

Central resource for those researching MacDermots: The MacDermot Clan Homepage provides online family trees and a notice board where you can post messages about your genealogical research on a MacDermot or variant surname. Also, the site has all sorts of membership information, including how to join and some of the benefits that are limited to members. Some of these benefits are an online registry of all members and their e-mail addresses, a service hosting personal home pages, and receipt of the official clan journal. Additionally, information about the clan's library contents is available, along with an online shop for products of interest to those researching a MacDermot line.

Peacock Family Association of the South

www.surnames.com/organizations/ peacock/default.htm

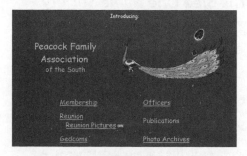

This site has an online database for anyone researching Peacocks: Regardless of its name, membership in this family association is open to anyone who is interested in the surname Peacock. The Web site identifies resources available from the association, including information about reunions and membership, photographs of some ancestors and from past reunions, GEDCOM files pertaining to Peacocks, and various downloadable files.

D-14 Government Sites

The Rutledge Family Association

www.rootsweb.com/~rutledge/

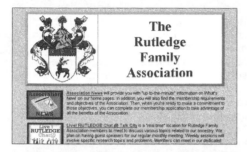

Look here for information on Rutledge families: Here you'll find information about membership in the Rutledge Family Association, as well as instructions for meeting others in the Rutledge Chat room to discuss your genealogical research. Also, you can find pages with Frequently Asked Questions, a glossary, online Family Group Sheets submitted by other Rutledge researchers, a list of association members and their e-mail addresses, and queries.

The Slee One Name Society

www.homeusers.prestel.co.uk/naylor/
slee.htm

A place to visit if you're researching a Slee: The Slee One Name Society page explains what the society is, how to join, and the benefits of membership. Two of the benefits include a newsletter and look-up services in the Society's databases. A sample article from the newsletter is on the Web page so you can get an idea of the regular contents of the publication. Also, the Web site includes a searchable index of some Slee ancestors.

Watkins Family History Society

iinet.net.au/~davwat/wfhs/index.html

An essential site to visit for Watkins researchers: The Watkins Family History Society collects and organizes genealogical information on all Watkins worldwide. Its Web site has a register where you can identify yourself as a researcher of the Watkins surname, as well as provide details about the particular Watkins line you are looking for and collecting information on. You can also search the Web site to see who else may be researching the same Watkins family line. You can post general messages or queries on a message board, and you can also read what others have posted. You can join a mailing list in order to participate in further discussions on the Watkins surname. Additionally, the Web site explains how to join the society and what some of the benefits of membership are, including a searchable database of Watkins worldwide from which information is taken for the membership newsletter.

Government Resources

If you're like us, you probably groan and grumble about paying taxes and sometimes even wonder what exactly the government is using your good tax dollars for! Maybe you are lucky and all you have to do is go down to your local library or courthouse where you find efficient operations and friendly government employees who give you the assurance that your tax dollars are being well spent. With the increasing popularity of the Internet, it is now a little easier for some of us to see our tax dollars at work — helping spread useful information along the superhighway. Here are some sites — either created by government

entities or containing government-related information and records — that contain helpful information for genealogists.

Ancestry HomeTown: Social Security Death Index

www.ancestry.com/ssdi/advanced.htm

Search the Social Security Death Index online: The United States government (through the Social Security Administration) assigns a unique nine-digit number to everyone who lives and works in the United States. The purpose of this number is to track who is eligible for Social Security benefits (sort of a supplemental retirement income) once they reach a certain age. This practice began in the 1930s. Whenever a claim for death benefits is filed with the Social Security Administration, the government adds the person's name and some other information to the Master Death Index. If your ancestors lived and worked in the United States, the Social Security Death Index can be useful in your genealogical pursuits, and Ancestry's online interface to search the index makes it easy to check and see if your ancestors are included. To search the database of over 50 million names, go to the search site (www.ancestry.com/ssdi/advanced.htm) and enter your ancestor's name. (Only the last name is required, but knowing the first name can be helpful.) Also, to narrow the search, complete any of the other fields on the form if you have that information (Social Security number, state in which Social Security card was issued, last known residence address, date of birth, and date of death). After you complete as much of the form as possible and click on the "Submit" button, Ancestry gives you a list of persons matching your search. Besides the person's name, the list includes the date born, date died, residence, address where the person's last Social Security benefit was sent,

Social Security number, state in which the person's Social Security card was issued, and date that the card was issued.

Archives of Mechelen (Belgium)

www.tornado.be/~marc.alcide/archief/
archiefe.htm

Look here to discover the types of records held by the Archives: This site provides general information about the hours and holdings of the Archives of Mechelen. Some of the records held by the Archives include birth, death, marriage, population, and parish registries, property records, tax lists, and a registry of abandoned children.

Australian Archives

www.aa.gov.au/

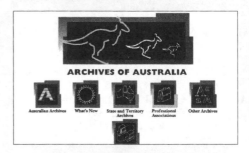

All you need to know about the Australian Archives can be found here: The mission of the Australian Archives is to preserve Commonwealth records and make them accessible to the public. Some of the Archives' services include public reference, an archival library, and maintaining personnel records of those Australians who served in World War I. The Web site provides information about the Archives' holdings, publications, exhibitions and events. It also provides the street addresses for each of the Archives' offices in the capital cities of each of the states.

D-16 Government Sites

Other Australian Sites to Check Out

Archives Authority of New South Wales
www.records.nsw.gov.au/

Queensland State Archives
www.archives.qld.gov.au/

South Australia Gopher
gopher://aa01.aa.gov.au:70/11/
State%20and%20Territory/
State%20Records%20%28South%20Australia%29

Archives Office of Tasmania
www.tased.edu.au/archives/archives.htm

Public Record Office of Victoria
home.vicnet.net.au/~provic/Welcome.html

Library and Information Service of Western Australia
www.liswa.wa.gov.au/

Western Australia Gopher
gopher://aa01.aa.gov.au:70/11/
State%20and%20Territory/
Public%20Records%20Office%20%28WA%29

Australian Capital Territory Gopher
gopher://aa01.aa.gov.au:70/11/
State%20and%20Territory/
Australian%20Capital%20Territory%20Archives

Northern Territory Gopher
gopher://aa01.aa.gov.au:70/11/
State%20and%20Territory/
Northern%20Territory%20Archives%20Service

Canadian Archival Resources on the Internet

www.usask.ca/archives/menu.html

Identifies archives in Canada: Canadian Archival Resources on the Internet provides just that — an index of archives in Canada that have Web sites. In addition to some basic information about the types of archives, this site has links to each of the archival resources identified. The various archives are categorized as

provincial, university, municipal, religious, medical, and other. Also, they are cross-categorized by region (western, central, eastern, and national).

Danish State Archives

www.sa.dk/

Discover what the Danish archives has to offer: The Danish State Archives home page is, as you would expect, in Danish. It provides general information about the Archives, its publications, and its film center.

General Register Office (Northern Ireland)

www.nics.gov.uk/nisra/gro/

Check here for information about vital records in Northern Ireland: The General Register Office (GRO) maintains statutory registers of vital events — births, deaths, and marriages. Although the registers themselves are not available for public use, you can order copies of certificates that contain information from the registers. This site explains in detail exactly what is available, how to order copies of certificates, what you must include when requesting certificates, and the costs for doing so. Additionally, the site provides some vital statistics for 1996, and the addresses and hours for the District Council Registration Offices.

General Register Office for Scotland

www.open.gov.uk/gros/groshome.htm

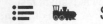

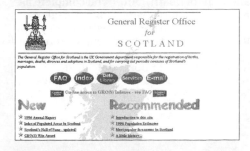

An easy-to-use site with all sorts of information about vital records in Scotland: The General Register Office (GRO) is the government agency responsible for registering births, deaths, marriages, divorces, and adoptions in Scotland. It is also responsible for conducting censuses of Scotland's population. The GRO's Web site is very well organized and easy to use. It has helpful Frequently Asked Questions (FAQs), an alphabetical index identifying records and how to use them, annual reports and statistical information about the GRO, and services that the GRO offers (including researching on behalf of genealogists who cannot visit the GRO and evening visits for genealogical groups). Most exciting for genealogists with Scottish ancestors is a recent development. In April 1998, the GRO made available on the Web a fully searchable index of Scottish birth and marriage records (1553 to 1897) and death records (1855 to 1897).

Library of Congress

www.loc.gov

Visit the Library of Congress online to see the American Memory collection: Although not officially recognized as the national library of the United States, this is what the Library of Congress has become since its inception in 1800. The Library now holds approximately 15 million books, 39 million manuscripts, 13 million photographs, four million maps, 3^1/$_2$ million pieces of music, and half a million motion pictures. The Library of Congress Web site explains its many Research Tools, including searchable Library of Congress catalogs, country studies and area handbooks, a database with information pertaining to U.S. military personnel who were killed, missing in action, or imprisoned in Southeast Asia during the Vietnam conflict, and U.S. Copyright office records from 1978 to the present.

Of special interest is the American Memory: Historical Collections section of the site. Part of the Library of Congress National Digital Library Program, American Memory provides digitized and transcribed historical documents that you can view on the Internet. The collection is divided into these categories: photographs, written materials, motion pictures, maps, and sound recordings.

National Archives and Records Administration: United States

www.nara.gov/

The Genealogy Page provides a variety of information about NARA's holdings: Briefly stated, the mission of the National Archives and Records Administration (NARA) is to provide access to evidence documenting the rights of American citizens, actions of federal officials, and the national experience. Among the resources at NARA's Web site are a couple of sections of special interest to genealogists. The Genealogy Page provides information about records held by NARA pertaining directly to individuals — including census returns, military service records, and passenger lists. The section explains how to use NARA and its resources in your genealogical research. You may also find interesting the section containing information about historical records for government agencies, particularly if events surrounding or prompted by one of these agencies had a direct impact on your ancestors and/or the area in which they lived. NARA has regional facilities across the United States that contain microfilmed copies of the records of interest to genealogists. Their Web sites (which provide their hours and locations as well as identifies resources held by the branch) can be found at the following addresses:

D-18 Government Sites

Northeast Region: Boston
www.nara.gov/regional/boston.html

Northeast Region: Pittsfield, Massachusetts
www.nara.gov/regional/pittsfie.html

Northeast Region: New York City
www.nara.gov/regional/newyork.html

Northeast Region: Bayonne, New Jersey
www.nara.gov/regional/bayonne.html

Mid Atlantic Region: Center City Philadelphia
www.nara.gov/regional/philacc.html

Mid Atlantic Region: Northeast Philadelphia
www.nara.gov/regional/philane.html

Southeast Region: Atlanta
www.nara.gov/regional/atlanta.html

Great Lakes Region: Chicago
www.nara.gov/regional/chicago.html

Great Lakes Region: Dayton
www.nara.gov/regional/dayton.html

Central Plains Region: Kansas City
www.nara.gov/regional/kansas.html

Southwest Region: Fort Worth
www.nara.gov/regional/ftworth.html

Rocky Mountain Region: Denver
www.nara.gov/regional/denver.html

Pacific Region: Laguna Niguel, California
www.nara.gov/regional/laguna.html

Pacific Region: San Francisco (San Bruno)
www.nara.gov/regional/sanfranc.html

Pacific Alaska Region: Seattle
www.nara.gov/regional/oseattle.html

Pacific Alaska Region: Anchorage
www.nara.gov/regional/anchorag.html

National Personnel Records Center: St. Louis
www.nara.gov/regional/stlouis.html

National Archives of Canada

www.archives.ca/

An online index of Canadian Expeditionary Force personnel is a main attraction at this site: The National Archives of Canada Web site states the agency's purpose is to preserve the memory of the nation and government of Canada and enhance a sense of national identify. The site provides information about researching on location and contains detailed descriptions of the types of records that the Archives holds. Among the many resources are civil registrations of births, marriages, and deaths dating from the 19th century, passenger manifests from 1865, immigration documents for people who arrived in Canada from U.S. borders, some naturalization records dating 1828 to 1850, and petitions for land. Of particular interest to those with ancestors who served in the military is an online index of about 620,000 personnel folders for the citizens who enlisted in the Canadian Expeditionary Force (CEF) during World War I. The personnel folders contain various documents including attestation and enlistment papers, medical records, discipline and pay records, and discharge papers. You can search the index online; if your search is successful, you can order copies of the documents from the personnel folder. The Web site explains how to do all of this. It also provides the locations of five Archives' sites (Winnipeg, Halifax, Vancouver, Montreal, and Saskatchewan).

National Archives of Ireland

www.kst.dit.ie/nat-arch/

Learn about the Great Famine and review convict transportation information here: The National Archives of Ireland Web site contains information to help you prepare to research in the Archives. It includes instructions for using the census returns, primary valuation (also known as *Griffith's valuation* — these are records pertaining to leased properties), and tithe applotment books (information collected in order to determine how much a person was required to tithe to the Church of Ireland). You can also find detailed information about the availability of birth, marriage, and death records, as well as wills. The site also provides historical facts and identifies records that are available pertaining to the Great Famine. The Transportation Records section provides a history of transporting convicts from Ireland to Australia between 1788 and 1868, in addition to having the searchable database where you can look for convicts by name and obtain information (such as the nature of their offenses and document reference numbers).

Public Record Office (England, Wales, and the United Kingdom)

www.pro.gov.uk/

Visit here to see what the Public Records Office offers: Founded in 1838, the Public Records Office (PRO) serves as the national archives for England, Wales, and the United Kingdom. It preserves the records of the government and the courts, and makes those records accessible to the public. Among the resources that are explained at the PRO's Web site is information specifically for genealogists. You can find general information

about the Family Records Centre (address, hours, holdings), its publications, paid research services that are available, and referrals to other agencies and organizations that may help you with your research. Additionally, there is a helpful section called Family Fact Sheets, which provides detailed information about researching a particular type of ancestor in the United Kingdom — such as one who served as a soldier, sailor, police, or one who was an immigrant or ship passenger.

Public Record Office of Northern Ireland

proni.nics.gov.uk/

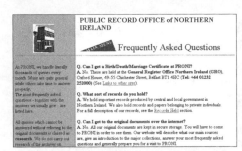

Learn how you can use the Public Records Office of Northern Ireland: The Public Record Office (PRO) of Northern Ireland is the official depository for records of government agencies, courts, and other public offices, as well as for records contributed by businesses, institutions, churches, and individuals. The PRO's Web site provides general information about the office, its resources and how to use them, publications, and exhibitions and events.

Local Connections

By now, you have probably discovered that most of the information about your ancestors for which you are looking was recorded at a local level — in the towns, counties, parishes, or states where they lived. Online sites are available that can help you whether you live near to or far from the areas where your relatives hailed. You'll want to look for sites that have a local flavor to them. They contain information and, in some cases, records that are specific to a geographical area. Here are some examples.

Australasian-Genealogy Web Resources: Australasia

home.vicnet.net.au/~AGWeb/ agweb.htm

Here you can access to links to all sorts of resources for Australian research: The purpose of the Australasian-Genealogy Web (AGWeb) is to link together and provide access to regional genealogical resources. In addition to providing links to sites that are members of the network, it links to non-member sites that have information pertaining to Australia. Of special interest to genealogists research-ing ancestors from the area is its section on Categories and Records. It is here that AGWeb contains transcribed files that you can view online or download for use. The categories include aborigines; civil registration; convicts; directories and almanacs; land records; local government records; manuscripts, letters, and diaries; newspapers; occupational records; passenger arrivals and departures; family histories and biographies; local histories; research directories and indices; shipping;

and genealogy-related. Not all the catego-ries have files associated with them at this time, so you'll want to check back periodically to see what's been added.

CaribbeanGenWeb

www.worldgenweb.org/Carib/ index.html

Links to resources for the Caribbean: CaribbeanGenWeb intends to have Web sites set up for each island in order to provide information about (and links to) genealogical resources on the Internet that pertain to that particular island. Additionally, the main CaribbeanGenWeb page provides links to some resources that pertain to the Caribbean in general.

CanadaGenWeb Project

www.geocities.com/Heartland/6625/ cngenweb.html

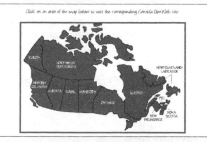

Click on an area of the map below to visit the corresponding Canada GenWeb site

Links to resources for Canada: The CanadaGenWeb Project states its mission as helping researchers find the enormous amount of Canadian information that is available through the Internet. It is modeled after the USGenWeb project and has links to each of the main pages for the provinces/territories of Canada. Each of the territorial pages then has links for county/district pages, which provide links to resources for those areas. Additionally,

the CanadaGenWeb page has a historical timeline of Canada and some facts and trivia about the country.

EuropeGenWeb and Former Soviet Union

www.worldgenweb.org/eurogenweb/ index.html

Links to resources for Europe and the former Soviet Union: EuropeGenWeb provides information about and links to the WorldGenWeb pages for countries that are located in Europe. Each of the WorldGenWeb pages for such countries then provides information and links to genealogical resources on the Internet that pertain to that country, as well as links to any state/county/province pages that fall under the particular country.

GENUKI: UK + Ireland Genealogy

midas.ac.uk/genuki/

A valuable site for anyone researching ancestors in and from the United Kingdom and Ireland: GENUKI is a service that is intended to be a "virtual reference library" of primary historical information in the United Kingdom and Ireland. And it is just that! The creators of GENUKI provide a comprehensive information service that covers all aspects of genealogy in the United Kingdom and Ireland, yet remains coherent and easy to use. Its structure is a four-level hierarchy corresponding to locality — from the British Isles as a whole down to each country within, to each county, to each parish. Its links are to sites that contain actual primary information, indices of such information, or transcriptions or electronic images of actual records. Some of

the subjects covered in GENUKI are archives and libraries, cemeteries, census, church records, civil registrations, colonization, heraldry, military, probate records, and taxation.

International Internet Genealogical Society

www.iigs.org/

A virtual genealogical society that you can join: This site is available in ten languages. The International Internet Genealogical Society's (IIGS's) purpose is to assist the genealogical community in finding new and better ways to preserve and present records and information on the Internet to share with others. This site explains in detail the services and resources that are available from IIGS. Two of the ongoing projects include an IIGS University, which holds online classes about genealogical research, and an Internet Relay Chat, where genealogists can go to discuss research and ideas.

MidEastGenWeb

www.worldgenweb.org/ mideastgenweb/index.html

Links to resources for the Middle East: MidEastGenWeb provides information about and links to the WorldGenWeb pages for countries that are located in the Middle East. Each of the WorldGenWeb pages for such countries then provides information and links to genealogical resources on the Internet that pertain to that country, as well as links to any state/ county/province pages that fall under the particular country.

D-22 Local Connections

Perry-Castañeda Library Map Collection

**www.lib.utexas.edu/Libs/PCL/
Map_collection/Map_collection.html**

Outstanding collection of maps: The Perry-Castañeda Library Map Collection at the University of Texas at Austin has online copies of various continent, country, state/territory/province, and county outline maps. This main Web page provides links to pages for several continents and countries, as well as outline county maps for the state of Texas. It also has historical maps and city maps.

SouthAmGenWeb

**www.worldgenweb.org/SouthAm/
index.html**

Links to resources for South America: SouthAmGenWeb provides information about and links to the WorldGenWeb pages for countries that are located in South America. Each of the WorldGenWeb pages for such countries then provides information and links to genealogical resources on the Internet that pertain to that country, as well as links to any state/county/province pages that fall under the particular country.

United States Internet Genealogical Society

www.usigs.org/

A virtual genealogical society for those in the United States: The United States Internet Genealogical Society (USIGS) is just that — an online genealogical society. Its Web site provides a history of the fairly new organization and explains its current projects.

USGenWeb

www.usgenweb.org

Links to resources for the United States: The stated purpose of USGenWeb Project is to provide Web sites for every county in every state in the United States. Each of these Web sites is tasked with identifying genealogical resources that are available on the Internet for its particular county. This main site provides links to all the state pages which, in turn, provide links to existing county pages. It also contains information about the USGenWeb's Archives project (where it is now storing FTP files for each state), and explains how you can become involved in the USGenWeb.

World Factbook Master Home Page

**www.odci.gov/cia/publications/
factbook/index.html**

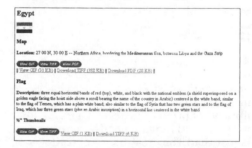

Find information about countries worldwide: The Central Intelligence Agency's World Factbook site provides information on every country and ocean in the world. The country pages are organized regionally and all are accessible from this main page. Each country page includes a map and the geographical location of the country, as well as detailed information about the country's flag, geography, people, government, economy, transportation, communication, and defense. The

pages for the oceans contain a map and geographical location, as well as information about the ocean's geography, economy, and transportation.

WorldGenWeb Project

www.worldgenweb.org/

Links to resources by country: The goal of the WorldGenWeb Project is to have a Web site for every country in the world that would contain information about and links to genealogical resources on the Internet.

One-Name Studies

Unlike personal Web pages, which provide you with detailed information about an individual's research and particular branch of a family, one-name studies give you a wide range of information on one particular surname. Usually the information presented at these sites is not constrained by geographic boundaries — in other words, the site may have information about the surname in several different countries. You will typically find that one-name studies have types of information that include histories of the surname (including its origins), variations in spelling, heraldry associated with the name, and databases and queries submitted by researchers worldwide.

Chicken Family Histories

ourworld.compuserve.com/homepages/ Chicken_Matthews/homepage.htm

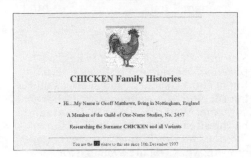

A must-see site for anyone with Chicken ancestors: Chicken Family Histories is "intended to be a focus for ALL Chickens and their descendants across the world." The Master Coop tells you about the origins of the Chicken surname and the Chicken Scratchings section has information about some better-known Chickens. Geoff Matthews, the site's creator, also provides a narrative genealogy on his Matthews-Chicken ancestors and the surnames of some of his other ancestors. The various poultry graphics and play-on-words at this site make it fun to visit even if you're not a "Chicken-chaser!"

Beard/Baird Genealogy

www.outfitters.com/~chelle/chelle.htm

Check out the forum for those researching Beards/Bairds and variations on these surnames: Beard/Baird Genealogy contains a collection of information and links to other resources on the Beard and Baird surnames, and variations. The site has a discussion group, a genealogy forum where you can post and read queries pertaining to Beards/Bairds, several online biographies, historical information about some Beards/Bairds and places named for them, and lots of other goodies.

The Gyllenhaal Family Tree Project

**www.voicenet.com/~egyllenh/Html/
treepage.html**

Visit this site to learn more about the Gyllenhaal surname: This is an international effort to collect and share as much information as possible on the Gyllenhaal surname. Most of the current information on the site relates to descendants in Sweden and North America. There is a growing GEDCOM file available for viewing at the site, as well as information on the surname and Coats of Arms. You can also find online biographies and photographs of some Gyllenhaals, and transcriptions (in Swedish and English) of the letter ennobling Nils Gunnarsson Gyllenhaal in 1672.

Kelton Family HomePage

**rampages.onramp.net/~ekelton/
index.html**

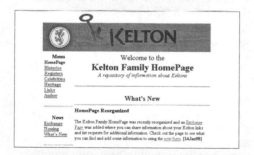

A repository for information on the Kelton surname: The Kelton Family HomePage is intended to serve as a repository for any information pertaining to families with the surname Kelton. It has an exchange section where you can post questions and general information about your Kelton ancestors, along with your e-mail address so that others may contact you directly.

Additionally, it has sections with histories about some Kelton families, family registers, stories about some famous Keltons and contemporary naming patterns, and links to other sites of interest to those researching the Kelton name. This site is easy to navigate and has online forms you can use to submit any information you have on Kelton ancestors.

Maule Family History Home Page

www.maule.u-net.com/home~1.htm

Check out the variety of information here on the Maule family: The Maule Family History Home Page has historical information about the origins of the surname and histories of the families in various countries, as well as information about some of the Coats of Arms. A research page has information about the family, queries and responses to queries, and a place to post messages when you are looking for particular long-lost Maules. You can also find biographies of several Maule ancestors and an index of personal information about male Maules born prior to 1900 (first name, date of birth, date of death, and places in which he lived).

Thompson One Name Study

www.geocities.com/Athens/2249/

Look here to read online histories of some Thompsons: The Thompson One Name Study site focuses on collecting and making available for users information about all Thompsons (and variations of the surname) in northeast England. The site includes some downloadable records for some Thompsons from the United Kingdom, as well as information about the origins of the surname, Coats of Arms,

the one-name study project in general, and researchers of the Thompsons. You can also find several online histories of various Thompsons.

Walsh Family Genealogy

pw2.netcom.com/~walshdw/index.html

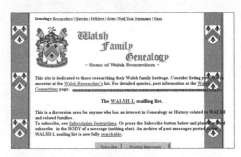

Information about Walshes all over the world: Walsh Family Genealogy is a site dedicated to sharing information about the Walsh surname and families world-wide. You can register as a researcher and identify the Walsh ancestors you are looking for information about, post messages and queries about your research, and join the Walsh-L mailing list to participate in discussions. The site also has sections with some online Walsh family trees, searchable indices and lists of information (cemetery, marriage, passenger lists, and land records), and information about the origins of the surname and Coats of Arms.

Wilkinsons on the Web

www.wilkinsons.com/Wilkinsons.html

Site has a variety of information on Wilkinsons: Here you can find a central-ized location for genealogists researching the Wilkinson surname to come together and share information. The Genealogy Page of the Wilkinsons site explains how

you can use the site and contribute to it. It includes a database of Wilkinsons and related families, a list of documents of interest to those researching the name, information about the origins of the name, and links to other Internet re-sources pertaining to Wilkinsons. The list of documents includes notes for each document indicating whether someone else has a copy of it and is willing to look up information for you. The site also has sections with information about the Coat of Arms, names and e-mail addresses of Wilkinsons who are on the Internet, announcements of interest to Wilkinson researchers, and an online transcription of William Augustus Wilkinson's diary.

Personal Web Sites

Personal Web sites usually provide information about an individual's or family's specific research interests, and they are the most common type of surname-related sites you will find. Generally, a personal Web site has information about a particular branch of a family. The format and presentation of this information can vary greatly. Some personal Web pages merely list the surnames that the site maintainer is researching; others contain the GEDCOM file of the site maintainer. And others have narrative histories about the family and areas in which they lived.

Given that there are thousands and thousands of personal Web pages, we had a difficult time narrowing our choices for this directory. A lot of good personal pages contain detailed and useful infor-mation. We chose these sites because they each provide a variety of information about the maintainer's interests and research, they are well-organized and easy to use, and they show that the

maintainer cares a lot about genealogical research and sharing information with others.

The Ashworth Family Page

www.murrah.com/gen/ashworth.htm

Visit this site for information about Melungeons, Lumbee Indians, and Red-bones: The Ashworth Family Page provides a narrative about the descendants of James Ashworth of Craven County, South Carolina. Included in the narrative are the surnames of some other families that married into the Ashworths, information about the Ashworths' role in the American Revolution, and their moves to South Carolina, Louisiana, and Texas. The controversy surrounding the Ashworths' race provides for very interesting reading at this site! There are excellent explanations of and references to other sites with more information about Melungeons, Lumbee Indians, and Redbones.

Brigette's Genealogy

www.geocities.com/Heartland/1590/ genalogy.htm

A site to check out if you have Lynn/Linn ancestors: Brigette's Genealogy page is broken down into many areas related to her personal research. She has several sections on her Lynn/Linn family research in which she provides a lot of information that she has collected. Her hope is that sharing what she has will encourage you to contact her (if you have information about the Lynns/Linns in the counties she's identified, of course), and you can work together to research further. Her site also includes sections that have information about Lynn/Linn lines that she is not researching but about which others have contacted her — including information about a Lynn Family Newsletter and links to other Web pages.

Chenoweth Family Site

www.accessone.com/~jegge/ chenweth.htm

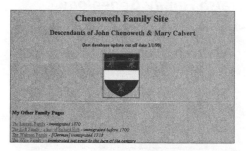

Check out the database of descendants from John Chenoweth and Mary Calvert: This site has extensive resources on the Chenoweth family, including an online database of the descendants of John Chenoweth and Mary Calvert, and some descendant reports, too. You can find background information on the genealogy itself and the Coat of Arms, discussions about disputes among researchers over information that is presented online, and explanations of areas in which John Egge (the site creator) is looking for information. The site also has sections with specific information about Chenoweths who served in the Civil War and other wars. You can find snail mail (regular mail) and e-mail addresses for other researchers interested in Chenoweths. We found it quite nice to see that there's a section that graciously cites the sources of the information contained on the Web site.

Jeff Alvey Genealogy and Other Good Stuff

www.fred.net/jefalvey/

Visit this site for information about heraldry: Jeff Alvey shares an index of the persons contained in his genealogical

database, as well as historical information about various Alveys and the origins of the surname. Two unique resources at this site are an informative section about heraldry and an index of names that appear in the book, *The Chronicles of Newgate*, which has information about inmates and others associated with the Newgate prison in London.

The Mabry Family

www.execpc.com/~dcollins/mabry.html

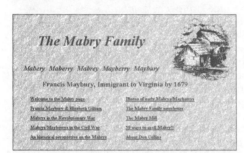

Read here about the Mabry family in America: Don Collins, the creator of the Mabry Family Web site, shares with you lots of information about the Mabry (and various spellings) family in America. The site has a list of descendants of Francis Maybury and Elizabeth Gilliam, who were married in Virginia in 1685. It also has information about various Mabrys who fought in the American Revolution and Civil War, a chronology of events in which Mabrys were involved, information about the Mabry Family newsletter, and several online photographs of Mabrys. You can also find a list of various spellings of the surname and a history of the Mabry Mill in Virginia, as well as several resources to help you research your Mabry family — including queries, a list of books, and a schedule of family reunions.

McCutchan

www.mccutchan.org/

Check out the information about descendants from Samuel McCutchen: In addition historical narrative about the migration of McCutchans from Scotland to Ireland to the United States, the McCutchan genealogy Web site contains information about the various spellings of the surname and one of the family tartans. The site also includes descendant charts for Samuel McCutchen and some of the other family lines that Bill McCutchan, the site's creator, is researching. Additionally, there is an online photo album, a guest book where you can post messages (including messages with information about the McCutchan line you are researching), and links to other sites of interest to those researching the McCutchan surname.

Mike Schwitzgebel's Genealogy Pages

genealogy.org:80/~mschwitz/

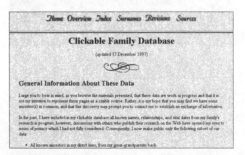

Look here for information about Schwitzgebel research: In addition to sharing a GED2HTML copy of his GEDCOM file, Mike Schwitzgebel has an online photo album and information about the origins of his surname, a Coat of Arms, and an international family reunion being planned for the year 2000.

D-28 Professional Researchers

He also identifies the main goals of his current research for you to review to see if you have any information that may help him and other researchers. We were impressed with Mike's open and gracious acknowledgments of the work by other researchers from whom he's received information about the Schwitzgebels. This is an excellent example of citing one's sources and giving credit where credit is due!

Nafzger Genealogy Home Page

sailfish.exis.net/~tjnoff/

Here you can see some reports of Nafzger family lines: Jay Noffsinger, the site's maintainer, shares some of his Nafzger (and related surnames) genealogy with you in the form of online versions of his two books, an online photo album, and reports containing information from his genealogical database. He also provides a guest book where you can register and indicate the Nafzger line that you are researching.

Professional Researchers

There may come a time when you need to hire a professional researcher to pursue your genealogy of a particular family line. Maybe you have exhausted all your leads on that family line, or you no longer have the time to devote to research, or the records you need are in a distant land and you have neither the time nor the money to travel there just to look for paper. A lot of research services are available — some from reputable companies, others from individuals who just want to help others.

The following is a list of just a few professional research services that are available in different parts of the world.

Chapter 4 provides more information about professional researchers and being careful when choosing one, and it walks you through how to find a list of professional researchers in a particular area where you need research done.

A+ Genealogy Research Service

www.genealogy-research.com/

$

Read about A+ Genealogy Research Service's one-week option: A+ Genealogy Research Service offers services in the United States and Canada. Their Web site provides detailed information about the services they offer, the costs of their services, records they use to look up information, and what you can expect to get in a final report from them (including charts). A+ offers a "one-week option" to help you decide whether it is worth hiring them to research for you. In the "one-week option," A+ researchers do a cursory review of some records and files looking for your ancestor's name. If they find quite a bit of information and believe you will benefit from their services, they tell you so in their report. Likewise, if they don't find much on your ancestor and are afraid that their services won't be beneficial to you, they report that, as well. For more specific information about their "one-week option" report, visit their Web site.

Adelaide proformat

www.users.on.net/proformat/ jaunay.html

$

Research help in Australia, the United Kingdom, Europe, and North America: Adelaide proformat was formed in 1994. Although Adelaide proformat specializes in helping Australians with their genealogical research and researching Australian

resources for those who do not live there or cannot travel there to do their own research, they offer research services in the United Kingdom, Europe, and North America, as well. Adelaide proformat offers services consulting and researching, looking for documents, preparing family histories, and drawing family trees.

Family Tree Genealogical and Probate Research Bureau Ltd.

www.familytree.hu/

$

Research help in the former Austro-Hungarian empire: Family Tree Genealogical and Probate Research Bureau Ltd. was formed in Hungary in 1988. Their researchers work in Hungary, Slovakia, Austria (Burgenland), Transylvania (part of Romania), Croatia, Slovenia, former Yugoslavia (Banat), and the Ukraine (Sub-Carpathia). In addition to explaining how they research, their Web site explains how historical Hungary varies from contemporary Hungary and how that affects genealogical research in the area; the site also provides details about Jewish genealogy and probate searches in the area. Family Tree also offers a service called Root Tours, where they arrange for you (and a group if you'd like) to tour the countries in the former Austro-Hungarian Empire and conduct your own genealogical research.

Garrison Communications

iccu6.ipswich.gil.com.au/comm/garrison/

$

Research help in Australia, England, Scotland, and Wales: Garrison Communications offers research services in Queensland, Australia and England, Scotland, and Wales. Their Web site explains exactly where they conduct their research into your ancestry, what types

of records are available, and the costs for various research services. Garrison Communications also offers publishing services on the Internet in which they design a genealogical home page for you.

Lineages, Inc.

www.lineagesnet.com/catalog/
 services.asp

$

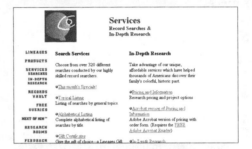

Research help in the United States: Lineages, Inc. was founded in 1983 to provide genealogical research services and products nationwide in the United States. The Lineages Web site provides detailed information about using their research services, including what you can expect upon hiring them to the costs of their services. One of the things you can expect if you do hire them to conduct some research for you is an extensive report explaining how they researched your ancestors, copies of records they used, and ancestry charts and family group sheets reflecting your line of descent.

Molander's Genealogy Service

www.algonet.se/~family/

$

Research help in Norway and Sweden: Molander's Genealogy Service helps you trace your family in Sweden and/or Norway. Molander's services include

conducting look-ups in church records and other written sources, as well as at archives in the area, and supplying to you detailed information about the community in which your ancestors lived and the people with whom they associated. Although Molander's Web site provides basic information about their services, you have to contact them directly by mail or phone (at the address and phone number provided on their Web site) for more information and the costs of their services.

Scottish Family Research

www.linnet.co.uk/linnet/tour/
   67015.htm

$

Research help in Scotland: Scottish Family Research uses base information that you provide (birth, marriage, or death details about a Scottish ancestor) and researches many genealogical sources in Scotland to put together a report for you. Their service includes using civil registrations, census returns, and old parish registers. The Scottish Family Research home page provides detailed information about their services, what information about your ancestor is initially required, costs of their services, and what you can expect to get in the report.

Threshold Concepts, Inc.

www.xmission.com/~tconcept/
   genhome.htm

$

Research help in the United States: Threshold Concepts, Inc. specializes in research services in Salt Lake City, Utah and Washington, D.C. Their Web site explains what research services they offer, as well as their other services: restoring and preserving photographs and documents, and preparing and publishing family histories, among others. Their Web site includes the costs for each of their services.

Search Engines

You've probably been hearing about the Big Guys (the major search engines, that is) ever since you first thought about going online. Search engines are programs that search large indices of information gathered by robots (sometimes called *spiders*) that are sent out to catalog resources on the Internet. Typically, the search engine has an interface form where you can enter keywords to search for in the search engine's index. The engine then runs a search of its index and returns its findings to you online with links directly to the pages where the search engine's robot identified the keywords.

Although we don't recommend starting your online genealogical research using one of the major search engines (please review Chapter 3 for the reasons), we recognize that if you hit a brick wall in your research, a search engine may be the only place left to go for some leads. Maybe the comprehensive sites didn't identify enough resources pertaining to a particular religious or ethnic group, and the searchable genealogical pages had only surname information, so where do you turn? To the Big Guys, of course.

We have a couple of recommendations for you before you take the plunge and conduct a search on one or more of the major search engines. Because it is likely that a search on one name or word will result in thousands — even hundreds of thousands — of results, we recommend that you follow the particular engine's instructions for narrowing your search. Typically, this means using more than one word in your search and avoiding really common words altogether. (For instance, you don't want to include "the," "a," and "of" in your search, or you will get an unmanageable number of results if the

search engine doesn't automatically ignore those words.) For each of the search engines identified here, we've tried to provide the instructions for narrowing your search, as well as identify any quirks about the particular engine that we think are helpful. However, it is still a good idea for you to review the information that the search engine site provides online because we may have missed some points that can make your search even more successful!

AltaVista

www.altavista.digital.com

Using tabs at the top of the search box in AltaVista, you can choose to use different parts of the site, including a subject directory of the database, people search, business search, and a translator (where you can have a phrase or URL that you type into a form translated into another language). The directory of subjects has titles such as society and politics, people and chat, and hobbies and interests. From the subject listing, you can select from sub-menus until you find the topic you are looking for. Or, if you prefer, you can just put keywords in the search form to have the search engine look through AltaVista's index of Web sites for possible matches.

AltaVista allows you to search its index in a variety of ways. You can use keywords, phrases, or questions, as well as require (by using a plus sign: +) or exclude (by using a minus sign: –) certain words and look for "wildcard" words (by using an asterisk: *). Also, it lets you look for exact phrases (by using quotation marks), search its entire database of identified Web sites, limit your search to just Usenet newsgroup postings for the most recent two weeks, or limit your search to sites written in particular languages. Unless you are looking for case-sensitive words, AltaVista recommends that you type all

words in lowercase for better search results. For information about AltaVista's special function searches and use of special and multinational characters, visit its Help section.

Lycos

www.lycos.com

Lycos has a guide in which it categorizes sites that have been identified by its robot, as well as has a search engine that looks through the entire Lycos database of identified World Wide Web sites or just sites that you specify. The guide is divided up by common topics, such as entertainment, government, home/garden, people, and travel. You can click through the subjects and their sub-menus to get down to sites of interest. Or you can use the search engine to look for keywords.

Lycos recommends that you use carefully selected words when using the search engine in order to control the number of results you get. Also, Lycos supports using phrases (you put the exact phrase in quotation marks), excluding words (you use a minus sign: –), and requiring certain words (you use a plus sign: +). After Lycos has generated a list of search results, you can "search the search," which creates a subset of sites taken from the original search results, or have Lycos show you only those sites for which your keyword appears in the title.

Lycos has Web pages hosted in several countries: the United States, Germany, the United Kingdom, France, the Netherlands, Italy, Switzerland, Belgium, Sweden, and Spain. Hence, if you so desire, you can access Lycos where the text is a language other than English.

D-32 Search Engines

Infoseek

www.infoseek.com

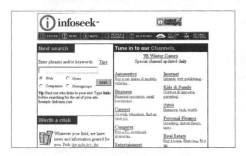

Infoseek has a directory of Web sites included in its database that you can click through using "channels" (or subjects in the directory) like the good life, kids and family, and travel. You can choose from the channels to get to sub-menus, where you can select more specific topics on down to links to actual sites. Or you can use the search engine to look for particular keywords in the Infoseek database.

Infoseek's help section for conducting searches is called "Tips." It explains that Infoseek supports simple word searches as well as searches with required words (you use a plus sign: +), words of lesser importance (you use a minus sign: –), and exact phrases (you use quotation marks). You can choose to search Infoseek's entire Web database, or just sections with information about news, companies, and newsgroups. Infoseek's advanced searches include searching within a search, looking for your keyword(s) in the titles or URLs of sites, identifying all pages within a Web site, or finding Web sites with similar topics to your keyword.

If you speak French, you're in luck! Infoseek is available in French, in addition to English. All you have to do is click on the "Infoseek speaks French!" link in the new search box on Infoseek's main page.

WebCrawler

www.webcrawler.com/

WebCrawler has a menu of subjects from which you can choose to find information on a particular topic. WebCrawler calls the subjects "channels." You click on a particular channel (such as computers and Internet, entertainment, and home and family) to get to get to a sub-menu, where you can select more specific topics, on down to links to actual sites. Or you can use the search engine to look for particular keywords in the WebCrawler database.

WebCrawler supports simple word searches, as well as searches with required words (you use a + or the word AND), excluding words (you use a – or the word NOT), and exact phrases (you use quotation marks). It also has an advanced feature where you can clarify whether to include or exclude multiple words by using parentheses.

The WebCrawler, which is a service of Excite, Inc. has links to Excite search engines in Australia, France, Germany, Japan, the Netherlands, Sweden, and the United Kingdom.

Excite

www.excite.com

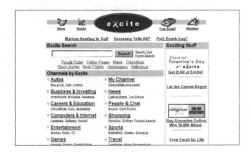

Excite has a directory of "channels" (or subjects) from which you can choose to look for sites of interest to you. Like the other search engines with directories, you click on the subject of interest which

takes you to a sub-menu where you can select a more specific topic to get down to links to actual sites on that topic. Some of Excite's channels include computers and Internet, lifestyle, and people and chat. Or you can use the search engine to look for particular keywords in Excite's databases of Web sites.

The Excite search engine uses something called Intelligent Concept Extraction to find relationships between the keyword(s) that you enter and other words or concepts. So instead of getting results that have only your keywords, you get results for your keywords plus any words that Excite thinks are related to those keywords. You can search Excite's database of World Wide Web sites, its Web guide (which is a database of sites selected as the best of their kind by Excite personnel), NewsTracker, City.Net, and the Usenet newsgroups. The results of your search are ranked in order of relevancy — which means Excite tells you that it thinks a particular site is a certain percent relevant to what you're looking for. Excite supports plain word searches, as well as searches with required (you use a plus sign: +) or excluded (you use a minus sign: –) words, and searches for exact phrases (you use quotation marks). It also supports Boolean Operator searches where you can use the words AND, NOT, OR, and parentheses to indicate to the search engine to include or exclude certain types of sites and words.

Excite has Web pages hosted in several countries: the United States, Australia, France, Germany, Japan, the Netherlands, Sweden, and the United Kingdom. So you can use the engine in languages other than English if you so desire.

HotBot

www.hotbot.com

In addition to the search engine part, the HotBot site has a directory, called Cybrarian, from which you can choose

topics of interest to click your way down to Web sites about those topics. However, the directory does not include all the World Wide Web sites that are indexed in HotBot's database. Rather, the directory has only a listing of sites that the Wired editors think are the best on those particular topics.

The HotBot search engine allows you to search indices of its database including information on all identified World Wide Web sites, Usenet newsgroups, top new sites, businesses, people, e-mail addresses, classified advertisements, domain names, stocks, discussion groups, and shareware. HotBot's search form is really easy to use as you don't have to remember to use + and – to include or exclude words, or quotation marks to look for an exact match to a phrase. Instead, HotBot has a pull-down menu that gives you all your options for the search. You can specify whether you want HotBot to look for sites by date, continent, and/or to include certain media (such as images, audio, video, or shockwave). Also, you tell HotBot how you want to see the results of your search — the number of results to view at one time and how much information to include. If the basic HotBot search does not do the trick for you, you can use HotBot's SuperSearch, which is a more advanced system for searching.

Searchable Pages

Searchable genealogical pages are just what they sound like — they are Web sites where you can search for a particular keyword by using a search engine or by following a hierarchical menu through the site to the information you are looking for. Generally, searchable pages are relatively easy to navigate because they have a search field that is readily apparent, or they have clear instructions for

D-34 Searchable Pages

using the hierarchy. Most searchable pages are surname-related or contain queries (about surnames, particular families, or geographic-areas). Here are a few that you may wish to examine.

FamilyFinder Index

www.familytreemaker.com/ffitop.html

Search 147 million names: Family Tree Maker's FamilyFinder Index is a database of names that is searchable online. It contains over 147 million names from census records, marriage records, Social Security death records, family trees, and various other sources. Each entry in the index includes the person's last name, first name, estimated dates, location, and archive type (the type of resource from which the information was taken). The archive type links you to more information about obtaining a copy of the particular resource. You can search the FamilyFinder entries one of three ways. First, you can use the "Search Expert" form, where you insert a name in a field and then click search to see if that name is in FamilyFinder. Second, you can scroll through the list of names (alphabetical by last name) by clicking on the "Previous Page" or "Next Page" buttons. Or third, you can enter the name you are looking for in a field below the list and scroll directly to the part of the alphabet where that name would appear.

Gendex

www.gendex.com/gendex/

An index of some five million names: Gendex is a site with a server that indexes hundreds of World Wide Web pages containing genealogical data. The index contains some five million names and brief biographical information about those persons for whom the information

is available. The biographical information includes dates and places of birth and death. The entries also include contact information for the individuals who registered the Web sites from which the data was obtained, and links to the actual sites. You can use the Gendex search engine to search the database by surname, or you can click through the alphabet to find surnames. Access to use Gendex is available on two levels: unregistered users (free access) and registered users (pay for use). Registered users are given priority access for searching Gendex, search filters that enable them to customize their searches, and the ability to modify how the data resulting from a search is displayed on their computers.

GeneaNet: Genealogical Database Network

www.geneanet.org/

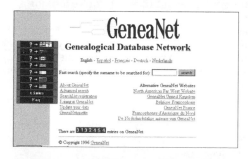

Search a database that identifies surname and location information worldwide: GeneaNet is dedicated to compiling a database indexing all genealogical resources worldwide and making it available for public access using Internet technology. You can do simple or more complex surname searches of the site using its search engine. The results it generates include the surname, dates of the records, location where the person was found or resided, and links to the provider of the information so that you

can contact that person. One really nice feature of this site is that it is offered in more languages than just English. You can access it in French, Spanish, Dutch, and Belgian.

SurnameWeb

www.surnameweb.org/

A central index of surname-related sites: SurnameWeb is intended to serve as a central collection point for information about Internet resources pertaining to surnames worldwide. It contains an index of sites that are set up as Surname Resource Centers, which are basically one-name study sites devoted to particular surnames. The Surname Registry portion of the site is an index of surnames found across the World Wide Web on various types of sites (personal Web pages, family histories, geographic-specific sites, and so forth). Although the site does not have a search engine, you can use its hierarchy to find information. All you have to do is click on the section you wish to review (Surname Resource Centers or Surname Registry) and then select links to subsections organized alphabetically until you find the surname for which you are looking.

Software

Aha. Now we get to the growing world of genealogical software! Over the past couple of years, we have seen huge expansion in the area of genealogical software — from commercial databases, to mapping programs, to freeware and software that lets you manipulate your GEDCOM. Whether you are looking to buy your first genealogical organization program, upgrade to a program that is more powerful, or make some sort of enhancement to your genealogical files, you are interested in what software is available and what it has to offer you! Here is a list of all the genealogical software databases we are aware of, as well as a few specialty-type programs we thought you'd be interested in.

Genealogical Databases

Ancestors and Descendants

www.aia-and.com/

Ancestor and Descendants (Version 1.55) is available on Windows 3.1 (and above), MS-DOS, and OS/2 platforms. It produces over 100 reports, including family group sheets, pedigree charts, and source lists. For more information, contact Adventures in Ancestry, Inc., 10714 Hepburn Circle, Culver City, California 90232-3717, e-mail: Dan@AIA-AnD.com

Ancestral Quest

www.ancquest.com/

Ancestral Quest (Version 2.1) is available for the Windows 3.1 (and above) platform. It produces ahnentafel reports, family group sheets, pedigree charts, and wall charts. Each database can contain 65,000 individuals. The CD-ROM version includes the Hammond Maps of the World, Konica Picture Show, and a genealogy resources list. For more information, contact Incline Software, P.O. Box 17788, Salt Lake City, Utah 84117, email: aqinfo@ancquest.com

D-36 Software

Brother's Keeper

**ourworld.compuserve.com/homepages/
Brothers_Keeper/**

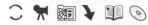

Brother's Keeper is available for the Windows 3.1 (Version 5.2F) and MS-DOS platforms. Reports include ahnentafel, pedigree charts, family group sheets, and a timeline. Each database can contain up to 1,000,000 individuals. Versions come in English, French, Norwegian, Danish, Swedish, German, and Dutch. For details, contact John Steed, 6907 Childsdale Avenue, Rockford, Michigan 49341, e-mail: 74774.650@compuserve.com

Create Family Trees Quick and Easy

**www.individualsoftware.com/
consumer/conqnetree.htm**

Create Family Trees Quick and Easy is available for the Windows 95 platform. Reports include Ancestor charts, descendant charts, and family group sheets. For more information, contact Individual Software Incorporated, 4255 Hopyard Road, #2, Pleasanton, California 94588, e-mail: webmaster@individualsoftware.com

Cumberland Family Tree

www.cf-software.com/

Cumberland Family Tree is available for Windows 3.1/95 and MS-DOS platforms. Versions include 2.29 (Windows), 4.1i (MS-DOS). Thirty-one types of reports are available including ahnentafel, pedigree charts, family group sheets, and descendant charts. Each database can hold 1,000,000 individuals. Software includes a date calculator and relationship calculator. Reports can be generated in Danish, Dutch, Finnish, French, German, Italian, Norwegian, Portuguese, Spanish, and

Swedish. For more information, contact Cumberland Family Software, 385 Idaho Springs Road, Clarksville, Tennessee 37043, e-mail: ira.lund@cf-software.com

EZITREE

www.ram.net.au/users/ezitree/

EZITREE is available for the MS-DOS platform. Reports include ancestor charts, descendant charts, and family group sheets. The number of individuals allowed per database is 99,999. Software includes relationship calculator. For more information, contact Rex Toomey, P.O. Box 84, Berowra, New South Wales, 2081 Australia, e-mail: ezitree@babelsoft.com.au

Family Explorer

www.commercial.com/kinware/

Family Explorer is available for the Windows 95/NT platform. Reports include ahnentafel, register, lineage, and custom. For details, contact M.J. Weeks, 6 Palmer Terrace, Gansevoort, New York 12831, e-mail: support@kinware.com

Family Heritage Deluxe

**www.imsisoft.com/familyheritage/
heritagedeluxe.html**

Family Heritage Deluxe (Version 2.0) is available for the Windows 95 platform. The following reports are available: ancestor, descendant, family group sheets, and custom. The software includes Family Publisher, Corel Photo House, Ancestry Genealogy Library, and Social Security Death Index. For more information, contact International Microcomputer Software Incorporated, 1895 Francisco Blvd. East, San Rafael, California 94901, e-mail: sales@imsisoft.com

Family History System

fhs.tallahassee.net/

Family History System (1997 Update) is available for the MS-DOS platform. Reports include ahnentafel, descendant, box charts, and tiny tafel. The number of individuals allowed in a database is 32,000. The software also includes a relationship calculator. For details, contact Phillip E. Brown, 834 Bahama Drive, Tallahassee, Florida. 32311.

Family Matters

members.aol.com/matterware/
    index.html

Family Matters (Version 3.31a) is available for the Windows 3.1 (and above) platform. Reports include pedigree and descendant charts. The software has Soundex, relationship, and birth/age calculators. For more details, contact Matterware, P.O. Box 2221, Valrico, Florida 33595, e-mail: matterware@aol.com

Family Origins

www.parsonstech.com/genealogy/
    products.html

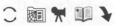

Family Origins (Version 6.0) is available for the Windows 3.1 (and above) platform. Reports include pedigree charts, family group sheets, descendant charts, kinship, and wall charts. You can have an unlimited number of names in each database. It includes a family reunion planner, cemetery records form, research log, place finder, databases of the royal houses of Europe, and source manager. For more information, contact Parsons Technology, Inc., P.O. Box 100, Hiawatha, Iowa 52233, e-mail: webmaster@parsonstech.com

Family Reunion

www.famware.com

Family Reunion (Version 97.0) is available for the Windows 95 platform. Reports include ahnentafel, pedigree, descendant, family group sheets, and life span lists. For details, contact FAMware, 8822 South Aspen View Drive, West Jordan, Utah 84088, e-mail: FAMware@accessintl.com

Family Scrapbook

users.southeast.net/~vesd/fsbabt.html

Family Scrapbook (Version 3.0) is available for the MS-DOS platform. Reports include book and custom charts. The number of individuals allowed per database is 999,999. For more information, contact Visionary Endeavors Software Development, P.O. Box 330439, Atlantic Beach, Florida 32233, e-mail: vesd@southeast.net

Family Ties

individual.downloadstore.com/prod-
    ucts/d00876.html

Family Ties (Version 4.0) is available for the Windows 3.1 (or higher) platform. It includes ancestor, descendant, and family group sheets. Added features that you can find are automatic backup and verification of conflicting or duplicate information. For more details, contact Individual Software Incorporated, 4255 Hopyard Road, #2, Pleasanton, California 94588, e-mail: webmaster@individualsoftware.com

Family Tracker

www.surfutah.com/web/famtrak/
    famtrak.html

D-38 Software

Family Tracker (Beta 7) is available for the Windows 3.1 platform. Reports include pedigree and family group sheets. You can have 32,000 individuals in each database. For additional information, contact Rex Myer, 575 N Seven Peaks Blvd. #3, Provo, Utah 84606, e-mail: rex@SurfUtah.com

Family Treasures

www.famtech.com/fa00001.htm

Family Treasures (Version 3.23e) requires Windows 3.1 (or higher). Reports include ahnentafel, pedigree, individual sheets, family group sheets, timeline, descendant, life span, and calendar. You are allowed up to 999,999 individuals. Additional items include date and age calculator, duplicate entry flags, and TWAIN-compatible scanner interface. For more details, contact Family Technologies, P.O. Box 309, Westfield, NY 14787-0309, e-mail: info@famtech.com

Family Tree Maker

www.familytreemaker.com/

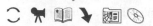

Family Tree Maker is available for Windows (Version 4.4) and Macintosh (Deluxe Edition II) platforms. Reports include ancestor, descendant, kinship, calendar, and family group sheets. The number of individuals allowed per database is 2,000,000. Features of the software include the FamilyFinder index, a How-to Guide, and spell checking. For more information, contact Brøderbund Software, Inc., P.O. Box 7865, Fremont, California, 94537.

Gene

www.ics.uci.edu/~eppstein/gene/

Gene (Version 4.2.1) is available for the Macintosh platform. Reports include ancestor, calendar, and relationship charts. For details, contact David Eppstein, e-mail: eppstein@ics.uci.edu

Genealogical Information Manager

www.mindspring.com/~dblaine/ gimhome.html

Genealogical Information Manager (Version 3.17) is available for the MS-DOS platform. Reports include family group sheets, pedigree, and descendant charts. The software also includes the ability to split the database. For more information, contact D. Blaine Wadsen, 4692 Bentley Place, Duluth, Georgia 30136, e-mail: dblaine@mindspring.com

Genius

www.gensol.com.au/genius.htm

Genius is available on the Windows 3.1 (and higher) platform. The program's current version is 1.50.11. Reports include descendant, pedigree, individual information sheet, and family group sheets. You can have 5,000 individuals per database. The software includes built in back up and restore. For details, contact Genius Solutions, P.O. Box 720, Woodridge Queensland 4114, Australia, e-mail: webmaster@gensol.com.au

Genus

www.mediabase.fi/suku/genupgb.htm

Genus (Version 2.13) is for Windows 3.1 (or higher). Reports include ancestor, descendant, and family group sheets. You may enter an unlimited number of individuals into each database. The program is available in Dutch, English, Finnish, French, German and Swedish. For more information, contact Business Computer of Finland, Ltd., Lonnrotinkatu 12A, FIN-87100 KAJAANI, Finland, e-mail: helpdesk@mediabase.fi

Généatique

www.cdip.com/geneatiq.htm

Généatique is designed for the Windows 3.1/95 platform. Reports include ancestor and descendant charts. The program only comes in the French language. For more information, contact the Centre de Développement de l'Informatique Personnelle, BP 27, 1 bis rue du Haut-Tertre, F-95550 Bessancourt, France.

Generations Deluxe Edition

www.sierra.com/titles/genealogy/

Generations Deluxe Edition runs on the Windows 3.1/95 platform (Version 1.0). Reports include ancestor and descendant charts. For details, contact Sierra On-Line, Inc. 3380 146th Place, SE Bellevue, Washington 98007, e-mail: home@sierra.com

Heritage

www.eskimo.com/%7Egrandine/
   heritage.html

Heritage (Version 3.11) is available for the Macintosh platform. Reports include ancestor, descendant, and family group sheets. For more information, contact Thomas Grandine, e-mail: grandine@eskimo.com

Heredis

www.heredis.com/

Heredis (Version 98) is available for the Windows and Macintosh platforms. Available reports include ahnentafel, descendant, pedigree, and anniversary lists. The number of individuals allowed per database is 2,500. The program is only available in the French language. For more information, contact BSD CONCEPT, 10 Parc-Club du Millénaire - F - 34036, Montpellier Cedex 1, France, e-mail: bsd@mnet.fr

KinQuest

www5.interaccess.com/orelleweb/
   kinquest.htm

Kinquest (Version 5.0) is available for the MS-DOS platform. Reports include ahnentafel and family group sheets. You can have two billion names in each database. For details, contact Orelle Corporation, P.O. Box 643, LaGrange, Illinois, 60525, e-mail: kinquest@orelle.com

D-40 Software

Kith and Kin

**ourworld.compuserve.com/homepages/
SpanSoft/**

Kith and Kin (Version 3.1) is available for the Windows 3.1 (or higher) platform. Reports include ancestor, descendant, and census reports. You can place 16,383 individuals in each database. For more information, contact SpanSoft, 11 Rowan Terrace, Cowdenbeath, Fife, KY4 9JZ Scotland, e-mail: SpanSoft@compuserve.com

Legacy

www.legacyfamilytree.com/

Legacy (Version 2.0) is available for Windows 3.1 (or higher). Reports include ancestor, ahnentafel, descendant, pedigree, family group sheets, calendar, timeline, and individual. Software includes date calculator, Soundex calculator, source clipboard, and blank forms. For more information, contact Millennia Corporation, P.O. Box 1800, Duvall, WA 98019, e-mail: WebMaster@MillenniaCorp.com

LifeLines

**www.genealogy.org/~ttw/lines/
lines.html**

LifeLines (Version 3.0.2) is designed for UNIX and related systems. Reports include register, pedigree, family group sheets, and tiny tafels. For more information, contact Tom Wetmore, e-mail: ttw@shore.net

Master Genealogist, The

www.whollygenes.com/

The Master Genealogist is available for Windows and MS-DOS platforms. The current versions are 3.5 (Windows) and 1.2a (MS-DOS). Reports include ahnentafel, descendant, family group sheets, individual, register, and custom. Software includes a research log and date calculator. For more information, contact Wholly Genes Software, 6868 Ducketts Lane, Elk Ridge, Maryland 21075, e-mail: tmg@whollygenes.com

My Family History

**www.ozemail.com.au/~pkortge/
MFH.html**

My Family History (Version 1.02) is available for the Windows 3.1 (and higher) platform. Reports include descendant, family group sheets, pedigree, and individual summary. The number of individuals per database is limited to 3,000. Software includes relationship and age calculators. For more details, contact Black Fire Technology, P O Box 817, Capalaba Queensland 4157, Australia, e-mail: pkortge@ozemail.com.au

Oedipus II

**web.inter.nl.net/hcc/L.G.Lamain/
odp95.htm**

Available for the Windows platform (Version 4.16). Reports include ancestor, descendant, and family group sheets. The software is in Dutch. For details, contact Besteldienst HCC Genealogie gg, Prins Clausstraat 11, 2691 CR 's-Gravenzande, Netherlands, e-mail: benkorff@wxs.nl

Parents

**ourworld.compuserve.com/homepages/
NickleWare/**

Parents (Version 4.6) is available for the Windows 3.1 (or higher) platform. Reports include ancestor, descendant, family group sheet, and custom reports. For more information, contact NickleWare, P.O. Box 393, Orem, Utah 84059, e-mail: 72730.1002@compuserve.com

Personal Roots

www.expertsoftware.com/roots.htm

Personal Roots (Version 1.0) is available for Windows 3.1 (or higher). Reports include ancestor, descendant, pedigree, family group sheets, and custom reports. For details, contact Expert Software, Inc., 800 Douglas Road, Coral Gables, Florida 33134, e-mail: sales@expertsoftware.com

Relativity II

www.gdatasys.com/rel_ind.htm

Relativity II (Version 1.0) is available for the Windows platform. Reports include individual event sheet, pedigree, ahnentafel, descendant, and modified register. For more details, contact Guardian Data Systems Inc., 516 Swain Ave., Elmhurst, Illinois 60126, e-mail: sales@gdatasys.com

Reunion

www.leisterpro.com/

Reunion (Version 5.0) is available for the Macintosh platform. Reports include pedigree, family group sheets, register, timeline, and ahnentafel. You can input 30,000 individuals in each database. Software includes research logs, date calculator, and blank forms. For additional information, contact Leister Productions, P.O. Box 289, Mechanicsburg, Pennsylvania, 17055, e-mail: info@LeisterPro.com

Ultimate Family Tree

www.uftre

Ultimate Family Tree is written for the Windows 3.1 (or higher) and Macintosh platforms. The three versions of the product include Basic (Windows, Macintosh), Plus (Windows), and Deluxe (Windows, Macintosh). Reports include family group sheets, pedigree, and individual charts. It includes blank forms and form letters, World Photo Studio, historical United States gazetteers, Family Tutor, and Family Album Maker. For more information, contact Palladium Interactive, 899 Northgate Drive, Fourth Floor, San Rafael, California 94903, e-mail: webstar@palladium.net

WinFamily

www.jamodat.dk/

WinFamily (Version 5.0) is available on the Windows 3.1 (or higher) platform. Reports include pedigree, family group sheets, and custom. Each database may have up to 16,000 individuals. The program is available in Danish, Norwegian, Swedish, Finnish, Czech, French, German, Dutch, and English. For details, contact JamoDat, Dr. Dagmarsvej 34, 3650 Ølstykke, Denmark, e-mail: jamodat@jamodat.dk

D-42 Software

Windows into PAF

**ourworld.compuserve.com/homepages/
phoenix/WIPafhom.htm**

Windows into PAF (Version 0.92) is available on the Windows 3.1 platform. Reports include pedigree, family group sheets, ahnentafel, and descendant. For additional information, contact Gary R. Phoenix, 21662 N 61 St. Ave., Glendale, Arizona, 85308, e-mail:
phoenix@compuserve.com

Miscellaneous Utilities

DeedMapper

www.ultranet.com/~deeds/factsht.htm

Mapping land records: Direct Line Software produces DeedMapper, which is a program that allows you to transfer information from land records to maps that you can see and use on your computer.

GED2HTML

www.gendex.com/ged2html/

Converting GEDCOM to HTML: GED2HTML is Gene Stark's popular program for converting your GEDCOM file into an HTML file that you can post on the World Wide Web.

GED2WWW

**pw2.netcom.com/~lhoward/
ged2www.html**

Converting GEDCOM to HTML: GED2WWW is Leslie Howard's freeware to convert GEDCOM files to HTML so that you can post your information on the Web.

GEDClean

**members.aol.com/tomraynor2/
gedclean.htm**

Cleaning your GEDCOM: GEDClean is Tom Raynor's freeware that helps you strip your GEDCOM file of information on living persons or particular other information that you specify.

Gedpage

**www.frontiernet.net/~rjacob/
gedpage.htm**

Converting GEDCOM to HTML: Gedpage is another software that you use to convert your GEDCOM files to HTML for posting on the Web. Rob Jacob wrote this program that provides output in the form of Family Group Sheets. And the software is available for Windows and Macintosh.

GenBrowser

**www.pratt.lib.md.us/~bharding/
rippleeffect/GenBrowser/
GenBrowser.html**

Searching for pertinent GEDCOM files and downloading them: Ripple Effect developed and sells GenBrowser, a software program that searches for and downloads to your computer GEDCOM files that it finds online and that meet specifications you enter. GenBrowser converts HTML pages that were generated from GEDCOM files back into GEDCOM for your use.

JavaGED

www.kersur.net/~ccooper/
javamain.shtml

Converting GEDCOM to Java: JavaGED is another program that converts GEDCOM files into Java Script and HTML for posting on the Web. It was developed by Chris Shearer Cooper and is available as shareware.

Sparrowhawk

www.tjp.washington.edu/bdm/
genealogy/sparrowhawk.html

Converting GEDCOM to HTML: Sparrowhawk is Bradley Mohr's GEDCOM to HTML converter for the Macintosh.

Surname-Related Resources

You are probably wondering how to find sites that pertain to the specific surnames in which you are interested. Wonder no more! Here are some sites that are indices of surname resources with explanations of what each has to offer.

Genealogy Resources on the Internet: Mailing Lists

members.aol.com/johnf14246/
gen_mail.html

Look here to find surname mailing lists: This section of Genealogy Resources on the Internet identifies mailing lists pertaining to particular surnames, sorted alphabetically. In addition to telling you

the name of the mailing list and exactly which surnames the list deals with, it tells you how to subscribe and post messages. Also, the site has general information about mailing lists.

Genealogy SiteFinder

www.familytreemaker.com/links/c/c-
people,surnames.html

Alphabetical and searchable list of surname sites: Genealogy SiteFinder is a comprehensive listing of genealogical sites found on the Internet. It is a cooperative project between Family Tree Maker Online and Helm's Genealogy Toolbox. This link to the People: Surnames section will take you to alphabetical indices of known surname-related sites. If the appropriate alphabetical index doesn't yield any pages of interest on a surname you are researching, try going to the main SiteFinder page and conducting a search on the site for your particular surname using the search engine.

The Guild of One-Name Studies

www.one-name.org/

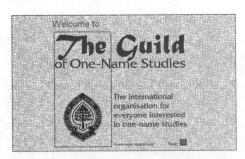

Site identifies registered one-name study sites: The Guild of One-Name Studies site is literally a guild of groups and online

sites that have registered as repositories for information pertaining to particular surnames. The Guild's Web site is broken down into five sections: Joining the Guild, First Time (background information on what a one-name study is and the purpose of the Guild), Help with Your Research, Surname Search, and Services to Members. The Surname Search section explains the register of one-name studies sites and links you to registered sites.

Online Genealogical Database Index

www.gentree.com/

Links to online databases: The Online Genealogical Database Index provides brief information about and links to genealogical databases on the World Wide Web. Most of the databases were created using GEDCOM files that have been converted to HTML. The index itself is organized alphabetically by the main surname of the database and does not include a complete listing of all surnames in the database.

SurnameWeb

www.surnameweb.org/

A central index of surname-related sites: The purpose of SurnameWeb is to make it easier for you to find any online resources pertaining to the surnames you are researching. It accomplishes this task by having a central location where people can register their surname-related Web pages. You can go to this main SurnameWeb page to find out more about hosting a surname page, as well as search the index of registered sites to find pages of interest to you.

Yourfamily.com

www.yourfamily.com/

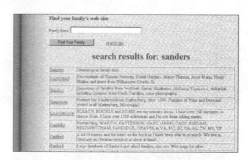

Search for family home pages: Among other services, Yourfamily.com provides a free, searchable index of family home pages. By entering the surname you wish to search and clicking the "Find Your Family" button, the search engine produces a list of links to pages that may meet your name specification. You can then look through the list and any accompanying comments about the sites to pick home pages to visit. Additionally, if you have a family home page that you wish to register with Yourfamily.com, this is the place to do it.

Part IV
The Part of Tens

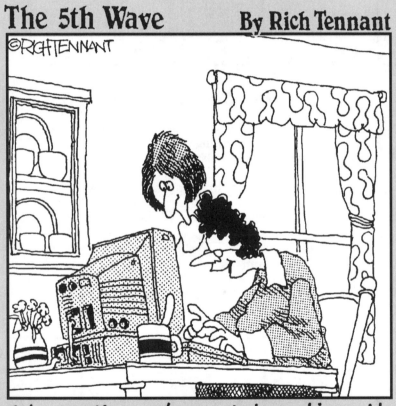

The 5th Wave   By Rich Tennant

©RICHTENNANT

"It's really quite an interesting site. There's roller coaster action, suspense, and drama where skill and strategy are matched against winning and losing. And I thought researching genealogy online would be dull."

In this part . . .

Ah, The Part of Tens — a staple of the *...For Dummies* books! Use the following chapters as quick references when you're looking for

Tips to get you smooth sailing in your research

Online periodicals that are quite useful

Places to visit when you're just getting started in your genealogical pursuits

Some things to ponder when designing your own genealogical Web pages

Chapter 12

Ten Genealogical Publications on the Internet

• •

In This Chapter

▶ Discovering genealogy publications available online

▶ Checking out newsletters promoting the study of family history

• •

*A*lthough this book covers the basics of researching your genealogy, new resources are constantly being discovered and new tools are constantly being created. To keep abreast of changes in the genealogical community, you may want to consult some of the journals and newsletters that are designed specifically for viewing on the Internet.

AfriGeneas News

    members.aol.com/gfsclint/Afrigeneas_News.html

AfriGeneas News traces its ancestry back to its premiere issue in June 1997. Its focus on African-American genealogical research is reflected in its articles that include:

✔ AOL Launches African American Resource Forum

✔ How The Slaves Celebrated Christmas

✔ The African Burial Ground Memorial And Interpretive Center

You can find other information at the site that includes dates and times of chats, book reviews, and a list of links to African-American resources on the Internet.

Best of DearMYRTLE

www.ancestry.com/home/Myrtlearch.htm

The Best of DearMYRTLE appears weekly with answers to genealogists' questions. The column, originally appearing on America Online, addresses topics such as:

- Researching Masonic Records
- Original Letters – Civil War
- American Genealogical Research at the DAR
- Cherokee by Blood

You can find past articles on the Ancestry, Inc. site back to May 8, 1997.

Eastman's Online Genealogy Newsletter

www.ancestry.com/home/eastarch.htm

Eastman's Online Genealogy Newsletter is a weekly column that covers current events in the online genealogy world. You can find information on new genealogical software, computer hardware, conferences, and World Wide Web sites. Recent topics include:

- Ged-Commander Version 2.1
- Free Historical Pictures on the Web
- Maryland Genealogical Society Conference
- SparQ Drive

Columns on the site date back to April 7, 1997. (See Figure 12-1.)

Family Tree Maker Online

www.familytreemaker.com/backissu.html

Brøderbund, Inc. maintains the Family Tree Maker Online site. Among the resources available on the site are articles on a number of genealogical topics. These topics are usually found in the lower right-hand corner of the

ancestry.com
Subscribe Now!
Find Your Ancestors
SEARCH:
All Databases
85 Million Names
Ancestry World Tree
3.5 Million Names
SSDI
58 Million Names
New Databases
Links to Other Sites
View Maps
SHOP ONLINE
Genealogy Software
CD-ROMs
Books
Supplies
Today's Special!
Buy Parson's Family Origins and get SSDI absolutely free!!
Click Here to order!
Eastman's Online Genealogy Newsletter
For the week of February 23, 1998
In This Issue:
- Family Tree Maker Version 4.4
- "AHN" for GEDCOM
- The 1998 "Mary Cornfoot Brehaut Award" Winner Is Announced
- Cyndi's List Moves
- OnBoard, an Online Resource for Genealogists
- Online BCG Roster Now Available
- Home Pages Highlighted
- Family Tree Maker Version 4.4
Broderbund released version 4.4 of their very popular Family Tree Maker genealogy program a couple of weeks ago. I had a chance to use it this week and decided to share my thoughts.
Family Tree Maker is reportedly the best-selling genealogy program in the world. Broderbund makes the program available in several versions, ranging from a Basic Edition for Windows that sells for $19.95 up to a

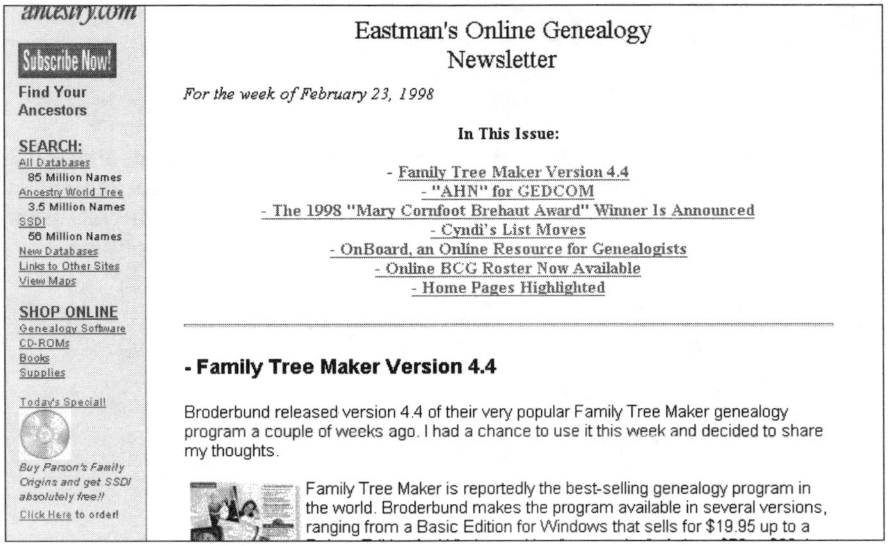

Figure 12-1: Eastman's Online Genealogy Newsletter includes articles on current events in the online genealogical community.

home page under the heading "In This Issue." Each issue contains two or three articles related to the same topic. For example, the February 1998 issue dealt with aspects of Internet genealogy. Articles included:

- Internet Glossary from Internet 101
- Computer Viruses and Genealogy
- Genealogy SiteFinder Quickly Links You to Thousands of Sites

For a list of back issues see `www.familytreemaker.com/backissu.html`

Family Tree Online

`www.teleport.com/~binder/famtree.shtml`

Family Tree Online is an online version of *The Family Tree,* a bimonthly publication by the Ellen Payne Odom Genealogy Library. It includes brief articles on genealogical-related subjects (such as "Help for African-American Researchers" and "Six Types of Marriages") and software reviews.

Global Gazette

www.globalgenealogy.com/gazette.htm

The Global Gazette, published biweekly by Global Genealogical Supply, includes articles that focus on the immigration and settlement of Canada, and on genealogical research in the countries from which Canadians originated. (See Figure 12-2.) The sections in the Gazette include:

- The Editor's Corner
- Routes to Roots
- Hints and Lists
- Tech Talk

Topics that appear include:

- Making the Genealogical Leap over the Atlantic
- The Challenge of Locating Vital Records in Ontario/Upper Canada/ Canada West. PRE - 1858. *(This is one article in a series on vital records for that area.)*
- Saskatchewan Residents Index 1,100,000 Records

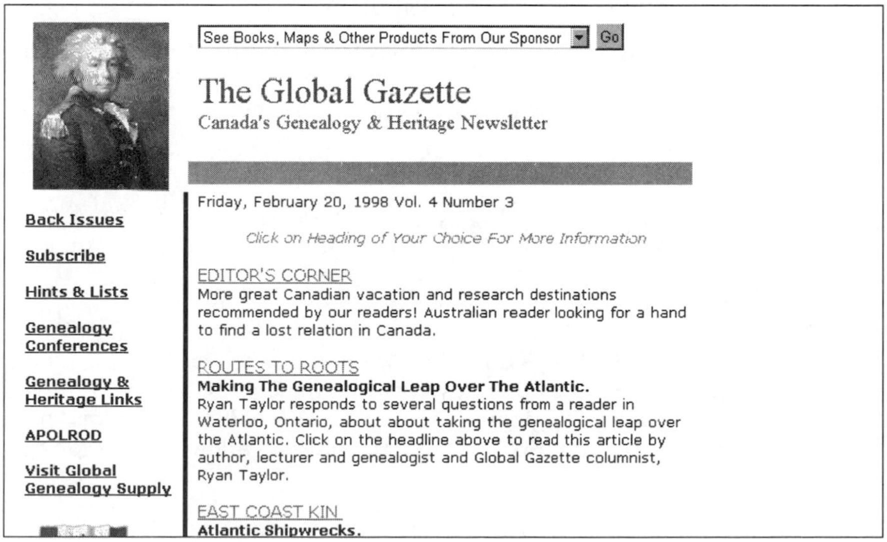

Figure 12-2:
The Global Gazette specializes in Canadian genealogy.

See Books, Maps & Other Products From Our Sponsor ▾ Go

The Global Gazette
Canada's Genealogy & Heritage Newsletter

Back Issues

Subscribe

Hints & Lists

Genealogy Conferences

Genealogy & Heritage Links

APOLROD

Visit Global Genealogy Supply

Friday, February 20, 1998 Vol. 4 Number 3

Click on Heading of Your Choice For More Information

EDITOR'S CORNER
More great Canadian vacation and research destinations recommended by our readers! Australian reader looking for a hand to find a lost relation in Canada.

ROUTES TO ROOTS
Making The Genealogical Leap Over The Atlantic.
Ryan Taylor responds to several questions from a reader in Waterloo, Ontario, about about taking the genealogical leap over the Atlantic. Click on the headline above to read this article by author, lecturer and genealogist and Global Gazette columnist, Ryan Taylor.

EAST COAST KIN
Atlantic Shipwrecks.

Journal of Online Genealogy

www.onlinegenealogy.com

We can't resist mentioning our own publication: the Journal of Online Genealogy. Honestly, it's a good resource! The Journal, a monthly World Wide Web publication, premiered in July 1996. Its mission is to promote the use of computers and the Internet in family history research. The Journal is offered in two formats: a low graphic edition and a high graphic edition — both editions have the same content. The genealogical community at-large submits articles that cover topics including advanced projects, beginner avenues, commercial sites, international efforts, newsgroups and mailing lists, online sites, societies, software, and technology (see Figure 12-3).

Shaking Your Family Tree

www.ancestry.com/home/Myraarch.htm

Myra Vanderpool Gormley's weekly column in the *Los Angeles Times Syndicate* is now available online on Ancestry Inc.'s World Wide Web site. Her column features a variety of genealogical topics, including:

- ✔ Tracing Ancestors in the British Army
- ✔ Pilgrims Remembered

Figure 12-3:
The high-graphic edition of the Journal of Online Genealogy, which promotes the use of computers and the Internet in family history research.

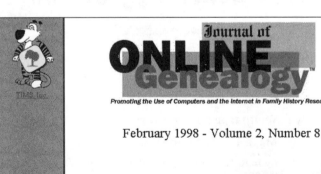

Journal of ONLINE Genealogy

Promoting the Use of Computers and the Internet in Family History Research

February 1998 - Volume 2, Number 8

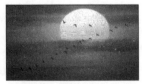

DEPARTMENTS
Advanced
Beginner
Commercial
Gentech
International
Newsgroups
Online Sites
Press Releases

GEDClean
Tom Raynor explains his GEDClean freeware program, which helps you remove information on living relatives from your GEDCOM prior to sharing it with others online.

Just for Kids: Tracing Your Family Tree
April Leigh Helm offers pointers to kids

SPONSORS

> ✓ Gravestone Chronicles: Art, History, and Genealogy
>
> ✓ When and How to Hire a Pro

You can find an archive of all her articles since May 8, 1997 on the site.

Southern Queries Genealogy Magazine (Web Edition)

`www.mindspring.com/~freedom1/sq/sq.htm`

If you're looking for information on your ancestors in the southern United States, Southern Queries is a place to start. This site has a Web Edition of selected articles from the companion print publication. Recent articles appearing in the magazine include:

> ✓ Your Medical Genealogy Can Save Your Life
>
> ✓ Crossing the Ocean in Salt Lake City
>
> ✓ Your Personal Archives
>
> ✓ Getting Help from Public Officials

Tri-City Herald Genealogy Online

`www.tri-cityherald.com/genealogy/`

At the Tri-City Herald Genealogy Online site, you can view past columns by Terence Day and Donna Potter Phillips. Columns by Day include topics such as:

> ✓ A Family's Wealth is in an Ancestor's Writings
>
> ✓ Computers Make Tedious Genealogical Work a Snap
>
> ✓ Census Records Solve Genealogical Mystery

Phillips's contributions cover subjects like:

> ✓ Scottish Church Records Offer Database on Past
>
> ✓ Grasp of History Can Help in Genealogy
>
> ✓ Don't Let Fire Singe Your Search

Chapter 13

Ten Things to Remember When Designing Your Genealogical Web Page

. . . .

In This Chapter

▶ Generating original and unique Web pages

▶ Conquering HTML

. . . .

Y ou don't want your genealogical Web page to look just like everyone else's, and you don't want it to contain almost exactly the same information. You want yours to be unique and useful to other genealogists so that a lot of people visit your site — and then recommend it to others. So what can you do to avoid the genealogical Web page rut that many authors find themselves in? Here we offer a few ideas and places to get help.

Be Unique — Don't Copy Other Web Pages

You want your home page to be set apart from all of the other genealogical Web pages that are out there, so you don't really have to be told not to copy other pages. Right? But when designing your own page, the pressure is on, and coming up with ideas for textual and graphic content can sometimes be pretty hard. That pressure sometimes makes it awfully tempting to take ideas from other Web pages that you like. Although it is acceptable to look to other pages for ideas on formatting and types of content, don't copy the pages! Web pages are copyrighted by the person(s) who created them even if they don't contain a copyright notice, and you could get yourself in trouble by copying them. (See Chapter 11 for more information about copyrights.)

The other reason you shouldn't copy other Web pages is that you want your page to attract as many visitors as possible and, in order to do this, you need to offer something unique that makes it worth peoples' time to stop by. After all, if your page has the same old information as another page that already exists, people have no need to visit your page. For example, because there are already several comprehensive genealogical sites (see Chapter 14), posting a Web page that merely has links to other genealogical pages doesn't make much sense. Likewise, if you're thinking about making a one-name study site on a surname for which there are already four or five one-name study sites, you may want to think about picking another one of the surnames you are researching to focus your home page on.

So check around and see what other genealogical Web pages offer, and then try to find something unique to put on your page. If you really want to post a surname page, think about making a page for your surname in a particular state or country. Or think about posting some transcribed records that would benefit genealogists who are researching ancestors from a particular county.

Include the Surnames You're Researching and Provide Your Contact Information

If the purpose of your Web page is not only to share the genealogical information you have collected but to get information from others as well, be sure to include a list of the names you're researching on your home page. While we encourage you to share your surnames, we also encourage you to share at least a little information about your ancestors with those surnames. Just a list of surnames alone isn't going to be very helpful to visitors to your home page. An online version of the information contained in your GEDCOM (that you create using GED2HTML or another similar program — see Chapter 11) will do because it will have an index of surnames that people can look through, which also has information about your ancestors with those surnames.

Also be sure to include your contact information so that people know how to get in touch with you to share data. At least provide your name and e-mail address so that they can contact you via electronic means to tell you what genealogical information they have collected and are willing to share with you.

Use Caution When Applying Colors and Graphics

Choose your colors and graphics wisely! While using some color and graphics (including photographs) helps your Web page stand out and make it more personal, be careful about using too much color or too many graphics. By too much color, we mean such bright backgrounds that you blind the visitors to your page, or backgrounds that drown out the colors you select for your links. You want your page to be appealing to others as well as to you, so before using neon pink or lime green, stop and think about how others will react.

The more graphics you use and the larger they are, the longer it takes for a computer to load them. (And animated graphics are even worse! Not only do they take a long time to load, but they can make your visitors dizzy and disoriented if you have several moving in different directions at the same time.) A couple of things affect how quickly computers load files, including graphical files — the amount of bandwidth of your Internet connection and the amount of space available on your hard drive. Waiting for a page to load that has more graphics than useful text content is frustrating. You can just about bet that people won't wait around, so it's better to make your page as user-friendly as possible from the beginning. Use graphics tastefully and sparingly.

The "Where to Go for Help" section later in this chapter identifies some online resources that lead you to sites with colors and graphics you can download and use on your Web page.

Be Careful What You Post

Be careful not to post any information that could hurt or offend someone. Respect the privacy of others and post information only on people who have been deceased for many years. (Twenty-five years is a good, conservative figure to use when in doubt.) Even then, be cautious about telling old family stories that may have an effect on persons who are still living. (For more information about privacy, see Chapters 10 and 11.)

Always Cite Your Sources

Always cite your sources when you put genealogical narrative on your Web page, or information from records you've collected or people you've interviewed. That way, anyone who visits your page and gets data from it knows

exactly where you got the information and can follow up on it if they need or want to. (Also, by citing your sources, you keep yourself out of trouble, because others may have provided the information to you for posting and deserve the credit for the research.)

Not All Web Browsers Are Created Equal

World Wide Web browsers interpret HTML documents differently depending on who created the software. Also, some Web browsers have HTML tags that are specific to the browser. So although you may create a Web page that looks great using Microsoft's Internet Explorer, it may look off-center or different in some other way when using Netscape. (And it will look a lot different in Lynx, which is a text-only browser.) Because of this problem, try not to use tags that are specific to any one browser when you are creating your Web page. And, whenever possible, test your page before posting it for public access by looking at it through several browsers. Better yet, use a testing service which allows the "experts" to look at your page and give you feedback! Yahoo! HTML Validation and Checkers page at www.yahoo.com/ Computers_and_Internet/Information_and_Documentation/ Data_Formats/HTML/Validation_and_Checkers/ provides a decent list of programs that will check your Web page for you and notify you about broken links.

To read more on browsers, see Appendix A.

Check and Recheck Your Links

If you include links on your home page to other Web pages you've designed or sites maintained by someone else, double-check them when you post your pages. Make sure that the links are working properly so that visitors to your page don't have problems navigating around sites you recommend or that support your home page. A lot of genealogical Web sites tend to be transient — the maintainers move them for one reason or another, or take them down entirely — so you should also check back periodically (once a month or so) to make sure the links are still working.

If you have a lot of links on your site and you don't have the time to go and check every single one yourself (which is a common scenario!), look to the Yahoo! HTML Validation and Checkers page at www.yahoo.com/ Computers_and_Internet/Information_and_Documentation/ Data_Formats/HTML/Validation_and_Checkers/. It identifies and links to a list of programs that will check your Web page for you and notify you about broken links.

Market Your Genealogical Web Page

After you have put together your Web page and posted it on your provider's server, you need to let people know that it exists so that they can stop by and visit your site. How do you do this? You can follow some of the same tips in Chapter 3 for marketing the research you've done on your surnames (using mailing lists if the site deals with particular surnames or geographic areas).

You can use a one-stop URL Registration site at the Genealogy Toolbox (genealogy.tbox.com/regis.htm) to register your Web page with the Genealogy Toolbox, Genealogy SiteFinder, Cyndi's List of Genealogy Sites on the Internet, the Genealogy Home Page, Genealogy Resources on the Internet, NetGuide: Genealogist's Guide to the Internet, and the RAND Genealogy Club. All of these are comprehensive genealogical Web sites that receive a lot of traffic from people looking for genealogy-related pages to visit.

Also, most of the major search engines have links to pages within their sites that allow you to submit the URL for a site you think should be added to their site. Of course, in the interest of saving time, you can visit Submit It! (www.submit-it.com/announce.htm). Submit It! offers a variety of announcement services, including one that allows you to submit your Web page information to about 20 search engines for free.

Helping Others Is Its Own Reward

Okay, we're not setting out to upset or offend anyone with this tip, but there is a good chance we will. We apologize in advance if we step on any toes, and will try to explain our point of view.

Don't go overboard promoting your home page on the actual home page for the sake of receiving awards from other sites, magazines, societies, or other sources. Post your genealogical home page with the intent of helping other genealogists and encouraging a sharing genealogical community — not to get a pat on the back. If you use the majority of your page to advertise your awards and beg people to vote for your site in popularity contests, you lose a lot of valuable genealogical space. (Space where you could be posting information that is useful to genealogists.) There's also a good chance you are turning visitors away — which defeats your purpose for self-promotion in the first place.

Now, we're not saying that you shouldn't acknowledge the awards that your site receives if it has good and sound genealogical content. We recognize that it's good business to give a little traffic back to the sites, magazines,

societies, or other sources that send visitors your way by awarding your page some honor. What we are saying is that you can acknowledge the honors you receive in a tasteful and humble manner. You don't have to plaster all the graphics for every single award across the top of your page. Rather, you can set up a separate Web page for awards and provide a link from your main page so that those who are interested in seeing your honors can go to that page.

Where to Go for Help

Chapter 11 tells you how to write some basic HTML and create a simple Web page, as well as about some HTML editors that are available from Web hosts. But maybe you want to learn more or want to be able to do fancier things with your Web pages. If this is the case, you should check out community colleges in your area or workshops that are being offered by local libraries or genealogical societies. Often, community colleges and workshops offer classes or sessions on how to make a Web page, which walk you through the basics of HTML — what the tags are, how to use them, and how to post a Web page.

If you don't want to take a course or attend a workshop and prefer teaching yourself beginning or advanced HTML, several books and online sites are out there to help you. One such book is *HTML For Dummies,* 3rd Edition, by Ed Tittel and Stephen James, published by the good people at IDG Books Worldwide, Inc. The following online sites have links to many resources for writing HTML, in addition to resources that have colors, backgrounds, graphics, and other things you can download that will help you enhance your Web page.

✔ **Yahoo's World Wide Web: Page Design and Layout** (www.yahoo.com/Computers_and_Internet/Internet/World_Wide_Web/Page_Design_and_Layout/)

✔ **Excite's Web Page Design** (www.excite.com/computers_and_internet/internet/web_page_design/)

✔ **Cyndi's Genealogy Home Page Construction Kit** (www.CyndisList.com/construc.htm)

Chapter 14
Ten Sites for Genealogy Beginners

In This Chapter

▶ Finding how-to sites
▶ Getting on mailing lists

Do census records make you feel senseless? Panicked at the idea of using the Soundex? Just plain confused about where to start? Here are ten sites that may relieve some of the anxiety you feel toward researching your genealogy.

Ancestors

```
www2.kbyu.byu.edu/ancestors/
```

The multi-part television show on genealogy, *Ancestors,* premiered in 1997. KBYU, the television station that produced the series, established a companion World Wide Web site that contains several resources for beginners. The first place to visit is the *Viewers Guide to Getting Started*. This guide has brief background pages for each of the ten episodes, including topics like getting started, looking at home, gathering family stories, the paper trail, libraries and archives, military and census records, African-American research, your medical heritage, high-tech help, and leaving a legacy.

Other nuggets you can find on the site include a resource guide with locations of genealogy resources in each state, a tips and tricks section, and several forms and charts that are useful in tracing your family history (these forms are available as GIF images or Adobe Acrobat files).

Ancestry HomeTown

`www.ancestry.com`

Ancestry, Inc., maintains this site modeled after a small town. Stop at the Ancestry Academy, which features over 30 online lessons for beginners interested in researching their genealogy. You can find several lessons on using Family History Centers and sample articles from one of the company's magazines, *Genealogical Computing*. At the library you can find online databases, but most are only available for a monthly fee. One free database at the Ancestry site that you may be interested in is the Social Security Death Index (SSDI) — especially if you are looking for someone in the United States in the 20th century (for more on the SSDI, see its entry in Chapter 13). Additionally, Ancestry has almost 400 databases that are accessible online to subscribers.

Beginner's Guide to Family History Research

`biz.ipa.net/arkresearch/guide.html`

Here you can find an online version of the book, *Beginner's Guide to Family History Research*. The site is organized along the lines of the book and contains 13 chapters, a glossary, a resource list, and bibliography. The topics discussed on the site include the following:

- Is Family History for You?
- Home and Family Sources
- Organizing Your Family Records
- Using Libraries and Archives
- Federal Census Records
- Courthouse Research
- Computers for Genealogists
- Military Records
- Ethnic Genealogy
- A Broad View of the Research Process
- Correspondence and Queries
- Sharing Your Heritage
- Special Interests

Family Tree Maker Online

www.familytreemaker.com

Family Tree Maker Online is a commercial site maintained by Brøderbund Software, Inc. The site contains a variety of resources for beginners and advanced researchers alike. Visit the Genealogy How-To Guide first, which takes you through three steps to beginning your genealogical journey. These steps include how to collect information on your family, how to get organized, and how to find missing pieces of family information. You can also find a directory of phone numbers and addresses, a genealogical dictionary, pre-made letters and forms to assist you in your research effort, and the Internet FamilyFinder service (for more information about Internet FamilyFinder, see Chapter 3).

This site also has a number of articles on various genealogical topics, a reference library of information on libraries, archives, and organizations, online genealogy classes, and the FamilyFinder Index (an index of names found in government records and family trees on CD-ROMs produced by Brøderbund).

National Genealogical Society

www.genealogy.org/~ngs/

The National Genealogical Society has a membership of more than 17,000 nationwide. At its Web site, you can find information on the society's home study genealogy course, conferences, Computer Interest Group (CIG), and other projects. Several reference materials are available on the site, including a list of genealogy bulletin board systems, numbering systems, the Genealogy Calendar (a calendar of genealogical events throughout the United States, Canada, and several other countries), and a list of tips for beginners.

The Present Meets the Past: Genealogy Instruction for Beginners, Teenagers, and Kids

`home.earthlink.net/~howardorjeff/instruct.htm`

This site offers basic information for starting your genealogical research. Sections of the site include instructions on where to begin, a list of questions to ask relatives, where to go for information, and what you'll need in your "research kit." Of special interest are two sections for children and teenagers who want to begin researching their family trees. Each section identifies projects for children and teenagers to complete. Also, the site has blank forms you can print off and use in your genealogical notebooks and files, along with a few links to some other unique sites.

Seven Steps to a Family Tree: A Beginners Guide to Genealogy

`www.agll.com/trivia/7steps.html`

The American Genealogical Lending Library has compiled seven steps that can aid you in constructing a family tree. These steps include organizing home and family sources, contacting relatives, writing for death records, following up on death records, and conducting several searches, including a federal census search, LDS library search, and state and county search. Each step contains information that is brief and to the point. Links to more in-depth material are within each of the steps if you need a more thorough explanation.

Treasure Maps

`firstct.com/fv/tmaps.html`

This site has several pages of interest to genealogists. Here you can find five steps to getting started, a tutorial on deciphering old handwriting, six steps to writing a successful query, and information on the U.S. Census. If you are contemplating a trip to a Family History Center, you can read articles on the Church of Jesus Christ of Latter-day Saints Research Outlines, a tutorial on the Family History Center, information on the FamilySearch collection, and

tips on how to order the Family History Library publications list. Treasure Maps also features a monthly newsletter covering tips on researching family history both online and through print sources.

GEN-NEWBIE-L

www.rootsweb.com/~newbie/

This is the home page for the GEN-NEWBIE-L mailing list. This mailing list is a forum for individuals who are new to computers and genealogy to discuss a variety of topics in a comfortable environment.

To subscribe to the GEN-NEWBIE-L mailing list, follow these steps:

1. **Open your favorite e-mail program and start a new e-mail message.**

2. **Type** GEN-NEWBIE-L-request@rootsweb.com **as the address to which you're sending the message.**

3. **Leave the Subject line blank, and type only the word** subscribe **in the body of your message.**

4. **Send your e-mail message.**

Soon you'll receive a confirmation message with additional details on unsubscribing from the mailing list and other administrative items. If you have questions about the mailing list, consult the home page for help.

For more on using e-mail, see Appendix A.

ROOTS-L

www.rootsweb.com/roots-1/

This is the home page for the ROOTS-L mailing list. If you're looking for an all-purpose mailing list on genealogy, ROOTS-L may be for you. ROOTS-L is the oldest and largest genealogical mailing list, having more than 10,000 subscribers. All types of genealogical issues are discussed on the list. On the mailing list's companion Web page, you can find subscription information, help files, a searchable archive of past ROOTS-L messages, and a brief history of the list.

To subscribe to the list, follow these steps:

1. **Open your favorite e-mail program and start a new e-mail message.**

2. **Type** ROOTS-L-request@rootsweb.com **as the address to which you're sending the message.**

3. **Leave the Subject line blank, and type only the word** subscribe **in the body of your message.**

4. **Send your e-mail message.**

Soon you'll receive a confirmation message with additional details on unsubscribing from the mailing list and other administrative items. (Check out Appendix A for more on using e-mail.)

You may want to consider subscribing to the digest mode of the ROOTS-L mailing list. Because it's one of the largest lists, your e-mail inbox may quickly fill if you receive every message that is posted to the list separately. *Digest mode* allows you to receive a single message with the text of several messages embedded within it periodically throughout the day. So instead of receiving some 50 to 200 messages per day, you may receive only five. For more information on subscribing to digest mode, see the ROOTS-L home page.

Chapter 15

Ten Tips to Genealogical Smooth Sailing

In This Chapter

▶ Identifying ways to enhance your genealogical research

▶ Recognizing pitfalls to avoid

*Y*ou want to make optimal use of your time when researching your genealogy — online and offline. Being time-efficient means planning well and keeping organized notes so that you don't get distracted by bad leads. Making the most of your time also means staying motivated when and if you do get distracted by a bad lead. Your genealogy is worth continuing. To help you plan, organize, and execute your research, here are some tips.

Start with What You Know

Sure, it seems basic. But it's worth repeating: When beginning your genealogy, start with what you know — information about yourself and your immediate family. Then work your way back in time using information from relatives and records that you've obtained copies of. Putting together the puzzle is a lot easier if you have some pieces first. If you try to start directly with your great-great-grandpa and all you know about him is his name, you're going to get frustrated very early in the process — especially if great-great-grandpa has a relatively common name like John Sanders or William Martin! Can you imagine trying to track down records on all the John Sanders or William Martins that would turn up in one year's census? (We believe in thoroughly covering the basics, so if you want to hear this again, go to Chapter 1.)

Get Organized

The better organized you are, the more likely your research efforts are to succeed. If you know ahead of time where you stand in researching your family lines, you'll be able to identify rather quickly which records or other materials you need about a particular surname, location, or time frame. This strategy enables you to get right down to the nitty-gritty of researching instead of having to spend the first hour or two of your research rehashing where you left off last time.

To help yourself get organized, keep a research log recording when and where you searched for information. For example, if you ran an Alta Vista search on the surname McSwain on March 12, 1998, and found three pages to visit, record that in your research log. Also record when you visited those three pages and whether they provided any useful information to you. That way, next time you're online researching your McSwain ancestors, you know you already ran an Alta Vista search and visited resulting pages so you don't need to do so this time. (Of course, you may want to check back some day in the future and run the search again to see if any new McSwain related sites have turned up. And again your research log will be handy because it can remind you whether you've already visited the resulting sites.)

You can print a copy of a research log at the Church of Jesus Christ of Latter-day Saints site (www.lds.org/Family_History/Research_Log.html). Although this particular log is intended for offline research, you can modify it yourself for your online pursuits — substituting the URL of a site you visit for the Location/Call Numbers section of the form. Or you can find a re-search table (which is basically a research log by another name) at the Family Tree Maker Online site (www.familytreemaker.com/00000002.html).

Always Get Proof

Don't trust everything you hear from other people or read in their books, reports, Web pages, or any other written form. Always be a little skeptical about secondhand information and seek to get your own proof of an event. That's not to say that if your Aunt Bettie gives you a copy of great-grandma's birth certificate you still need to go and get your own copy from the original source. It is to say, however, that if Aunt Bettie merely tells you that great-grandma was born in Hardin County, Kentucky, and that she knows this because great-grandma said so, you need to get a copy of great-grandma's birth certificate or some other primary record that verifies this fact.

If you assume that everything you hear or read is true, you're likely to get frequently distracted by bad leads. You could end up tracing an entire branch of a family you're not even related to. And just think of all the lost time that you could have spent working on your direct family line!

Always Cite Your Sources

We can't say this enough — always cite your sources! In other chapters (such as Chapter 13), we explore why citing your sources when sharing your genealogical information with others is a smart thing to do. We also touch on why citing sources is important for your own research — so important, in fact, that we reiterate the point here. Make sure that you know where, when, and how you obtained a particular piece of information about your ancestors in case you ever need to verify the information or get another copy of the record. Doing so saves you a lot of grief. It also brings you greater respect from others for your efforts.

For more information about citing your sources, we recommend you take a look at the articles offered at Family Tree Maker Online's Documenting Sources page (www.familytreemaker.com/issue19.html).

Focus, Focus, Focus

Don't put too many coals in the fire at once. If you're trying to remember all your ancestors in all your family lines and research them all at the same time, you are bound to get confused and burned out! Focus on one or two branches at a time — even better, focus on one or two people within a branch at a time. By maintaining a tight focus, you can still find information on other relatives in that family and collect records and data that pertain to others, but be able to do so without driving yourself crazy.

Share Information

One of the best ways to facilitate getting genealogical information from others is to share some information first. While most genealogists are rather sharing people to begin with, some still believe in protecting what they've discovered like closely guarded treasures — it's "every man for himself" in their minds. However, after they realize that you'll be giving information as well as getting it, some of them lighten up and are much more willing to share with you. By sharing information, you can save each other time and energy, as well as begin to coordinate your research in a manner that benefits both of you.

Sharing information is one area where the Internet has proven to be an invaluable resource for genealogists. It provides easy access for unconditional and conditional sharing of information among genealogists. Those of you who are willing to share anything you have can go online and post information to your heart's content. And in return, all you ask for is that the researchers who benefited from your site share interesting information with you. And for those of you who are a little more apprehensive about sharing what you know, you can post messages stating what you're looking for and that you're willing to share what you have with anyone who can help you.

 You have several different ways to share your information online. Many of these are covered in various chapters of this book. You can share in one-on-one e-mail messages, mailing lists, newsgroups, and Web pages, just to name a few of the means. Also, you can place classified advertisements at sites like Family Tree Maker Online's Genealogy Classified Ads (www.familytreemaker.com/adsfront.html) or post queries to sites like the Genealogy Toolbox's Query Central (genealogy.tbox.com).

Join a Society or Research Group

You've probably heard the phrase that two heads are better than one, right? Well, this theory holds true for genealogy. Joining a society or a research group allows you to combine research efforts with others who are interested in a particular surname or geographic location so that together you save time and energy getting documents that benefit everyone. A society or research group also provides you with a support group to which you can turn when you begin to get discouraged or whenever you want to share a triumph.

There are several ways to go about identifying genealogical societies and research groups you can join. Check out your favorite comprehensive genealogical site (see the *Genealogy Online Internet Directory* in this book for a list) and look under both the category that lists societies and the place category for the location where you live. Or, if you live in the United States, take a look at the Federation of Genealogical Societies home page at www.fgs.org (which identifies member societies by location) or the USGenWeb Project at www.usgenweb.org (which links to state pages that identify resources for the state and its counties).

If you live outside the United States, check out the WorldGenWeb site at www.worldgenweb.org to link to any resource pages for your country. These resource pages should include at least general information about societies in your area.

Attend a Conference or Workshop

Conferences and workshops that are hosted by genealogical societies can be a great resource for you! They can help you get organized, learn how to research in particular place or for specific records, and motivate you to keep plugging along with your research even if you have days where you feel you haven't accomplished a thing. Conferences and workshops also allow you to meet other researchers with whom you have something in common. Even if you aren't necessarily researching the same surname or geographic location, knowing others who enjoy researching means you have someone to go with to the local or state archives. Being in the company of someone you can share your genealogical successes and failures with is always nice.

Typically, conferences and workshops offer sessions that instruct you on various traditional researching topics. These topics typically include:

- Using local libraries and archives
- Finding and using land records
- Obtaining vital records
- Converting Soundex codes and using the census
- Publishing a genealogical report or book

Recently, there has been a trend of offering more and more computer-based sessions at conferences and workshops. Some of the sessions include:

- Using genealogical software
- Designing and posting your own genealogical Web page
- Joining online societies and mailing lists
- Presenting overviews of the Internet's genealogical offerings
- Using a computer in general

You can use your trusty computer and Internet connection to help find genealogical and historical conferences and workshops in your area. Just point your Web browser to the Genealogy Calendar (genealogy.org/PAF/www/events/). It is a comprehensive listing of upcoming events worldwide! If you're not up to browsing through the entire list, you can review it by location or month.

Attend a Family Reunion

Family reunions offer you a means to visit relatives you haven't seen in a long time and to meet new relatives you never would have known! Reunions are a wonderful opportunity to build your genealogical base by just chatting with relatives about old family stories, ancestors, and the like. Although a reunion doesn't feel like a formal interview, it can give you much of the same information as if you sat down and formally interviewed each of the people in attendance. Taking along a tape recorder or video camera is a good idea because you don't have to worry about writing down everything your relatives say right at that moment — you can just sit back and enjoy talking with your family. Plus, your genealogy is greatly enhanced by audio or video tape. (Just make sure that when you're going to tape a conversation, you have the permission of those relatives who are present and will be recorded on the tape.)

Family reunions also offer you the opportunity to share what you know about the family and exchange genealogical records and reports. If you know ahead of time that several of your relatives are also into genealogical research, you can better plan with them what records, pictures, reports, and other resources to bring. If you're not sure that any of your relatives are into genealogical research, we recommend you take a notebook with some printed reports and maybe a narrative family history or genealogy (if you've already put one together). Remember, your work does not have to be totally complete (in fact, it probably won't be!) or perfect in grammar for others to enjoy seeing what you've collected.

If you'd like more information about how family reunions can motivate you and help you in your research, you may wish to take a look at Family Tree Maker Online's Family Reunions articles (www.familytreemaker.com/issue1.html). To find out about family reunions, we recommend you watch the family association and one-name study Web sites of the surnames you are researching. Typically, these types of Web pages have sections set up for reunion announcements. Also, see the Reunions Magazine site (www.reunionsmag.com/).

Don't Give Up

You are going to have days where you spend hours at the library, archives, or on the Internet with what you think of as no research success whatsoever. Don't let those days get you down, and certainly don't give up! Instead of thinking about what you didn't learn about your ancestors on such days, think in terms of what you did learn — that your ancestors were not in that record for that particular place at that particular time. By checking that record, you have eliminated one more of the items on your "to do" list. And now, the next time you get ready to research, you know exactly where *not* to look for more information!

Part V
Appendixes

The 5th Wave   By Rich Tennant

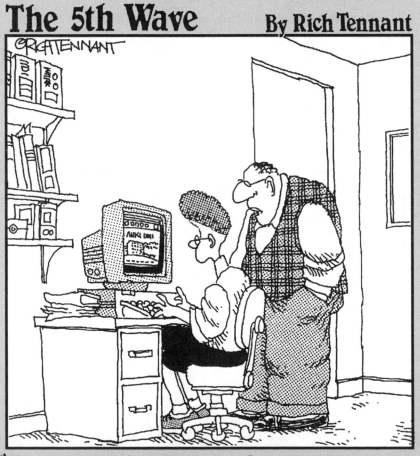

"I'm not sure I want to be claimed by a family whose home page has a link to the Zany Zone."

In this part . . .

*W*hether you skipped back here to get a quick review of something or you've diligently read through the entire book and find yourself near the end, the Appendixes provide additional resource information to help you with both your genealogy research and your quests on the Internet. Here you can find information about going online, a glossary of genealogical and online terms, and what you can find on the CD-ROM that accompanies this book.

Appendix A
Going Online

In This Appendix

▶ Covering your hardware and software needs

▶ Finding an Internet service provider

▶ Exploring your Internet resources

· ·

*B*efore we talk about what you need to go online and how to do it, we first need to explain what we mean by online. We use the term *online* to refer to gaining access to and then using the Internet. So what, then, is the Internet?

The *Internet* is a system of computer networks joined together by high-speed data lines called *backbones.* The Internet began as a smaller system of regional networks, called ARPANET, sponsored and used by the United States military in the 1960s. Over time, other government agencies and colleges and universities that were conducting research for the government were added to the network. And eventually, the Internet sprang forward and became accessible by the average person through Internet service providers (which we talk about later in the section "Getting an Internet Service Provider").

This appendix covers the equipment you need for your computer to be able to access the Internet, finding an Internet service provider to provide the access, and the types of resources that you find on the Internet after you're on it. Of course, the primary focus of this book is genealogy online — not the Internet and computer-use in general — so we just touch on the types of Internet resources available. In some cases, we do provide examples and details to help you out when you come across some common situations in your online genealogical research (situations like sending e-mail, joining mailing lists, and using newsgroups). And because we don't want to leave you in a lurch if you're trying to learn all you can about every Internet resource, we include some references to other books we think you'll be interested in if you want to know more about something in particular.

Is Your Computer Ready to Go Online?

If your computer is relatively new, it most likely came loaded with the hardware and software you need to access and effectively get around on the Internet. However, if you're using a computer purchased several years ago, you may have to add a piece of hardware or software in order to access and use the Internet. In general, you need to have a base system that meets the same requirements to run genealogical software (see Chapter 8 for more information), plus a modem and some communications software.

Modem on up

What is a modem, you say? A *modem* is a piece of equipment that enables your computer to talk to other computers through a telephone line. A modem can be internal (meaning you install it inside your computer) or external (meaning you plug it in to one of your computer's serial ports). A modem transmits information to and from your computer at a speed that is measured by the total number of characters, or *bits,* it can send or receive per second. Nowadays, modems have speeds ranging from 14,400 to 56,000 bits per second (also referred to as *bps*) — the higher the number, the faster the modem. Most Internet service providers recommend that you have a modem with a minimum speed of 14,400 bps. (For more on Internet service providers, move ahead to the section "Getting an Internet Service Provider" later in this chapter.)

To use a modem to access the Internet and talk with other computers, you need communications software that tells the modem what to do and also interprets information coming back into your computer. The exact kind of software you need depends on your modem and your Internet service provider (ISP). Check with your ISP to determine what exactly you need and how to get it, then double-check the owner's manual for your modem to ensure that the software is compatible with your modem. Most commercial ISPs (like America Online and CompuServe) provide you with free copies of the software you need to access and use any of the many online resources they offer.

Don't forget a telephone line

In addition to having a computer equipped with a modem, you need a telephone line to access the Internet. Using a jack-to-phone telephone cord, connect your modem to the wall jack so that the modem can use the telephone line to dial out and communicate with other computers. (Generally, you can find the modular plug to hook the phone cord into your modem on

the back of your external modem or on the back of your computer if you have an internal modem.) Your modem will then call your Internet service provider and gain access to the Internet for you.

You don't necessarily have to have a second telephone line in your house to access the Internet. You can use your regular line and phone number. However, there are a few things you may want to think about:

- ✔ If you subscribe to a call-waiting service, beware that call waiting can interrupt an online session, which can be very frustrating. When a call-waiting call rings through, your computer gets very confused and the consequences can be far from fun. The computer does anything from trying to answer the second line to disconnecting from your online service to shutting down completely. So if you have call waiting, we recommend you follow your communications software instructions or your phone company's instructions for blocking it while you're online.

- ✔ If you spend long periods of time online (which is extremely easy to do when you get into genealogical research and dialogues with other researchers), you may want to remind your relatives and friends that your computer sometimes uses that phone line to access the Internet. Letting them know that the line will be tied up saves them frustration and worry if they're trying to reach you and continually get a busy signal.

- ✔ If you have several phones hooked up on the line, remember to tell others in the household you're going to be online. When someone picks up an extension in the home, it can cut off your Internet connection.

Getting an Internet Service Provider

The choices seem endless when it comes to finding an Internet service provider (ISP). You have a choice among several types of access:

- ✔ Work or school
- ✔ Direct connection
- ✔ Commercial online service providers (local, national, or international)
- ✔ Freenets

Some services are free, while others charge a monthly fee but give you access to more resources and even some specialized resources. So how do you choose? You need to review all the available options in your area and determine which one offers the most of what you need.

Access from work or school

If you work for an office or attend a school that has an Internet connection, you may already have access to some or all of the resources available on the Internet, particularly e-mail and the World Wide Web. Whether you are allowed to use that access for personal, genealogical research depends on your company or school, of course. Many offices have reasonable policies against using company equipment and time for personal purposes, so be sure you know your company's policy before embarking on your genealogical pursuits online at work. If you work in an office that doesn't permit personal use of the Internet, you're with the majority of the population and need to get Internet access from your home.

Direct connection to the Internet

A direct connection to the Internet is just that — an Internet line comes directly into your home, and your computer is hooked directly into it. Because the line coming into your home is dedicated just to the Internet, you don't need to worry about having a phone line available or a modem to use that phone line. Typically, if you have a direct connection, you have a computer that's running at all times and may be acting as a *server* (a computer that makes information on its drives available for access by other computers). This server runs programs that know where to route visitors to your computer, and also lets you out onto the Internet to look at other sites and use other resources. For most online genealogists, the expense and technical knowledge that it takes to have and maintain a dedicated Internet line in your home makes having one unrealistic.

Commercial online service providers

Chances are, the names America Online, Prodigy, and CompuServe pop into your mind when we say commercial Internet service providers. While these are three of the better known providers, a lot more are available, and taking a look around to find the service that best meets your needs is worth the time. Commercial Internet service providers are companies or organizations that provide subscribers dial-up access to the Internet. They can be international, national, or local in scope. The services that the commercial ISPs offer vary, but typically all provide e-mail and World Wide Web access. Most of the major providers also have special interest groups and forums that members can participate in, as well as access to newsgroups. Many now offer space where you can post your own Web page. (For more information about designing and posting Web pages, see Chapters 11 and 13.)

Just because your aunt, brother, or best friend uses a particular commercial ISP doesn't necessarily mean that that same service is the best one for you. After all, you may have different needs. Your aunt may live in a metropolitan area where the provider has several telephone access numbers, whereas you may live in a rural community or isolated area where the provider does not have a telephone access number and you would get stuck with long-distance charges to use the same provider. Or your brother may subscribe to a provider that gives him only e-mail access, whereas you want to browse the World Wide Web and be able to keep abreast of the genealogy news-groups. Because your needs may be different, we recommend that you ask several questions when considering any ISP, whether it is a national, international, or local provider.

- What services — e-mail, World Wide Web access, space for a Web page, FTP (File Transfer Protocol, which is a way to transfer files from your computer to another, or vice versa, over the Internet), newsgroups, and so on — does the ISP provide?

- Does the ISP provide the software you need to access its system? Can you use your own software if you prefer?

- What is the ISP's pricing policy? Do they have a set rate where you get unlimited access? Or do they have a tiered system where you pay for a set number of hours of access per month, and then get charged a certain amount for each hour that you go over?

- Does the provider have local telephone access numbers available in the area where you live? If not, do they have free 800 telephone access numbers you can use, and, if so, do you have to pay extra for access to them? (The access numbers are the phone numbers your modem calls to log you into the ISP's servers so that you can get online.)

- If the ISP includes space for a Web page in your subscription, do they have support services to help you set up your home page?

- How does the ISP handle customer support? Do you have to post an e-mail message and, if so, how quickly do they respond? Or do you have to call a long-distance telephone number to speak to a customer service representative? What are the provider's hours of customer support?

Shop around to see who gives you the better deal and can best address your Internet needs — a local ISP or one of the national or international ones. You can find a local ISP a few different ways. You can look in your local phone directory or the newspaper, ask around among your friends and coworkers, or go to the directory Web site at www.thedirectory.org/, which has listings of ISPs by area code. And to help you comparison shop, here are the names and Web addresses (Web addresses are technically known as Uniform Resource Locators, or _URLs_) for several of the better-known commercial online services. (Keep in mind that these are not the only major providers available; they are just a sampling.)

- ✔ **America Online (AOL):** www.aol.com
- ✔ **CompuServe:** www.compuserve.com
- ✔ **Concentric:** www.concentric.net
- ✔ **Earthlink:** www.earthlink.net
- ✔ **Microsoft Network:** www.msn.com
- ✔ **Prodigy:** www.prodigy.com

Freenets

Freenets are Internet service providers that are locally based and offer access to people in the community either free-of-charge or for a minimal charge. (Yes, it is a contradiction to say that there may be a minimal charge for a freenet — which is why you also hear freenets called *community networks* these days.) Some freenets are able to give free access to individuals because they have corporate sponsorship, while others are associated with educational institutions. These days, freenets are rather hard to find, and they may limit the types of service available. For example, they may provide e-mail and FTP (File Transfer Protocol) access, but not offer World Wide Web browsing. To see if there's a freenet in your area, flip through your local phone directory or watch the newspaper. You may also want to ask at the local library or use a friend or relative's Internet access to check out the directory Web site at www.thedirectory.org/, which identifies ISPs by area code.

Types of Internet Resources

When preparing to go online, knowing the types of Internet resources available to you is helpful. By reviewing what the resources are and what they're called, you become more familiar with some terms that you may encounter on the Internet after you go online.

Bulletin Board Systems

Although Bulletin Board Systems (BBSs) technically are not Internet resources, you can get to some BBSs via the Internet. And as there are still quite a few BBSs dedicated to genealogical research, we thought it a good idea to tell you what exactly a BBS is. A *BBS* is a computer (or maybe more than one computer) that answers the telephone and communicates with other computers that call it, letting users of the other computers post information or messages to the BBS. Some BBS administrators began trading files with other BBSs as the systems became popular, and BBS networks were formed. The best known network of BBSs is FidoNet.

Some genealogical BBSs that may be worth your calling are still out there. Keep in mind, however, that for many BBSs, you still have to configure your computer to call the BBS's phone number. (Be aware that the phone number may be long distance!) To find out more about genealogical BBSs, what's available, and how to find and access them, visit Richard Cleaveland's Consolidated List of Genealogy Bulletin Board Systems (`www.genealogy. org/~gbbs/`).

If you want to know more about BBSs in general, *BBSs For Dummies,* by Beth Slick and Steve Gerber (IDG Books Worldwide, Inc.), may be the book for you.

Electronic mail

Electronic mail — commonly called *e-mail* — is just what it sounds like: Mail (or messages, if you prefer) that is sent from one person to another electronically over the Internet. Because you can communicate with others worldwide on any given topic (surname, geographic location, types of records, and so on), e-mail is the best Internet tool when it comes to genealogical research online.

How you get an e-mail program varies. If you subscribe to one of the commercial ISPs, the communications software that the ISP provides should have an e-mail client included. Or it's possible that an e-mail program came with your computer when you bought it, or you have one as part of your World Wide Web browser. And, of course, another way to get an e-mail program is to buy one or download one off the Internet. Regardless of how you got your e-mail client, most work generally the same way.

To use your e-mail software, install the program following the instructions provided with the software.

Sending e-mail

When it comes time to send your message, follow these general steps:

1. **Open your e-mail program.**

   You generally do this by double-clicking on the icon (the icon will vary depending on the program you're using) or using your Start program menu (depending on what operating system your computer uses).

2. **Click the button that lets you create a new message. (Or you can usually use a pull-down menu to tell the software you want to create a new message.)**

3. **In the To: field, type in the e-mail address for the person you want to send the message to.**

   The protocol for an e-mail address is this: (user name)@(name of the person's ISP). For example, April's e-mail address is: ahelm@tbox.com (ahelm is her user name, and tbox.com is her ISP through which she gets her e-mail messages).

   Depending on your e-mail program, you may be able to enter more than one person's e-mail address if you plan to send the message to more than one person. If you do have multiple addresses, separate each e-mail addresses with a comma or semicolon. Or (again depending on your program) you can use the CC: (meaning *carbon copy*) field to enter the addresses of the other people.

4. **In the Subject: field, type a brief note stating what the message is about.**

5. **In the message box, type the message you want to send to the other person.**

6. **When you've finished your message, click the Send button or use a pull-down menu to tell the software to send the message.**

Receiving and reading e-mail

When you first install your e-mail program, you're prompted with questions or dialog boxes to finish configuring your computer and ISP account to receive e-mail. After the configurations are set, e-mail that others send to you automatically arrives in your inbox, which sits on your ISP account and is accessible whenever you dial in to access the Internet. After you're logged into your ISP and have opened your e-mail inbox, you'll be able to read any messages you receive by double-clicking on the message line in the inbox or highlighting the message you want to read and clicking the Open button. (Of course, if you want to reply to the message after reading it, your e-mail software probably provides a Reply button or pull-down menu option to do so.)

Check out Chapters 3 and 9 for more information on using e-mail for particular genealogical purposes and to learn about *netiquette* (guidelines for communicating effectively and politely with e-mail).

To find out more about your particular e-mail software, consult the user's manual or other documentation that came with the software. The manual (or other documentation) tells you about special features the program has and how to use them. For even more information on using e-mail programs, we recommend *Internet E-Mail For Dummies,* by John R. Levine, Carol Baroudi, Margaret Levine Young, and Arnold Reinhold (IDG Books Worldwide, Inc.).

Finding e-mail addresses for other people

You're probably asking, "How can I get addresses for other genealogical researchers I want to communicate with via e-mail?" For the most part, you get e-mail addresses from people when they contact you, or when you post a message to a mailing list, post a query, or put up a Web page. However, there will be times when you're looking for someone's e-mail address and can't find it (whether you've lost it or never had it), which is when online directories come in pretty handy.

An *online directory* is just that — a listing of names and addresses (e-mail and/or regular mail depending on the directory) that you can access and search on the Internet. Most directories are accessible on the World Wide Web (we cover the World Wide Web in more detail later in this appendix). Here's how to use an online directory to look for a particular person's e-mail address.

1. **Open your World Wide Web browser.**

   You generally do this by double-clicking on the icon for the program or using the Start program menu.

2. **In the URL field of your browser, type in the Web address for the Four11 directory,** www.four11.com/

   The Four11 search page comes up. You're looking for an e-mail address, so use the top form called E-Mail Search. Notice that Four11 also offers a Phone Number Search where you can look for a person's phone number.

3. **In the First Name field, type in the person's first name (if you know it).**

   For the purpose of this example, look for April in the Four11 directory. In the First Name field, type in the name **April**.

4. **In the Last Name field, type in the person's last name.**

   Following our example, type in **Helm**.

5. **If you happen to know the *domain* (the name of the person's Internet service provider's computer), type it in the Domain field.**

   Most of the time, you won't know the domain name for the person's e-mail account — that's probably why you're looking for the e-mail address in the first place! So leaving this field blank is perfectly fine.

6. **Leave the SmartName box checked.**

   The SmartName box tells the search engine at Four11 whether or not to assume some things about the person's name. For example, it tells the search engine that you consider Bob to be a related name to Robert, so instead of searching only for those persons literally named Bob So-and-So, the search engine will look for all Bobs and Roberts with the So-and-So last name. Unless you know for sure that a person's name

isn't a diminutive or nickname, leaving this box checked is a good idea so that the search engine looks for any and all variations of certain names.

7. Click the Search button.

Four11 executes the search and brings up an E-Mail Search Results page showing any matches it found or informing you that it doesn't find anyone with that name. For each match, the Search Result page provides the person's name and e-mail location. Each name is a link to more information.

In this example, Four11 brings up three matches. Based on what you know, you choose the match you believe to be the right person. In this case, match number one is the April Helm you're looking for. Notice that her e-mail address is at `tbox.com`, but you don't see what her e-mail name is on this page.

8. Click the name of the person you think is the one you're looking for.

Click the first match, which takes you to a page with more detailed information about what Four11 has in its directory for this particular April Helm. Here you see that Four11 has April's full e-mail address as `info@tbox.com` and that it knows her e-mail address is in the United States.

Directories like Four11 are great when you're trying to track down the e-mail addresses for just a few people you want to contact. However, online directories do have their limitations! If you're searching for someone who has a common name — like John Martin or Elizabeth Smith — you're in for a challenge when you use an online directory. You need to know a little bit more about people with common names to effectively search for their e-mail addresses. Information like where they live is helpful. While Four11 provides the country where a person's e-mail address is, other online directories provide full address information.

Another twist to online directories that you may encounter is that they can turn up more than one e-mail address for the same person. If you'd run a search on Matthew's name instead of April's in the steps above, three or four of the many Matthew Helms who showed up on the results page would have been the Matthew you were looking for. (The reason for this is that Matthew has three or four different e-mail accounts.)

In addition to telling you about these quirks of online directories, we feel we must give you a warning here as well: Use online directories only to find others you know are into genealogy or from whom you know you can get specific information that will guide you in your genealogical pursuits. Unless you want to receive a lot of negative e-mail from people you don't know,

don't use an online directory to identify everyone who has a certain surname you're interested in and then e-mail them with questions of how
they're related to you or the ancestor you're researching. (We discuss this
tactic and why it isn't a good idea in more detail in Chapter 3.)

Mailing lists

Mailing lists are closely related to e-mail in that they involve e-mailing other
people, but en masse instead of one-on-one. (You may hear mailing lists
referred to as *listservs,* although technically Listserv is a software program
for managing mailing lists and not the mailing lists themselves.) Mailing lists
are formed by groups of people who share common interests. In terms of
genealogical research, the common interest may be a specific surname,
locality, or ethnic groups.

Here's how mailing lists work: You join (or subscribe to) a mailing list and
then receive any e-mail messages sent to the mailing list. (The list consists
of the e-mail addresses of each person who joins the group.) When you want
to send a message to the entire group, you send it to a single e-mail address
which, in turn, delivers your message to everyone who subscribes to the
list. When responding to a message posted by another subscriber, you can
send your response directly to the person who posted the first message or
to the entire mailing list. Which you choose to do depends on whether the
information you're sending is of interest to just that one person or to
everyone on the list.

We discuss mailing lists and posting queries to them in Chapter 3, along with
an example of how to subscribe to a mailing list. In general, to subscribe to
a mailing list, all you have to do is send an e-mail message to a designated
e-mail address with the word **subscribe** in the subject line. (If a particular
mailing list has different instructions for subscribing, the site where you find
information about the mailing list should tell you so and provide more
detailed instructions.)

For more information about mailing lists, including the ins and outs of how
they work and step-by-step instructions for subscribing or unsubscribing, we
recommend the *Internet For Dummies,* 5th Edition, by John R. Levine and
Carol Baroudi and *MORE Internet For Dummies,* 4th Edition, by John R. Levine
and Margaret Levine Young (both books published by IDG Books Worldwide,
Inc.).

Telnet

Telnet is a text-based program that allows you to log in to another computer
and view files or documents that are available for public access. You cannot
download the files, nor can you upload your files to the other computer. To

telnet to another computer, you must have a telnet client (software) or a World Wide Web browser (like Netscape and Internet Explorer) that launches a telnet client. (For more on browsers, see the World Wide Web section later in this chapter.)

As the World Wide Web became more popular over the past few years, telnet started to fall by the wayside, and most of the telnet sites that still exist and are of interest to genealogists are library card catalogs. However, even many of these card catalogs have made the move to the World Wide Web for access and use, and even those that haven't made the move can usually be linked to and viewed using your browser.

For more information about telnet and how to use telnet sites, take a look at *Internet For Dummies,* 5th Edition, by John R. Levine and Carol Baroudi and *MORE Internet For Dummies,* 4th Edition, by John R. Levine and Margaret Levine Young (both published by IDG Books Worldwide, Inc.).

File Transfer Protocol

File Transfer Protocol (FTP) is a way to transfer files from your computer to another, or vice versa, over the Internet. You must have software that enables you to FTP, and you can only log into other computers that allow FTP access. After you've logged into a computer that allows FTP access, you can download files that are available for FTP or, in some instances, upload your own file to that computer.

How you get to an FTP site on another computer to log in and download or upload files depends on the other site and the FTP software that you use. The general gist of it is this: Using your software, you tell your computer to FTP into the other computer. The other computer asks you for a log in and password, and then gives you access to the FTP files you're allowed to download. If, for some reason, you are not authorized to FTP into that other computer, it will reject your attempt. A lot of computer systems allow you to download things "anonymously," meaning that you can log in to a machine that you do not know the password for by simply typing **anonymous** for the username and your e-mail address for the password.

Some World Wide Web pages have FTP files available for downloading directly from the Web pages. All you have to do is click the link to the file, and your computer asks where you want the file saved.

For more detailed information about FTP, we recommend the *Internet For Dummies,* 5th Edition, by John R. Levine and Carol Baroudi and *MORE Internet For Dummies,* 4th Edition, books by John R. Levine and Margaret Levine Young (both published by IDG Books Worldwide, Inc.).

Gopher

Gopher was developed at the University of Minnesota as a way to hierarchically categorize data on the Internet. Gopher uses a series of text-based menus through which you can browse. You click on menu choices to get to other levels of information and eventually to the particular file or document you're looking for. Gopher was popular before the World Wide Web and has, for the most part, been replaced by Web sites.

You can get to and use Gopher sites several different ways. You can use a Gopher client (or software) or your World Wide Web browser. (Actually, because you can use your Web browser, Gopher software has basically become obsolete.) Depending on which way you go, your instructions for getting to Gopher sites will vary. However, the method for navigating within a Gopher site will be the same: Click on menu choices that take you to submenus down through the hierarchy.

For more information about Gopher sites and software, we recommend the *Internet For Dummies,* 5th Edition, by John R. Levine and Carol Baroudi, and *MORE Internet For Dummies*, 4th Edition, books by John R. Levine and Margaret Levine Young (both books published by IDG Books Worldwide, Inc.).

Newsgroups

Newsgroups are places to post messages of interest to groups of people at large. Newsgroups are similar to mailing lists in that you use e-mail to send a message that several people can read. However, instead of the message being sent individually to everyone on a mailing list, the message is posted to a news server, which in turn copies the message to other news servers. The other news servers wait for people who are interested in the topic to request the latest postings.

Newsgroups are categorized in hierarchies. Each hierarchy has a top-level label like `soc` or `alt`. Beneath the top level is a second hierarchy, followed by a third level, and so on. The majority of traffic pertaining to genealogical research flows through the `soc.genealogy` hierarchy (although some traffic does come through the `alt.genealogy` newsgroup).

We discuss newsgroups, their hierarchies, and posting messages to them in greater detail in Chapter 3, as well as provide information on how to access the newsgroups to read the messages posted on them. In general, there are a few ways to get to the newsgroups or the messages posted to them:

✔ If your Internet service provider (ISP) has a news feed, you can use a news reader that's configured to pick up the news feed and connect you to the news server. If you use Netscape or Internet Explorer, you already have a news reader as both browsers have them built in. (To use this method of access, we recommend you consult the manual or other instructions provided by your individual ISP to configure your news reader.)

✔ If your Internet service provider doesn't have a news feed or you don't have the software necessary to access it, you can get to some newsgroups through the World Wide Web (one such site is DejaNews at `www.dejanews.com`). (Using the Web is our preferred method of accessing newsgroups because it's easy and requires only a World Wide Web browser. For more on browsers, see the "World Wide Web" section coming up later in this appendix. To find out how to access and use DejaNews, keep reading.)

✔ If the newsgroup is gatewayed with a mailing list, you can receive the messages posted to the newsgroup through that mailing list. (*Gatewayed* means that traffic from the newsgroup is relayed to a mailing list and vice versa.)

Here's how to access a newsgroup and read it through the World Wide Web.

1. **Open your World Wide Web browser.**

   You usually do this by double-clicking on the icon for the program or using the Start program menu.

2. **In the URL field of your browser, type in the Web address for DejaNews,** `www.dejanews.com/`

3. **Click <u>Browse Groups</u>.**

   The link for Browse Groups appears just below the Search field on the DejaNews page.

4. **Select the <u>soc</u> link.**

5. **Scroll down the page until you see** `soc.genealogy` **and click the link titled <u>18 branches</u>.**

   From here, you can select any of the `soc.genealogy` newsgroups to explore the messages posted to the group, or after you've read some of the messages to get a feel for the newsgroup, you can click the <u>Post</u> link to send your own message to a particular `soc.genealogy` newsgroup.

Be sure to take a look at Chapter 3 for detailed information about posting to the newsgroups before you do so. Chapter 3 gives you a few guidelines on what to post and how to format your message.

World Wide Web

The World Wide Web is a system for viewing and using multimedia documents on the Internet. The documents that you view on the World Wide Web are written in a code called Hypertext Markup Language (HTML) that is translated into graphical pages (which may have sound and motion attached) by software called a World Wide Web browser. (For general information about features of a browser and how to use one, see the following section, "World Wide Web browsers." For more on HTML, take a look at Chapter 11.)

The pages of the multimedia documents usually have hypertext links that you can click to get to other sites. You can navigate the World Wide Web by typing in the address of Web sites — also called a Uniform Resource Locator (URL) — in the appropriate field of your browser and hitting Enter, or by clicking the links on a page to get to other pages.

On a side note, we want to let you know that although you hear the Web referred to as the Internet, the World Wide Web is not the Internet. The Web is a resource *on* the Internet; it doesn't make up the Internet all by itself. (Other sections of this appendix explain various Internet resources in addition to the Web.) The fact that many of these other resources are now accessible through the World Wide Web is true, but that doesn't make the Web the exact same thing as the Internet.

World Wide Web browsers

A World Wide Web browser is the software you use to view World Wide Web pages. The software converts text documents written in Hypertext Markup Language (HTML) into graphical documents you view on the Internet.

There are several different browser programs available. You can download some browsers for free off the Internet; others come loaded on your computer with software packages; some you buy separately; and still others come with your subscription to an online service provider. Most offer similar or standard navigation features, and almost all are easy to use.

Two of the more popular browsers are Netscape Navigator (see Figure A-1) and Microsoft Internet Explorer (see Figure A-2). Here are some of the common features of these two browsers and how to use those features:

> ✔ Notice that both browsers have a field near the top of the screen where you enter the address, or URL (Uniform Resource Locator), to get to a Web page of interest. Netscape calls its address field Location or Netsite, and Internet Explorer calls its field Address.

✔ The Stop button halts a page that's loading into your browser.

✔ The Back button on the button bar takes you back to the previous site you viewed. Similarly, the Forward button takes you forward to the site you were viewing before you hit the Back button.

✔ Netscape's Reload button and Internet Explorer's Refresh button load the page you're looking at again. If there were any changes to the page while you were online, reloading or refreshing the page picks up those changes and reflects them.

✔ The Print button prints a copy of the site you're looking at. If the Web page is too long to fit on one regular sheet of paper, the browser tells the printer where to split the Web page to print on multiple sheets of paper.

Shortcut list to specific sites.

Takes you to the previous site.

Takes you forward one site.

Loads the page again.

Help pull-down menu.

Prints a copy of the site.

Stops the page that's loading.

Enter URL here.

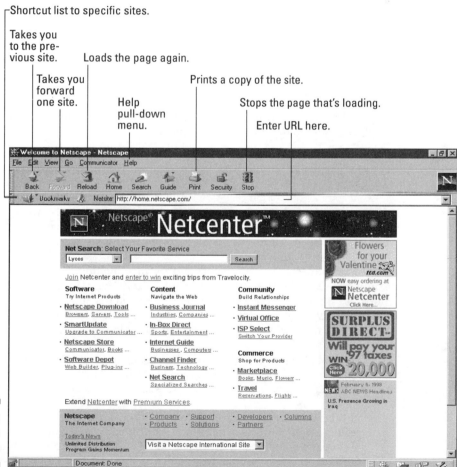

Figure A-1:
Netscape
Navigator.

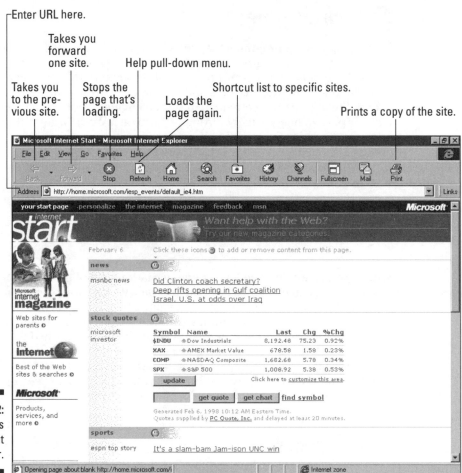

Enter URL here.

Takes you forward one site.

Help pull-down menu.

Takes you to the previous site.

Stops the page that's loading.

Loads the page again.

Shortcut list to specific sites.

Prints a copy of the site.

Figure A-2:
Microsoft's Internet Explorer.

✔ Netscape's Bookmarks and Internet Explorer's Favorites give you a shortcut list to sites that the software manufacturers think you may be interested in or looking for. Additionally, you can add your own book-marks for your favorite or frequently-visited sites by following the software's instructions for adding a bookmark.

✔ Both programs have Help pull-down menus for more information on using the browser and its features.

Search engines

Search engines are programs that search large indices of information that are gathered by robots sent out to *catalog* (sort and record) resources on the Internet. (*Robots* are programs that travel throughout the Internet and collect information on the various sites and resources that they run across.) You can access the information contained in search engines through an *interface* (a form or page online), usually through a form on a World Wide Web page.

Some of the better-known search engines are

- ✔ **Lycos:** www.lycos.com
- ✔ **AltaVista:** www.altavista.digital.com
- ✔ **HotBot:** www.hotbot.com
- ✔ **Excite:** www.excite.com

While each search engine has its own variations, all of them function similarly. All search engines have an interface with a form where you enter keywords to search for in the search engine's index. Each search engine then runs a search of its index, returning its findings to you online with links directly to the pages where the search engine's robot identified the keywords.

Chapter 3 explores genealogical-specific search engines as well and gives you a numbered example to run through. Check out the *Genealogy Online Internet Directory* for even more information on particular search engines.

Chat rooms

Chat rooms are Internet sites where you can log in and participate in real-time (or with just a few seconds delay) conversations. And although chat rooms aren't a resource you'll encounter and use a lot in your genealogical research, we did want you to know that they exist.

A few chat rooms are available to discuss genealogy specifically. Typically, the genealogy chat rooms (or in some cases, sessions that are prearranged) are hosted by or are available through the commercial Internet service providers (particularly America Online) or the Internet Relay Chat (IRC) network.

The IRC hosts several areas (called *channels*) where you find discussions about genealogy. To access and use a chat channel on IRC, you have to use chat software. For more information about the genealogy-related chat channels, visit the Home Page for Genealogy on IRC (www.genealogy.org/~jkatcmi/genealogy-irc/welcome.html). Not only does this home page tell you what's available, its FAQ (Frequently Asked Questions) section provides detailed instructions for downloading the chat software and joining chat channels as well.

Appendix B

What Does This Mean? (A Glossary of Terms)

● ●

Abstract: A brief overview or summary of what a document or Web site contains.

Administration: Handling of the estate of a person who died *intestate.*

Admon: Abbreviation for *administration*.

Ahnentafel: A well-known genealogical numbering system. Ahnentafel is a method of numbering that has a mathematical relationship between parents and children. The word itself means "ancestor" and "table" in German; also referred to as the *Sosa-Stradonitz System* of numbering.

Albumen print: A type of photograph that was produced on a thin piece of paper coated with albumen and silver nitrate and usually mounted on cardboard; typically taken between 1858 and 1910.

Ambrotype: A type of photograph that was printed on thin glass and usually had a black backing; typically taken between 1858 and 1866.

America Online: One of the most popular *commercial Internet service providers.*

Ancestor: A person from whom you are descended.

Ancestor chart: A chart that runs horizontally across a page and identifies a primary person (including that person's name, date and place of birth, date and place of marriage, and date and place of death), his/her parents, and then each of their parents, and so on until the chart runs off the page. Usually called a *Pedigree chart*.

Ancestral File: A *database* created and maintained by the Church of Jesus Christ of Latter-day Saints with millions of names available in family group sheets and pedigree charts; part of the *FamilySearch* collection of *CD-ROMs,* which are accessible at Family History Centers.

Archive: A physical location where historical documents and records are stored.

Automoderator: A computer program that determines whether a post to a *newsgroup* is appropriate, and if so, posts it to the newsgroup.

Backbones: High-speed data lines that support the *Internet*.

Banns: See *marriage banns.*

Baptismal certificate: A certificate issued by a church at the time of baptism; sometimes used to approximate birth in the absence of a birth certificate.

BBS: Acronym for *Bulletin Board System.*

Bibliography: A list of books or other materials that were used in research; also a list of books or other materials that are available on a particular topic.

Biographical sketch: A brief written account of a person's life.

Biography: A detailed written account of a person's life.

Birth certificate: A legal record stating when and where a person was born.

Bounty land: Federal land given to a person in exchange for military service or some other civic service.

Browser: See *World Wide Web browser.*

Bulletin Board System: One or more computers that answer a telephone in order to communicate with other computers that call. Bulletin Board Systems allow users of the other computers to post information or messages to them. Also called *BBS.*

Bureau of Refugees, Freedmen, and Abandoned Lands: Established in 1865, the bureau had programs to assist ex-slaves after the American Civil War. Also called *Freedman's Bureau.*

Cabinet card: A larger version of the *carte-de-visite* photograph; typically taken between 1865 and 1906.

Canon Code: A code that explains the bloodline relationship in legal terms by identifying how many degrees of separation (or steps) are between two people related by blood. Canon law counts only the number of steps from the nearest common *ancestor* of both relatives.

Carte-de-visite: A type of photograph that was a small paper print mounted on a card; collections were usually bound together in a photo album. Typically taken between 1858 and 1891.

CD-ROM: Acronym for Compact Disk – Read Only Memory; used in your computer's compact disk drive. A CD-ROM stores large amounts of information (including multimedia) that can be retrieved by your computer.

Census: The counting of a population undertaken by a government.

Census index: A listing of the people who are included in particular census records, along with references indicating where you can find the actual census records.

Charter: A formal or informal document that defines the scope of a *newsgroup.*

Chat room: An *Internet* site where you can log in and participate in real-time conversations.

Cite: To name the source of some information and provide reference to the original source.

Civil Code: A code that explains the bloodline relationship in legal terms by identifying how many degrees of separation (or steps) are between two people related by blood; civil law counts each step between two relatives as a degree.

Civil records: Government documents that contain information on the civic duties of your *ancestors,* proceedings of municipal governments, or any other records of your ancestors' interaction with the government; often found in local and state archives or courthouses.

Civil registration: Primary record of a vital event in life: birth, death, or marriage; for the most part, originals are kept by local governments. Also called *vital records* in the United States.

Commercial Internet service provider: A company or organization that supplies access to the Internet for a fee.

Community network: An *Internet service provider* that's locally based and offers access to people in the community free of charge. Also called *freenet.*

Comprehensive genealogical site: A Web site that identifies a large number of other genealogical sites containing information on a number of families, locations, or a variety of other genealogically related subjects.

CompuServe: A popular *commercial Internet service provider.*

Copyright: Copyright is the exclusive right of a creator to reproduce, prepare derivative works, distribute, perform, display, sell, lend, or rent his/her creations.

County clerk: The clerk of the county court that records or maintains records of transactions and events in that county. Sometimes called the county recorder.

Daguerreotype: A type of photograph that required a long exposure time and was taken on silver-plated copper; typically taken between 1839 and 1860.

Database: A collection of information that is entered, organized, stored, and used on a computer.

Death certificate: A legal record stating when and where a person died.

Declaration of intent: A sworn statement by a person who intends to become a naturalized citizen of the United States.

Deed: A document that records the transfer of ownership of a piece of property or land.

Descendant: A person who descended from a particular *ancestor*.

Descendant chart: A chart that contains information about an *ancestor* and spouse (or particular spouses if there was more than one), and their children and their spouses, grandchildren and spouses, and so on down the family line; it is usually formatted vertically on a page like a list.

Dial-up connection: A method of connecting to the Internet wherein your computer uses a telephone line to call in to an *Internet service provider*.

Digest mode: An option for receiving postings to some *mailing lists* in which several messages are batched together and sent to you instead of each message being sent separately.

Digital camera: A camera that captures images to memory instead of to film, and then downloads the images to your computer.

Digitized record: A copy or image of a record that has been made using electronic means (typically a *scanner* and computer).

Direct connection: An *Internet* line that comes directly into your home or business and is hooked up to your computer(s).

Directory: A collection of information about individuals who live in a particular town, city, county, or district.

Download: Getting a file (information or a program) to your computer from another computer.

Earthlink: A popular *commercial Internet service provider.*

Electronic mail: Messages that are sent from one person to another electronically over the *Internet.* Also called *e-mail.*

E-mail: Short for *electronic mail.*

Emigrant: A person who leaves or moves away from one country or region to settle in another country or region.

Enumeration district: The area assigned to a particular *enumerator* of the *census.*

Enumerator: A person who collected details on individuals during a *census.*

Estate: The assets and liabilities of a person who dies.

Family association: An organized group of individuals who are researching the same branch of a family or a particular *surname.*

Family association site: A Web page that is designed and posted by an organization devoted to researching a particular branch of a family or a specific *surname.*

Family group sheet: A summary of a particular family including biographical information about a husband, wife, and their children.

Family history: The written account of a family's existence over time.

Family History Center: Local branches of the *Family History Library.*

Family History Library: The Church of Jesus Christ of Latter-day Saints' main library in Salt Lake City, Utah. The Family History Library has the world's largest collection of genealogical holdings including print sources and microfilmed records, as well as records and other information shared by genealogical researchers worldwide.

Family History Library Catalog: A listing of records (books, films, microfiche, CDs, cassette tapes, videos, and microfilms) available at the *Family History Library* in Salt Lake City, Utah; part of the *FamilySearch* collection of *CD-ROMs,* which are accessible at *Family History Centers.*

Family outline report: A list of the descendants of a particular *ancestor*.

FamilySearch: A collection of *CD-ROMs* of information compiled by the Church of Jesus Christ of Latter-day Saints; it includes the Ancestral File, International Genealogical Index, Military Index, Social Security Death Index, and Scottish Church Records.

FHC: Acronym for *Family History Center.*

FHL: Acronym for *Family History Library.*

File Transfer Protocol: A way to transfer files from your computer to another, or vice versa, over the *Internet.* Also called *FTP.*

Flame: A verbal (written) attack *online*.

Forum: A subject-specific area where members post messages and files.

Fraternal order: A service club or organization of persons.

Freedman's Bureau: Abbreviated name for the *Bureau of Refugees, Freedmen, and Abandoned Lands.*

Freedman's Savings and Trust Company: Established in 1865, this was a bank for ex-slaves.

Freenet: An *Internet service provider* that's locally-based and offers access to people in the community free of charge. Also called *community network.*

Freeware: Software you usually obtain and use for free by downloading it off the *Internet.*

FTP: Acronym for *File Transfer Protocol.*

Full-format: An option for receiving postings to some *mailing lists* in which you receive every message that is posted individually instead of batched together in *digest mode.*

Gateway: Computer(s) that forward messages and route data between networks.

Gatewayed: When traffic from a *newsgroup* is relayed to a related *mailing list* and vice versa.

Gazetteer: Geographical dictionary that provides information about places.

GEDCOM: Acronym for *Genealogical Data Communication.*

Genealogical Data Communication: The standard file format for exporting and importing information between genealogical *databases;* intended to make data translatable between different genealogical software programs so that you can share your family information easily.

GenCount: A report that provides you with an *e-mail* indicating the number of times your selected *surname* appears in the *GenServ* system.

GENDEX: An index of *online* genealogical *databases* that were created using the GED2HTML program.

Genealogical society: An organized group that attempts to preserve documents and history for the area in which the society is located; often a genealogical society has a second purpose, which is to help its members research their *ancestors.*

Genealogy: The study of *ancestors, descendants,* and family origins.

GenSample: A list of the individuals who have posted records in the *GenServ* system pertaining to a *surname* you're interested in.

GenServ: A collection of *GEDCOM* files that's maintained on a central computer.

Geographic-specific Web site: A Web site that has information pertaining to a particular locality (town, county, state, country, or other area).

Glass plate negative: A type of photograph made from light-sensitive silver bromide immersed in gelatin; typically taken between 1848 and 1930.

Gopher: A way to hierarchically categorize data on the *Internet* using a series of text-based menus through which you can browse and click; developed at the University of Minnesota.

Henry System: A widely used and accepted genealogical numbering system, it assigns a particular sequence of numbers to the children of the *progenitor* and subsequent generations.

Hierarchy: In terms of a *newsgroup*, a hierarchy is the major grouping to which a newsgroup belongs; for example, `soc.genealogy.computing` belongs to the `soc` hierarchy.

Historical society: An organized group that attempts to preserve documents and history for the area in which the society is located.

Home page: A multimedia document that is created in *HTML* and viewable on the *Internet* with the use of a *World Wide Web browser;* also called a *World Wide Web page.*

HTML: Acronym for *HyperText Markup Language.*

HyperText Markup Language: The programming language of the *World Wide Web.* HTML is a code that's translated into graphical pages by software called a *World Wide Web browser.*

IGI: Acronym for *International Genealogical Index.*

Immigrant: A person who moves into or settles in a country or region.

Immigration record: A record of the entry of a person into a specific country where they were not natively born or naturalized.

Index: A list of some sort. An index can be a list of Web sites, types of records, or so on.

Interlibrary loan: A system in which one library loans a book or other material to another library for a person to borrow or use.

International Genealogical Index: A list of births and marriages of deceased individuals reflected in records collected by the Church of Jesus Christ of Latter-day Saints. The International Genealogical Index is part of the *FamilySearch* collection of *CD-ROMs* which are accessible at *Family History Centers.*

Internet: A system of computer networks joined together by high-speed data lines called *backbones.*

Internet service provider: A company or other organization that provides people with access to the Internet through a direct connection or dial-up connection. Also called *ISP.*

Intestate: A person who died without leaving a valid *will.*

ISP: Acronym for *Internet service provider.*

Kinship report: A list of family members and how they relate directly to one particular *ancestor,* usually kinship reports include the *Civil Code* and *Canon Code* for the relationship to the ancestor.

Land grant: Permission to purchase or a gift of land in exchange for military service or other civic service.

Land record: A document recording the sale or exchange of land; most land records are maintained at a local level where the property is/was located.

Lurking: Reading messages that others post to a *mailing list* without posting any messages of your own.

Maiden name: A woman's *surname* prior to marriage; sometimes reflected as "née" on records and documents.

Mailing list: An *e-mail* exchange *forum* that consists of a group of people who share common interests; e-mail messages posted to the list come directly to your e-mail in *full-format* or *digest mode;* the list consists of the names of everyone who joins the group. When you want to send a message to the group, you post it to a single e-mail address that subsequently delivers the message to everyone on the list.

Marriage banns: A proclamation of the intent to marry someone in front of a church congregation.

Marriage bond: A financial contract guaranteeing a marriage was going to take place; usually posted by the groom and another person (typically the father or brother of the bride).

Marriage certificate: A legal document certifying the union of two individuals.

Marriage license: A document granting permission to marry from a civil or ecclesiastical authority.

Maternal: Relating to the mother's side of the family.

Microfiche: A clear sheet that contains tiny images of documents, records, books, and so on; you must read it with a microfiche reader or other magnifying equipment.

Microfilm: A roll of clear film that contains tiny images of documents, records, books, and so forth; you must read it with a microfilm reader.

Microsoft Network: A popular *commercial Internet service provider.*

Military Index: A list of those killed in the Korean and Vietnam Wars; part of the *FamilySearch* collection of *CD-ROMs,* which are accessible at *Family History Centers.*

Modem: A piece of equipment that allows your computer to talk to other computers through a telephone line; modems can be internal (inside your computer) or external (plugged into one of your computer's serial ports).

Mortgage: Legal agreement to repay money borrowed with real property as collateral.

Muster record: A type of military pay record reflecting that your *ancestor* was present with a military unit at a particular time and place.

Naturalization: The process of becoming a citizen or subject of a particular country in a manner other than birth in that country.

Naturalization record: The legal document proving one is a naturalized citizen.

Netiquette: Simple guidelines for communicating effectively and politely on the *Internet.*

Newsgroup: A place to post messages of a particular focus so that groups of people at large can read them online; messages are posted to a *news server* which, in turn, copies the messages to other news servers.

News reader: Software required to read messages posted to a *newsgroup.*

News server: One or more computers that replicate *newsgroups* over the Internet.

Notebook computer: A compact computer that's portable.

Obituary: An account of one's death that usually appears in a newspaper or other type of media.

One-name study: A page on the *World Wide Web* that focuses on research involving one particular *surname* regardless of the geographic location in which it appears.

Online: Gaining access to and using the *Internet.*

Orphan: An infant or child whose parents are both deceased. In some early times and places, a child was considered an orphan if his/her father had died but the mother was still living.

Palmtop: A hand-sized computer that is portable and can contain some of the same programs that are housed on desktop computers.

Passenger list: Listing of the names of passengers who traveled from one country to another on a particular ship.

Patent for land: A document that conveyed the title of a piece of land to a new owner upon that person's meeting certain required conditions to own the land.

Paternal: Relating to the father's side of the family.

Pedigree chart: A chart that runs horizontally across a page, identifying a primary person (including that person's name, date and place of birth, date and place of marriage, and date and place of death), his/her parents, and then each of their parents, and so on until the chart runs off the page. Sometimes called an *Ancestor chart.*

Pension record: A type of military record reflecting the amount of a pension the government paid to an individual who served in the military during a particular war or campaign and was disabled or had financial need; pension records also showed the amount of pension paid to the widow or orphan(s) of such an individual.

Personal Web page: A page on the *World Wide Web* that was designed and posted by an individual or family.

Petition for land: An application your *ancestor* may have filed for a land grant.

Plat map: A map of lots within a tract of land.

Platinum print: A type of photograph with a matte surface that appeared to be embedded in the paper. Images were often highlighted with artistic chalk giving the photo a hand-drawn quality; typically taken between 1880 and 1930.

Primary source: A document, oral account, photograph, or any other item that was created at the time a certain event occurred; information for the record was supplied by a witness to the event.

Probate: Settlement of one's *estate* after death.

Probate records: Types of court records that deal with the settling of an *estate* upon one's death. Probate records include contested wills and *will* readings; often the file contains testimonies and the ruling.

Prodigy: A popular *commercial Internet service provider.*

Professional researcher: A person who will research your genealogy — particular family lines — or obtain copies of documents for you for a fee.

Progenitor: The furthest-back *ancestor* you know about in a particular family line.

Robot: A program that travels throughout the *Internet* and collects information about sites and resources it comes across. Also called a *spider.*

Roots Surname List: A list of *surnames,* their associated dates, and locations accompanied by the contact information for persons researching those surnames. Also called *RSL.*

RSL: Acronym for *Roots Surname List*.

Query: A research question that you post to a particular Web site, *mailing list,* or *newsgroup* so that other researchers can help you solve your genealogical research problems/challenges.

Scanner: A device that captures digital images of photographs and documents into your computer.

Search engine: A program that searches either a large index of information generated by *robots* or a particular Web site.

Secondary source: A document, oral account, or any other record that was created after an event took place or for which information was supplied by someone who was not an eyewitness to the event.

Service record: A type of military record that chronicles the military career of an individual.

Shareware: Software that you can try before you pay to license and use it permanently; usually you download shareware off the *Internet.*

Site: One or more *World Wide Web pages;* also called a *Web site.*

Social Security Death Index: An *index* of those persons for whom Social Security death claims were filed with the United States government. The Social Security Death Index is part of the *FamilySearch* collection of *CD-ROMs,* which are accessible at *Family History Centers;* also available *online* (at www.ancestry.com/ssdi/advanced.htm).

Sosa-Stradonitz System: See *ahnentafel.*

Sound card: An internal device on your computer that enables you to hear any audio that comes on software or audio files that you download off the *Internet.*

Soundex: A system of indexing the U.S. federal *census* that places names that are pronounced in a similar manner but spelled differently into groups; the Soundex code for a name includes a letter and then three numbers.

Source: Any person or material (book, document, record, periodical, and so on) that provides information for your research.

Spider: A program that travels throughout the *Internet* and collects information about sites and resources it comes across. Also called a *robot.*

Stereographic card: A type of photograph that was curved and rendered a three-dimensional effect when used with a viewer; developed in the 1850s.

Surname: A last name or family name.

Survey: Detailed drawing and legal description of the boundaries of a land parcel.

Tax record: A record of any tax paid, including property, inheritance, and church taxes; most taxes were collected at the local level, but the records have now been turned over to government archives.

Telnet: A text-based program that allows you to log in to another computer and view files or documents that are available for public access; you need a telnet client (software) to use telnet.

Thread: A group of messages with a common subject on a *newsgroup.*

Tintype: A type of photograph that was made on a metal sheet, and the image was often coated with a varnish; typically taken between 1858 and 1910.

Tiny tafel: A compact way to show the relationships within a family *database.* Tiny tafel provides a *Soundex* code for a *surname* and the dates and locations where that surname may be found according to the database.

Tract book: A book describing the lots within a township or other geographic area.

Transcribed record: A copy of the content of a record that has been duplicated word for word.

Uniform Resource Locator: A way of addressing resources on the *World Wide Web;* also called *URL.*

URL: Acronym for *Uniform Resource Locator.*

U.S. Colored Troops database: An *online database* of information on more than 230,000 soldiers of African descent who served in the U.S. Colored Troops; part of the Civil War Soldiers and Sailors System sponsored by the National Park Service.

Video-capture board: A device that enables your computer to grab images from your video camera.

Vital record: Primary record of a vital event in life — birth, death, or marriage; for the most part, originals are kept by local governments. Often called *civil registrations* outside the United States.

Warrant: A certificate to receive land when your *ancestor's* petition for a land grant was approved.

Web site: One or more *World Wide Web pages;* also called a *site.*

Will: A legal document that explains how a person wishes for his/her *estate* to be settled or distributed upon death.

Witness: One who attests that he/she saw an event.

World Wide Web: A system for viewing and using multimedia documents on the *Internet;* Web documents are created in *HyperText Markup Language (HTML)* and are read by *browsers.*

World Wide Web browser: Software that enables you to view *HTML* documents on the *Internet.*

World Wide Web page: A multimedia document that is created in *HTML* and viewable on the *Internet* with the use of a *World Wide Web browser;* also called a *home page.*

Zip disk: A computer disk that you use with an Iomega Zip drive; stores up to 100MB of data.

Appendix C

About the CD

● ●

*Y*ou'll find a variety of software on the CD-ROM to help you organize your genealogy with the help of your computer, navigate resources on the Internet, and share your own genealogical information on the Internet. This Appendix tells you a little about each of the programs and how to use them.

System Requirements

Make sure that your computer meets the minimum system requirements listed below. If your computer doesn't meet most of these requirements, you may have problems using the contents of the CD-ROM.

- ✔ A PC with a 486 or faster processor, or a Mac OS computer with a 68030 or faster processor.
- ✔ Microsoft Windows 3.1 or Windows 95, or Mac OS system software 7.5 or later.
- ✔ At least 16MB of total RAM installed on your computer.
- ✔ A CD-ROM drive — double-speed (2x) or faster.
- ✔ A monitor capable of displaying at least 256 colors or grayscale.
- ✔ A modem with a speed of at least 14,400 bps and an Internet connection.

If you need more information on the basics, check out *PCs For Dummies,* 4th Edition, by Dan Gookin; *Macs For Dummies,* 4th Edition, by David Pogue; *Windows 95 For Dummies* by Andy Rathbone; or *Windows 3.11 For Dummies,* 3rd Edition, by Andy Rathbone (all published by IDG Books Worldwide, Inc.).

Using the CD with Microsoft Windows

To install the items from the CD to your hard drive, follow these steps:

1. **Insert the CD into your computer's CD-ROM drive.**

2. **Windows 3.1 or 3.11 users: From Program Manager, choose File⇨Run.**

   Windows 95 users: Click Start⇨Run.

3. **In the dialog box that appears, type** D:\SETUP.EXE

   Replace *D* with the proper drive letter if your CD-ROM drive uses a different letter. (If you don't know the letter, see how your CD-ROM drive is listed under My Computer in Windows 95 or File Manager in Windows 3.1.)

4. **Click OK.**

   A license agreement window appears.

5. **Read through the license agreement, nod your head, and then click the Accept button if you want to use the CD — after you click Accept, you'll never be bothered by the License Agreement window again.**

   The CD interface Welcome screen appears. The interface is a little program that shows you what's on the CD and coordinates installing the programs and running the demos. The interface basically enables you to click a button or two to make things happen.

6. **Click anywhere on the Welcome screen to enter the interface.**

   Now you are getting to the action. This next screen lists categories for the software on the CD.

7. **To view the items within a category, just click the category's name.**

   A list of programs in the category appears.

8. **For more information about a program, click the program's name.**

   Be sure to read the information that appears. Sometimes a program has it's own system requirements or requires you to do a few tricks on your computer before you can install or run the program, and this screen tells you what you might need to do, if necessary.

9. **If you don't want to install the program, click the Go Back button to return to the previous screen.**

   You can always return to the previous screen by clicking the Go Back button. This feature allows you to browse the different categories and products and decide what you want to install.

10. **To install a program, click the appropriate Install button.**

    The CD interface drops to the background while the CD installs the program you chose.

11. **To install other items, repeat Steps 7 – 10.**

12. **When you've finished installing programs, click the Quit button to close the interface.**

    You can eject the CD now. Carefully place it back in the plastic jacket of the book for safekeeping.

Using the CD with Mac OS

To install the items from the CD to your hard drive, follow these steps:

1. **Insert the CD into your computer's CD-ROM drive.**

   In a moment, an icon representing the CD you just inserted appears on your Mac desktop. Chances are, the icon looks like a CD-ROM.

2. **Double-click the CD icon to show the CD's contents.**

3. **Double-click the Read Me First icon.**

   The Read Me First text file contains information about the CD's programs and any last-minute instructions you may need in order to correctly install them.

4. **To install most programs, just drag the program's folder from the CD window and drop it on your hard drive icon.**

5. **Other programs come with installer programs — with these, you simply open the program's folder on the CD, and then double-click the icon with the words "Install" or "Installer."**

   Sometimes the installers are actually self-extracting archives, which just means that the program files have been bundled up into an archive, and this self extractor unbundles the files and places them on your hard drive. This kind of program is often called an .sea. Double-click anything with .sea in the title, and it will run just like an installer.

   After you have installed the programs you want, you can eject the CD. Carefully place it back in the plastic jacket of the book for safekeeping.

What You Get on the CD

Here's a summary of the software on this CD arranged by category. If you use Windows, the CD interface helps you install software easily. (If you have no idea what we're talking about when we say "CD interface," flip back a page or two to find the section, "Using the CD with Microsoft Windows.")

If you use a Mac OS computer, you can take advantage of the easy Mac interface to quickly install the programs.

Genealogy programs

AniMap Plus 1.6 Demo Version (Windows 3.1/95)

This is a demonstration version of the AniMap Plus County Boundary Historical Atlas for Windows program. AniMap is an interactive historical atlas that helps you track your family's movements and county boundary changes over time. Information about the full program is available at www.goldbug.com/AniMap.html

Brother's Keeper 5.2B (Windows 3.1/95)

Brother's Keeper 5.2B is genealogical shareware that allows you to store information about your family and create charts and reports using that information. It includes versions in English, French, Norwegian, Danish, Swedish, German, and Dutch. If you decide you want to keep and register your copy after trying it out, you can follow the instructions at the Brother's Keeper for Windows Web site (ourworld.compuserve.com/homepages/Brothers_Keeper/).

Brother's Keeper 5.2F (MS-DOS)

This is the MS-DOS brother program to Brother's Keeper 5.2B (described earlier). It is a genealogy shareware program that stores data on your ancestors and allows you to create charts and reports. It includes versions in English, French, Norwegian, Danish, Swedish, German, Finnish, and Dutch. If after trying the shareware you decide to keep and pay for it, the Brother's Keeper for DOS Web site (home.sprynet.com/sprynet/steed/) provides instructions for you to follow.

Family Tree Maker 3.02 (Windows 3.1/95)

This is a basic edition of the popular genealogical software Family Tree Maker from Brøderbund Software, Inc. It is fully functional, allowing you to organize, store, and use charts and reports for information on your family. Using it is the best way to decide whether you'd like to upgrade and purchase a standard or deluxe edition of Family Tree Maker, both of which offer

more features and enhancements. For a comparison chart between the basic, standard, and deluxe editions, visit `www.familytreemaker.com/ftmvers.html`

GED2HTML (Windows 3.1/95)

This is Eugene Stark's infamous program to convert your GEDCOM to an HTML file so that you can post data contained within it on the World Wide Web. It is shareware that you must register if you decide to keep it when the trial period is over. The GED2HTML Web site (`www.gendex.com/ged2html/`) provides additional information about the program.

GEDClean 2.11 (Windows 3.1/95)

GEDClean is freeware developed by Tom Raynor. It assists you by stripping information about living persons from your GEDCOM file per your specifications. For more information about GEDClean, check out `members.aol.com/tomraynor2/gedclean.htm`

GenBrowser 1.05 (Windows 95)

GenBrowser is shareware that searches the Internet looking for sites with genealogy indices created using GEDCOM files. It retrieves the information that you request and converts the HTML back to GEDCOM for you to use with your genealogical database. For more information about GenBrowser features and how to register your copy if you decide to keep it, see `www.pratt.lib.md.us/~bharding/rippleeffect/GenBrowser/GenBrowser.html`

Reunion v.5 (Mac)

This is the demonstration version of the popular genealogical program for Macintosh. It allows you to document, store, and display information about your family. The demo version limits you to information about 35 people. If after using the demonstration version, you find that you like Reunion, you can purchase the full version. For more information about Reunion, visit its Web site at `www.LeisterPro.com/Default.html`

Sparrowhawk 1.0 (Mac)

Sparrowhawk is Macintosh shareware that converts your GEDCOM file into HTML so that you can post part or all of it on the Web. Its Web page provides detailed information about the program — how to use it and how to register it if you decide to keep it after the trial period. The Web address is `www.tjp.washington.edu/bdm/genealogy/sparrowhawk.html`

Internet tools

Anarchie 2.0.1 (Mac)

Anarchie 2.0.1, from Stairways Shareware, is a Macintosh shareware File Transfer Protocol (FTP) program that you can use to find files on the Net and copy files between your Mac and a computer on the Net. FTP programs were more useful before the World Wide Web took hold and made finding and downloading files a snap. FTP programs are still handy, however, for activities not supported by the Web, such as uploading your own files and Web pages. To register the software or to learn more about the product, check out the Web site at www.share.com/share/peterlewis/index.html

Eudora Light 3.01 and v 3.1 (Windows 3.1/95 and Mac)

Eudora Light from Qualcomm, Inc., is a free, powerful e-mail program. If you have an Internet e-mail account, you can use Eudora Light to send e-mail to and receive e-mail from any of the tens of millions of other people around the world who are connected to the Internet. In addition to text messages, Eudora Light lets you attach files to e-mail, so that you can use it to transmit electronic pictures, sound clips, or any other kind of data stored in files. To learn more or to puchase the more-powerful commercial version of Eudora, go to the Web site at www.eudora.com

Free Agent 1.11 (Windows 3.1/95)

If your Internet service provider has a news feed and you want to access the soc.genealogy and alt.genealogy newsgroups the traditional way (not using the Web), this is a program that will help you! Free Agent, from Forté, Inc., is a free Windows program that lets you read and participate in ongoing group discussions that take place on the Internet via Usenet newsgroups. Tens of thousands of newsgroups exist, devoted to virtually every topic under the sun, ranging from knitting to high finance and from dating to decoding DNA, and Free Agent is one of the best programs available for accessing them. Among the great features of Free Agent is its capability to let you read newsgroup articles offline, which could conceivably save you Internet connection charges and phone charges. For more information about how to use Free Agent, visit their Web site at www.forteinc.com

HomeSite 3.0 (Windows 95)

HomeSite 3.0, from Allaire, is a popular shareware HTML editor for Windows 95. If you're interested in creating your own Web page, this program makes creating and editing documents with HTML, the programming language used to make a Web page, a breeze. Get more information on HomeSite at www.allaire.com

HotDog (Windows 95)

HotDog, from Sausage Software, is a powerful but easy-to-use Windows shareware program that helps you create Web pages. This is shareware from Sausage Software that you can use and evaluate for 30 days before having to decide whether to purchase it. For more information about HotDog, visit the program's Web site (www.sausage.com).

HTML Web Weaver Lite (Mac)

This is a shareware version of Miracle Software's commercially available World Wide Web Weaver. Though it doesn't have many of the stronger features of its commercial sibling, HTML Web Weaver Lite is easy to use and takes up only a bit of your hard drive space and memory, making it a perfect editor for older Macs. To learn more or to purchase the commercial version, check out the Web site at www.miracleinc.com

Internet Explorer 4.0 (Windows 95)

Internet Explorer 4.0, from Microsoft Corporation is the latest version of the popular Web browser from Microsoft, including support for CDF-based Web channels. In addition to Active Channels, Explorer 4.0 includes components that allow Windows users to use the Active Desktop as well as Active Screen Savers. To learn more or to check for updated versions, go to the Microsoft Web site at www.microsoft.com/ie

Net Nanny v 3.0 (Windows 3.1/95)

NetNanny is just what it sounds like. It's a program that monitors and blocks Internet content that is unsuitable for your children (or other young viewers). This is a 30-day free trial version; you can also find information at www.netnanny.com. According to Net Nanny developers, the software enables you to monitor, screen, and block access to anything residing on, or running in, out, or through your PC, online or off. Net Nanny offers two-way screening in real-time and you decide what to screen with the help of a site list. You can also control access to World Wide Web addresses, newsgroups, IRC channels, FTP sites, e-mail, non-Internet bulletin board services (BBSs), words, phrases, and personal information (addresses, credit card numbers, and so on).

Netscape Navigator 4.0 (Windows 3.1/95)

Netscape Navigator 4.0, from Netscape Communications Corporation, is the latest and greatest Web browser from the folks at Netscape. It features enhancements such as faster start-up time, faster loading plug-ins and Java applets, and drop-down menus for quicker and easier navigation. The latest HTML standards are also supported in this version. For more information about the Navigator family of products, go to the Web site at home.netscape.com/navigator/index.html

WebWhacker (Windows 3.1/95 and Mac)

WebWhacker, from Blue Squirrel, allows you to save Web pages (the text, graphics, and HTML links) to your hard drive so that you can open and view them quickly and offline. The copy on your CD-ROM is a demonstration version and will expire after you've used it for a little while. If you like it after trying it for a while, you can puchase the software from the Web site at www.bluesquirrel.com/whacker/

WS_FTP LE 4.5 (Windows 3.1/95)

WS_FTP LE 4.5, from Ipswitch, Inc., is a free (for noncommercial use) Windows File Transfer Protocol (FTP) program. With it, you can transfer files (also called uploading and downloading) between your PC and a computer on the Internet that supports FTP. Why would you need it? It is handy if you want to download an FTP copy of a GEDCOM file from someone's Web or FTP site or upload your Web page to your Internet service provider's server. To learn more, check out the Web site at www.ipswitch.com

Multimedia tools

Acrobat Reader 3.0 (Windows 3.1/95 and Mac)

Acrobat Reader 3.0, from Adobe Systems, is a free program that lets you view and print Portable Document Format, or PDF, files. The PDF format is used by many programs that you find on the Internet for storing documentation because it supports the use of such stylish elements as assorted fonts and colorful graphics. You can also get more information by visiting the Adobe Systems Web site (www.adobe.com).

GraphicConverter 2.8 (Mac)

GraphicConverter 2.8, by shareware author Thorsten Lemke, is a Macintosh program that lets you view images in virtually any graphics format that you're likely to encounter on the Internet. It lets you convert the most common Windows, DOS, Amiga, and Atari computer images to Macintosh formats and vice versa; and it provides a rich set of image-editing options. The latter two features are especially useful if you're interested in creating your own Web pages. For more information, check out the Lemke Software Web site at members.aol.com/lemkesoft

Paint Shop Pro (Windows 3.1/95)

Paint Shop Pro, from JASC, Inc., is a multipurpose graphics tool for Windows. This superb shareware program lets you view images in virtually any graphics format that you're likely to encounter on the Internet. In addition, it lets you edit and crop images, convert images from one file format to

another, and even create pictures from scratch, which all can be useful in helping to create your own World Wide Web pages. Visit the program's Web site (www.jasc.com/psp.html) for more information.

Utilities

CleanSweep Deluxe (Windows 95)

Clean Sweep Deluxe from Quarterdeck is a tryout version of Quarterdeck's commercial uninstaller software. This program gets rid of all the system files associated with any program installed by Windows. This fully featured trial version operates for 30 days and can remove programs running on Windows 95. For more information on CleanSweep Deluxe, visit the Web site (www.qdeck.com).

StuffIt Expander 4.0.1 (Mac)

StuffIt Expander 4.0.1, from Aladdin Systems, Inc., is an invaluable file-decompression shareware utility for the Macintosh. Many files you find on the Internet are compressed, or shrunken in size via special programming tricks, both to save storage space and to cut down on the amount of time they require to be downloaded. You may also occasionally receive compressed files as e-mail attachments. After you have a compressed file on your hard disk, you should use StuffIt Expander to decompress it and make it useable again. To learn more, check out the Web site at www.aladdinsys.com

DropStuff with Expander Enhancer (Mac)

DropStuff with Expander Enhancer 4.0 is a complementary product that not only creates StuffIt archievies, but also enables StuffIt Expander to handle a wider variety of compression formats and to decompress files more quickly on Power Macintosh computers. For more information about StuffIt Expander and DropStuff with Expander Enhancer, visit the Web site at www.aladdinsys.com

WinZip 6.3 (Windows 3.1/95)

WinZip 6.3, from Nico Mak computing, is an invaluable file compression and decompression Windows shareware utility. Many files that you find on the Internet are compressed, or shrunken in size via special programming tricks, both to save storage space and to cut down on the amount of time they require to be downloaded. You may also occasionally receive compressed files (ZIP files) as e-mail attachments. After you have a compressed file on your hard disk, you can use WinZip to decompress it and make it useable again. To learn even more about WinZip, visit the program's Web site (www.winzip.com).

Know the Difference Between Freeware and Shareware

Freeware is a program that the creator makes available for public use on a free-of-charge basis. Usually you download freeware off of the Internet (although there are some exceptions through which you can get freeware — like on this CD-ROM) and it does not require that you register your copy. You can use freeware for as long as you like with no obligations!

Shareware is another story. Shareware is not free — it is commercial software that you are allowed to use on a trial basis for no charge. After the trial period is over, you must decide whether to keep it and pay for it. If you decide not to keep and pay for the shareware, you delete it from your computer. (Sometimes the copy you downloaded becomes unusable upon expiration of your trial period.) If you decide to buy the shareware, you should follow the registration instructions that come with it.

Using the Directory Links

The *Genealogy Online Internet Directory* in this book provides a lot of URLs for sites that we recommend you visit to get an idea of what is available in various categories. Rather than make you flip page by page through the Directory to find these URLs and go to visit these sites, we thought we'd save you some time and paper cuts! We've put links on the CD-ROM to all of the sites identified in the Directory! Isn't that convenient? Here's what you need to do to use these links:

1. **With the CD-ROM in your drive, launch your Web browser.**

2. **Using the File pull-down menu in your browser, select the option that allows you to open a file.**

   An Open dialog box pops up.

3. **Select the LINKS.HTM file either by clicking on it (if it appears in the dialog box) or by typing the filename and path in the field.**

   The filename and path includes the letter for your CD-ROM drive, and then the filename — it looks like this: D:\LINKS.HTM if your CD-ROM drive is D:\

4. **Click on a link for any site you want to visit.**

   This opens a second browser window taking you to the Web site you've selected. The links page remains open in the original browser window so that you can toggle back to it to select another link. Each time you

select a new link, the Web site selected pops up in that second browser window — so don't worry that you're going to end up with several browser windows open at one time.

If You've Got Problems (Of the CD Kind)

We've tried our best to compile programs that work on most computers with the minimum system requirements. But your computer may differ, and some programs may not work properly for some reason.

The two most common problems are that you don't have enough memory (RAM) for the programs you want to use, or you have other programs running that are affecting installation or running of a program. If you get error messages like `Not enough memory` or `Setup cannot continue`, try one or more of these methods and then try using the software again:

- **Turn off any antivirus software that you have on your computer.** Installers sometimes mimic virus activity and may make your computer incorrectly believe that it is being infected by a virus.

- **Close all running programs.** The more programs you're running, the less memory is available to other programs. Installers also typically update files and programs; if you keep other programs running, installation may not work properly.

- **In Windows, close the CD interface and run demos or installations directly from Windows Explorer.** The interface itself can tie up system memory or even conflict with certain kinds of interactive demos. Use Windows Explorer to browse the files on the CD and launch installers or demos.

- **Have your local computer store add more RAM to your computer.** This is, admittedly, a drastic and somewhat expensive step. However, if you have a Windows 95 PC or a Mac OS computer with a PowerPC chip, adding more memory can really help the speed of your computer and enable more programs to run at the same time.

If you still have trouble installing the items from the CD, please call the IDG Books Worldwide Customer Service phone number: 800-762-2974 (outside the U.S.: 317-596-5430).

Index

• B •

(continued)

IDG Books Worldwide, Inc., End-User License Agreement

READ THIS. You should carefully read these terms and conditions before opening the software packet(s) included with this book ("Book"). This is a license agreement ("Agreement") between you and IDG Books Worldwide, Inc. ("IDGB"). By opening the accompanying software packet(s), you acknowledge that you have read and accept the following terms and conditions. If you do not agree and do not want to be bound by such terms and conditions, promptly return the Book and the unopened software packet(s) to the place you obtained them for a full refund.

1. **License Grant.** IDGB grants to you (either an individual or entity) a nonexclusive license to use one copy of the enclosed software program(s) (collectively, the "Software") solely for your own personal or business purposes on a single computer (whether a standard computer or a workstation component of a multiuser network). The Software is in use on a computer when it is loaded into temporary memory (RAM) or installed into permanent memory (hard disk, CD-ROM, or other storage device). IDGB reserves all rights not expressly granted herein.

2. **Ownership.** IDGB is the owner of all right, title, and interest, including copyright, in and to the compilation of the Software recorded on the disk(s) or CD-ROM ("Software Media"). Copyright to the individual programs recorded on the Software Media is owned by the author or other authorized copyright owner of each program. Ownership of the Software and all proprietary rights relating thereto remain with IDGB and its licensers.

3. **Restrictions on Use and Transfer.**

   (a) You may only (i) make one copy of the Software for backup or archival purposes, or (ii) transfer the Software to a single hard disk, provided that you keep the original for backup or archival purposes. You may not (i) rent or lease the Software, (ii) copy or reproduce the Software through a LAN or other network system or through any computer subscriber system or bulletin-board system, or (iii) modify, adapt, or create derivative works based on the Software.

   (b) You may not reverse engineer, decompile, or disassemble the Software. You may transfer the Software and user documentation on a permanent basis, provided that the transferee agrees to accept the terms and conditions of this Agreement and you retain no copies. If the Software is an update or has been updated, any transfer must include the most recent update and all prior versions.

4. **Restrictions on Use of Individual Programs.** You must follow the individual requirements and restrictions detailed for each individual program in Appendix C of this Book. These limitations are also contained in the individual license agreements recorded on the Software Media. These limitations may include a requirement that after using the program for a specified period of time, the user must pay a registration fee or discontinue use. By opening the Software packet(s), you will be agreeing to abide by the licenses and restrictions for these individual programs that are detailed in Appendix C and on the Software Media. None of the material on this Software Media or listed in this Book may ever be redistributed, in original or modified form, for commercial purposes.

5. Limited Warranty.

(a) IDGB warrants that the Software and Software Media are free from defects in materials and workmanship under normal use for a period of sixty (60) days from the date of purchase of this Book. If IDGB receives notification within the warranty period of defects in materials or workmanship, IDGB will replace the defective Software Media.

(b) IDGB AND THE AUTHORS OF THE BOOK DISCLAIM ALL OTHER WARRANTIES, EX-PRESS OR IMPLIED, INCLUDING WITHOUT LIMITATION IMPLIED WARRANTIES OF MERCHANTABILITY AND FITNESS FOR A PARTICULAR PURPOSE, WITH RESPECT TO THE SOFTWARE, THE PROGRAMS, THE SOURCE CODE CONTAINED THEREIN, AND/OR THE TECHNIQUES DESCRIBED IN THIS BOOK. IDGB DOES NOT WARRANT THAT THE FUNCTIONS CONTAINED IN THE SOFTWARE WILL MEET YOUR REQUIREMENTS OR THAT THE OPERATION OF THE SOFTWARE WILL BE ERROR FREE.

(c) This limited warranty gives you specific legal rights, and you may have other rights that vary from jurisdiction to jurisdiction.

6. Remedies.

(a) IDGB's entire liability and your exclusive remedy for defects in materials and workmanship shall be limited to replacement of the Software Media, which may be returned to IDGB with a copy of your receipt at the following address: Software Media Fulfillment Department, Attn.: *Genealogy Online For Dummies,* IDG Books Worldwide, Inc., 7260 Shadeland Station, Ste. 100, Indianapolis, IN 46256, or call 800-762-2974. Please allow three to four weeks for delivery. This Limited Warranty is void if failure of the Software Media has resulted from accident, abuse, or misapplication. Any replacement Software Media will be warranted for the remainder of the original warranty period or thirty (30) days, whichever is longer.

(b) In no event shall IDGB or the author be liable for any damages whatsoever (including without limitation damages for loss of business profits, business interruption, loss of business information, or any other pecuniary loss) arising from the use of or inability to use the Book or the Software, even if IDGB has been advised of the possibility of such damages.

(c) Because some jurisdictions do not allow the exclusion or limitation of liability for conse-quential or incidental damages, the above limitation or exclusion may not apply to you.

7. U.S. Government Restricted Rights. Use, duplication, or disclosure of the Software by the U.S. Government is subject to restrictions stated in paragraph (c)(1)(ii) of the Rights in Technical Data and Computer Software clause of DFARS 252.227-7013, and in subparagraphs (a) through (d) of the Commercial Computer–Restricted Rights clause at FAR 52.227-19, and in similar clauses in the NASA FAR supplement, when applicable.

8. General. This Agreement constitutes the entire understanding of the parties and revokes and supersedes all prior agreements, oral or written, between them and may not be modified or amended except in a writing signed by both parties hereto that specifically refers to this Agreement. This Agreement shall take precedence over any other documents that may be in conflict herewith. If any one or more provisions contained in this Agreement are held by any court or tribunal to be invalid, illegal, or otherwise unenforceable, each and every other provision shall remain in full force and effect.

Installation Instructions

Please see Appendix C for full details on the CD and its contents.

Using the CD with Microsoft Windows

1. **Insert the CD into your computer's CD-ROM drive.**

2. **Windows 3.1 or 3.11 users: From Program Manager, choose File⇨Run.**

   Windows 95 users: Click Start⇨Run.

3. **In the dialog box that appears, type** D:\SETUP.EXE

   Replace *D* with the proper drive letter if your CD-ROM drive uses a different letter.

4. **Click OK, read the license agreement, and then click the Accept button if you want to use the CD.**

5. **Click anywhere on the Welcome screen to enter the interface and see the categories.**

6. **To view the items within a category, just click the category's name to see a list of programs in the category.**

7. **For more information about a program, click the program's name (and be sure to look at the program's readme file).**

8. **If you don't want to install the program, click the Go Back button to return to the previous screen. To install a program, click the appropriate Install button.**

9. **When you've finished installing programs, click the Quit button to close the interface.**

Using the CD with Mac OS

1. **Insert the CD into your computer's CD-ROM drive.**

2. **Double-click the CD icon to show the CD's contents.**

3. **Double-click the Read Me First icon to read information about the CD's programs and any last-minute instructions you may need in order to correctly install them.**

4. **To install most programs, just drag the program's folder from the CD window and drop it on your hard drive icon.**

5. **Other programs come with installer programs — with these, you simply open the program's folder on the CD, and then double-click the icon with the words "Install" or "Installer."**

   Just double-click anything with .sea in the title, and it will run just like an installer.

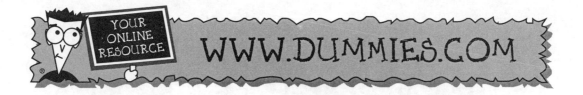

YOUR ONLINE RESOURCE

WWW.DUMMIES.COM

Discover Dummies Online!

The Dummies Web Site is your fun and friendly online resource for the latest information about ...*For Dummies*® books and your favorite topics. The Web site is the place to communicate with us, exchange ideas with other ...*For Dummies* readers, chat with authors, and have fun!

Ten Fun and Useful Things You Can Do at www.dummies.com

1. Win free ...*For Dummies* books and more!
2. Register your book and be entered in a prize drawing.
3. Meet your favorite authors through the IDG Books Author Chat Series.
4. Exchange helpful information with other ...*For Dummies* readers.
5. Discover other great ...*For Dummies* books you must have!
6. Purchase Dummieswear™ exclusively from our Web site.
7. Buy ...*For Dummies* books online.
8. Talk to us. Make comments, ask questions, get answers!
9. Download free software.
10. Find additional useful resources from authors.

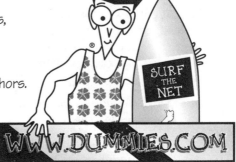

Link directly to these ten fun and useful things at **http://www.dummies.com/10useful**

For other technology titles from IDG Books Worldwide, go to **www.idgbooks.com**

Not on the Web yet? It's easy to get started with *Dummies 101*®: *The Internet For Windows*® *98* or *The Internet For Dummies*, 5th Edition, at local retailers everywhere.

IDG BOOKS WORLDWIDE

Find other ...*For Dummies* books on these topics:

Business • Career • Databases • Food & Beverage • Games • Gardening • Graphics • Hardware
Health & Fitness • Internet and the World Wide Web • Networking • Office Suites
Operating Systems • Personal Finance • Pets • Programming • Recreation • Sports
Spreadsheets • Teacher Resources • Test Prep • Word Processing

IDG BOOKS WORLDWIDE BOOK REGISTRATION

We want to hear from you!

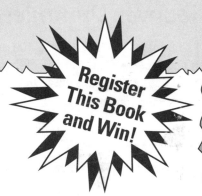

Register This Book and Win!

Visit **http://my2cents.dummies.com** to register this book and tell us how you liked it!

- Get entered in our monthly prize giveaway.

- Give us feedback about this book — tell us what you like best, what you like least, or maybe what you'd like to ask the author and us to change!

- Let us know any other ...*For Dummies*® topics that interest you.

Your feedback helps us determine what books to publish, tells us what coverage to add as we revise our books, and lets us know whether we're meeting your needs as a ...*For Dummies* reader. You're our most valuable resource, and what you have to say is important to us!

Not on the Web yet? It's easy to get started with *Dummies 101*®: *The Internet For Windows*® *98* or *The Internet For Dummies*®, 5th Edition, at local retailers everywhere.

Or let us know what you think by sending us a letter at the following address:

...*For Dummies* Book Registration
Dummies Press
7260 Shadeland Station, Suite 100
Indianapolis, IN 46256-3945
Fax 317-596-5498

™

BESTSELLING
BOOK SERIES
FROM IDG